Anything Goes

Anything Goes

A History of American Musical Theatre

Ethan Mordden

OXFORD
UNIVERSITY PRESS

OXFORD
UNIVERSITY PRESS

Oxford University Press is a department of the University of Oxford.
It furthers the University's objective of excellence in research,
scholarship, and education by publishing worldwide.

Oxford   New York
Auckland   Cape Town   Dar es Salaam   Hong Kong   Karachi
Kuala Lumpur   Madrid   Melbourne   Mexico City   Nairobi
New Delhi   Shanghai   Taipei   Toronto

With offices in
Argentina   Austria   Brazil   Chile   Czech Republic   France   Greece
Guatemala   Hungary   Italy   Japan   Poland   Portugal   Singapore
South Korea   Switzerland   Thailand   Turkey   Ukraine   Vietnam

Oxford is a registered trade mark of Oxford University Press
in the UK and certain other countries.
Published in the United States of America by

Oxford University Press
198 Madison Avenue, New York, NY 10016

Library of Congress Cataloging-in-Publication Data
Mordden, Ethan
Anything goes : a history of the American musical / Ethan Mordden.
pages   cm
Includes bibliographical references and index.
Discography: (pages).
ISBN 978-0-19-989283-9 (alk. paper)
1. Musicals—United States—History and criticism. I. Title.
ML1711.M732   2013
782.'40973—dc23   2013000208

Portions of the material on *The Wizard of Oz* first appeared in *The Baum Bugle*, Volume 28,
Number 3; the *Gypsy* discography was used, in somewhat different form, in my blog,
Cultural Advantages. All illustrations courtesy of the Billy Rose Theatre Collection,
The New York Public Library for the Performing Arts, Astor, Lenox, and
Tilden Foundations; Culver Pictures; and private collections.

3 5 7 9 8 6 4

Printed in the United States of America
on acid-free paper

CONTENTS

Acknowledgments   *vii*
Introduction   *ix*

PART ONE: The First Age
1. Source Material   *3*
2. The Age of Burlesque   *19*
3. At the Turn of the Century   *33*

PART TWO: The Second Age
4. The Witch of the Wood and the Bamboo Tree   *51*
5. Victor Herbert   *72*
6. The New Music   *83*
7. The Variety Show   *98*

PART THREE: The Third Age
8. The Structure of Twenties Musical Comedy   *109*
9. The Structure of Twenties Operetta   *120*
10. Dancing in the Dark   *130*
11. Blue Monday Blues   *143*
12. The Rodgers and Hammerstein Handbook   *157*
13. Something to Dance About   *182*
14. After *West Side Story*   *202*
15. The Sondheim Handbook   *223*

PART FOUR: The Fourth Age
16. Devolution   *247*
17. That Is the State of the Art   *258*

For Further Reading   *281*
Discography   *291*
Index   *323*

ACKNOWLEDGMENTS

To my faithful agent and friend, Joe Spieler; to Jon Cronwell and Ken Mandelbaum for giving me access to arcane research material; to Anne Kaufman; to Ian Marshall Fisher and Tom Vallance for helping me get close to *Mexican Hayride* and *The Day Before Spring*; to wise Geoffrey Block; at Oxford, to my old pal Joellyn Ausanka and my sterling editor, Norm Hirschy.

INTRODUCTION

When the composer-lyricist Frank Loesser became famous, in the middle of the twentieth century, two forms dominated Broadway music theatre, musical comedy and the more ambitious musical play. Loesser's form, in *Where's Charley?* and *Guys and Dolls*, was musical comedy. But he wrote his next piece, *The Most Happy Fella*, as an opera. True, much of it conformed to the practices of musical comedy, for example in the hoot-and-holler dance number "Big D" and the use of spoken dialogue. However, the romantic portions of the score were extremely lyrical, even ecstatic, and some of the ensemble writing surpassed even the standards of operetta. Then, too, the overture was no song medley but a prelude of leitmotifs, so volatile that it jumps from *Allegro giocoso* ("joyous") to *Moderato e misterioso* to *Largamente* ("grandiose") to *Allegro* and so on every few measures, as if only the most expansive composition could prepare the public—not merely to see a show but to *listen* to it.

Then the curtain rose on a restaurant at closing time. The music is marked *Dolente* ("pained"), but it is actually rather noncommittal in tone, strangely unevocative after, say, *Oklahoma!*'s tiny tone poem of dawn on the prairie or *Wonderful Town*'s orchestral tweaking of a thirties piano riff. But then a vamp breaks in, *Pesante* ("Heavy"), in brisk 4/4: grumpy and resentful, the very sound of endless trudging under the weight of laden trays. A waitress takes stage for the evening's first vocal, "Ooh! My Feet!," sarcastic and almost bitter yet, in its gamy honesty, likable.

This is Cleo, the sidekick of the heroine, Amy (who is called "Rosabella" till one spoken line before the show's finale). A customer Amy can't recall has left a note and a bit of jewelry for her—object: matrimony—and, after a longish musical scene with Cleo made of dialogue and *arioso* mixed together, Amy gets the Heroine's Wanting Song, "Somebody, Somewhere." It aches with vulnerability, not only in the lyrics but also in the hesitantly soaring music. Partway through it, Amy moves downstage, the traveler curtain closes behind her, and stagehands rush in to clear the restaurant set for the show's first full-stage location and the title song. Now we meet

Amy's secret admirer, Tony, who is not the shy young man she has imagined but a much older specimen, ebullient and generous at *Tempo di Tarentella* but, we sadly realize, too unattractive physically for a love plot.

Thus, three songs into the narrative, we are caught up in a worrisome conflict, not least because Amy and Tony have been *musically* presented to us as appealing personalities. The next number, "Standing on the Corner," brings out the musical-comedy Loesser and introduces Cleo's incipient mate, Herman. "Saturday," he sings, disarmingly, "and I'm so broke": so he and his buddies hang out and cruise instead of dating. The number is almost pure pop, easy listening in its close-harmony quartet—but Herman's solo sections give us, once again, a character in the tune as well as in the words: affable and eternally optimistic, a soft target for the others to pick on. As two girls pass by, Herman and Clem pointedly look them over, and Clem then tells Herman, "Yours was awful!"

A plot point: Amy has sent Tony her picture, and he must send his in return. She won't like what she sees, he fears, and now Loesser sings his fifth principal to us—Joe, Tony's foreman, a friendly hunk with, nevertheless, "something cold and possibly brutal," as Loesser warns in the stage directions, "behind the smile in his eyes." Tony is going to send Amy Joe's picture, turning his courtship into a fraud—but we don't know that yet. All Loesser gives us is "Joey, Joey, Joey," Joe's own particular Wanting Song, scored with slithery, unstable harp and celesta runs. The music is sensitive yet dominating: beautiful and disturbing, like Joe himself. And so Loesser concludes his chain of establishing numbers. Now we know everyone in the story, what he or she needs or is capable of.

This is what the American musical had been working up to for some one hundred years, and all its artistry dwells in the historian's key buzz term "integrated": the union of story and score. Once a mere collection of songs and now a pride of fully developed numbers supported by incidental music, intros and development sections, and musical scenes mixed of speech and song, the score not only tells but probes the story, above all unveiling its characters. As we'll see, there were integrated American shows around the turn of the twentieth century—*Robin Hood, El Capitan, The Prince of Pilsen, The Red Mill*. Yet the business model continued to tolerate specialty material to spotlight performers and extramural interpolations to humiliate the evening's designated authors. Even *Show Boat*, more or less officially America's first great musical, in 1927, includes specialties and interpolations. Still, when *Show Boat* was integrated it was *very* integrated, and the practice of integration was already catching on. *The Student Prince* and *The Desert Song*, directly preceding *Show Boat*, are absolutely integrated shows . . . in their scores. For the historian recognizes other aspects of integration—of dance as a thematic and psychological instrument, experimental in the 1930s and fully executed in *Oklahoma!* in 1943; of production style, introduced in *Allegro* and *Love Life* in the late 1940s and revisited in *Cabaret* and *Company* a generation later.

Much of this may seem like ancient history to some readers. But I was there for a good deal of it, and I vividly remember certain bits of staging that one cannot glean from surviving documents. When very young, I memorized a show's score through its cast recording and became so intimate with its continuity that I could so to say photograph the stage action in my mind when I saw the play itself. I still remember being startled when the original *Most Happy Fella* Cleo, Susan Johnson, sang, about her littlest toe, "the big son-of-a-bitch hurts the most!," because on the disc she left out the no-no term. Years later, interviewing Agnes de Mille for a book on Rodgers and Hammerstein, I found her wary—her relationship with them soured on *Allegro*—but I won her confidence by recounting, second by second, the opening sequence of one of her later shows, *Goldilocks*: how the curtain rose on a theatre exterior that then broke into halves sailing off into the right and left wings to reveal the Boys and Girls paired off and, upstage, Elaine Stritch sitting on a moon. Mollified (actually, I think she was a little shocked), de Mille grew voluble.

So there is more to "research" than ransacking the archives. As other interviews for the Rodgers and Hammerstein book revealed, one quickly learns who Knows Stuff and who is carving a graven image of himself or has no memory function. The dowager empress Dorothy Rodgers didn't know stuff: her relationship with her husband's career comprised no more than attending the premieres with him. But Stephen Sondheim knew plenty; better, he knew Oscar Hammerstein. John Fearnley, a Rodgers and Hammerstein production associate, was rich in recollection about putting on and even writing the shows. Jamie Hammerstein, Oscar's younger son, assisted on and thus knew much about *Flower Drum Song*. But more: he revealed that his father complained that, in the 1930s and 1940s, organizations were constantly springing up, recruiting Names for their advisory board. These outfits invariably claimed to be politically progressive, but many were communist fronts and even those that weren't were simply drains on Oscar's concentration time for his work. It was the reason he wrote *Allegro*—to show how life in the Great World lures a man away from his purpose on earth.

Such insights from those who were in one way or another part of the history obviously help fill out the chronicle. Further, Ted Chapin of the Rodgers and Hammerstein organization gave me access to material relating to the early composition of such works as *Show Boat* and *The King and I*; seeing what the authors rejected brings one closer to what they discovered about a show as they felt their way into it.

I should mention as well the unique figure of the gay mentor, who in my case were former chorus boys and stage managers who carried with them a treasury of anecdotes and recollections and were glad of a new audience for them. My descriptions of shows that precede my own theatregoing owe everything to them, for, make no mistake, the chorus people have a larger perspective on a show than the leading players do, distracted as they are by the demands of their parts. And no one knows a show like its stage manager.

Elaine Steinbeck, for example, had a story about *Oklahoma!* Eventually John Steinbeck's wife, she was in 1943 Elaine Anderson, one of *Oklahoma!*'s stage managers; the story finds her at a Saturday rehearsal when, for the first time, director Rouben Mamoulian and choreographer Agnes de Mille decided to "put Act One together." In those days, musicals were cast with separate singing and dancing choruses, to be combined on stage to appear more or less versatile, though in fact the singers sang (and moved a little) and the dancers danced (and lip-synched or so). They rehearsed separately, the singers and principals with the director and the dancers with the choreographer, each squad unaware of what the other squad would be doing.

Of course, at some point early on, the two "halves" of the production would be brought together, and this was the day. Keep in mind that, while *Oklahoma!* proved to be a unique and influential piece after it opened, at this point the cast thought of it simply as an unusual show (because of its frontier setting and dialect) with wonderful songs. De Mille's dancers scarcely even knew what the plot was about.

So, when Will Parker followed the "Kansas City" vocal by showing off the new two-step—"the waltz is through," he announces. "Ketch on to it?"—and the watching cowboys joined in, the cast saw something more than a dance. *Oklahoma!* looks in on a community in transition, its tribal folkways to be suppressed in favor of statehood and membership in an ethnically diverse nation. The Oklahomans' world will change, and "Kansas City" illustrates this as much in dance as in song.

A bit later came the heroine's feminist anthem, "Many a New Day," and *its* follow-up dance, a mixture of caprice and tenderness, expressing in movement what lyrics and music cannot. As Mamoulian and de Mille ran the rehearsal, Elaine noticed how astonished the performers had become. What marvelous experiment had they fallen into? *Oklahoma!* was more than unusual: enlightening. Even at this early stage, in a bare room to an upright piano, it was unmistakable that *Oklahoma!* was going to make fabulous theatrical history.

Hammerstein was in the country that weekend, but Rodgers was in town, at home, and Elaine ran to a telephone, rang him up, and said, "You better get down here quick."

PART ONE

The First Age

CHAPTER 1

⌒

Source Material

The first musical was *The Beggar's Opera*, produced in the theatre at Lincoln's Inn Fields in London, in 1728. To give the work modern billing, its book and lyrics were by John Gay and its music was by Johann Christian Pepusch. Or, more precisely, either Gay or Pepusch selected sixty-nine popular airs of the day and Gay fitted to them new words to express his characters' thoughts, to develop atmosphere, or even to advance plot action. Perhaps because the script continuously slips in and out of mostly very short vocals, Gay at first wanted the actors to sing without accompaniment, but in the end Pepusch gave them instrumental backing, becoming the first orchestrator in the musical's history.

Or was *The Beggar's Opera* the very first? It was certainly the first lasting success in its form, **ballad opera**. There had been light musical-theatre pieces before 1728, but not till ballad opera can we speak of works like unto what we think of as a musical: an enacted story bearing some relationship with our daily life and "lifted" by songs that *belong* to the story.

Gay's intention was to satirize the Italian opera that had monopolized the interest of London's trend setters. This mode of the moment, the *opera seria* of the émigré George Frideric Handel, treated the amorous and political intrigues of nobles in exotic places: crusaders, sorceresses, the high hats of Greek mythology. John Gay's "opera" reversed the terms. In place of heroes: criminals. In place of arias in Italian: ditties in English. *Opera seria* delighted in the rivalry of princes: Gay's protagonist is Macheath, a bandit, and his rival is the underworld boss Peachum (a pun on "Peach 'em," meaning "Turn the felons in for the forty-pounds-a-head reward").

Riffraff! *Opera seria* featured triangle love plots, again among the courtly; Gay offered Peachum's daughter, Polly, and the daughter of the keeper of Newgate Prison, Lucy Lockit—both wives of Macheath, who has at least six that we know of. To the tune of "Oh, London Is a Fine Town," Gay wrote "Our Polly Is a Sad Slut!," and, when the two women meet in confrontation, "Good-morrow, gossip Joan" turns into Polly's "Why how now, Madam Flirt," to which Lucy replies, "Why, how now, saucy Jade; Sure the Wench is Tipsy!" Theatre historian Simon Trussler likens *The Beggar's Opera* to a print by Hogarth: "so rich in incident, interpolation, and low-life impropriety as to upset conventional expectations of dramatic art, but . . . thought-provoking in its simultaneous likeness and unlikeness to life."

Above all, *The Beggar's Opera* is a remarkably consistent work; as we'll see, many musicals before, say, the 1890s were if anything superb in their lack of consistency, especially in America. Minutes before *The Beggar's Opera*'s final curtain, with Macheath about to be hanged, two members of the company come forth to debate this dire conclusion in a piece determined to be popular:

> PLAYER: The Catastrophe is manifestly wrong, for an Opera must end happily.
> BEGGAR: Your Objection, Sir, is very just; and is easily remov'd . . . in this kind of Drama [i.e., in Handelian opera], 'tis no matter how absurdly things are brought about. —So—you Rabble there—run and cry a Reprieve.
>
> . . .
>
> PLAYER: All this we must do, to comply with the Taste of the Town.

The Beggar's Opera tickled London, to put it mildly. It played 62 performances in its first season, unprecedented for the age, and all but commanded imitation. Benjamin Britten scholar Eric Walter White noted that "at least 120 ballad operas were produced during the period 1728–38." But ballad opera began to evolve. Inevitably, musicians would realize personal cachet in composing rather than arranging and in constructing musical scenes instead of a chain of songlets.

This leads us to the so-called **Savoy Operas** of Arthur Sullivan and W. S. Gilbert, which appeared over a quarter of a century, from 1871 to 1896.* These comprise, almost inarguably, the most influential suite of musicals the English-speaking world was to know for seventy years, till the age

---

*"Savoy" denotes the theatre built for their production, in 1881.

of Rodgers and Hammerstein and, after, Sondheim-Prince. One notes traces of *The Beggar's Opera* in Gilbert and Sullivan, in the satiric tone and the close relationship between script and score. Further, the music in both really suits the characters. Just as Polly and Mrs. Peachum duet, in "O Polly, You Might Have Toy'd and Kist," in tones of mother and daughter, the one forgiving and the other beseeching, so does, for instance, Sullivan's setting of the Mikado's "My Object All Sublime" mark him as ponderously implacable. Yes, it's in the words. But the number's relentlessly marching rhythm intensifies their meaning, with a jumpy little vamp that suggests how eagerly this ogre looks forward to his next grisly exaction of justice. Thus, the composer is a dramatist, even if *The Beggar's Opera*'s "composer" was a miscellany of prefabricated melodies.

At that, it is worth pointing out that Gay's lyrics are very much in character for his various principals, an amazing achievement considering that the profession of lyricist for the popular stage did not truly exist till Gay invented it. *Opera* had librettists, of course—poets more often than not. But keying popular music into character songs started with *The Beggar's Opera*; even Gilbert didn't specify his characters' lyrics as keenly as Gay did his. True, Gilbert's wit is a summoning concept in the musical's history; in his own way, he has never been outdone. Still, many of his people sound like each other—or, rather, they all sound like Gilbert.

Nevertheless, the Savoy titles are highly evolved from ballad opera, most particularly in grander musical structures. They usually start with a chorus featuring one or the other gender—*HMS Pinafore*'s men in "We Sail the Ocean Blue" or *Patience*'s "Twenty Love-sick Maidens We"—then build through the first act to a bustling finale full of many distinct parts. Further, the chorus work is crucial to the action, whether gondoliers, bridesmaids, or even ghosts. The vocal demands on nearly all the principals are well-nigh operatic, whereas actors can fake their way through some of *The Beggar's Opera*'s roles, even Macheath, which has been played by such non-musical actors as Michael Redgrave and (on film) Laurence Olivier.

In 1871—again, the very year in which Gilbert and Sullivan launched their partnership, with the now mostly lost *Thespis*—Gilbert made an English translation of Jacques Offenbach's *Les Brigands* (The Bandits, 1869). It was not performed (either in London or New York) until 1889, but it suggests an early link between English "comic opera" and Offenbach's form, which he dubbed "**opéra bouffe**," a French translation of the Italian *opera buffa* (literally, "comic opera"). However, *opéra bouffe* is nothing like *opera buffa*. Nor is it like French *opéra comique*, a genre that varied in style from era to era but was never in any real sense *comic*. "It is impossible," says critic Martin Cooper, "to find any English translation [for] the term *opéra comique*.

'Comic opera' suggests something quite different." Indeed, a popular confusion mistakes the French *comédie* as meaning "comedy" only, when it in fact means "drama" generally.* The difference between opera and *opéra comique* is not that one is serious and the other comic but that *opéra* is purely musical and *opéra comique* a dramatic work with music.†

Yes, *opéra comique*, depending on the era, might include a comic part, usually the Ridiculous Servant. In André Grétry's "beauty and the beast" piece *Zémire et Azor* (1771), the menial Ali dithers in fear or nods off when he is needed, and that may have been amusing enough for the age—but his music is just like that of everyone else in the work, devoid of comic character. Later, in the early 1800s, an outstanding *opéra comique* like *La Dame Blanche* emphasizes the sentimental and mysterious, but still there is no comic content.

And yet, after John Gay's deliriously wicked jesting in ballad opera, is there nothing in *French* music theatre before Offenbach that can truly be called funny? Fun is the soul of musical comedy—and there is an Exhibit A, Jean-Philippe Rameau's *comédie-ballet Platée* (1745). Here, at least, is an overtly absurd plotline: a benighted though harmless swamp monster believes herself beloved of Jupiter. In the fashion of bygone times, the work has a lot of fun at the expense of this mythical cocktail waitress to the stars, and ends by flattening her self-esteem as if she were a villain. Rameau, an extremely resourceful composer, does place some musical silliness here and there, such as animal sounds, from frogs to donkeys. Even so, not till our own times, in a 2002 staging by Laurent Pelly at the Paris Opéra, could *Platée* emerge as a *funny* piece, at that entirely through Pelly's ingenious interpretations of ancient operatic usages. Setting the action entirely in a theatre-within-the-theatre, Pelly crazed everyone up: Mercure was all silver, from shoes to hair glitter, and the diva La Folie wore a gown made of music sheets. In her solo showpiece, she enjoyed a particular note of such round and golden tone that she signaled the conductor, Marc Minkowski,

---

*Thus the name of the French National Theatre, the Comédie-Française, not a house of comedy per se. This usage applies to Romance languages in general. In Italian, the chief of a theatre troupe is the *capocomico*, and Dante's *Divina Commedia* is not a jokebook, but a poetic "drama" about the afterlife.

†The famous difference between the two—that *opéra* has recitative (in effect, "sung" dialogue) and *opéra comique* speech between the numbers—is a generic technicality of no importance. *Opéra* had the more glamorous voices, with characters drawn from the leadership class, striving for glory. *Opéra comique*, for less imposing voices, dealt with middle-class or peasant characters striving for love. Thus, Gounod's *Faust*, originally an *opéra comique* (1859), was revised as a grand opera (1869)—for a number of reasons but, really, because its subject, drawn from one of Western Civilization's most exalted classics, was too vast for the smaller form.

not to interfere even as he tapped his watch (though he did blow her a kiss when it was over). Or: Act Three couldn't begin till a frog, sitting in a stage box, signaled Minkowski to get going.

All this creates a marvelous show without the slightest editing of what Rameau wrote. Still, it derives from Pelly's imaginative responses to the music and not from the music itself. *Platée* as written is droll, just as *The Beggar's Opera* is scathing in the thrust-and-parry style of Restoration comedy and Gilbert and Sullivan is occasionally biting but more often simply whimsical.

But Offenbach is *zany:* in his music. For the first time, the uproarious and sexy and even transgressive attitudes that identify the musical throughout its various ages move into the voices and pit—yodeling, crazy "wrong" notes, tone-deaf bands, vocal evocations of a train trip, a blizzard, kissing. Any composer would call up a military march when warriors tread the stage; Offenbach was the first to concoct goofy ones.

Above all, it was Offenbach who instituted pastiche composition and the quoting of other composers as essential to the very sound of a musical. He loved Spanish characters, because Spaniards sing boleros, and of course Germans supply the yodeling. If no Germans are handy, anyone can yodel, as the tenor Paris does in *La Belle Hélène* (1864), to evoke a Bacchic air as he abducts Helen. In Offenbach's upside-down world, the two leads in *Orphée et Euridice* (1858) torture each other sadomasochistically. They gleefully reveal adulterous liaisons—and, boy, does she hate his music. "Mercy!" she cries, when he launches his "latest concerto"—and, he gloats, "It lasts an hour and a quarter." And he proceeds to fiddle it: a sugary, droopy thing, pretty if you like to hear salon music and grotesque if you'd rather die—which, of course, Euridice eventually does.

Thus Offenbach overturns the rules for decorum and beauty in art and for, above all, a reverence for the classics. "No more nectar!" the gods cry in the same work, during a Mt. Olympus uprising. "This regime is boring!" When Jupiter's thunder fails to faze them, he asks, "What about morality?"

Morality? From *him*? One by one, Diana, Venus, and Cupid review his erotic capers in music that has the uncanny sound of children blackmailing a grownup. With its mincing little steps and hip-swivelling after-phrase, it is infantile yet knowing, the wagging finger of your comeuppance. There simply hadn't been music like this before.

Now, isn't this Simon Trussler's aforementioned "simultaneous likeness and unlikeness to life"? It's the transformation of believable human behavior into exaggeration and fantasy. And that will prove to be the sine qua non of the American musical in its Golden Age—*Of Thee I Sing, Du Barry Was a Lady, On the Town, Finian's Rainbow, Guys and Dolls, Hello, Dolly!*.

Offenbach's use of pastiche was especially influential, giving the American musical a variety of texture and a wealth of "meanings" not found in comparable genres of other cultures. It keeps the musical fresh, mischievous, adaptable. When Victor Herbert defines his Italian heroine (naughty) Marietta with the ebullient "Italian Street Song," or when John Kander gives *Chicago*'s prison matron a Sophie Tucker number in "When You're Good To Mama," they expand their soundscape while referencing memes that help the audience place the character more or less instantly. We get it: Marietta has brought to the French America of New Orleans the zest of Italian life; the matron is tolerant of the appetites of the human condition, especially her own.

Pastiche takes many forms. Sometimes the music toys with a spoofy citation, as when George M. Cohan quotes "Yankee Doodle" in "The Yankee Doodle Boy"; when Cole Porter unveils another of his parody country-western numbers (as in "Friendship"); when *The Pajama Game* sets a scene in a place called Hernando's Hideaway just so it can program a Latin number because Latin numbers were trending at the time; or when orchestrator Jonathan Tunick studs *A Little Night Music*'s "A Weekend in the Country" with a quotation of the first seven notes of Richard Strauss' *Der Rosenkavalier*: the most romantic of operas gracing the most romantic of musicals.

And note how vigorously *My Fair Lady* pursues this use of styles to capture Edwardian England. The clash of social orders that informs the action is given voice when Doolittle's "With a Little Bit Of Luck" and "Get Me To the Church On Time" brawl with the impeccably ducal languor of the "Ascot Gavotte" and the sheer whirling richness of the "Embassy Waltz." Doolittle is music hall, rough and rash: honest. The fine folk sing en masque but dance with abandon, as if they can be honest only in a ballroom, where no outsider can see.

Then too, "The Rain in Spain" executes a musical pun in a *Tempo di Habanera* that breaks into a jota for the ensuing dance, for the age's social cautions are so rife that Eliza and her two protectors can bond only in music so "foreign" that it protects them from their own intimacy. Similarly, the narrative about the interfering Zoltan Karpathy in "You Did It" rings in Lisztian Hungarian Rhapsody, right down to a *spiccato* violin solo and outright quotation, isolating Karpathy as not a Hungarian but a schemer, a villain, a creature outside the community of musicals, where opposites like Eliza and Henry Higgins meet cute, wage war, and fall in love. This musical imagery extends to even a quotation of "London Bridge Is Falling Down," in the strange little buskers' dance that opens the show. Why? To sound out the show's title: "My fair lady!"

Gilbert and Sullivan had no rivals; is the same true of Offenbach? There was—to a very limited extent—one, Florimond Ronger. Working mononymously as Hervé, this composer-librettist-performer launched his career a bit before Offenbach, who in any case had emigrated from Cologne, Germany, at the age of fourteen in 1833 and thus had some assimilating to do before he could compete in the French music world. Hervé's huge list of works begins in 1842, but Offenbach quickly overtook him, especially once he gave up one-acts for full-length works, some of which comprise the very center of the French repertory in the musical: *Barbe-Bleue* (Bluebeard, 1866), *La Vie Parisienne* (Parisian Life, 1866), *La Grande-Duchesse de Gérolstein* (1867), *La Périchole* (1868), the aforementioned *Les Brigands, La Fille du Tambour-Major* (The Drum-Major's Daughter, 1879), as well as the two just cited.

In the end, Hervé became an Offenbach imitator himself, for his rudimentary compositional style was not able to host his sense of humor: Hervé's fun lay entirely in his words. His history spoof *Chilpéric* (1868) even bears Offenbach's unique generic designation as an *opéra bouffe* and appropriates Offenbach's typical parodies of grand opera, especially its most dogged convention, the *Grand Duo* (here for King Chilpéric and his light of love, Frédégonde, both out of authentic sixth-century chronicle), with its restless changes of tempo culminating in a Big Tune. (Hervé sets it to an Offenbachian cancan.) Hervé's *Le Petit Faust* (1869), a spoof of Goethe, borrows Offenbachian casting, with its "ténor comique" as Faust, its "Trial" (after the so to say "talksinging" comedian Antoine Trial), as Valentin, and its trousered soprano, a "chanteuse légère," as the Devil. It's not that Hervé's music is completely artless; his *Faust*'s second-act prelude contains a tiny concerto for flute and orchestra, and the act then opens in a clever mockup of Gounod's *Faust*'s Kermesse choruses. Nevertheless, Hervé was no Offenbach, and no one else has been to this day.

Most important, Offenbach's genius forced him to extend the boundaries of *opéra bouffe*. At various times, he wrote on the grand scale, including one out-and-out opera in the fashionable vein of the nature-and-magic adventure, *Die Rheinnixen* (The Fairies of the Rhine, 1864), for Vienna. However, his masterpiece, unfinished at his death (at the age of sixty-one, in 1880), was a kind of exalted *opéra bouffe*, satiric, touching, and eerie all at once: *Les Contes d'Hoffmann* (The Tales of Hoffmann, 1881). Ostensibly a review of a poet's doomed loves, the work in fact demonstrates the artist's isolation in a world run by occult, disruptive forces. It was too intimate to be a grand opera, too crazy and experimental to be an *opéra comique*, and too romantic to be an *opéra bouffe*: an unprecedentedly rich work, billed as an *opéra fantastique*. Because *Hoffmann* was thrown together after Offenbach's death in a corrupt and simplified version, and because much of *Hoffmann's* most glorious music was lost till relatively recently, we are finally realizing that it is not only one of the unique inventions but also the exhibition piece in how the popular lyric stage—the musical—is infinitely protean, inspiring its practitioners to effect genre breakouts. They expand their musical structures, twist the fun show into the serious show without losing the fun, reinvent the purpose of the musical: *Show Boat, Cabaret, Follies*. And note that all three of these paradigmatic classics deal heavily in pastiche or quotation, from *Show Boat's* black spiritual through *Cabaret's* "suggestion without imitation" of Weimar Berlin to *Follies'* retrospective of the Songs They Don't Write Any More.

Call it the audacity of talent. When Gilbert and Sullivan and Offenbach simultaneously take hold of American stages in the back third of the nineteenth century, their influence on the musical becomes, quite simply, tremendous. We know this because it was only after exposure to the European musical that the American form began to favor full-length story scores: the very basis of the musical as we know it today.

Before the European invasion, the American musical comprised primitive forms enjoying relatively little artistic development—the **minstrel show**, for instance, dominant in the nineteenth century's middle third and moribund in most theatre capitals by the 1890s (though minstrel troupes toured successfully into the early 1900s). George M. Cohan twice tried to revive the form on Broadway, in 1908 and 1909. Both tries failed—yet *Ziegfeld Follies of 1919* featured a star-filled tab minstrel show for its first-act finale that proved the highlight of everyone's favorite *Follies*, and the trope of actors made up in blackface, hymning the supposed joys of plantation life, sneaked into Hollywood musicals in the 1930s and 1940s. The stage, too, has never quite given it up: in the finale of Kurt Weill and Alan Jay Lerner's *Love Life*, in Charlemagne's war council in *Pippin*, even providing the staging concept for the recent Kander and Ebb show *The Scottsboro Boys*.

These sometimes scathing resuscitations use minstrelsy intellectually; in the 1800s, it was simply a way of creating musicals without full-scale stories. These were variety shows, made of songs, dances, and jokes united by subject matter—black life and love in the southland—and performed by not only whites but (till the 1870s) by men only. Thomas D. Rice is credited with the inspiration for the iconic black character in a song-and-dance medium. Yet it was Dan Emmett, the composer of the first more-or-less hit songs in this field (including "Blue Tail Fly" and the very anthem of minstrelsy, "Dixie") who directed in 1843 the first quartet billed as the Virginia Minstrels: the first minstrel show. "If Rice was father of the American minstrel," says historian Julian Mates, "then Emmett was father of the American minstrel show."

The quartet expanded, and the "burnt cork" makeup and outlandish costuming of colorful "finery" or tailcoats with shirt collars hitting the ears became essential. From a single act, the minstrel show grew to three. The

First Part, as it was called, remained the key event: a semi-circle of men backing up, at center stage, the Interlocutor and, at the sides, the two end-men. These were Mr. Bones (playing two semi-attached bone-like substances producing a castanet crackle) and Mr. Tambo (on the tambourine). "Gentlemen," cried the Interlocutor at the start, "be *seated!*" He then announced the numbers and worked the jokes with the endmen, all in stage-southern dialect, repeating the set-up lines so the public wouldn't miss the punchline. The jokes were traditional, often virtually pointless. On an early Victor 78 treating a miniature First Part, Mr. Tambo tells of an uncle so mean he won't feed his chickens.

"*Won't feed the chickens?*" the Interlocutor repeats.

Yes, and one poor hen was reduced to eating sawdust and shavings at the saw mill.

"*Sawdust and shavings?*" the Interlocutor cries, because apparently the audience hasn't yet turned on their hearing aids.

Yes, and then she laid a dozen eggs. And when they hatched, "Eleven of them had wooden legs and the other was a woodchuck!"

Which is immediately followed by hideous yawk-yawk laughter from everyone on stage and percussive punctuation from the Messrs. Tambo and Bones.

The Second Part, known as the "olio," was a variety show made of anything from song and dance spots to crazy novelty acts by the entertainment industry's outliers—playing tunes on glassware filled with contrasting levels of water, say, or barnyard imitations. One thing the public could count on was the "stump speech," modeled on the politician's pompous rhetoric but filled with doubletalk, allusions to everything from the Bible to the latest scandal, and aimless fill-in phrases such as "due to de obvious fact dat," which merrily led from one topic to another without a blip of continuity. "Usually given by one of the endmen," says minstrelsy historian Robert C. Toll, the stump speech "was a discourse as much on the infinite possibilities for malaprops [*sic*] as the chosen subject." These flights of eloquent gibberish were rendered with acrobatic flash, often culminating in the speaker's crashing off the podium to the floor. Toll pinpoints a modern practitioner of this lost art in the actor and recurring Johnny Carson television talk-show guest "Professor" Irwin Corey, so a few of my readers may actually have seen the very last of the stump speakers, albeit without the blackface makeup and fake southern dialect.

The Third Part brought forth a playlet supporting more song spots, reserved in particular for the Old Favorites, perhaps "My Dusky Rose," a ballad fit for close harmony; a sentimental piece such as Stephen Foster's "Old Folks At Home"; or a fast choral number like "Climb Up, Ye Chillun,

Climb." Sometimes the Third Part offered a spoof of some literary or dramatic work (especially *Uncle Tom's Cabin*), anticipating the form of burlesque, which itself led (under the tutelage of Gilbert and Sullivan and Offenbach) to American musical comedy. This places minstrelsy's Third Part as one of the musical's founding outfits.

Thus, an entertainment machine was run on just a few moving parts, and as time went on, rival companies outdid one another, particularly in size. John H. Haverly, the manager who dominated the minstrel scene in the 1880s with over a dozen different troupes touring the nation, introduced the monster minstrel show in Haverly's Mastodon Minstrels. Here was where a deathless show-biz advertising idiom was introduced, in Haverly's "40, Count 'Em, 40!": the number of his "stars."

"The minstrel show was the backbone of American popular entertainment for over half a century," says Julian Mates. Further, it was at first the only American form that really was a musical—that is, it blended singing and "acting" into a relatively unified whole. As to its influence, it is very likely that it was the minstrel show that first disseminated ragtime—in the late 1880s and 1890s—when ragtime could otherwise be heard only in saloons and dives.

Were there American story musicals in these very early years? Historians cite a surprising number of them, such as *The Archers* (1776), on the William Tell saga; or *The Seven Sisters* (1860). The former intrigues for its timely revolutionary subject, as the Swiss Tell defies the Austrian Gesler with Colonial fire—and its librettist-lyricist,* William Dunlap, was a prolific playwright and the first major historian of the American stage. But *The Archers'* music, by Benjamin Carr, is almost entirely lost; it's difficult to assess the work. As for *The Seven Sisters*, it is not clear whether it even had a score beyond dance music and choruses.

At that, most of the shows named as musicals in the mid-nineteenth century were really plays with a smattering of song and dance. Virtually

---

*The word "libretto" is ambiguous; does it denote only "the book" or "the book and the lyrics together"? Originally, the libretto was the verbal content of an opera. By extension, it meant, as in Webster's Third International Dictionary, "the text of a work of musical theater"—in other words, the book and lyrics together. Some users make a distinction: the libretto, to them, is dialogue only. Taking *My Fair Lady*'s "Wouldn't It Be Lovely?" as an example, the refrain's spoken cue line, "Where'ya bound for this spring, Eliza? Biarritz?," is part of the libretto, and its sung reply, "All I want is a room somewhere," is part of something else. This seems to me awkward and diffuse, but it has long since become standard usage: the *libretto* is the book of a musical, to be considered separately from the *lyrics* of a musical. Thus, Alan Jay Lerner, who wrote all of *My Fair Lady*'s words, is not the show's librettist but its librettist-lyricist. While we're at it, the "score" refers to the music and lyrics together, not the music alone.

every theatre had an orchestra—this remained the norm through the 1920s—because one reason why people went to theatres in the first place was to hear music. As long as the band was available, why not add to its accustomed duties in playing before and after the show and during the intervals? Why not let performers air their musical specialties? Why not, indeed, hire musical performers for this very purpose in the first place? *A Glance at New York in 1848* and *New York As It Is*, both in 1848, are often mentioned as proto-musicals, partly because their most important figure, F. S. Chanfrau's celebrated portrayal of Mose the Fire B'hoy, anticipates the heavily Irish character of early Broadway musicmaking, by Harrigan and Hart, George M. Cohan, and Chauncey Olcott among many others. Note the spelling of Mose's sobriquet: this uncouth little devil, a burst of vernacular realism that thrilled his real-life counterparts in the peanut gallery, belongs to one of the city's volunteer fire brigades, and "B'hoy" records the Irish-immigrant pronunciation of "boy." Yet these two Mose shows—there were others in the series—contained only seven ditties each.

A very typical musical show of this era is *The Naiad Queen; or, The Mysteries of the Lurlie Berg!* (1841), another of those-nature and-magic tales, billed as "a mythological and romantic drama." The authors, W. E. Burton and a composer called simply Mr. Woolf, are unknown to fame, but the star, in the title role, was Charlotte Cushman, an opera singer who lost her voice and re-employed herself as America's first prominent actress. *The Naiad Queen*'s program lists only three vocal numbers, but there were eight dances, including "Military Evolutions" (uniformed women showing off a marching drill, a stock item in musicals till the 1920s) and a corps of nymphs in "Beautiful Scarf Movement."

In other words, this is a mating of drama and dance, not a musical as we use the term. It reminds one of the Old Vic's spectacular staging of *A Midsummer Night's Dream* in 1954, with actors and dancers: Robert Helpmann and Moira Shearer were Oberon and Titania, Stanley Holloway was Bottom, and the company landed at the Metropolitan Opera, for extra prestige. But it wasn't a musical. If it had been, the characters would have been singing on and off throughout the action; obviously, they weren't. Either they were speaking Shakespeare or dancing to (and singing a tiny bit of) Mendelssohn.

And that brings us to what is generally thought of as the first American musical, *The Black Crook* (1866), which wasn't the first anything and wasn't even a musical. Nevertheless, the history has to start somewhere, and *The Black Crook* was a smash hit of such vast proportion that it serves as a marker, a first bullet-point in the catalogue of precedents. And of course there is the wonderful legend of how a visiting European ballet troupe was to play the Academy of Music when the theatre burned down, forcing the dancers to join forces with a crazy melodrama in a rival theatre, Niblo's Garden, and an alchemy of horror thriller and beauteous display mixes up the "first musical." Lately, some historians have debunked the tale as a fantasy, but they're wrong. What legend tells is almost exactly what happened.

My authority is a very short book published many years after the event, *The Naked Truth: An Inside History of* The Black Crook. The author, Joseph Whitton, isn't clear on his role in the production, saying only that he had "a connection to the financial department of Niblo's Garden." From his close view of the saga, Whitton would seem to have been the box-office manager— but also a confidant of William Wheatley, who ran Niblo's Garden. As Whitton fills out the bare bones of the legend, managers Henry C. Jarrett and Harry Palmer had gone to Europe some time in early 1866 to hire "the most accomplished artistes and the prettiest women . . . from the leading theatres of London, Paris, Berlin, and Milan." Here Whitton corrects the legend slightly, for Jarrett and Palmer hired not just ballet people but actors and singers. Whitton cites among others Millie Cavendish of Drury Lane, George Atkins of Sadler's Wells, Rose Morton and Mary Wells of the Lyceum Theatre, contralto Annie Kemp, "pantomimist" Hernandez Fuller (*recte*, according to *The Black Crook's* program, Hernandez Foster). Obviously, Jarrett and Palmer had more than just ballet in mind, and when they returned to New York, in the summer of 1866, they approached William Wheatley with an offer—this is Whitton again—"to join them in the production of a spectacular drama [at Niblo's Garden], in which their Ballet would be introduced."

Wheatley agreed—and he had the drama, yet another of those nature-and-magic stories, this one very reminiscent of Carl Maria von Weber's opera *Der Freischütz*, about a nice guy, a nice girl, and a bad guy in league with hell and featuring a scene in which the devil himself is conjured up in spooky ritual. This was *The Black Crook*, a play by Charles M. Barras. Jarrett and Palmer resented Barras' exorbitant terms, and they suggested a revision of *The Naiad Queen*. However, Wheatley seems to have wanted a novelty, and by the time he talked Jarrett and Palmer around, all three men must have sensed that they were in on something not just new but big, because they spent $10,000 to buy out the contract of the Ravel family, French acrobats-*cum*-dancers who had been headlining in America for a generation, and whose engagement at Niblo's Garden had six weeks left to run. With a huge company imported from Europe at great expense (and already on salary), it was imperative to free Wheatley's stage for rehearsals and, especially, to work out the special effects with which the three partners expected *The Black Crook* to distinguish itself.

Ten thousand dollars was a stupendous amount in 1866. *The Black Crook* itself, loaded as it was with sets, costumes, and "transformation" scenes (in which one locale more or less dissolved into another before one's eyes), only cost $55,000 altogether.* A colossus in every way, the show lasted over five hours on opening night, September 12, 1866, and ran for 474 performances, which had never happened before. Broadway had not yet become the absolute focus of American theatre, and long runs were generated over the course of a multi-city tour, not in a single venue. To keep a theatre with a seating capacity of 1,762 open with a single work for, in this case, sixteen months was unheard of, especially as *The Black Crook* was really one more entry in the now longish line of phantasmal plays-with-ballet. However, Wheatley, Jarrett, and Palmer did innovate, in three ways: their show was indeed quite a spectacle; their show had popular elements that suggest a primeval form of musical comedy; and their show was sexy.

It was those ballet girls. All one saw, really, was the outline of their legs in flesh-colored tights under their skirts. Still, in 1866, that'll do it. "Nothing in any other Christian country, or in modern times, has approached the indecent and demoralizing exhibition at Wheatley's theatre," the New York *Herald* thundered. "There [were] similar places and scenes in Pompeii just as that city was buried beneath the eruption of Vesuvius."

So everybody immediately bought tickets. In fact, Joseph Whitton believes that the *Herald*'s publisher, James Gordon Bennett, was deliberately provoking guilty-pleasure ticket buying to thank Wheatley for having taken Bennett's side in his feud with P. T. Barnum. Whether that's true or not, *The Black Crook* did become a hit at least partly through notoriety, enlivening many a Sunday sermon and becoming the topic that, to the ladies' delighted alarm, could scarcely be broached in mixed company. Indeed, this bashing of *The Black Crook* by censors and soul savers marks it as roguish, rebellious, and culturally subversive—the very qualities that the American musical was to seize as its own, as we'll presently see.

Interestingly, Whitton does not mention the burning of the Academy of Music, the event that forced the merging of the ballet-and-acting troupe with *The Black Crook* in the first place. Still, Jarrett and Palmer had to have had a contract with the Academy, because they could not possibly have gone to the trouble of contracting talent in four European countries and hauling them back to America without having secured a place to play in when they returned. They obviously didn't have one with Niblo's Garden till they proposed partnering up with Wheatley—so it must have been with the Academy, the only other New York theatre with a stage large enough to suit their ambitions. The probable timeline supports this speculation, for

---

*For some reason, the press reported the capitalization as $50,000, and the figure has dogged the annals ever since. Whitton insists it was the higher number.

in order to pack in the ocean voyage to Europe, visit four cities, take in the shows to audition the talent, and then shepherd the new company back across the sea, Jarrett and Palmer must have been gone a good three months—before which they would have signed their contract with the Academy of Music and during the first weeks of which the Academy suffered its conflagration.

But what of *The Black Crook* itself? Why isn't it a musical even when it anticipates aspects of the musical? For one thing, it had very few vocal numbers, at least in 1866. But, remember, Jarrett and Palmer had sought out not only dancers but specialists of the light musical stage, for instance the aforementioned Millie Cavendish, who played the heroine's servant, Carline. This part, of the genre known to British play production as the Singing Chambermaid, could be counted on for a merry song regardless of the plot particulars. Indeed, amid all the dastardly intrigue of *The Black Crook*'s several bad guys and the ethereal wonders of the fairy kingdom, Carline (and her vis-à-vis, Greppo, lackey of the black crook himself, Hertzog) supplied a saucy undertone.

Certainly, Barras' script needed it, as witness the posturing diction. The setting is the Hartz Mountains in 1600, and we begin outside Dame Barbara's cottage. Rodolphe enters, claps his hands three times, and the lovers meet:

> AMINA: (looking out a second-floor window) Surely I heard his well-known signal. Hist, who's there?
> RODOLPHE: Tis I, Rodolphe!

Rodolphe, a painter, has been trying to raise money by selling his art, but has had no luck.

> AMINA: (aside) Poor, dear Rodolphe, he knows not the worst—the heaviest blow is yet to come.

That's because Barbara, Amina's foster-mother, has promised her to evil Count Wolfenstein. After Barbara shoos Rodolphe away, the local girls enter, among them Carline, who gets to deliver what may be the first Unbelievably Contrived Number Cue in the musical's history:

> CARLINE: But come, while 'Mina is making ready, let's rehearse our Festival Dance.

It's as good a reason as any. Carline's activity sheet includes also making fun of Barbara:

BARBARA: Then you—you think me graceful, eh?

CARLINE: (to audience) As a hippopotamus.

On their London visit, Jarrett and Palmer presumably caught Millie Cavendish at Drury Lane singing "You Naughty, Naughty Men," which she had commissioned from composer George Bicknell and lyricist Theodore Kennick for her exclusive use. When Cavendish came across the Atlantic, she packed the song, a primitive little carol rattling along on almost non-stop eighth notes (but observe the extremely ahead-of-its-time enjambment in the last two lines):

> You may talk of love and sighing,
> Say for us you're nearly dying,
> All the while you know you're trying
> To deceive, you naughty, naughty men.

Barbara plays comedy, too, with Von Puffengruntz, Wolfenstein's valet. It is not too early in the musical's saga for there to be a homely woman trying to trap a pompous man into marriage, a convention for the next three generations. In a bit of foolery, Dragonfin—a monster in the service of Stalacta, the Queen of the Golden Realm—rises up through a trap door between Barbara and Von Puffengruntz. (Dragonfin was played by Hernandez Foster, singled out a few pages ago as one of the recruits on the English leg of the European talent search.) The two mortals are self-consciously looking away, and when Von Puffengruntz tries to take Barbara's hand, he unknowingly gets Dragonfin, who shakes with silent laughter.

VON PUFFENGRUNTZ: Poor frightened thing, how she trembles.

Then he looks at the hand he is holding. Hmm. That doesn't seem ladylike, does it? Von Puffengruntz's gaze slowly travels up the arm till he spies Dragonfin's face, panics, and races off—all in mime. Barbara, mouing and preening beside Dragonfin, has no idea what has happened:

BARBARA: (flirtatiously) You'll promise not to tread on the Fraulein von Skragneck's bunion? (Aside) Poor fellow, joy has made him speechless.

It may well be that Millie Cavendish's song and the comedy spots were *The Black Crook*'s secret weapons—the folderol that helped some of the public get through the hours of ballet, no to mention Barras' Sturm und

Drang dialogue. "Trash," the critics called it. "Rubbish." The plot was as coarse and rowdy as a Spielberg dinosaur. Nevertheless, the show was the biggest hit in theatre history; and such a precedent demands a follow-up. Not a sequel, but a second experiment of comparable nature—a *Carousel* (after *Oklahoma!*), a *Camelot* (after *My Fair Lady*).

So Jarrett and Palmer put on a "second" *Black Crook* at Niblo's Garden in 1868 as *The White Fawn*, with a script by James Mortimer. In this "fairy burlesque spectacular extravaganza," King Dingdong imprisons his daughter, Princess Graceful, in a tower from which she escapes into the arms of Prince Leander (a trouser role, in the style of the day, played by Lucy Egerton). *The Black Crook*'s satanic intrigue was set aside for the purer atmosphere of Storybookland, yet the same combination of melodrama, ballet, and elaborate decor ruled the stage. This time, however, there were more than just a few songs, including early examples of what would prove one of the musical's most useful expedients, the establishing number. Think of "Why Can't the English?," "I Put My Hand In," "The Worst Pies in London." *The White Fawn* offered the analogous, if risibly obvious, "I'm King Dingdong" and "Prince Leander Is My Name."*

Lasting 176 performances, *The White Fawn* was a smash hit, hut no phenomenon. Nor did the title itself develop any reverberation. Among melodrama-dance spectacles, it was *The Black Crook* that the public demanded, in revival tours that kept beefing up the vocal menu to compete with the full-fledged musicals of the 1880s and 1890s. In the end, *The Black Crook* became the summoning title for the era, just as, later, *My Fair Lady* would; the defining work of the time, event theatre, the piece that playgoers had to collect and others at least know about.

Then, too, coming right after the end of the Civil War, *The Black Crook* stood at the entrance to the new economic and social epoch in American life, the day of robber barons and railroad wealth and upward mobility within both the middle and fashionable classes. The show thus marks the start of the musical's First Age, from 1866 to 1899, when primitive genres were elaborated or retired and when European imports dazzled the public with their integration of song and story. This is where the saga really begins.

---

*Offenbach and Gilbert and Sullivan are filled with establishing numbers. Think of "I'm Called Little Buttercup" or, in its own strange way, the song of the mechanical doll in *The Tales of Hoffmann*, which is not only her establishing song but virtually her entire part. However, at the time of *The White Fawn*, Offenbach was only just being heard in America, and Gilbert and Sullivan hadn't even met. An outstanding precedent for the establishing number can be found in Mozart's *Die Zauberflöte* (The Magic Flute), in Papageno's entrance number, a virtual calling card: "The bird catcher am I . . . "

CHAPTER 2

ᖍᕽ

The Age of Burlesque

There is something worth examining in that billing of *The White Fawn* as a "fairy burlesque spectacular extravaganza." The last word, properly reserved for shows on the grand scale, became so misapplied by managers boosting their pokey little productions that the word lost all meaning. *The White Fawn* was also, we note, a burlesque—and this word needs discussion. Although **burlesque** was the very distant forerunner of the degraded art of strippers and low comics that we visit in the last scenes of *Gypsy*, it took a long time and a lot of devolution to get there. In the early 1900s, for instance, burlesque was simply a variety show featuring performers of the lowest rank and emphasizing young women in only slightly revealing outfits. A burlesque theatre was the neighborhood show shop, about as far from what "Broadway" meant as a cocktail napkin is from an illuminated medieval manuscript.

However, before that, in the time of *The White Fawn*, burlesque was a spoof of a literary or dramatic work with mostly women performers—cast, every manager claimed, for beauty if not talent—in a script delineated in rhymed couplets, its humor concentrating on puns. And this brings us to the queen of early burlesque and America's first musical star, the English Lydia Thompson, actor-manager of the celebrated "British Blondes."

Thompson's troupe made their American debut in New York at Wood's Museum* in 1868 with *Ixion!; or, The Man At the Wheel*, Ixion being a fabled Greek king who boasted of having seduced Hera and took his punishment bound to a revolving wheel. Thompson played the role, and, as so often in

---

*Many early American theatres were housed in buildings denoted as "museums" to deflect puritanical criticism with the trappings of an educational experience—artifact displays, lecture series, and the like.

Western art, Greek and Roman names for the gods were carelessly intermingled; characters included Bacchus and Ganymede but also Jupiter
(Zeus). Generally, in burlesque, the fun centered on modernizing ancient
times or exotic places with the peeves and delights of the public's daily life.
This gave an original flavor to the scripts, and each season brought novel
topics to reference. The scores, however, were the usual grab bag of pre-
existing music, sometimes tricked out with new lyrics. Raids on the classics
were popular as well: *Ixion!* included an orchestral medley from Verdi's *Il
Trovatore*, just fifteen years old at the time.

Thompson enjoyed a long career, and in due course her offerings grew
musically more expansive. *Robinson Crusoe* (1877), with Thompson again in
the name role, contained numbers listed in the program as "Concerted
Piece," "Quartette à la Marionette," and "Grand Ensemble." But the comedy,
as before, was slick and daring for the day. In 1869, a Chicago newspaper
editor accused Thompson of using the stage "for the exhibition of coarse
women and the use of disreputable language unrelieved by any wit or humor," and Thompson retaliated by horsewhipping him outside his house.
Burlesque historian Robert C. Allen calls Thompson "the figurative mother
of Sophie Tucker and Mae West"—that is, of independent women who
tested the legal limits of bourgeois protocols about gender. "From *Ixion* [sic]
on," says Allen, "burlesque implicitly raised troubling questions about how
a woman should be 'allowed' to act on stage . . . and about the relationship
of women onstage to women in the outside, 'real' world."

Not all burlesques were subversive. Most simply threw everything they had
at a designated target as a schoolboy heaves a snowball at a banker's top hat.
In 1844, Michael William Balfe's opera *The Bohemian Girl* played the Park Theatre; a year later came *The Bohea Man's Girl*—the burlesque, of course. Virtually all theatregoers had seen tragedian Edwin Forrest's perennial vehicle
Metamora; or, The Last of the Wampanoags (1829); now they could enjoy *Met-A-
Mora; or, The Last of the Pollywogs* (1848). Longfellow and Shakespeare took
their turns, in *Hiawatha; or, Ardent Spirits and Laughing Waters* (1856), which
drew largely on Italian opera for its music; and *Shylock: A Jerusalem Hearty
Joke* (1853). In an 1857 revision, *Shylock; or, The Merchant of Venice Preserved*,
the score borrowed the big tune from Auber's *opéra comique Fra Diavolo*,
known in its English translation as "On Yonder Rock Reclining." Here its first
line was "In yonder house is dining . . ." There were even topical burlesques, as
in *King Cotton; or, The Exiled Prince* (1862), "a new, national, quizzical, local,
farcical, musical, dramatical burlesque extravaganza in one act, nine scenes,
suitable to the times." The characters ran from Jefferson Davis the First, King
of Cotton, to Ponce de Leon, the scene was laid in Secessia, and the numbers
included a chorus of Federals, "Oh, Jeff Davis, Have We Caught You!"

Most early burlesques were one-acts; *King Cotton* was preceded by a scene from Shakespeare and followed by a farce. By the 1870s, however, burlesque had been graduated to full-length works, some with original scores. And here, at last, we find the first American musical (at any rate, the first famous one): Edward Everett Rice and J. Cheever Goodwin's *Evangeline; or, The Belle of Acadia* (1874). Once again, Longfellow provided the subject matter, his tragic poem of 1847 on the forced emigration from their homeland of the lovers Evangeline and Gabriel. Separated, the two travel the American continent in search of each other; in one ghoulishly tender sequence, Evangeline and her party camp in hiding on the Mississippi shore while an unknowing Gabriel sails past them. After years, while nursing the sick in an almshouse, Evangeline recognizes Gabriel. Sleeping, he utters her name and dies. "This is the forest primeval" is *Evangeline*'s first line, and at the end Longfellow returns to the image, telling how some of the exiles have returned to Acadia, repeating the sad story of the two sundered sweethearts:

> While from its rocky caverns the deep-voiced, neighboring ocean
> Speaks, and in accents disconsolate answers the wail of the forest.

One immediately sees the possibilities: the heroine's picaresque can take her anywhere the audience would enjoy seeing her, such as the far west and even Africa, and, as Longfellow gave her a cow, why not put two men into a cow suit to caper about as (so billed) the Heifer? Gabriel has a mother, Catherine, played by a man in drag, and, for that touch of novelty, the authors added in the Lone Fisherman, "a patient and singularly taciturn toiler of the sea," the program explained, "with a natural tendency to hook whatever comes within reach." Turning up in scene after scene in contradiction of geographical logic, ever gazing out to sea through his telescope, the Lone Fisherman became much better known than any character in *The Black Crook* or Lydia Thompson's shows. James S. Maffitt, himself an author and actor-manager, succeeded to the role sometime during its twenty-five-year history, as did George K. Fortescue to that of Catherine; both virtually based their careers on this one work. Further, it became a proving ground for future stars: Henry E. Dixey and Francis Wilson broke in their curriculum vitae as halves of the Heifer in the late 1870s.

By then, Rice and Goodwin were billing their show as an "opera bouffe," with an expanded score now running to some thirty numbers, though these weren't necessarily programmed in every performance. The music is unimpressive: "Thinking, Love, Of Thee," the heroine's first number, gets through an entire refrain on little more than four chords. Yet some of *Evangeline*'s song titles suggest a story score, especially the ensembles and, obviously, Evangeline's very apropos "Where Art Thou Now, My Beloved?," sung during her African visit.

We should note as well "I'm in Lofe Mit a Shveet Leedle Girl," the German-dialect song of one Captain Dietrich, "a 'Dutch' mercenary in the British ranks, who shows no mercy, being a mercy-nary cuss." He's a minor character, but it's a major point: the musical in general was to stereotype Europeans as stock figures—especially as immigrants in America—playing on their accents and malapropisms for humor. In *Evangeline*'s day, they were Scandinavians and Germans. ("Dutch" is simply a corruption of *deutsch* ["German"]). Later, Irish, Italian, black, and Jewish stereotypes emerged. Although the intention was to create fun at a minority group's expense, the long-range effect was, paradoxically, to socialize and assimilate alien peoples through familiarity. Stereotyping precedes sensitive portrayal, which engenders equality and a share of political power. Writing in a totally different context, H. G. Wells called this "let[ting] daylight into the temples." Bizarre as it may sound, such sophisticated works as *Fiddler on the Roof* and *Parade* are founded on the cultural penetration of the Dutch-comic team of Weber and Fields, who will be along shortly.

Unlike the musical's other founding titles, *Evangeline* played only one long run in New York, lasting half a year on a visit in 1885. This show was a *national* favorite. But another such broke *The Black Crook*'s record and then, in revival, enjoyed another gigantic run, yet faded away so completely that, unlike *Evangeline* and even *The Black Crook*, it left absolutely nothing behind. We can call it the most obscure smash hit in the musical's history: *Humpty Dumpty* (1868).

The main reason is that its genre died out very, very suddenly just when *Evangeline* was enjoying a vogue and *The Black Crook* was still doggedly touring. *Humpty Dumpty* was a **pantomime**, an irritatingly confusing term whose history starts in Italian commedia dell'arte, moves to France and thence to England, where pantomime is still an annual Christmastime event. However, modern pantomime resembles nineteenth-century pantomime in only the storybook subjects and the eclectic music using pre-existing materials. From ancient burlesque, it adopts the Principal Boy and the Drag Dame we met up with in *Evangeline*'s Gabriel and Catherine. Otherwise, today's English pantomimes are unique only for their traditional audience participation, especially in warning actors when something dangerous threatens (such as a spider coming down behind an innocent) and arguing with, for instance, Cinderella's step-sisters, who insist, "Oh, yes, it is" to the public's shouted "Oh, no, it isn't!" till the step-sisters throw a picturesque tantrum.

Humpty Dumpty was nothing like that, but it's difficult to say exactly *what* it was. An episodic mixture of fantasy and the everyday and filled with exhibition sequences from roller skating and circus acts to ballet and an exploding steamboat, the show centered on the reportedly matchless abilities of its star, George L. Fox. His title role had nothing to do with sitting on a wall and all the king's horses; the scenes took place in a "Vale of Fertility" and "The Retreat of the Silver Sprites" but also "Humpty's Grocery" and "Lunch Room Down Town." As always in old pantomime, the show started like other musicals, then underwent a magical bit in which a fairy transformed the leads into commedia figures who played the rest of their parts in dumb show (except when they sang). Hernandez Foster, *The Black Crook*'s silent comic monster Dragonfin, would have been right at home in *Humpty Dumpty*.

Virtually all show biz at this time was a performer's medium, but pantomime was especially so. One might even call it George L. Fox's medium, because, after dementia drove him from the stage, pantomime instantly collapsed. The Humpty of the first national tour, Tony Denier, kept the show going here and there. Still, without Fox's drawing power, there was no reason to create any new works in this line.

Then, too, pantomime, like the ballet spectacles, was expensive to capitalize. Burlesque was tidier and thus attractive to managers—and in the 1870s, **farce** offered the stingiest form of musical yet. Farce didn't even need to produce a score: the manager hired a small company, each to contribute his or her specialty, like a band of Millie Cavendishes. In her case, it was "You Naughty, Naughty Men" dropping in on *The Black Crook*, but it might be any song or two, a dance, an acrobatics display, a recitation. The musical farce was a play containing a talent show.

Reciting was Nate Salsbury's specialty, and Salsbury, as actor-manager and playwright, is called the creator of the American farce musical. He provides us with another of our landmark titles, *The Brook* (1879), a single act expanded to two in 1881 and a cheapskate manager's dream of a show: just two sets, no chorus, and five lead roles taken by, as historian Gerald Bordman puts it, "shouters and buffoons." Billed as Salsbury's Troubadors, they did largely hold together as a unit through not only *The Brook*'s years of touring but on to *Three of a Kind!* (1883) and *The Humming Bird* (1887). Salsbury was in the shows, though as author he wrote only *The Brook*. "Pic-nic grounds for a dinner in the woods" was the set description in the original program: the party arrives, finds that all the food has been contaminated during the trip, and opens a chest to discover not the hoped-for watermelons but . . . theatrical costumes! Well, on with the motley, and, after performing, the party packs up and sets off for home.

Insistently heralded as "farce comedies," these were in fact musicals with hodgepodge scores—a new topical number on, say, the dos and don'ts of train travel, or the patter trio from Gilbert and Sullivan's *Ruddigore* that ended up also in *Thoroughly Modern Millie* over a century later, or a "Plantation Song" called "Swinging on a Gospel Gate."

Farces became the rage, and if Nate Salsbury was their father, Charles H. Hoyt became their master. Hoyt had a gimmick: his titles began with the indefinite article: *A Bunch Of Keys* (1883), *A Parlor Match* (1884), *A Black Sheep* (1896), *A Day and a Night in New York* (1898). Manager Florenz Ziegfeld's first Broadway production was a revival of *A Parlor Match*, in 1896, with the original stars, Charles Evan Evans and William F. Hoey. The latter played a crazy tramp who "haunts" a house and sang a hit interpolation, "The Man Who Broke the Bank at Monte Carlo," the kind of number for which the word "rollicking" might have been invented.

Monte Carlo has nothing to do with being a tramp or haunting a house, but farce was the player piano of musical comedy, always open to a hot number of any kind. Ziegfeld really intended his *Parlor Match* as the debut venue for his first musical-comedy star, "étoile de Paris" Anna Held, who appeared as one of the spirits in a séance scene to sing the somewhat less than spiritual "Come and Play With Me," along with encores at the public's demand. Ziegfeld invented the use of PR as the engine that drives stardom, and while Evans and Hoey were the show's leads, Mlle. Held was the reason the audience was there, keyed up by Ziegfeld's drumming bulletins on the enticingly hedonistic abandon of Held's lifestyle, eventually to include a mysterious jewel robbery and a daily enjoyment of—innocents, please leave the room—milk baths! *Yes!* To pleasure the skin and revel in the guiltless freedom of the appetitive existence. The method was headlines, the content was sin, the reaction was mass curiosity, and the result was sensation.

Even so, farce's outstanding hit was a different Hoyt title, *A Trip To Chinatown* (1891), billed as "An idyll of San Francisco" and, at 657 consecutive performances in New York alone, our biggest success yet. It can also to be credited with the musical's first gigantic song hit, the "Memories" of its day, Charles K. Harris' "After the Ball," a nostalgic piece interpolated sometime during the run. It tells of an old bachelor who broke off his engagement with his life's love because he—wrongly—thought her faithless. A story ballad, "After the Ball" runs on a structure in which each of three verses advances the narrative while the repeated chorus remains the same—a static nineteenth-century format that the twentieth-century musical would retire. In fact, the old story ballad became so antique that *Show Boat* used this very number to place a scene chronologically. When it is announced as "an old favorite," the audience instantly understands that the scene recalls a time when story ballads were still sung—when heroines like Magnolia Ravenal would appear in an evening gown with a feathered fan to transform cabaret into the Story Hour.

A Trip To Chinatown's plot is almost painfully simple. The setting is San Francisco. In Act One, some young people plan to attend a ball while alibiing to curmudgeonly Uncle Ben that they're merely going to take in the sights of Chinatown. Oh, it's perfectly innocent. Mrs. Guyer, a widow (a favorite character in musicals, always assumed to be ahead of the curve in worldly matters) will chaperone. But Uncle Ben has designs on the widow.

Act Two is set in a chic restaurant, where Uncle Ben awaits the widow in vain and does shtick comedy with an uncooperative waiter while, unbeknown to him, the young people enjoy themselves in the next room. (Nobody gets to the ball, which, in any case, is raided by the police.) Uncle Ben's bill is a hundred dollars, but he has lost his wallet . . . and here many a historian chimes in with how much A Trip To Chinatown anticipates the Harmonia Gardens restaurant scene in Hello, Dolly!. Indeed it does: the old curmudgeon who has lost his money, the young people he knows but can't see (and one of them, in both shows, is his niece), the widow. Even more interesting is how much of the stock humor that the musical would still be using well into the twentieth century was already in play in the 1890s—the crazy names, for example, a notable feature some fifty years later in On the Town, with its Lucy Schmeeler and Claire De Loon. The leader of Chinatown's young crowd is Rashleigh Gay, his best friend is Wilder Daly, Uncle Ben's hypochondriac friend is Welland Strong, the waiter is Slavin Paine, and of course Mrs. Guyer is so named because a widow knows how to "guy" (fool) the men. (She also gets into male disguise at one point.)

Or take this exchange, whose play on the word "taste" is standard musical-comedy fun even today. In the restaurant, the supposedly moribund Welland Strong is asked to order for the young people's party:

WELLAND: I fear the taste of a dying man may not exactly suit your fancies.
WILDER: I don't know. I never tasted one.

Chinatown's core numbers (before the huge New York run and years of touring added various interpolations), composed mainly by Percy Gaunt to Hoyt's lyrics, were wholly unintegrated. At regular intervals, someone would simply cue up a song, as when, at the restaurant, Rashleigh's girl friend, Flirt, cries out, "Say, everybody! Tony [Uncle Ben's niece] knows the song the orchestra's playing. I want you all to listen." Or consider the ramp-up to "The Pretty Widow":

RASHLEIGH: The widow's more fun than any girl I know. Say, Wilder, I don't believe a woman is ever at her best till she becomes a widow.

WILDER: The boys all seem to think she's in her prime, anyway. That's a great song Billy Barker wrote and dedicated to her.

And the two then dig in:

> Do you know her?
> Have you met her?
> If so, you'll ne'er forget her,
> The pretty little widow with the laughing eyes of brown.

It's a slim score, too, for the show had far more book than music. Even so, *A Trip To Chinatown* counted hit tunes besides "After the Ball." "Reuben and Cynthia" and the clodhopping waltz "(On) The Bowery," popular long after their day, are ridiculously simplistic. But a minstrel number entirely by Gaunt, "Push Dem Clouds Away"—a description of the heavenly life—bears a disarming naiveté. The young people and Mrs. Guyer introduce it in Act One:

> Old Gabriel's horn will toot and roar,
> When you push dem clouds away!
> There'll be no dudes around the stage door,
> When you push dem clouds away!

Discussions of musical farce seek its truest source but also its expressive summit in the work of Harrigan and Hart, though Edward Harrigan, the actor-manager-playwright of the concern, generally termed each work as a "local comedy" or "local play." The "local" was not used lightly, for the series of shows that Harrigan and his acting partner, Tony Hart, presented from just before to just after the 1880s was obsessed with New York immigrant life. Here was a counter to Dutch comedy in something larger: Irish stereotypes at once broad and nuanced, for the fun of it, but also to taste of life as lived. E. J. Kahn, Harrigan and Hart's biographer, tells us that the company would appear not in costumes but in clothes bought right off the backs of Irish immigrants as they stepped out of Castle Garden, the immigration processing station, and that the Garden itself was set on Harrigan's stage more than once. "Good old Ned!" the crowd would cry at a line that struck them with the wonder of self-recognition. Some historians want to date the founding of the American musical from Harrigan and Hart simply because here the musical discovered its unique content, in a sociology of New York's evolving ethnicity: *The Mulligan Guards' Ball* (1879); *The Mulligans' Silver Wedding* (1880); *Cordelia's Aspirations* (1883), which are social; *McNooney's Visit* (1887), which leads him to be mistaken for a burglar; *Reilly and the Four Hundred* (1890), another mixup between the Irish and Society. The playwright Dion Boucicault, famed for unusually realistic melodramas often set in Ireland, told Harrigan, "You have done for the Irish in New York what I have done for the Irish in Ireland."

The Harrigan and Hart enterprise was like a family. Some of the company were married—had, in fact, met on the job—and they held together over the years like a stock company, at least until Tony Hart brought his Yoko Ono onto the scene. The new Mrs. Hart nourished acting ambitions, and ultimately Hart broke up with Harrigan and struck off on his own, unsuccessfully. The two men's era lasted less than a generation even with a lock audience, for there was just so much to be got out of a single milieu—even a single family, Dan and Cordelia Mulligan and their brood. No other major writer or writing team pursued so limited an agenda, but no others had to: when Harrigan stepped out of type for *Mordecai Lyons* (1882), as a Jewish pawnbroker, his public balked.

Further, as so often in the First Age, the Harrigan and Hart shows weren't really musicals. Some had a handful of tunes, others only a few more than that—and the songs were atmosphere pieces, not character numbers. For all its banality, the *Evangeline* score tries to give voice to its characters at very certain turns in the plot, whereas the Harrigan and Hart songs, composed by Dave Braham to Harrigan's verses, are all of a "boys and girls together" type: "The Mulligan Guard," as Dan's militia turns out on parade; "The Babies On Our Block," "The Widow Nolan's Goat," "Maggie Murphy's Home," where "A bedroom and a parlor is all we call our own."

In fact, there was very little genuine music theatre in America until Gilbert and Sullivan and Offenbach showed theatregoers what a musical really was, with greatest impact in the late 1870s and early 1880s. Offenbach had been heard from as early as 1867, when *La Grande-Duchesse de Gérolstein* played New York for an astonishing 156 performances in the original French. In fact, the public enjoyed Offenbach partly because few understood what his characters were actually saying; later, when they heard what the randy Grand Duchess, the adulterous Helen and Paris, and that sexual racketeer Zeus were up to in English translation, there was outcry.

Gilbert and Sullivan are circumspect about fleshly pleasure. More to the point, Sullivan utterly overtook the sophomoric sounds of the native forms and Gilbert was everyone's first taste of wit in the libretto. Such was the appeal of *HMS Pinafore* in its premiere season of 1878–1879 that it didn't just make a hit on Broadway: it saturated the theatre district in multiple showings. Besides a run of 175 performances at its main home, the Standard Theatre, it enjoyed good stays also at the Broadway and Fifth Avenue Theatres and in two *different* productions at the Lyceum, a German version, short runs at the Olympic and Wallack's, a staging by a black troupe at the Globe, a double-teaming of adult and children's casts at Haverly's Lyceum (after which the adults departed and the kids took over for 57 performances), and, naturally, a burlesque version, by the San Francisco Minstrels, *His-Mud-Scow Pinafore*, a big deal at 92 performances at Niblo's Garden.

Theatregoers went Gilbert-and-Sullivan mad, and each next Savoy title nourished their love of this very new form of musical, smart and sly and musically persuasive. Then, too, unlike the faerie of *The Black Crook* and the dizzy contortions of burlesque, the Savoy style offered satires on sociopolitical themes. They were, to use a concept of the 1960s, "relevant." Many shows made topical references: here was a full-fledged topical conversation. Gilbert and Sullivan's *Patience*, named for a milkmaid torn between two trendy poets, seemed to be a spoof of Oscar Wilde, who was even then—in 1881—making his Personal Appearance in America under the management of Richard D'Oyly Carte, Gilbert and Sullivan's manager in both England and the United States. As Wilde's biographer Richard Ellmann puts it, "Carte expected *Patience* to give a fillip to Wilde's lectures, and the lectures to give a fillip to *Patience*." *Patience* is really a spoof of trendiness per se, not of Wilde—but the presumed Wildean character (actually a composite of artsy public figures), Reginald Bunthorne, has a line about walking down Piccadilly "with a poppy or a lily in your medieval hand." And didn't Wilde do just that? "To have done it was nothing," Wilde eventually remarked, "but to make people think one had done it was a triumph." Still, isn't there a strong sense of Wilde in his late-in-the-second-act confrontation with his rival, one Archibald Grosvenor, when Bunthorne is about to pronounce a curse?:

GROSVENOR: Oh, reflect! You had a mother once.
BUNTHORNE: Never!
GROSVENOR: Then you had an aunt.

Whereupon Bunthorne goes completely to pieces.

Then as now, the most popular Savoy title was *The Mikado*, first given here in 1885, initiating a cycle of American musicals set in the East: *The Begum* (1887), *Wang* (1891), *Panjandrum* (1893), *The Rainmaker of Syria* (1893), *Tabasco* (1894). The appeal to writers was easy to understand: exotic customs gave them instant comedy material. *Wang*, by *Evangeline's* primary librettist, J. Cheever Goodwin (who was now working with composer Woolson Morse), anticipated the plot premise of *The Merry Widow*, as all intrigue to secure a widow's fortune . . . in Siam. But "Ask the Man in the Moon" told where the show really took place, with references to "the L roads" (New York's elevated railways) and "the Washington Arch." Again, the scores were infantile, so while such shows were very successful, the historical momentum lay with European models with their integrated scores and true-voiced singers: **comic opera** was the term for them now.

Consider the 1880–1881 season. There were helpings of Harrigan and Hart; yet another revision of *Evangeline* and revivals of *The Black Crook*, *Humpty Dumpty*, and *The Brook*; a burlesque of *Carmen*; and *Fritz in Ireland*, the latest entry in a series focusing on yet another immigrant group that began with *Fritz, Our Cousin German* (1870), starring J. K. Emmet.

These and a few trifles constituted the American shows, and, of them all, only *Evangeline* was truly a musical, with its evening's worth of songs, at least some of which were embedded in the action so tellingly that without them the work would implode. This was something that comic opera supplied as a rule. In a mere two years after the appearance of *HMS Pinafore*, the story show with its story score had colonized Broadway.

Thus, Gilbert and Sullivan were represented by more of *Pinafore* and, to boot, *The Pirates of Penzance* (which inspired two burlesques), and there were no fewer than fourteen productions of continental pieces. These counted new works and revivals, about half in the original and half in translation: Offenbach, Lecocq, von Suppé, Genée, Strauss. Planquette and Audran enjoyed double mountings of their *Les Cloches de Corneville* and *La Mascotte* (respectively), in both French and English.

Then, near the start of the following season, the Casino Theatre opened— the first American playhouse built specifically for musicals. Dominating the southeast corner of Broadway and Thirty-Ninth Street, well north of the theatre district of the day, the structure combined a facade of Venetian Gothic with a Moorish tower at the corner matching the interior's decor, something like a seraglio seating 1,300. The very size of the place emphasized the proportions of comic opera, not so much in spectacle as in the importance of the chorus and the expanded orchestra.

The Casino was a palace of comic opera, an acknowledgment that a major form deserved a major showplace. But first, just to make this difficult for us, burlesque threw a last party with one of the biggest hits of the era, setting a new long-run record at 603 performances: *Adonis* (1884). A spoof of the Pygmalion and Galatea legend, *Adonis* starred Henry E. Dixey as a statue come to life, entrancing so many would-be lovers that he seeks relief by turning back into marble. The score was the usual ragbag of old music with new words, though Edward E. Rice did some fresh composing. William F. Gill wrote the script in a breathless, anything-for-a-laugh style that at times goes into free-associative gabble. Here's Adonis crazing around with Rosetta, described in the program as "The happy possessor of a clear conscience and a soprano voice" and played by Amelia Summerville, a specialist in physically abundant young women:

> ADONIS: (rushing on and falling into Rosetta's arms) I am hemmed in by my pursuers . . . But fear not, Rosetta, I will never be taken alive. Rather than that I would eat pies of your making and die of indigestion.

Rosetta wants Adonis to save himself through masquerade.

> ROSETTA: My wardrobe is extensive.
> ADONIS: (noting her waistline) It would have to be.

Only *Humpty Dumpty* had so promoted the talents of its star, for *Adonis* was devoted to the trim and handsome but endlessly sassy Dixey—and to some twenty disguises that he slipped into and out of, to his imitations of everyone from a Harrigan and Hart type to the English Shakespearean Henry Irving, and not least to Dixey's kicky dancing. Dixey and his fellow leads took the show to London, a most unusual event for an American musical, and the star seldom strayed from his signature role for the next twenty years. On one of Dixey's last New York appearances, in 1884 at the Casino, his famous "fadeout" curtain in which he reassumed his original pose as the statue was followed by a unique exhibition by the bodybuilder Sandow, a real-life Adonis. The young Florenz Ziegfeld was in the Casino that night; noticing how animated the audience became as Sandow flexed, preened, and went into his unique standing back-flip, Ziegfeld decided to manage Sandow as a show-biz attraction. This eventually led Ziegfeld to the aforementioned revival of *A Parlor Match* and, ultimately, to a producing career in the musical outranking in influence that of all other non-writers except Hal Prince.

Adonis marked the end of old-fashioned burlesque, which soon devolved into a girls-and-comics revue format in rundown neighborhood venues and, later, into the tawdry stripper shows that most Americans think of when they hear the word "burlesque." European comic opera was sweeping the American musical stage, and now comes the first enduring *American* comic opera, a potboiler for some fifty years and occasionally staged today, as a niche ceremony by companies as devoted to the Old Ways as Druids were in the days of Camelot.

This is Reginald De Koven's *Robin Hood* (1891), written for a touring stock troupe, the Boston Ideal Opera Company. The Bostonians (as they were commonly called and eventually renamed) were formed right at the start of comic opera's heyday, for a production of *HMS Pinafore*, and they define the genre's vocal demands in their repertory, which included both comic operas and such "lighter" outright operas as *L'Elisir d'Amore*, *Le Nozze di Figaro*, and *Martha* (all in English). Indeed, much of *Robin Hood* sounds like opera when it doesn't sound like Johann Strauss. A men's sextet in Act Two, "Oh, See the Lambkins Play!," starts as a sturdy glee and then breaks into a sprightly waltz with "Ho! then for jollity, fun and frivolity" that would feel right at home in *Die Fledermaus'* party scene.

That isn't an homage: the soundscape of Strauss, Lecocq, and their colleagues created the palette with which American comic opera loved to paint: it brought relief from the dowdy tinkle of *Evangeline* and its like. Burlesque and farce had the fun; comic opera had the prestige. The Europe-trained De Koven was the compleat musician, orchestrating his scores himself and composing genuine operas, *The Canterbury Pilgrims* (for the Met) and *Rip Van Winkle* (for Chicago). Critics thought him no more than workmanlike, but *Robin Hood*, at least, has tang, and it even got one last hearing on Broadway as late as 1944, albeit in a poor staging that banished the piece thereafter to the twilight of minor venues.

Robin Hood's libretto, by Harry B. Smith, offers no surprises to those even dimly familiar with Maid Marian, the Sheriff of Nottingham (the comic role, for the Bostonians' Henry Clay Barnabee), the ample Friar Tuck (who leads the show's second most popular number, "Song of Brown October Ale"), the romantic Allan-a-Dale (a trouser role, with the show's *most* popular number, "Oh, Promise Me," interpolated for the Bostonians' pet mezzo, Jessie Bartlett Davis), Little John, Will Scarlett, and of course the bandit nobleman title role himself. Oddly, the Bostonians weren't keen on the piece at first, throwing the premiere together out of odds and ends. In his memoirs, Smith tells us the production cost $109.50, and the Robin Hood, Edwin Hoff, played in his *Il Trovatore* Manrico suit.

Nevertheless, the music caught on, the Bostonians put it into heavy rotation on their tours, and much of it served as a model for other writers in the field. The opening fair scene, with its introduction of various groups and individuals, each in a different musical setting, anticipates comparable openings in a number of evolved forms, from *Naughty Marietta* and *Show Boat* through *Strike Up the Band* and *Allegro* to *Wonderful Town* and *Li'l Abner*. Further, the lengthy first-act finale in which plot zigzags drive the music—again in contrasting musical paragraphs—appears to enter the American musical's vocabulary at this time. The three-act *Robin Hood* has two such, so dramatically effective that the finaletto, as it was called, became all but de rigueur in even the least ambitious of musicals into the 1930s.

Most important, De Koven gave *Robin Hood* consistency of tone. There are only a few very pointed touches of pastiche, yet it all somehow suggests "England at the time of Richard I." While antiquing away with horn calls and marches, De Koven created something the American musical may not have had before, atmosphere. There were more successful comic operas at the time, but none remained as popular for as long as *Robin Hood* did. Its music even entered demographic knowledge far beyond that of the average theatregoer when "Oh, Promise Me" became the wedding hymn of choice for some three generations. This gives us a hint of the musical's growing power to assert control of the national songbook, and to enjoy cultural impact far greater than that of any other theatrical form in any other Western country.

CHAPTER 3

❧

At the Turn of the Century

As the First Age drew near its end, much of the generic jumble we have been witness to was cleared away. That loony-kazoony genre known as pantomime vanished, along with dancing plays like *The Black Crook*. European comic opera inspired a body of American comic opera, meanwhile making the author team of composer and librettist-lyricist significant as never before: because an intimate relationship between script and score had become elemental in the making of musicals.

However, where in all this was **musical comedy**, comic opera's vernacular counterpart? It had arrived, quite suddenly, in the early 1880s, as a spruced-up burlesque imitating Gilbert and Sullivan. *Cinderella At School* (1881), written entirely by *Wang*'s composer, then known as Henry Woolson Morse, and based on T. W. Robertson's play *School*, is the first work I can trace to bill itself as a "musical comedy," though the term did not catch on till the early 1900s. From the opening chorus, "Green Are the Waving Branches," to the last solo, after a regatta, "Columbia Won the Race Today," *Cinderella At School* utilized a story score with some thirty numbers while juggling two sweetheart couples and a bad guy, Dr. Syntax. The future Adonis, Henry E. Dixey, played him during *Cinderella At School*'s second season, when the role of the Schoolmistress was recast, in a touch of burlesque, as a man in drag—*Evangeline*'s George K. Fortescue. Yet another important performer, De Wolf Hopper, who had played the title role in *Wang*, played also the title role in a complete rewriting of the show as *Dr. Syntax* (1894), when it was billed as a "comic opera."

Thus, the very identity of what were becoming the two chief forms—musical comedy and comic opera—was a slippery one. Was musical comedy something like burlesque but further modernized? A lowdown comic opera? At times, it seemed to be anything with a few vaudevillians and a voiceless soubrette who was charming her way to the top. Perhaps *The Belle Of New York* (1897) is instructive: billed as a "musical comedy," it became famous as one, to the point of embodying the type. Was this because of the raffish characters from the Bowery and Chinatown? The modest vocal demands? Or simply the very ordinariness of the plot, about a Salvation Army lass (Edna May) involved with a dissolute society boy (Harry Davenport) in danger of being disinherited by a grouchy papa?

Harry Davenport is our first performer readers may be acquainted with, for his long career took him to Grandpa Smith in MGM's *Meet Me In St. Louis*. However, it was eighteen-year-old Edna May in *The Belle*'s title part who became a song-and-dance star, for the show, unappreciated on Broadway, was taken to London and had a sensation, making May the belle of the West End. As the only genuinely refined character among the principals, she of course would sing soprano, her voice to ring out on high at the usual first-act finale. Most of her colleagues got songs of limited range, presumably to allow producer George Lederer to hire entertainers rather than legit singers; David Warfield, a lead character billed as the "polite lunatic" Karl von Pumpernick, appeared only in book scenes.

Revived in London six times into the 1940s, *The Belle Of New York* caught on in the United States entirely on the road and with amateur groups, though the Shuberts mounted a revision as *The Whirl of New York* in 1921 that did reasonably well at 124 performances. *The Belle*'s score did produce a few standards, not least the heroine's first number (after a surprisingly late entrance in the last third of Act One), "They All Follow Me." Framed as a revivalist's march and egged on by tambourine, the song is the confession of a soul-saver too pretty to be effective. She conquers not souls but hearts:

CHORUS: Follow on! Follow on! When the light of faith you see.
VIOLET: But they never proceed to follow that light,
    But always follow me!

If on sheer reputation alone, *The Belle of New York* is a landmark title. Its authors, on the other hand, are known to archivists only: composer Gustave Kerker and librettist C. M. S. McLellan, who worked at this time as Hugh Morton. The pair wrote eight shows together around the turn of the century, a typical Broadway collaboration in that Kerker came from Germany and McLellan was British: this was the era of partnerships between continental composers and English or American wordsmiths.

Another such duo was Gustav Luders (from Bremen) and Frank Pixley (from Richfield, Ohio), who generally worked in established formats, from fantasy to the trope of the American getting into trouble in foreign parts. In *The Burgomaster* (1900), Peter Stuyvesant (the ubiquitous Henry E. Dixey) wakes up in modern-day New York. *King Dodo* (1902) revolves around an elixir of youth. *The Prince Of Pilsen* (1903) tells of a Cincinnati brewer mistaken for a real prince who is courting the brewer's daughter. *Woodland* (1904) sounds unusual at first, for the entire cast is birds. But it's the same old plot—a prince loves a commoner and the king says no—even if the royals are eagles and the sweetheart is a coloratura nightingale. Like Gustave Kerker, Luders laid out his own orchestrations. But he lacked imagination; all his scores sound alike. Oddly, though they have the fully developed musicality of comic opera, they were billed as musical comedies.

The Prince Of Pilsen was the outstanding Luders-Pixley hit, running 143 performances and, while touring, returning to New York once a year from 1904 to 1907. A beloved show, it fell right into grooves cut deep by others: in a husband-hunting widow out of Gilbert and Sullivan, in a tenor prince with cohort of carolling students, in its waltzing "Message of the Violet," an "I love you" song by other means. Above all, it had the brewer, a typical Dutch comic with the fractured English, observing the native folkways and getting his temperament ruffled. "Efery man," he notes, of Europe in general, "mit nodings to do is a prince." Then, meeting an English lord on the short side, the brewer declares, "Ofer here nobody is a plain man. Even de vaste material is labeled." *The Prince of Pilsen* was so rife with cliché that it was as if the public domain had written an operetta. Yet it held the stage till the more ecstatic music of Romberg and Friml appeared, and remained a title of some minor power till it finally disappeared in the 1950s.

Of the American composers of comic opera, Reginald De Koven was never able to turn out another *Robin Hood*, though *Rob Roy; or, The Thistle and the Rose* (1894), again in collaboration with Harry B. Smith, was a huge hit in its day. Like *Robin Hood*, it had a "famous" part, the Mayor of Perth, who—like the Sheriff of Nottingham—got all the fun stuff. Still, *Rob Roy's* music, though seasoned with an appealing Scots flavor, failed to ingratiate itself beyond its time. De Koven was prolific, giving Broadway twenty-four scores (a few others did not come in), including a *Robin Hood* follow-up, *Maid Marian* (1902), complete with Henry Clay Barnabee again as the Sheriff. And De Koven was part-manager, entering into a deal with the Shuberts to raise up a classy line in comic opera at their brand-new Lyric Theatre on Forty-Second Street. Further, De Koven was of tony family (from Chicago) in a time when such things mattered. And we already know about his excursions into grand opera. If anyone could lend American comic opera prestige, De Koven was the man. Yet in the end, he enjoyed his little era and then, but for *Robin Hood*, was gone.

John Philip Sousa illustrates the opposite paradigm, for the so-called march king had terrible trouble maintaining a catalogue in comic opera. With his work largely undervalued or unproduced, he had but one hit—and he still has it, as this work is received with thanks wherever comic operas are still performed, from the Ohio Light Opera to Goodspeed Opera House: *El Capitan* (1896). Playwright Charles Klein wrote the script and Thomas Frost collaborated with Sousa on the lyrics, but the music really does sweep all aside as Sousa fills the piece with crazy fun in an almost Offenbachian way. De Koven's *Robin Hood* music summarizes story and characters generally; Sousa really digs into character, especially in his treatment of the lead role, Don Medigua. One might call his the title part but for a technicality: there is no title part, for El Capitan has been killed before the conductor strikes up the overture.

Disguise and mistaken identity were the choice plot fillers of the age, especially when narratives threatened to sag in the second act. But Don Medigua pretends to be somebody else for virtually every minute of *El Capitan*, right up to the last few moments before the finale. As the incipient Viceroy of Peru, he decides to confuse an insurrection by posing as the dread—and late—mercenary called only El Capitan. The joke lies in the difference between the frantic, blustering Don Medigua and the ferocious brigand his subjects believe him to be. It is not that Don Medigua's many solos are particularly compelling, but that his music rounds out a figure who, in his spoken lines, is a dull Ko-Ko in a suit of armor, Gilbert and Sullivan without the wit. Sousa excelled, too, in ensembles. The rebel heroine Estrelda leads one, "Onward! Patriotic Son!," that develops into a dashing quodlibet, as she sings one strain, the chorus baritones sing another, the sopranos imitate trumpets, and the tenors whistle, all at once.

El Capitan is easily the best American work we have met up with so far; it also brings us back to De Wolf Hopper, the original Don Medigua and literally the biggest star of the age at six feet, three inches and two hundred thirty pounds. A comic, Hopper nevertheless fielded a thundering basso profundo to send every lyric to the top of the house. Hopper was useful in everything—Gilbert and Sullivan, European comic opera, Weber and Fields burlesque (to be dealt with presently), variety bills at the vast Hippodrome. He even took over the non-singing comic role of Lutz, the valet, in the original production of *The Student Prince*. Hopper was Howja-Dhu (in the aforementioned "Hindoo comic opera" *The Begum*; others were Klahm-Chowdee and Myhnt Jhuleep), Wang, Mr. Pickwick, *Iolanthe*'s Lord Chancellor, the Pied Piper. One would call him beloved but for his habit of treating his public as a captive audience while he roared into "Casey At the Bat" at his curtain call. True, it's better than Mandy Patinkin's singing forty hours of Yiddish folk songs with the theatre's door locked, to name another self-indulgent performer. But today Hopper is mainly known for having given his name to six wives at a time when a single divorce was startling. One of the six, *née* Furry, became the Hollywood gossip queen Hedda Hopper.

By this time—the mid-1890s—exotic-setting comic opera was a dominant form, especially when an American could be dropped in among the natives for ironic commentary comparing their folkways with ours, in the *Prince of Pilsen* manner. Victor Herbert first won notice for a pair in this genre, *The Wizard of the Nile* (1895) and *The Idol's Eye* (1897), both with librettist-lyricist Harry B. Smith and starring comedian Frank Daniels. Actually, Daniels played a Persian in the first show, a fake wizard obsessed with parlor tricks that usually don't work. He visits Egypt in time to save it from drought, unfortunately with an inundation: the second act is set on the roof of Ptolemy's palace, where everyone has gone to avoid drowning. Daniels' character was Kibosh (pronounced Kih-*bosh*), and Smith may have invented this once popular word, widely misspoken during World War I in a phrase promising to "put the *ky*-bosh on the Kaiser."* Also common was Kibosh's personal catchphrase, "Am I a wiz?," with which small-town wags would drive their friends crazy, and Daniels, along with an imaginative production full of scenic wonders from pyramid to crocodile, made *The Wizard of the Nile* a hit. There were as well two very popular numbers, a waltz quintet, "Star Light, Star Bright," and Daniels' tale of his love for a human contortionist, "My Angeline."

After 105 performances at the Casino, *The Wizard of the Nile* went off on a long tour; two years into it, Daniels asked Herbert and Smith for another *Wizard*; they obliged with *The Idol's Eye*, in which Daniels, now as an American, arrived by hot-air balloon in India. Here the gimmick was two rubies: one makes everybody love you and the other makes everybody give you the death penalty. Naturally, the gems keep getting mixed up; you never know which one you have till it's too late. Along with the Brahmins, Nautch Girls, and occupying British inevitable in Broadway's India, Smith gave Herbert a crew of Westerners all set for pastiche numbers, including a Cuban complete with operatic cadenza. Or why not a Kiss Duet, "Pretty Isabella and Her Umbrella"?:

> I know a blue-eyed maiden with the usual hair of gold
> And her very pretty name is Isabella.
> And everywhere that maiden goes, if day be hot or cold,
> She always takes a big white sun umbrella . . .

Whereupon the two singers hide behind an umbrella making smooching noises.

*Webster cites "kibosh" with "origin unknown."

One reason the "exotic" show was so popular was the chance it gave composers to create exotic music, and Herbert excelled in this as nobody else. *The Idol's Eye*'s second act opens with a chorus-and-dance sequence that rises to a passionate intensity almost comparable to parts of *Porgy and Bess*. All the same, the show focused on Daniels' amiable lampoon of tribal formalities:

> HIGH PRIESTESS: The Brahmins must be given a ruby for you to be set
>   free.
> DANIELS: Anybody got a ruby he's not using?

Daniels even had a number referencing *The Wizard of the Nile*'s "My Angeline," when he refuses to be tattooed for sacrifice:

> DANIELS: I knew a tattooed man once, and those tattoos caused a
>   problem . . . Oh, here, I'll tell you all about it . . .

Launching the verse, he actually alludes to his real life as an actor:

> Do you remember Angeline,
> That heartless human snake,
> Who won my heart in another part,
> And gave that heart a break?

The song is "The Tattooed Man." It tells how Angeline fell for his illustrations and gave him her savings—but he ran off with the fat lady:

> It's certainly true you can beat a tattoo,
> But you can't beat a tattooed man!

The number was so popular that Herbert and Smith gave Daniels a third show in this series, *The Tattooed Man* (1907). All were billed as comic operas—the classy title of the times.

But Herbert was unique in segregating the comic from the opera, tilting a work's musical style toward one or the other. In *The Serenade* (1897) and his first lasting hit, *The Fortune Teller* (1898), Herbert emphasized the romantic. In the Frank Daniels vehicles, he slipped in bits of musical slapstick, as when the 4/4 verse of "The Tattooed Man" galumphs into 6/8 for the chorus.

No doubt, Herbert got more than a little help from Harry B. Smith, who would be called the father of all librettist-lyricists but for historians' disdain for him. Is it because he was so prolific, working on over three hundred shows? Or is it the curiously unruffled tone in his autobiography? A book collector, he entitled it *First Nights and First Editions*, as if reading was as fulfilling to him as creating. He seems so impartial about everything; we like a little angst in our artists. True, Smith's era is not celebrated for wit and point in its librettists. Even its composers get relatively little attention, except for Herbert. In fairness to Smith: though conventional, he used the conventions well, and some of his lyrics toot along with saucy charm.

We last left burlesque dissolving into history as musical comedy absorbed it. But it did enjoy an Indian summer in the double bills of Weber and Fields around the turn of the century. Their opaquely titled shows, such as *Fiddle-Dee-Dee* (1900) and *Twirly Whirly* (1902), offered, first, a very loosely plotted one-act built around set-piece songs and sketches, and, second, the actual burlesque, always of the latest hit play: *Cyrano de Bergerac* as *Cyranose de Bric-a-Brac*, *Barbara Frietchie* as *Barbara Fidgety*. The Weberfields troupe, as they were known, played their midweek matinees, most unusually, on Tuesday just so they could attend the Wednesday matinee of the next show they were planning to spoof.

A favorite target was the inevitable Big Scene. The French backstager *Zaza*, a David Belasco hit of 1899 for Mrs. Leslie Carter, featured an encounter between the actress heroine and her adulterous lover's little girl, whose dear little charm so sentimentalizes Zaza that she changes her mind about destroying his marriage. The Weberfields crew retained the scene almost line for line, but recast the little girl as a giant French poodle.

Joe Weber and Lew Fields were Dutch comics of the Jewish variety, easily the most famous of their kind during their heyday, which lasted from the mid-1890s till a bitter parting in 1904. Some of the humor that they invented lives on in the repartee of Marx Brothers movies, as when Fields uses the word "etiquette" and Weber replies, "Who et a cat?" Or try this exchange at table, between Weberfields stooge David Warfield and Weberfields beauty Lillian Russell:

RUSSELL: (to waiter) You might bring me a demi-tasse.
WARFIELD: Bring me the same, and a cup of coffee.

Their biographer Felix Isman records a classic routine. Fields, tall and thin, is the pack leader; Weber, short and rotund, is the eternal dupe. They play as, respectively, Myer and Mike:

MIKE: I receivedidid a letter from mein goil, but I don't know how to writteninin her back.

MYER: Writteninin her back? Such an edumuncation you got it? . . . How can you answer her ven you don't know how to write?

MIKE: Dot makes no nefer mind. She don't know how to read.

In their own small theatre on Broadway and Twenty-Ninth Street, Weber and Fields seemed to plow all their earnings into their productions, for they could clear only marginal profit even with sellout houses because of the star salaries they had to pay. Lillian Russell was at the end of her career when she joined the Weberfieldses for *Whirl-i-Gig* (1899), but hers was still a box-office name and it came dear—even if she played only half the evening because her public thought her too chaste to take part in burlesques. Though everyone loved working for them, Weber and Fields were constantly losing their best people to more glamorous bookings: because the Weber & Fields Music Hall was so prominently attended that to appear there was to invite the interest of rival managers.

The pair had another headache: the Rogers Bros. (as they were billed). Exactly coeval with Weber and Fields, Gus and Max Rogers were thought to be imitators of such relentless study that, once heard at the Music Hall, the "etiquette" and "demi-tasse" jokes were sure to turn up in the next Rogers Bros. show. Worse, the Rogerses were managed by Weber and Fields' enemy, Abraham Erlanger, the ruthless dictator of the monopoly known as the Theatre Syndicate. With control of most of the biggest and best playhouses, Erlanger could set the Rogers Bros. and their travelogue plots into highly favorable bookings, with more elaborate production values than Weber and Fields could offer. Advertised as farces and, later, musical comedies, *The Rogers Bros. in Wall Street* (1899), *The Rogers Bros. in London* (1903), *The Rogers Bros in Panama* (1907), and so on were not burlesques per se but rather more grandly scaled likenesses of what Weber and Fields put on in their first half. It might even be that the vindictive Erlanger had commissioned these knockoffs to irritate Weber and Fields, among the few prominent managers to refuse to kowtow to him.

Even the Rogerses' scores were imitations. Weber and Fields used composer John Stromberg and lyricist Edgar Smith, and the Rogerses had, mainly, composers Maurice Levi and Max Hoffmann. But one cannot tell the two series apart by their songs. We know "Come Down Ma Evenin' Star" is a Weberfields piece (from *Twirly Whirly*) because a famous tale goes with it: Stromberg dies just before Lillian Russell is to sing it onstage for the first time and she breaks down while doing so. And we know "The Belle of Murray Hill" is from a Rogers escapade—*In Wall Street*, in fact—because it's a blatant echo, now of Harrigan and Hart, in its vapid salute to "Sweet Nellie Kelly" and waltz-clog refrain. When important musicals get by with such limp songs, we realize that the score as such has not truly become elemental yet—at least not in musical comedy.

One development of the time was nomenclatural. **Extravaganza**, which formerly could denote anything from a vaudeville act to a Passion Play, had finally settled on a specific format. This was the fairytale spectacle, a blend of pantomime, burlesque, and musical comedy aimed at family audiences, with wisenheimer jokes about modern mores and politics and, for the kiddies, high jinks and slapstick. We have to sneak over into 1903, in the Second Age, to sample two of the most outstanding examples of the form. One was the biggest musical-comedy hit of its decade (that is, not counting comic opera), and the other was the only extravaganza to survive, if marginally, to the present day: *The Wizard of Oz* and *Babes In Toyland*.

The Wizard, based of course on L. Frank Baum's children's tale, was from the start Baum's project. He wrote book and lyrics to Paul Tietjens' music, following his original storyline: Dorothy, the Scarecrow, the Tin Woodman, and the Lion (a pantomime animal, rather like *Evangeline*'s heifer) set off on a quest that ends with Dorothy's return to Kansas. However, Baum eliminated the Wicked Witch of the West, so effective in driving the action in the 1939 MGM movie adaptation, and the show's narrative thus lost its bite. Still, the stagestruck Baum knew how musical-comedy books should go. At one point, the Scarecrow takes a tumble:

SCARECROW: There's a hole there.
DOROTHY: Why didn't you go around it?
SCARECROW: The way I went was quicker.

Tietjens, however, was a dull composer and Baum's lyrics were at times horribly lame:

> For I'm Dorothy,
> Little Dorothy,
> Whose home is the prairie wide;
> And always I'll be Dorothy,
> Whatever may betide.

This was an attractive package all the same, and manager Fred Hamlin accepted it for his Grand Opera House in Chicago, passing the property over to Julian Mitchell, the very first of the major director-choreographers. Mitchell was to stage early Victor Herbert and late George M. Cohan, Weber and Fields burlesques, Florenz Ziegfeld's first *Follies* revues, and, lasting into the mid-1920s, a black show, *The Chocolate Dandies*, and—this time choreographing only—a Marilyn Miller vehicle, *Sunny*. It was Mitchell who turned *The Wizard of Oz* from a pleasant little show into a high-powered special event with magical effects, a large cast of principals new to Baum, and so many interpolations, added in and replaced during the show's ten years on stage, that *The Wizard of Oz* was a musical without a score. *Show Boat* and *Follies* have collected alternate and extra songs over time through revisions, but each has a core of essential numbers—an "Ol' Man River" or "Who's That Woman?"—without which they could not function. *The Wizard* has no equivalent, because Mitchell replaced most of the Tietjens-Baum numbers with new ones by composer A. Baldwin Sloane working with two different lyricists, and even then socked in specialty numbers by others. Thus, to cover a scene change, the Scarecrow and Tin Woodman appeared, without explanation of any kind, in nautical garb on a dinky little boat to sing Theodore F. Morse and Vincent Bryan's "Hurrah For Baffin's Bay":

The Bo'sun asked a Polar bear would she eat off his hand,
But Polar bears talk Polish and she did not understand;
She chased him up a mountain peak, she acted very tough
When she made him jump the precipice, he knew it was a bluff . . .

Mitchell's script changes crowded Baum's original characters off the stage for long periods, as a crew of eccentrics chased around in a plot to restore King Pastoria to the throne of Oz.* Mitchell's new characters included the "lady lunatic," Cynthia Cynch; the poet Sir Dashemoff Daily (a trouser role, in the burlesque tradition); Sir Wiley Gyle; General Riskitt; and Tryxie Tryfle. Mitchell added also a second mime animal, Dorothy's new pet (replacing the book's Toto), Imogene the cow. This was not a frolicking two-man operation as in *Evangeline*, but rather a single acrobat doubled over in a cow suit, rather like the one that Chad Kimball played in the 2002 revival of Stephen Sondhem's *Into the Woods*. As for Baum's rather midwestern little Wizard, Mitchell bent him into an ethnic caricature, "Dutch" during the Chicago run (to please the sizable German-Scandinavian population), and then, for New

---

*It was news to Baum: authority figures in his Oz were women, fairies, witches, or little girls who take trips to right wrongs. Ironically, two years later, when Baum wrote the first Oz sequel, *The Marvelous Land of Oz*, he incorporated Pastoria in some passing references. Then, twenty-one years after that, Ruth Plumly Thompson, the new Oz author after Baum's death, thought back to the musical—for many, a more vivid memory than trivia in the books—and developed Pastoria as the hero of *The Lost King Of Oz*.

York, an Irish rogue out of the Harrigan and Hart catalogue, with the dry sarcasm that reflected the Gaelic tone of New York humor. Thus, when the leads first met the Wizard:

WIZARD: What's this? Strangers here.
SCARECROW: Yes, little Dottie.
WIZARD: You all look a little dotty.

Mitchell drew heavily on the merrily inane masquerading that bolstered many a musical's plot right into the 1940s, as when Pastoria and Tryxie round up lion and cow to pose as a "one-ring circus." Pastoria becomes Signor Gonzabo, the Lion Tamer and Tryxie is the bareback rider Bouncerine. Tryxie also got the show's outstanding song hit, "Sammy," by composer Edward Hutchison and lyricist James O'Dea (who himself was to marry a lyricist, Anne Caldwell). Like most of *The Wizard*'s score, "Sammy," a ballad with a light touch of ragtime, simply showed up in the narrative. There is no Sammy any more than there is a Bill in *Show Boat* to go with the song "Bill." And that would bother the character-conscious Hal Prince if he had to stage "Sammy" today. But it didn't bother anyone in 1903:

> Did you ever meet the fellow fine and dandy,
> Who can readily dispel your ills and woes?
> Did you ever meet the boy who's all the candy
> Where'er he goes?

Mitchell's keenest coup was casting Fred Stone and Dave Montgomery as the Scarecrow and Tin Woodman. Already bonded as a double act, the pair had played Broadway in a Gustave Kerker–Edna May musical, *The Girl From Up There* (1901), though this time May was no belle of New York but a pirate's moll who had just been defrosted after five hundred years on ice at the North Pole. Montgomery and Stone (in their chosen billing order) were pirates, too, but the show gave them no career traction and they were soon back in vaudeville. It was *The Wizard* that put them over as a box-office sellout attraction, from the flamboyant costuming to their remarkable plastique, Stone's weightless blundering next to Montgomery's metal solemnity. Stone's entrance was one of those memories that theatregoers would fondly refer to long after: perched high over his cornfield, contorted and lifeless, he convinced audiences that he was literally a stage dummy.

As Stone recalled it in his memoirs, on opening night in Chicago, Dorothy (Anna Laughlin) had to give so many encores of "Carrie Barry (will you be mine?)" that when she finally got around to letting Stone down in the following book scene, his limbs had gone to sleep and he flopped helplessly about the stage. Thereafter, he apparently retained this "business" (the old term for "shtick") to suggest the movements of a creature with no center of gravity, a true Baumian Scarecrow. Later, in the third act, Mitchell used an old stage trick to simulate the putting together of the Scarecrow's sundered body parts. Stone was standing in a black box, his body hidden in black masking. At a distance, in theatre lighting, he was invisible. Then, as each body part was passed into the box, Stone removed the appropriate section of the masking, making it look as if each limb were actually being reunited with the rest of him. "Let me have an arm next," he cried. "I want to scratch my nose."

All of this—Montgomery and Stone, the enjoyable cascade of specialty numbers, and such visual spectacles as the opening tornado sequence or the soothing of the dangerous Poppy Maidens under a blanket of snow— made *The Wizard of Oz* a smash. The show's historian, Mark Evan Swartz, calls it "one of the most profitable shows mounted in Chicago up to that time," paying off "by the seventh week of [the] run." Success on that level changes industry practice: *The Wizard* offered tickets as much as a month in advance. In a day when almost all theatregoing save family outings on holidays was walk-in business, tickets were usually sold on the day of the performance, mainly within two or three hours of curtain time. This is where the concept of a public's being "turned away" at the box office comes from: at some point in a hit show's afternoon, the Standing Room Only sign went up, and when even standing room was sold out, would-be spectators were thus turned away.

The Wizard of Oz opened in Chicago on June 16, 1902 (incidentally the "Bloomsday" on which James Joyce's *Ulysses* takes place). This was not the start of a Broadway-bound tryout tour, as Chicago was a theatre capital in its own right. Still, the piece was too big not to dare America's theatrical center, and after 125 performances in Chicago and a Midwestern tour, *The Wizard* opened a new theatre on Broadway on January 21, 1903, the Majestic. This was not the current Majestic, home of *The Phantom Of the Opera*, but a now demolished building in Columbus Circle, a few steps southeast of the main entrance of the Time-Warner Center.

In fact, this Majestic was not really a Broadway house, because "Broadway" ran more or less from the Weber & Fields Music Hall through Herald Square up to Forty-Second Street. "About the only way to get [to the Majestic] was by four-wheeler," Stone recalled in his memoirs.

The New York critics, unlike those in Chicago, gave *The Wizard of Oz* very mixed reviews. Alan Dale of the New York *American* liked the new theatre but called the show "absolutely inexplicable," citing "evil comedians with infamous puns [and] jokes that Noah would have routed out of the Ark." But the public loved it, and two road companies were assembled, one drawn from the New York cast after it had played its 293 performances and the other freshly assembled. Montgomery and Stone left the production after four years, though they were so identified with it that Baum's publishers, Reilly & Britton, used a green-tinted photograph of the pair in their Oz makeup on the endpapers of *The Marvelous Land Of Oz*—green, of course, being the color of Oz's capital, the Emerald City.

In one form or another, including a slightly cut-down version and taking in return visits to both New York and Chicago, *The Wizard of Oz* played the United States for seven years. Throughout that time, it kept losing and accumulating numbers—"I Love You All the Time," "Can't You See I'm Lonely?," "The Tale of a Monkey" (added for a replacement Cynthia, Allene Crater, who became Mrs. Fred Stone), "Little Nemo and His Bear" (after Winsor McCay's visionary comic strip *Little Nemo In Slumberland*, with a piquant "whistling" effect on the last line: "Just Nemo"—tootle ootle—"and his bear." *Chord* !). Thus, *The Wizard of Oz* exaggerated a tendency to look upon the music in musicals as not a fixed element of production but something permanently unstable. The core numbers would provide some narrative continuity, like *The Wizard*'s "Poppy Song," an innocuous choral waltz. But then, what difference did it make what Poppy Girls sing? It was the interpolations that gave the show energy, as when Montgomery and Stone's "Baffin's Bay" was dropped in favor of the comparably out-of-narrative "Football," the stars banging each other up acrobatically in gridiron togs.

Hamlin and Mitchell planned *Babes in Toyland* as a kind of replica of *The Wizard*: starting with another disaster pantomime (here a shipwreck) that leads to an adventure in a quaint and spectacular fairyland, with two guys in animal suits (a spider and a bear, which get into mortal combat; the bear wins), and even Bessie Wynn, *The Wizard*'s Dashemoff Daily, again in trousers as Tom Tom, the Widow Piper's Son. For a fresh touch, celebrities from children's bedtime stories—the males all young women in drag—haunted the stage, from Tommy Tucker to Red Riding Hood, and there was a good deal less of the topical humor that dotted *The Wizard*. In a genre that typically set smart-alec commentary on current events into storybookland, *Babes In Toyland* was unusually consistent in tone.

For instance, *The Wizard of Oz* really was a farce with a sudden blast of guignol at the climax, when Pastoria takes everyone prisoner and brings on a hooded executioner with an ax. But *Babes in Toyland* was a good-versus-evil parable from beginning to end. The two babes, Alan (William Norris) and Jane (Mabel Barrison, Tryxie Tryfle in *The Wizard*'s Chicago run), have a greedy uncle who plans to force Contrary Mary into marriage and, worse, murder his two wards for their inheritance. The uncle stalks them throughout the action, joining forces with the Master Toymaker—not the absentminded professor one might expect but Toyland's dictator.

The greatest difference between *The Wizard* and *Babes* lies in the latter's authors, for *Babes* was the work of Victor Herbert and Glen MacDonough—and if MacDonough was at best an acceptable wordsmith, Herbert was the composer of the age and *Babes* one of his most popular scores. One still hears the "March of the Toys" today, along with that autumnal hymn to lost childhood, "Toyland," whose dreamy refrain starts with a whisper of magic on an unexpected sixth tone of the scale. While *The Wizard* ran on a fickle miscellany of songs, *Babes*—after dropping and adding a few between Chicago and New York—offered a reasonably fixed set of numbers, and all by Herbert and MacDonough.

Interestingly, very little in *The Wizard*'s score has anything to do with Oz. *Babes*, however, sings of the lore and fears of children. "Never Mind, Bo-Peep, We Will Find Your Sheep" gives Herbert a chance to introduce a melody and then hand it to the chorus while the soprano sings a descant over it, a regular feature of Herbert's shows, widely imitated. "In the Toymaker's Workshop" is a minuet scored for rattle, whistle, a doll's "Mama!," and various toy-animal eructations from crowing to mooing. "Go To Sleep, Slumber Deep," when Alan and Jane are lost in the Spider's Forest, treats the little ones' nighttime terror of the unknown: turn off the dark.

There were a few glitches, as when Contrary Mary got a solo with chorus, "Barney O'Flynn," about her love for a lad from County Clare. And, she adds, " 'Tis the wild ones come from there." That's good to know, but why is a Mother Goose character in love with someone from the real world, other than to give the Irish-born Herbert one of his countless pieces of Hibernian pastiche? Then, too, bowing to a fashion of the day, the authors presented William Norris with the thoroughly extraneous "Song of the Poet," in which he put "Rock-a-Bye, Baby" through transformations: as a Cockney maid with spoken catchphrases, as a John Philip Sousa march, in a takeoff on the Sextet from *Lucia di Lammermoor*, and in ragtime, *Tempo di Cakewalk*. *Babes* even had a number spoofing the latest diet craze, "The Health Food Man." "Against all lamb and ham and jam his eloquence was tidal," we learn. And "He said dessert was sudden death and soup was suicidal." Alas, he dies of starvation, though, in any case, the number was dropped before New York. That it was written at all reminds us how slippery was extravaganza's sense of setting, even in a piece as relatively coherent as this one.

Indeed, *The Wizard of Oz* and *Babes in Toyland* arrived when the musical was finally undergoing developments that would bring it into line with what we of today think of as musicals. Comic opera would turn into the more graceful and passionate operetta of Rudolf Friml and Sigmund Romberg; farce became full-fledged musical comedy. Yet extravaganza never grew up. It got out of date and rare, and its strengths were passed on to other forms: musical comedy swallowed up the anachronistic and topical banter, while operetta and revue seized the visual spectacle. Still, extravaganza was a performer's medium, so Montgomery and Stone, and then Stone by himself (after Montgomery's untimely death) kept the form on the must-see list well into the 1920s. By then, however, the authority of the writers became so paramount that even the quality of the book mattered, creating influential stylists who were neither composer nor lyricist. Not coincidentally, by the late 1930s, except for sporadic stagings of *Babes in Toyland*—invariably with updated, musical-comedy style scripts—extravaganza had vanished, never to return.

PART TWO

The Second Age

CHAPTER 4

⌒∿⌒

The Witch of the Wood
and the Bamboo Tree

It is not too early in the musical's age to observe a major throughline: the interdependence of the musical's two essential forms, the romantic and the satiric. Or the one with musical ambitions and the one with a populist agenda. Or the beautiful show and the crazy show. On one hand, you have *Camelot*. On the other, you have *The Producers*. We can diagram the two streams of development thus:

Burlesque → musical comedy, in the spirit of Offenbach.
Comic opera → operetta → musical play, in the spirit of Mozart.

However, each era counts works that blend the two forms. *Show Boat* is musically ambitious and treats serious themes, but its book, especially in Act One, has a musical-comedy tone. *Oklahoma!* is a musical comedy undergoing psychoanalysis, with a grand patriotic theme beyond the scope of a fun show. *New Girl In Town* is Eugene O'Neill with pop tunes, *Cabaret* the Nazi musical comedy. And *Follies*? Beautiful and crazy at once.

This ontological revolution has already begun in the first two decades of the twentieth century: the Second Age, when forms were both consolidating and evolving. Yes, this was happening in the First Age as well—but not so pointedly. Setting aside for the moment the variety show we call "revue," we see the musical tending to be either romantic or satiric even as the two extremes borrow from each other so casually that at times it becomes difficult to tell comic opera from musical comedy. Well, there is one way, though it vastly oversimplifies: if the composer went to a conservatory or studied in Europe, he probably wrote comic opera. Everyone else wrote musical comedy.

Sometimes even the manager—or, as he was often called now, the producer—didn't know which of the two forms he was producing. "Colonel" Henry Savage announced Alfred G. Robyn and Henry M. Blossom Jr.'s *The Yankee Consul* (1904) as a "comic opera." But it's called a "musical comedy" on the title page of the score. Another in the "Americans in exotic places" genre, *The Yankee Consul* told of Abijah Booze, our man in Puerto Plata, Santo Domingo. Booze was played by Raymond Hitchcock, already established as a Wily Rube: straw-chewing, slow-moving, rough-voiced, and so folksy that he turned the native American type into an ethnicity. One seldom saw actors of this kind in comic opera, especially as Hitchcock had no singing voice to speak of. His *Yankee Consul* numbers were talkathons— "Ain't It Funny What a Difference Just a Few Hours Make?" or "In Old New York," on the flaws of every other city, exactly the sort of turn Sondheim recalls in *Follies'* "Ah, Paris!" The two sweetheart leads, naval officer Jack (Harry Fairleigh) and local bolero singer Bonita (Mrs. Hitchcock, Flora Zabelle), sang legit; their "Tell Me (thou lov'st but me)" is even called, rather operatically, a "love duet" in the score. This is comic opera for certain. But then out come the chorus girls in pink tights—and that was pure musical comedy.

A. Baldwin Sloane, whom we just met replacing Paul Tietjens on *The Wizard of Oz*, was no longhair. Yet when he and Sydney Rosenfeld built *The Mocking Bird* (1902) around the old number that opera sopranos favored when asked to sing something "popular," it was "a romantic comic opera." True, "Listen To the Mocking Bird" no longer holds any cultural importance even to the few who know it. In 1902, however, this oddly twittering lamentation for a dead love occupied that odd space between regal art and lowdown art that we think of as kitsch. It claims a sort of dowdy dignity. Okay: a comic opera. But then Sloane unveils "What's the Matter With the Moon Tonight? (It don't seem the same old moon)," a close-harmony ballad fit for a minstrel show. Another musical comedy.

Perhaps musical comedy was simply the earthier form, on the risqué side. Ivan Caryll and C. M. S. McLellan's *The Pink Lady* (1911) and *Oh! Oh! Delphine* (1912) were each billed as a "musical comedy," and the erotic does rather hover over the action. *The Pink Lady* tells of a satyr loose in Paris stealing kisses, and *Delphine*'s heroine has a jealous husband and a parrot cawing, "Oh! Oh! Delphine" whenever she thinks of another man. The authors even got a title song out of it, as a trio for the reproving husband, the conciliating yet helplessly vivacious Delphine, and, yes, the parrot. "Psha! you're wildlike," Delphine sings to her spouse, "I'm most childlike!" Yet

Delphine was based on a French farce, about as childlike as Victor Hugo chasing the cook: musical comedy.

Just to confuse us, Caryll was one of the conservatory guys. He not only studied in Europe, but came from Europe. And here's extra class: the "pink lady" was played by Hazel Dawn, an accomplished violinist who fiddled during the show. And when a certain Philippe Dondidier is accused of being *The Pink Lady*'s lecherous mystery man, Caryll built the scene into a whirlwind of an ensemble to delight a music professor, "Donny Didn't, Donny Did (No, I didn't! Yes, he did!)." Julian Mitchell staged it with the cast moving up and down an ornate double stairway, and the music was as elaborate as the set: comic opera.

Or perhaps comic opera was simply musical comedy with an opera singer in it, such as *The Firefly* (1912), written for Emma Trentini. She was a member of the Manhattan Opera Company when the Metropolitan Opera bought off its impresario, the senior Oscar Hammerstein. Freed of her Musettas and Neddas, Trentini joined other Hammerstein colleagues in his production of Victor Herbert's *Naughty Marietta* (1910). Written for opera singers!: *that*, truly, is a comic opera, and it's Herbert's most expansive score, more so even than his two operas, *Natoma* and *Madeleine*. Then Herbert and Trentini had a falling out—inevitably, for Trentini fought with everyone—and she ended up in not Victor Herbert's but Rudolf Friml's *The Firefly*. To us moderns, the very title conjures up bygone operetta, but that word wasn't yet in use, and the *The Firefly* really is a comic opera, without a Moon Song or chorus girls in tights.

Trentini played a street singer who gets taken up by the yachting class, disguises herself as a boy, is accused of theft, goes off to study voice, and returns in glory as a prima donna. And the firefly? The firefly is . . . love! (because it "glimmers by, and dies while it is gleaming"). Friml's wordsmith was Otto Hauerbach (later Harbach), very given to poesy in his lyrics—another sign of comic opera—and this might be *the* worst book written for a famous title, pursuing a clunky storyline with unshakable resolve. Not surprisingly, MGM's version, with Jeanette MacDonald and Allan Jones, retained nothing of the show but its title and key numbers, most of them Trentini's: "Love Is Like a Firefly," "When a Maid Comes (knock, knock, knock, knock) Knocking at Your Heart," and a real soprano showpiece, "Giannina Mia," a lush serenade with an A strain that could have come right out of a sketch book that Victor Herbert lost in the subway.

Friml would get to operetta—the modernized comic opera—in due course. But the "other" Friml, Sigmund Romberg, was already there, more or less, in *Maytime* (1917). Romberg worked for the Messrs. Shubert—and J. J., the Shubert brother who put on the musicals, had a habit of buying the rights to German musical shows, commissioning literal translations into English, and then changing everything. *Maytime* was one such. The original, *Wie Einst Im Mai* (Once Upon a Maytime, 1913), told of parted lovers whose grandchildren, seventy-five years later, finally redeem the original romance with their own love. For unity, all three sets of lovers sang "Das War in Schöneberg im Monat Mai," and a comic character's "Heissge-liebtes Firlefänzchen" was reprised and updated to each act's era, reflecting dance trends from gavotte to polka (and, in a 1943 revision, a rhumba, as Nazi Germany was cultivating South America).

Those two musical ideas and the outline of the plot (moved from Berlin to New York) was all that Sigmund Romberg and his collaborator, Rida Johnson Young, retained from the German piece. Writing a completely new score, they changed even the nature of the two numbers they used as models, for "Das War in Schöneberg" is not remotely as rapt and hungry as *Maytime*'s "Will You Remember?" (the one that starts with "Sweetheart, sweetheart, sweetheart"). Marlene Dietrich recorded "Schöneberg"; she'd as soon sing "Will You Remember?" as fall for a student prince. The aesthetic, again, is Change Everything. *Maytime*'s comic character—who merrily ages, marries, and remarries while the other principals die off, sang not one single dance number altered in reprises but three different numbers, first a vigorous clog hop ("It's a Windy Day on the Battery"), then a minstrel number ("Jump Jim Crow"), and finally a waltz ("Dancing Will Keep You Young").

Shubert didn't give *Maytime* an elaborate production. But the cast was big, to play the many figures who bob in and out of a narrative spanning three generations, and the leads were fine—tenor Charles Purcell and melting soprano Peggy Wood as the first and third pair of sweethearts. William Norris (just mentioned as one of the title parts in *Babes in Toyland*) was the ever-aging roué. And somehow the show struck a nerve, perhaps because Young's love-song lyrics were less sappy than the norm, or Romberg's music was less stuffy. The waltzy "Battery" number has a good rhythmic drive, and "Jump Jim Crow"—new for *Maytime* but using the concept and title of an ancient minstrel song—manages to be piquant rather than antique.

In short, *Maytime* felt new. It was, in effect, one of the first of the twenties operettas. *The Firefly* was still mired in comic-opera practices, and for all the opportunities it gave Trentini it isn't a very romantic piece. *Maytime*, with its thwarted love sadly postponed for two generations till a long-lost deed is accidentally recovered and the grandchildren sing a last reprise of "Will You Remember?," veritably aches with squandered happiness. At 492 performances, it was one of the longest-running shows in the musical's history to that time, behind *A Trip To Chinatown* and *Adonis* but ahead even of *The Black Crook*.*

Another show set in New York led on from comic opera to operetta even more surely than *Maytime*, though it is now one of the great unsung scores, *Apple Blossoms* (1919). Composed by two men, Fritz Kreisler and Victor Jacobi, to the libretto of William LeBaron, *Apple Blossoms* blended a gala musicality into a very modern story. Nancy (Wilda Bennett) and Philip (opera tenor John Charles Thomas) are forced to wed to please her uncle; outwardly obedient, they agree to an open marriage. But their nuptial duet, "You Are Free," sounds cold only in its lyrics. After a conversational 4/4, the number moves into waltz time on "Love is just a game that two are playing"—still cynical, yes, but to passionately lyrical music. The very sound of it tells us that these two worldly I-don't-cares are already hopelessly in love.

Co-composed shows were not uncommon at the time. Victor Herbert, Rudolf Friml, Sigmund Romberg, Vincent Youmans, George Gershwin, Irving Berlin, and Jerome Kern are just some of the musicians who wrote half a score at least once. But it's a wonder that producer Charles Dillingham was able to get not only the eminent Jacobi but Kreisler, the outstanding violin virtuoso of the day. Their music blended beautifully, as the classical Kreisler revealed a gift for snazzy syncopation in "A Widow (that captures the men)" and "A Girl, A Man, A Night, A Dance," while the more pop-oriented Jacobi reveled in the charm song in "Brothers," a how-to on passing off a forbidden date as a family outing, *Allegretto grazioso*. The *Apple Blossoms* score is also one of the first beautifully orchestrated musicals (presumably by Kreisler and Jacobi), so intricate that the Harms vocal score

---

*For many years, it was believed that a second company of *Maytime* played New York simultaneously with the first. However, there was always something suspicious about the tale, as no writer could name the performers in the second troupe. Besides, after those crazy seasons of multiple stagings of *HMS Pinafore* and the like, when has a Broadway show sprouted a second production during its original run? Why would this have happened only once? And why *Maytime* and not an even bigger hit—*A Trip To Chinatown*, say, or, while we're at it, *Oklahoma!* or *My Fair Lady*? In the latest updating of Gerald Bordman's *American Musical Theatre*, Richard C. Norton writes, "Careful research by Stanley Green has shown the story to have no basis in fact." As for how it originated, I have a theory. The Shuberts moved *Maytime* three times during its original run. The first time, they shunted it from the Shubert to the Forty-Fourth Street, directly opposite. Someone must have passed by when the Forty-Fourth Street's marquee announced *Maytime* but the Shubert's marquee had not yet been changed to herald its next occupant (Augustus Thomas' post–Civil War melodrama *The Copperhead*, starring Lionel Barrymore) and was still advertising *Maytime*. That someone might have concluded that *Maytime* had thus reproduced like an amoeba. This mistake, which eventually took in almost every writer (including, to his shame, your reporter), would seem to have first gone into print on page 271 of David Ewen's *Complete Book of the American Musical Theater*, in 1958.

troubled to indicate middle voices, high violin fill-in lines, and the like, an unheard-of nicety till then. This was, in every way, a forward-looking show, so much so that although it reserved two spots for a dance team having no role in the script, this pair would take a main part in the evolutionary earth-quake that would jump-start the Golden Age: Fred and Adele Astaire. Romberg's *Maytime* had billed itself as "a play with music," but *Apple Blossoms* announced itself, unblushingly, as an "operetta," the form that really didn't exist till the 1920s of *The Student Prince*, *Rose-Marie*, and *The New Moon*.

The work that most influentially renovated comic opera was, with *The Wizard of Oz*, one of the two biggest hits of the first decade of the twentieth century, Franz Lehár's *Die Lustige Witwe* (The Merry Widow), seen on Broadway at the New Amsterdam in 1907 for 416 performances, a huge stay in a huge house. Ethel Jackson and Donald Brian played Hanna (glamorized as Sonia) and Danilo, and it is these two roles, really, that fomented the revolution. Comic-opera romantic leads were songbirds, like Robin Hood and Maid Marian, but Sonia and Danilo were also comedians. They created the musical's first *interesting* love plot, because Lehár gave them such personal vivacity that they united what had previously been two separate job descriptions: being charming and being silly. The widow is capricious and mocking, as in her establishing song, "In Marsovia,"* sung with a flock of admiring fortune hunters—for what self-respecting musical would feature a beautiful young widow without her own personal bank? The number is a comparison of the widow's simple country ways with the worldly Parisian style. "Men are all the same, I *can* see," she observes, "you all beat your wives I fancy." And yet the widow is also entranced by romantic notions, as in her narrative of the enthralling "witch of the wood," "Vilja." Danilo is suave and womanizing in "Maxim's," but vulnerable in his extended solo in the second-act finale, "There Were Once Two Prince's Children." These two express their love in sarcasm, grumpy flirting, and even insults—at one point, he virtually tells her to go to hell, a shocking violation of the cautions of the age. This pair would be a handful even for a juggler, yet Lehár harmonizes them perfectly in the famous *Merry Widow* Waltz that sneaks in early on and then returns, a shimmering valentine, to tie up the plot.

*This was another imposition on the German text: the widow's native land was originally Pontevedro. The first English translation, used in both Great Britain and the United States, had lyrics by Adrian Ross and an uncredited book. Richard C. Norton notes that it is "variously ascribed to Edward Morton or Basil Hood." That version was *the* version for over two generations, and when other writers finally offered new English, Sonia and Marsovia vied with the original names or variants. Joan Sutherland widowed as Anna from Pontevedria. The original text to *Die Lustige Witwe*, while we're crediting, was by Victor Léon and Leo Stein from a French play by one of Offenbach's main collaborators, Henri Meilhac.

In short, *The Merry Widow* was a rebuke to comic opera for having left all its fun to grotesques. *The Widow*'s most immediate effect lay in its innovative merchandising, leading to the Merry Widow hat, the Merry Widow corset, the Merry Widow cigar. It was a national craze. During the show's post-Broadway tour, the Chicago Sunday *American* ran a cartoon on the matter entitled "When the Town Goes Crazy," exaggerating the Widow spinoffs: a prizefighter enduring the "Merry Widow Jolt," a bar offering the "Merry Widow free lunch," even the "Merry Widow peanut stand."

However, the show's long-range effect was to inspire more ambitious characterization of the love plot in the Big Sing musicals (as opposed to musical comedy). One senses the inspiration of Sonia and Danilo in the many bickering sweethearts of twenties operetta, where the temperature runs so high that lovers may be politically hostile—not simply quarrelsome but representatives of dueling ideals.

Broadway's producers suddenly took to patrolling European capitals in search of the next *Merry Widow*, though they usually settled for German and Austrian hits in their London versions. Thus, producer Charles Frohman gave New York the British adaptation of Leo Fall's *Die Dollarprinzessin* (The Dollar Princess) in 1909, while trying to edge the piece into *Merry Widow* territory. For one thing, his leading man was New York's Danilo, Donald Brian, and Frohman interpolated numbers designed to beef up Fall's music with Leháresque interpolations. These included a march sextet by Jerome Kern and the *Widow*'s translator, Adrian Ross, "Red, White and Blue," whose spirit echoed that of the *Widow*'s march *septet*, "Women."

And *The Dollar Princess* was a hit. Still, nothing challenged the *Widow*'s eminence as a romantic lark at once stimulated and soothed by music. There were to be no other *Widows*, not even from Lehár. As I've said, the 1920s was operetta's heyday—yet *Paganini* and *Der Zarewitsch*, still among Lehár's most popular scores, from 1925 and 1927, respectively, were not given here. *Das Land des Lächelns* (The Land of Smiles), Lehár's second most successful piece, with a Japanese background even more ceremonial than *The Mikado*'s, closed twice on the road here till it finally turned up on Broadway in 1946 as *Yours Is My Heart*. Even with the essential Lehár tenor, Richard Tauber, it limped along for a month before giving up. But then, central-European operetta had crashed because of anti-German sentiment during World War I. *American* operetta might dare a German setting with success, as we'll see. But operetta written by the enemy was more or less *verboten* and never really recovered. Indeed, as an odd footnote to all of this, Charles Frohman went down on the *Lusitania*, sunk by a German U-boat in 1915.

English musicals, on the other hand, were very much a part of American theatregoing in the Second Age. Formally, they were all of a kind, billed as either "musical comedy" or "musical play" yet aiming at a kind of comic opera interrupted by music-hall turns. Characters would use a few non sequitur cue lines and a crowbar to insert a specialty number into the continuity, giving the shows a Gilbert and Sullivan air cut with the latest in show-biz smarts. Composers Sidney Jones, Lionel Monckton, Leslie Stuart, and Ivan Caryll led this corner of the repertory, and they must be faulted for allowing the G & S format to devolve. In place of Gilbert's wit was a kind of functional clever-ness, vitality without imagination, and Sullivan's keen characterizations gave way to all romantic leads sounding alike, all sidekicks sounding alike, and all choruses sounding alike. Consider—those of you who know the Savoy titles—how different *Patience*'s twenty "love-sick maidens" sound from *Rud-digore*'s chirping bridesmaids. Or think, in *HMS Pinafore*, of the sailors' shyly quizzical *Gotcha!* and the Captain's answering hesitation that Sullivan slips into his setting of "What, never?" and "Well, hardly ever!"

It's precision: and now it was over, replaced by, for example, "The Inter-fering Parrot," in Jones' *The Geisha* (1896, U.K. and U.S.), one of those self-contained story numbers, beginning, "A parrot once resided in a pretty gilded cage." It's pure vaudeville, with no connection to *The Geisha*'s convo-luted plot concerning Brits in Japan. Stuart's *Florodora* (1899; 1900), on romantic and business dealings surrounding a perfume made on a Philip-pine island, has a few, too. "Willie Was a Gay Boy," another story song, sung by the sidekick, Angela (May Edouin in New York), includes a whistling solo, first by Angela, then by an offstage tenor, and at last by the chorus, all jammed up in the wings as the stage manager cued them in.

Story songs were handy because they could be plopped in just about any-where. Monckton and Caryll's jointly composed *The Girls of Gottenberg* (1907; 1909) is notable for the only New York appearance by London's big-gest musical star, Monckton's wife, Gertie Millar, in her original role of Mitzi, and for being based on a real-life incident. London's musicals were anything but realistic, being obsessed with the mating of shopgirls and lords. However, in 1906 a Prussian shoemaker passed himself off as an army captain and, given the German reverence for military uniforms, he briefly took over the town of Köpenick. This is the plot of *The Girls of Gottenberg*—so how does the number "Two Little Sausages" fit into the plot? Well, you know, Germans do like sausages. Monckton composed the song, a coy duet in gavotte tempo, to his own lyrics:

> Once in the window of a ham and beef shop
> Two little sausages sat!
> One was a lady and the other was a gentleman,
> Sausages *are* like that!

It's a cute little piece, still heard today in Britain. So is "Moonstruck," another Monckton-Millar specialty, this one from *Our Miss Gibbs* (1909; 1910). But it is worth noting that, for all their success, the English musicals left scarcely a note behind in the United States.

There was one exception, another of those compartmentalized numbers having no communication with the plot. This one didn't even slither in on some pretext. It simply happened: six men in gray and six women in pink and black, bearing parasols, appeared from opposite wings, prancing in time to a beguiling vamp. The two lines then formed couples, to flirt to an oddly ever-changing vocal that kept breaking into a new melody without repeating the previous one. "I must love someone," sang the girls, to which the men replied, "Then why not me?" And off they danced to that effervescent vamp, as the public cheered for encore after encore; as the town dudes booked box seats to arrive just in time for the number, leaving directly after; as news stories swirled around the original six women: Vaughan Texsmith, Marie L. Wilson, Agnes Wayburn, Marjorie Relyea, Daisy Greene, and Margaret Walker.

The *Florodora* Sextette!: so spelled in this mannered time, when shirts and collars were purchased separately, when a lady had "limbs," not legs, and when only riffraff would sing a mere Sextet. "Tell Me, Pretty Maiden" (which Leslie Stuart composed to his own lyrics) was the actual title, and if the music is never heard any more, the words "*Florodora* Sextette" remain a summoning term even so, not so much for English musicals per se as for a time when Broadway produced the nation's rock stars. For some thirty years, that Sextette held pride of place in American culture. For starters, Stuart's next show, *The Silver Slipper* (1901; 1903) included another Sextette, "Come Little Girl (And Tell Me Truly), and three of the girls were of the original *Florodora* six. (The other three had married millionaires, and they all did, eventually.) Fanny Brice got a number out of it in *Ziegfeld Follies of 1920*, called "I Was a Florodora Baby," picturing herself as the Sextette's loser: "Five darn fools got married for money," she recalls. But "I got married for love!" And Marion Davies made an early talkie, *The Florodora Girl* (1930), that reenacted the original staging in a special Technicolor reel.

Still, why did the rest of these mostly very successful shows fade so quickly? They may have been a bit dainty for American tastes, but they were very strong in one element: the book. As if reproving American musical comedy for its dependence on self-contained skits plopped into the action, the English musicals pursued their storylines—in the scripts, at least—with determination.

And yet the outstanding American author of musical comedies took nothing from the English model. On the contrary, he scorned anything European. This was George Michael Cohan, the compleat thespian: he wrote the book, rhymed the lyrics, composed the music, capitalized and staged the production, often starred in it, and stopped just short of running the candy counter. He was genial with those he liked and scathing with those he didn't, Irish-American in the most robust sense—merrily Irish and fiercely American—and an uncanny combination of underplaying and cavorting. The Cohans we know from James Cagney (in *Yankee Doodle Dandy*) and Joel Grey (in *George M!*) are incorrect. The real Cohan filled the playhouse with a confidential delivery at times no louder than a stage whisper. He spoke rather than shouted, much less sang, his numbers. He didn't bark at the public: he drew them in with such controlling subtlety that, when he read lines, the house got quiet enough to hear lint collecting in pants cuffs. His stagings were showy; he wasn't. Rather, he was unpredictable. And it was Cohan who initiated the revolution in American popular song that led to Irving Berlin and Jerome Kern, then to Cole Porter, the Gershwins, Vincent Youmans, Rodgers and Hart, and all the others. New York's critics found him irritating at first, then put up with him, and finally learned to appreciate him, because, whatever one thought of his curious blend of urban conceit and country corn, he was unique in a business that loves the unique above all. It's not an overstatement to call George M. Cohan the soul of musical comedy when it first took on its enduring form, right now, in the early years of the Second Age.

True, Cohan worked partly in the spoken drama as well; he even reached the American actor's summit of playing Eugene O'Neill (in his one comedy, *Ah, Wilderness!*). But Cohan made his history in musical farce, even if by 1900 the notion of a spoken play with a few songs had become outmoded. Cohan got one hit out of the genre: *Forty-Five Minutes From Broadway* (1906) has only a handful of numbers, and the middle act (of three) has no singing at all.

However, this was not enough musical for Cohan, who would never hoof when he could prance or walk when he could strut—and his musicals were extensions of himself. Cohan's shows were stuffed with song and dance—"Cohanized," to use his own term. Unfortunately, he was basically writing the same show over and over, because his themes were, really, nags. The Cohan material is like a high school senior's yearbook blurb. Pet Peeve: the affected, the pretentious, the disloyal, the opportunistic. Definitive Line: "When a fellow's on the level with a girl that's on the square." Favorite People: my mother, my father, and my sister. Most Admires: George M. Cohan.

A Cohan show was fast and dancey, and so reveled in its musicalcomedyness that characters sometimes commented on the action to the audience. Of course, they were all plotted around Cohan's obsessions. For instance, his love of simple instincts untouched by materialism: *Forty-Five Minutes From Broadway*'s heroine's solo, "Mary's A Grand Old Name," is not only self-righteous about being called Mary ("There is no falseness there"), but upbraids any Marie for masquerading ("She'll surely bleach her hair").

Now, the music is very gentle, anything but judgmental in tone. Yet the lyrics are an accusation. Cohan sees treachery everywhere—even, come 1919, in the actors' union striking for the most basic rights. Cohan takes the concept of the simple life being the American ideal to the nth power, as *Forty-Five Minutes'* Mary destroys the will that would have made her rich because her boy friend refuses to marry an heiress. Victor Moore, eventually the whining, bumbling partner of William Gaxton in Gershwin and Porter shows, played the boy friend, called Kid Burns, and Cohan and Moore got a successful sequel out of him in *The Talk Of New York* (1907), on another Cohan obsession: nobly taking the blame for someone else's misdeed.

And of course there was the patriotic Cohan. Like Irving Berlin later, Cohan was accused of excessive flag-waving, but love of country—and, again, suspicion of Europe—runs through his work like an animating force. In *Little Johnny Jones* (1904), Cohan played an American jockey unfairly believed to have thrown a race; typically, this happens in snooty England, and Johnny remains there to clear not only his reputation but that of America as well. He is, as he explains in "The Yankee Doodle Boy," the "real live nephew of my Uncle Sam's" and the antithesis of phoney—one of Cohan's favorite attack words. Phoneys lie, cheat, and steal. Worse, they put on airs. And they don't revere the flag.

But is Cohan's nationalism based on a genuine love of democratic ideals or simply egomania in disguise? Certainly, Cohan's patriotic songs are immensely persuasive, with a crude but irresistible vigor. "The Yankee Doodle Boy" is an exhibition piece in the sheer newness of Cohan: nothing like its stamping, confident display was ever heard before. Show-biz "I" songs tend to self-glorification, but this was something new: *autobiographical* self-glorification. The song's first line runs "I'm a Yankee Doodle Dandy," and the last three words form the title of Warner Bros.' Cohan bio: because Cohan was that dandy. And note the song's pastiche allusions, becoming more and more essential to the musical at this time, as Cohan quotes both "The Star Spangled Banner" and "Yankee Doodle" itself.

Further, *Little Johnny Jones* included a tremendous coup de théâtre in the original production, when Johnny learned that a buddy has the proof to exonerate him. On the wharf at Southampton, Johnny sends off a departing ship with "Give My Regards To Broadway"—a "Yankee Doodle Boy" in show-biz terms. Blackout. Then the lights come up on Johnny alone on the dock, watching the ship, in miniature, sailing on the horizon. Johnny awaits a signal that the vindicating evidence has been found, the firing of a rocket on board the ship. Leaning on a pier-head, facing upstage, Johnny watches the boat steam from stage right to the left, and, just as he and we begin to despair, the rocket goes off. And Johnny brings down the act curtain with a last chorus of "Give My Regards To Broadway," calling out rather than singing the words, swaggering rather than dancing, the Cohan hero and the Cohan republic bonded in a thrill of self-affirmation. When Cohan built his own theatre, at Broadway and Forty-Third Street, in 1911, he decorated the interior with paintings showing great moments from his shows. There was one over each of the three side boxes, left and right, and another overlooked the street doors. But the one over the proscenium, right in the center of George M. Cohan's Theatre where everyone could see it, preserved that vindicating act finale of *Little Johnny Jones*.

Starting in vaudeville as Master Georgie of The Four Cohans, George got to Broadway at the age of twenty-two, in *The Governor's Son* (1901), an expansion of one of the family's vaudeville sketches. Cohan naturally took his family along with him, and there was a role for his then wife, Ethel Levey. The run was typical: a mere 32 performances, though the piece came back in 1906 for another two months. But that was New York, a tough stand; Cohan's key public lived in the provinces.

The "road"—the old term for the various bookings in the life of a production beyond its New York season—was still very active in the early 1900s, before movies, radio, and at last television contracted it. A show might play Broadway for two or three months but last for years on tour. Still, to a man like Cohan, at once sentimental and ambitious, the Road was an adjunct to the part of show business that mattered, for the very word "Broadway" was his own personal brag. To stroll through the theatre district and accept the congratulations of "the gang at Forty-Second Street" and to "mingle with the old time throng," as he sings in "Give My Regards To Broadway," was to feel love from one's peers. Not from journalists and, worse, intellectuals, but from show folk: real people.

In time, Cohan's shows earned longer runs in New York. He was a Presence, and his song hits were *big*, virtually national anthems. To stabilize the business side of his art, Cohan joined up with Sam H. Harris, one of the smartest of the new breed of producer. "Cohan & Harris" became a favored brand even before "F. Ziegfeld, Jr.," not for spectacle but for showmanship. It was characteristic of Cohan to be not just partner but best friends with Harris: everything was personal with Cohan. And in 1919, when Equity shut Broadway down in a strike for recognition and

Harris went, as Cohan saw it, soft on the union, Cohan broke up the partnership.

Even Cohan's plays were personal; that's why he was in them. Again, he *was* the Yankee Doodle Dandy. He even took over Victor Moore's role in *Forty-Five Minutes From Broadway*, in a 1912 revival, because Cohan was Kid Burns, too: and *George Washington Jr.* and *The Man Who Owns Broadway* and *The Yankee Prince*, to cite other Cohan titles.

Cohan could get an entire show out of nothing more than Romeo and Juliet and a spoof of Americans who flock to Europe because it's *rilly* so European, my dear. "The Cohan & Harris Comedians in a Musical Frivolity" was the billing for *The American Idea* (1908), in which the "Dutchman" Budmeyer seeks a continental nobleman for his daughter and the Irishman Sullivan wants a princess for his son. (The kids love each other, but when did fathers in search of high-hat "Society, propriety" care about something as natural as love?) A sidekick playing Mr. Fix-it decides to get involved:

> SIDEKICK (To audience): If I only knew some crazy Frenchman.
> PIERRE SOUCHET (merrily entering): Tra la la, la la la.
> SIDEKICK: There's one now.

This "We're all in a musical comedy" attitude, a carryover from burlesque, could arguably be seen as a distant precursor of the modern Concept Musical. As I've said, this was a Cohan specialty, but it runs through the fun shows all the way along—in Ed Wynn's playing the emcee in his revues so he could shmooze with the public between (and sometimes during) the acts, or when Lucille Ball, confronted by a short, chubby, bald man in *Wildcat* (1960), asked him, "D'jou ever know a guy named Fred Mertz?" We even see it in the first film musicals, heavily influenced by Broadway, when Maurice Chevalier angrily, ironically, or amusedly gets rhetorical with the audience.

Cohan himself wasn't in *The American Idea*, but there was a Cohan role, billed as a Mysterious Man (Hugh Mach). He, too, addresses the public, as in his second-act entrance:

> MYSTERIOUS MAN: Several hours later, he appeared in the lounging
> room of the big hotel . . .

or, later, to cue in the second-act finale, "American Ragtime":

> MYSTERIOUS MAN: At that moment, a crowd of Americans entered
> the lounging room, and the air was filled with ragtime . . .

The Mysterious Man retains this omniscient voice to conclude the plot, when the two kids end up together and the sidekick announces his own marriage. Forbidding it, the Mysterious Man unmasks himself as

GRACE: William Waxtapper, my husband!
MYSTERIOUS MAN: Screamed the woman as she staggered toward him.
GRACE: I thought you were lost at sea.
MYSTERIOUS MAN: She stammered. No, he replied, it was a jolly hoax
    on my part.

Literally three lines later, they're all singing the finale.

For all his innovations—and they were many—Cohan really did harp away on his themes, especially in his music and lyrics. He seems at times to have only a dozen numbers in him—the event song ("The Easter Sunday Parade," "The Belle of the Barber's Ball"), the "Let's have fun" song ("Push Me Along in My Pushcart"), the American song ("I Want To Hear a Yankee Doodle Tune"), the true-blue song ("Those Wonderful Friends," "Go Home Ev'ry Once in a While"), the name song, the place song, the song song. *The American Idea* even repeated a song concept Cohan had introduced earlier that year in *Fifty Miles From Boston*, a name song we still hear today, "Harrigan." One of the two fathers sang his own "That's me!" number, "Sullivan."

On the other hand, cliché song genres were the very meat of the musical's dinner in the Second Age. The most obvious is the Moon Song, useful in adding a chaste little thrill of the erotic because these songs all occur at night, when Boy not only Meets Girl but steals a kiss. *The Wizard of Oz* accumulated so many different numbers over its years of touring that it counted at least one example of almost every song genre, and its Moon Song, sung by Sir Dashemoff Daily, was "The Moon Has His Eyes on You (so be careful of what you do)." The moon thing got so insistent that when Ira Gershwin mocked lyric platitudes in the movie *Delicious* (1931), his first line ran, "Blah, blah, blah, blah moon." Yet the form continued healthy, as in "How High the Moon," from *Two For the Show* (1940), even if the staging context was not sparking in the dark but Londoners surviving another night of the Blitz.

Most Second Age song genres were moribund or dead by 1920, but they were ubiquitous before then, especially just after the turn of the century. There was the pastiche series, in which a melody is taken through stylistic variations—opera, then ragtime, and so on. We've already seen one of these curiosities in *Babes in Toyland*'s comic transformations of "Rock-a-Bye, Baby." Gustav Luders and Frank Pixley specialized in another short-lived format, the animal fable—"The Tale of the Turtle Dove," "The Tale of a Bumble-Bee" (who proves faithless to his loving clover flower), even "The Tale of the Seashell."

Most popular of all was the rag number; musical comedy wasn't musical comedy without one, though rags found their way into comic opera as well. *Madame Sherry* (1910)—so gently musicalized that its hit tune was a sweet little "Polka française" "Ev'ry Little Movement (has a meaning all its own)," suffered a rag insert. Karl Hoschna and Otto Hauerbach wrote *Madame Sherry*, but it was Phil Schwartz and Harold Atteridge who pepped the show up with "The Dublin Rag," with a bagpipes-like droning in the bass and the inevitable mention of the Blarney Stone. "Oh, oh, you cutey," the lyric ran, "you Irish beauty."

A longer-lasting genre was the comic novelty—not a character number such as *Kiss Me, Kate*'s "Always True To You in My Fashion," but a chance frolic bobbing up out of nowhere, usually with a trick title made of cockamamie logic. Try this taste of "Who Paid the Rent For Mrs. Rip Van Winkle (when Rip Van Winkle went away)?," from *The Belle Of Bond Street* (1914), a revision of an English show, *The Girl From Kay's* (1902; 1903):

> She had no friends in the place,
> Had no one to embrace,
> But the landlord always saw her with a smile on her face.

The most useful of these song types was the New Dance Sensation, because it provisioned some smart exhibition hoofing or even the ensemble dance riot that became de rigueur in the 1910s. By a wonderful irony, the New Dance Sensation always promised to give instructions in how to perform the latest ballroom craze and then blithely said next to nothing about the actual steps. Even the decryptors of Bletchley Park, who conquered the German Enigma Code in World War II, would not have been able to crack the secret message in, for example, "The Broadway Glide," from *Ziegfeld Follies of 1912*. Bert Grant and A. Seymour Brown wrote this tribute to the "swing" and "sway" of Times Square:

> See the old tragedian and young soubrette,
> There's a Dutch comedian and suffragette.

Okay, let's all do it. Tell us how. And Brown proceeds to praise the dance without describing it. "You will want to take it up, take it up, take it up," he crows—but the execution remains an enigma wrapped in a mystery.

They were all like that—the walk, the toddle, the hop. Rudolf Friml offered "The Dixiana Rise," Jerome Kern "The Edinboro Wriggle." Even the staid Reginald De Koven got into the act. He may even have started it: "The Boulevard Glide," from *The Beauty Spot* (1909), could be the earliest example of the form.

By far the most common of these genres was the so-called coon song— or, really, the whole range of stereotyped minority-group numbers, taking in also Irish, Italian, Jewish, and German subjects. They were easy to write, because they came with a prefabricated vocabulary—the Swanee, the shamrock, spaghett', Cohen owes me ninety-seven dollars, Herman and his beer saloon—and, like the pastiche numbers, they broke up the very limited texture of Second Age composition with novel sounds. *The Wizard of Oz* offered "Daisy Donohue" and "Good Bye Fedora," but it was the coon song that got into everything, with its quaint "negro" dialect and ragtime flourishes. We're not surprised to find "Ma Starlight Queen" in *The Rogers Bros. in Harvard* (1902), because like the others in the series it billed itself as a "vaudeville farce" and thus served as a carry-all for every current in show biz. But even comic opera made room for these southern-idyll numbers, where they might have seemed like curiosities but for their go-everywhere popularity. *The Idol's Eye*—a Victor Herbert title, remember—had "Talk About Yo' Luck," and the avian *Woodland* featured "If You Love Me, Lindy," albeit in a rather extravagated vocal arrangement.

These three titles were written by each show's authors, but very often the genre numbers were the work of outside contributors. These of course were the "interpolations," routinely denounced by historians as an affront to integration. But the interpolation was likely to be the song hit that propelled a show to success through sheer musical publicity. Producers and music publishers conspired to boost business in this way, for the piano and sheet-music concerns stood among America's most powerful interests. Until the acculturation of radio in the 1920s, the only way most Americans could hear music was by going to the theatre or making it themselves on the home keyboard. So the piano, music sheets, and Broadway were in an essential alignment.

Further, the sheets themselves were a glory of the age, king-size at eleven by fourteen inches and bearing attractive colored covers, an art in themselves. And note that a singer who introduced a song would appear on those covers, taking his star billing right into folks' homes.

Thus, Broadway's singing leads also supported the interpolation system. But Victor Herbert went to war with it—with, really, Marie Cahill while she was interpolating in *It Happened in Nordland* (1904). Herbert was in the pit one night, proudly leading his orchestra in his music. And let it be said that he troubled to compose, to Glen MacDonough's lyrics, a specialty number for Cahill, three strophes of sarcasm called "She's a Very Dear Friend Of Mine." It showed off Cahill's comic gifts, mocking a chum singing Carmen's

Habanera with flat notes; observing, of another chum's supposed sable coat, "Here, pussy, pussy, pussy!"; and imitating a third chum's love of the trendy Delsarte aesthetic movement with an imitation of the Delsarte "attitudes," crying, "Vibrate!" and "Now devitalize!"

It was an interpolation, one might say, by the house team. However, Cahill preferred Marie Cahill Numbers, baptized in the copyright of starry glamor. These were specialties, weren't they? What's special about a number that's part of the score? Cahill didn't sing only Victor Herbert. Cahill sang Tin Pan Alley, all of it—"Under the Bamboo Tree" in *Sally In Our Alley* (1902), "The Glowworm and the Moth" and "Navajo" in *Nancy Brown* (1903), "The Hottentot Love Song" in *Marrying Mary* (1906), "The Arab Love Song" in *The Boys and Betty* (1908), "The Turkish Love Song" in *Judy Forgot* (1910). Coyly erotic, touring the genres from coon song to rag, these personalized pieces gave the star a chance to thrust the show aside and get intimate with her public. No longer Nancy Brown or Betty, she became Marie Cahill, Seriocomic!* And Cahill had a secret weapon: she most often worked for her producer husband, Daniel V. Arthur.

But *It Happened In Nordland* found Cahill under different management, and on the night that Herbert led the show, he refused to conduct Cahill's interpolation and she refused to skip it. *Impasse!*

As the story goes, Herbert disdainfully handed his baton to the concertmaster: Here, *you* conduct this drivel! Shaken, Cahill left the stage. A minor player, Pauline Frederick, was promoted to replace Cahill, an odd note in the saga because Frederick was to become famous as a silent film star. More oddly, Frederick was then replaced by Blanche Ring, another seriocomic, with a penchant for interpolating Blanche Ring Numbers. Hers varied more widely than Cahill's, and Ring fielded a stronger instrument, ideal for the stomping rhythm she reveled in, as in "Yip-I-Addy-I-Ay!," added to *The Merry Widow and the Devil* (1908) by ringers John H. Flynn and Will D. Cobb. The show was one of the last of the burlesques, produced by Joe Weber after his breakup with Lew Fields, but Weber billed it as a "satire," as if turning against the very taxonomy of his former partnership. Marked "Tempo di Valse," "Yip-I-Addy" is a rough clog dance of a piece, so raucous in tone that Ring launched each "Yip" with a rising glissando of notes—"Eeeee-*yip*-i-addy-i-yay-i-yay!"—like a rocket hurtling to heaven. We can visualize Ring swaying in time to the music, one hand swishing her skirt and a grin

---

*This was the old term for talent too rich for sweetheart roles. The nearest modern parallel would be Barbra Streisand or Gilda Radner, performing Their Very Own Television Special in their bedroom at the age of ten as they dreamed of changing the rules for woman-lead show biz.

on her face as she holds center stage of the art of musical comedy. It's a great song and a great performance, and it tells us why interpolations were so popular: the rest of a score might be workmanlike, but this was *music*.

Cahill and Ring could be seen as decendents of Lydia Thompson, but she was a revolutionary while Cahill and Ring were mainstream. Theatre audiences in Thompson's youth were predominantly male, enjoying an atmosphere heedless of social and religious cautions. Cahill and Ring played to gender-equal, middle-class family audiences. To put it another way, Thompson's stage was primitive in every respect, back in the First Age of *Black Crooks* and *Humpty Dumptys*; Cahill and Ring are modern enough to have played, respectively, in shows by Cole Porter and the Gershwins.

At the same time, the Second Age saw an expansion of the talent pool from Lydia Thompson's day, in which immigrants or their children began to challenge the natives. Raymond Hitchcock and Fred Stone and David Montgomery represented traditional theatre casting. Al Jolson represented the newcomers—he was actually born in Eastern Europe—and along with his coevals Fanny Brice and Eddie Cantor he often cast a more observant eye upon American culture than Americans did: because the outsider has perspective.

Like Hitchcock and Montgomery and Stone—and George M. Cohan, for that matter—Jolson played comic roles, where personality mattered more than vocal tone. Of course, Jolson was a singer, touted by some as the voice of the age. But his timbre was rough, even unattractive. Worse, he relentlessly added distracting extra words to kick a lyric along, and he so toyed with note values that songs he introduced were not properly heard till someone else got to them.

All the same, his delivery was intensely charismatic, with a hectoring "sell it to the last row in the balcony" address that embraced the entire auditorium. Even while singing, he danced, clapped his hands, and, famously, knelt with arms wide and beseeching, crying, "*Mammy!*" You've heard of flop sweat. Jolson had hit sweat, tearing his ego apart before your eyes the better to thrill you. Cheer him, and he'd cry, "You ain't heard nothin' yet!" as he ripped into the next one.

Playing in blackface as Gus—a stable boy, servant, or simply a vagabond wisenheimer—Jolson starred in *The Whirl Of Society* (1912), *The Honeymoon Express* (1913), *Dancing Around* (1914), *Sinbad* (1918), and *Big Boy* (1925), among other Winter Garden hits for the Shuberts. The black makeup marks the influence of the minstrel revue (and the jokes were corny, too). But these were, in fact, book musicals, in which a subservient supporting cast sang the very derivative core numbers while Jolson reveled in interpolations.

In *Robinson Crusoe, Jr.* (1916), Gus was a Long Island socialite's chauffeur, who joins his boss in a dream of surviving stranded on a desert island. The show's composer was Sigmund Romberg, but Jolson didn't sing much Romberg. Jolson sang specialties, throwing them in and out as he fancied: "Yaaka Hula Hickey Dula," "Down Where the Swanee River Flows," "Tillie Titwillow," "Now He's Got a Beautiful Girl (but he's worried to death all the time)," and "Where Did Robinson Crusoe Go With Friday on Saturday Night?" The last-named, a frantic one-step, epitomizes the insert number in its self-sufficient, narrative-defying gaiety. To hear Jolson's 78 is to imagine him prancing and whooping it up as he envisions the social opportunities:

On this island lived wild men in cannibal trimmin'.
And [*Jolson adds:* you know] where there are wild men, there must be
 wild women!

Big as Jolson was, one star was bigger, on Broadway if not in Hollywood. She, too, could sing and dance—both hoofing and ballet. And she could act. Further, she was a looker, in the modest yet radiant girl-next-door mode, with a fabled stage presence that lit up the house the second she entered: Marilyn Miller. Raised in a vaudevillian family, Miller was just shy of fifteen when she hit Broadway, in a Shubert revue. Florenz Ziegfeld stole her away three years later for the *Follies*, then repositioned her as a heroine of story shows. The first of these was the emblematic smash hit of the Second Age, though it premiered at the start of the Third: *Sally* (1920).

Everything about this show was old, but everything else, so to say, was new, for Ziegfeld was a revolutionary conservative. Miller wasn't *Sally*'s star, but rather its co-star, opposite comedian Leon Errol, as a waiter who helps orphan Sally attain show-biz stardom and a Society scion in the love plot. So it was the old story of the sweetheart and the clown, the very essence of the musical. Before directors and choreographers, before even the notion of a newly written score, there was Lydia Thompson and George L. Fox. What Ziegfeld did was to bind their very different arts in a single work, just as his *Follies* revues centered on showgirls and comics.

Sally was Ziegfeld's first story musical bearing author credits we recognize today: book by Guy Bolton, music by Jerome Kern (with a ballet by Victor Herbert), lyrics by P. G. Wodehouse and B. G. De Sylva (among others). It had originally been a small piece—called, in fact, *The Little Thing*. Kern, Bolton, and Wodehouse had planned it as part of their series for the Princess Theatre (a landmark genre we will get to presently). But Ziegfeld never put on anything small. He saw the musical as something important and demanding, glamorous above all. Small was real life; the musical was a fantasy. The leading lady must be not only a great entertainer but an ideal of youthful beauty, and the leading man not a hunk but a comic—a great one, with a distinctive style. It was a heterosexual's golden dream of art, where the woman is his date and the man a harmless accessory instead of a rival. And when *Sally* had concluded its 570 performances at the New Amsterdam and toured with its New York cast virtually intact for another year and a half, it became synonymous with the term "smash hit." What *My Fair Lady* was in the 1950s, *Sally* was in the 1920s.

It was a great show, but not a great work. The score gives the heroine three wonderful numbers: "Wild Rose" (a big scene, as she dances with a line of tuxedoed men while disguised as a Russian femme fatale at a Society party), "Look For the Silver Lining" (the Cinderella credo number), and "Whip-Poor-Will" (a nostalgic duet with the Society boy). Yet the last two had been written for another project, and the rest of *Sally*'s score is third division. The title number is an idiotic mess; when Warner Bros. filmed *Sally* as Technicolor super-special, in 1929, with Miller opposite Joe E. Brown, they slipped in a new title song, by studio writers, and it's a vast improvement.

If Hollywood journeymen can outrank Jerome Kern, the musical's greatest composer in the period after Victor Herbert's heyday, something's wrong. And what went wrong, really, was Ziegfeld. His focus was always on the beauty of it all, not on composers. Ironically, Kern's greatest score—and, to that point, Broadway's greatest musical—was a Ziegfeld production, *Show Boat*. It arrived a mere seven years after *Sally*—but by then Ziegfeld realized that the theatregoing public had discovered a new essential in the making of musicals: a first-division score.

Still, where does composition end and producing begin? Who really wrote "Wild Rose"—Kern and his lyricist, Clifford Grey, or Ziegfeld and his notion that Marilyn must get an exhibition number with the chorus boys? "Look For the Silver Lining" and "Whip-Poor-Will" were the beauty of Sally/ Marilyn; "Wild Rose" was her power: as the boys adore her and she basks in and further provokes that adoration while leading them in the dance and singing in her oddly rich soprano, top-heavy with extra tone on the notes leading up to her trusty high F. Did Ziegfeld commission this gala—at times frenzied—showpiece, or did Kern and Grey come up with it on their own? Was *Sally* written or Ziegfelded? Does "Wild Rose" sound like Sally or does Marilyn sound like "Wild Rose?"

There is footage of Federico Fellini directing a scene of his *Satyricon* (1970) involving a sexual get-to-know-you among Martin Potter, Hiram Keller, and Hylette Adolphe, in which we see Fellini sculpting his art with commands and gestures. "Hiram, *su*," he urges, his hand bringing Keller up from a reclining position, and "Martin, *giu*," he coaxes, his hand now smoothing Potter down. Shooting silent, as was standard in Italy at the time, Fellini can substantiate his vision shot by shot, literally *making* the movie—and that's how Ziegfeld made his musicals.

Nevertheless, the composer and lyricist are about to take over the history, right in the middle of the era of Ziegfeld and Miller. But first, let us backtrack to trace the rise of the important score and how it redesigned the way a musical told its story.

CHAPTER 5

ᴏᴧᴏ

Victor Herbert

If Harry B. Smith was more or less the dependable but uninspired lion king of librettist-lyricists, Henry Blossom, nine years Smith's junior, was the young tiger. Though Blossom tended to write for the more accomplished composers in comic opera, he had a musical-comedy mentality. The aforementioned *Yankee Consul* that couldn't decide whether it was a Big Sing show or a Zany Fun show was Blossom's, and on his eight collaborations with Victor Herbert, Blossom often led his partner into the crazy stuff.

Their most lasting hit, *The Red Mill* (1906), is in fact a musical comedy containing a comic-opera love plot and a haunted mill complete with a mezzo direly intoning "The Legend Of the Mill" in e minor, *Molto misterioso*. The musical-comedy identification inheres particularly in the two leads, for this was the follow-up title for Montgomery and Stone after *The Wizard of Oz*. They played Americans stranded in a Dutch village, unable to leave till they pay for their lodgings. Once again, it was the "Americans in Exoticland" trope. Stone was "Con" Kidder and Montgomery "Kid" Conner, out of the grotesque Oz look and free to extemporize in rehearsals till they ran the action, though they actually had little to do with the plot per se, concerned with young lovers, old lovers, and that looming, cursed mill.

Let's look at Act One, pausing, as we enter the Knickerbocker Theatre, on Broadway and Thirty-Eighth (and long since demolished) to admire producer Charles Dillingham's unique PR manifestation of a windmill with moving arms, outlined in electric light. It was Broadway's first mobile illumination, and the talk it inspired supposedly contributed to the show's 274 performances.

After the overture, the curtain rises on one of those opening choruses, as Dutch boys paint and Dutch girls model for them. Various principals then enjoy establishing numbers. The soubrette, Tina, sings with her girl friends a quick march, "Mignonette," in praise of the immense social success of a "bleached brunette" with "a figure that would make a saint forget." The number has nothing to do with the story, but hearing from the soubrette—secondary to the heroine but a livelier personality, the forerunner of Ado Annie, *Brigadoon*'s Meg Brockie, and *Kiss Me, Kate*'s Lois Lane—is always fun.

Next come two authoritarians, the owner of the Red Mill Inn and the town's Burgomaster. They're both fathers: respectively of Tina and of the heroine, Gretchen. The plot thickens, for Gretchen loves a ship captain improbably named Doris (this is always changed in revivals), but her father has implacably betrothed her to the district governor. Comic villains, the pair nevertheless enjoy a swinging duet, "You Never Can Tell About a Woman," running through the stereotypical talking points of the day— she's unreasonable and emotional, yet rules the world:

> The men may fancy still, that they have the strongest will
> But the women have the strongest "won't!"

A circus acrobat in his youth, Stone made a specialty of executing at least one physical stunt in each of his shows. In *The Red Mill*, he had two, the first on his entrance, falling backward down an eighteen-foot ladder. (It was managed with padded trousers that gripped the ladder's sides to control what appeared to the audience to be a sudden accident.)

We'll get to the second stunt in due course. Just now it's time for another extraneous number, for the two stars and the soubrette, a song and eccentric dance called "Whistle It," which is what you do instead of swearing when you're upset. The vocal line is part lyrics and part whistling, as when one Willie Jones tried to carve a stick of dynamite into a flute:

> He started on his boring with a piece of red-hot wire,
> Of course it was an awful chance but Willie took a "flier,"
> Now this is the selection that was rendered by the choir . . .

And they whistle the funereal final phrase.

But it's time for the typical musical-comedy Worldly Older Woman (Allene Crater, Fred Stone's wife) to step in with her establishing number, "A Widow Has Ways." In all, this is an awfully dilatory way to run a plotline. By this time in other shows, Mrs. Anna has started confronting the King in earnest, Henry Higgins is reclassifying Eliza, and two Mormon elders are converting Uganda. Even when *The Red Mill*'s sweethearts finally duet, in "The Isle of Our Dreams," the story is all but motionless, especially when, to fill out the act, Herbert and Blossom contrive an offstage automobile collision between a Brit and his six daughters and a Frenchwoman and her six sons. All of them enter for an ensemble, the madame storming at the Englishman in French till the twelve kids get friendly in a gavotte, "When You're Pretty and the World Is Fair (Why be bothered by a thought or care!)."

All told, the music is wonderful, and Montgomery and Stone, freed from *Oz*'s busy narrative, gad about playing sketch comedy and passing daffy remarks about Dutch treats and arranged marriages. Later, in Act Two, they will weight-train *The Red Mill*'s skinny plot by disguising themselves, first as an Italian organ-grinder duo and then as Sherlock Holmes and Dr. Watson—but just now comes the first-act finale, wherein Stone pulls off his second acrobatic stunt. To separate Gretchen and Doris, the Burgomaster has locked her in the haunted mill. As night falls, Herbert reprises snatches of the act's tunes while the audience enjoys the show's first helping of genuine plot suspense. Surely someone is going to rescue Gretchen— and that would be Doris, right? After all, he's the hero. A flunkey guards the mill door, but he finally falls asleep. *Ha!* Time for Doris to tiptoe in and . . . no—Gretchen appears at an upper window with a Big Ballad Coming Up look on her face. The number is "Moonbeams," one of Herbert's loveliest melodies, with a piquant little trick in the refrain: the jumpy sixteenth notes Herbert often used as breathless little syncopations. Herbert's biographer Neil Gould points out something extra special in the verse, a replica of the accompaniment Schubert employs in "Gretchen am Spinnrade," the Spinning Song from Goethe's *Faust*. "Is this portrayal of the two Gretchens," Gould asks, "perhaps one of the great musical puns in the literature?"

Now the townsfolk gather, demanding that Gretchen be released. However, no one but the audience knows that Stone has just pulled off his second stunt: rescuing Gretchen by holding her in one arm, catching on to one of the windmill's moving wings with the other arm, and sailing to earth to hide. (Doris is nowhere to be seen in all this; apparently he's a lover, not a fighter.) Meanwhile, the Burgomaster has entered the mill, turns back, and cries, "Gone!" The chorus echoes him, and the orchestra bangs out the music of the "Whistle It" dance as the curtain falls on the only thirty seconds of plot in the whole act.

Almost nothing happens in the second act as well, except the Governor arrives to sing one of the show's outstanding numbers, "Every Day Is Ladies' Day With Me." Montgomery and Stone get their big number, too, a Bowery waltz called "The Streets of New York," during which the pair put on an informal boxing exhibition that Stone had worked out with ring champ John L. Sullivan. Still, it is the Governor and the widow who enjoy the score's most interesting number, "Because You're You." Its distinction is a continuous filigree of interlocking lines, so that the last note of her first line occurs on the first note of his.* Clearly, Governor and widow will form a couple, so the authors simply declare Doris the heir to a fortune, the usual musical-comedy solution to a courtship problem, and the curtain falls on one of the busiest non-stories of all time.

Producer Dillingham billed *The Red Mill* as "a musical comedy," and he was right. Today, Victor Herbert is the CEO of operetta, but while he did start off in comic opera, he worked in every available form (including revue) from *Babes in Toyland* on. Further, his phenomenal national presence as the man who spanned classical and popular music—who else wrote for both the Metropolitan Opera and Paul Whiteman's band?—credentialed him to authenticate each of these forms through his unique approach to them. His coeval D. W. Griffith was to American cinema as Victor Herbert was to the musical: grammarian, innovator, and debate-club coach. He is sometimes praised as having led the musical's transition from its European roots to a more American sound, for instance in his many ragtime numbers. *The Red Mill* has one, "Good-a-Bye, John,"† for Montgomery and Stone during their "Italian" sequence.

However, Herbert had been singing in his own style almost from the beginning, with a heavy use of rubato and, again, that fastidious sprinkling of sixteenth notes that is less European than Herbertian. More important, he reshaped the very structure of American song, shortening the verse and lengthening the chorus till his heirs, from Irving Berlin and Jerome Kern to Rodgers and Hart and the Gershwins, had a more dramatically protean format to work with. Looking at it as Before and After, the Before was "Yip-I-Addy-I-Ay!" and the After was "My Heart Stood Still."

Herbert has been overpraised in one very limited way. Till the recent interest in the orchestration of musicals, it was "common knowledge" that only Victor Herbert and, later, Kurt Weill scored their shows. This is incorrect.

---

*The form became popular starting in the 1940s, a specialty of Frank Loesser in particular, as in "Baby, It's Cold Outside," "Make a Miracle," "Happy To Make Your Acquaintance." (Loesser's protégés Richard Adler and Jerry Ross tried it in *The Pajama Game*'s "Small Talk.") But "Because You're You," two generations earlier, might well be the first of its genre.

† This number has been dogged by a tale that it was actually written by others. However, it was published under Herbert's name at a time when interpolations were invariably brought out under their true authors' byline. The notion that Herbert needed to lift a tune instead of drawing from his bottomless well of melody is so absurd it does not bear pursuing.

As I've said, self-orchestrating composers were almost routine in comic opera—and, decades after, composers such as Marc Blitzstein and Leonard Bernstein took a decisive role in their shows' scoring even when they didn't actually write out the charts.

However, even the compleat musician employed assistants. Arthur Sullivan allowed his music director to arrange a few of the (less interesting) Savoy overtures, and Herbert's compositions were so nationally pervasive in so many different forms—band medleys of his show scores, for example—that Herbert could not be troubled to arrange them all himself. That's why God made assistants—mainly Otto Langey, in Herbert's case, but there were others. And while Langey was lightening the master's burden in these supplementary arrangements, he might well have stepped in to help orchestrate Herbert's show scores. At the start of the 1905–1906 season, Herbert composed three musicals that launched their tryout within a single five-week period: *Miss Dolly Dollars* on August 30 in Rochester, *Alice and the Eight Princesses* on September 14 in Buffalo, and *Mlle. Modiste* on October 7 in Trenton. Are we to believe that Herbert wrote and scored three works at the same time? At that, the *Alice* show, a combination of *Alice in Wonderland* and *The Twelve Dancing Princesses*, was so violently revised before Broadway that the Lewis Carroll figures were discarded (though the piece came in as *Wonderland*) and the score was all but rewritten.

So Herbert could not possibly have done all his own orchestrations. Yet note that he had so influenced the styling of the national sound that an assistant could duplicate Herbert's autograph without anyone's noticing: Herbert was, in effect, America's composer. He wrote forty-one Broadway shows (besides making substantial contributions to various Ziegfeld titles), and we might call him the Father of the Musical but for his having arrived too soon: before there were librettists to match his stature.

Nevertheless, Herbert dominated the Second Age as no composer dominated an era till Stephen Sondheim's collaborations with Hal Prince appeared, in the 1970s. Herbert's ability to vary a single score is astonishing. He gave Ziegfeld's revue *The Century Girl* (1916) the expected waltzes and marches (the latter taking in "When Uncle Sam Is Ruler Of the Sea" and "The Romping Red Heads," a curious piece about toys coming to life at night), but also unique forays into period pastiche (a gavotte for "Marie Antoinette") and pounding minor-key primitivism for a ballet, "The Stone Age."

Above all, Herbert tackled head-on the question of what form music must take in a romantic piece and a satiric piece. He infused romance with the Big Sing, trimmed satire with sass. Thus, the comic opera *The Princess "Pat"* (1915), a romantic comedy set among Long Island country-club folk, tilts toward the grand gesture, as in the "Neapolitan Love Song," given in

Italian and composed in the soaring lines that would serve as the lingua franca of twenties operetta, with its "Indian Love Call" and "Softly, As in a Morning Sunrise." Yet *The Princess "Pat"* makes do with a silly story about an American (Eleanor Painter) who has married a prince and does a little flirting now and then.

"Indian Love Call" and "Softly" belong to tales of murder and revolution, respectively; their music soars because their narratives do. But "Pat"s librettist, the redoubtable Henry Blossom, gave Herbert a lot of Europe in the storyline, for Pat is an Irish girl and her husband is Italian—and Europe, to Herbert, meant lots of that "extra" music that could run away with a show, turning a slightly romantic comedy into a *romance*. Herbert and Blossom gave the show's jester, Al Shean, the prancing "I Wish I Was an Island in an Ocean of Girls," but that "Neapolitan Love Song," starting as a wheedling barcarolle and moving into a passionate tango in the chorus, really sets the show's tone, for the evening was studded with grand ensembles and high-flying vocal lines. Perhaps Herbert felt a tale of the idle rich getting into idiotic mischief needed a musical buildup, strengthening his characters with strong music.

Conversely, in *Miss Dolly Dollars* (1905), a musical comedy about an American heiress adventuring in England and France, Herbert mixed just a bit of high-end singing into a fun-filled, snazzy score. His heroine, Lulu Glaser as Dorothy Gay, the daughter of a "Condensed Soup magnate" and catnip to fortune hunters, was a less expansive singer than Eleanor Painter in the first place. Still, the whole *Dolly Dollars* score is amusing rather than lyrical, as when Dolly duets with a German Army officer who speaks no English. Harry B. Smith gave them a bilingual lyric in which they converse using those constipated sentences favored by phrase books—"Has your cousin the shoes of the sailor?" and the like. And of course Herbert had to include a ragtime number, "American Music ('Tis Better Than Old Parsifal To Me)," always a sign that the show in question was—like *The Red Mill*— essentially satiric rather than romantic.

In other words, Herbert towered over his coevals because he rationalized the helter-skelter musical. Even extravaganza, the most undisciplined of the genres, seems almost Tolstoyan in its organization when Herbert writes one. True, *Babes in Toyland*'s score gets a bit vaudevillian at times. But now comes a Herbert extravaganza that enjoys almost absolute story unity, *Little Nemo* (1908).

Remember that number in *The Wizard of Oz*, "Little Nemo and His Bear," on Winsor McCay's comic-strip hero? Each night, the youngster would dream that he was joining his beloved Princess in the kingdom of Slumberland, sometimes to attend wondrous balls but sometimes undergoing nightmares of colossal pictorialism: climbing through the insides of an upside-down palace, seeing a vegetable garden go monster-size in nine panels, riding one's bed as it gallops through the town on rubber legs. Then, in the last square, Nemo would awaken, sometimes pulled out of bed by an impatient parent.

Herbert, with the ever-ready Harry B. Smith, gave McCay's dreamer his own musical, complete with the denizens of Slumberland, familiar to readers of the *New York Herald*: the Princess; Dr. Pill in his three-foot-tall top hat; the Candy Kid; and of course the unspeakable Flip, a latter-day Mose the Fire B'hoy, whose specialty was creating a rumpus during the most elegant Slumberland ceremonials.

Nemo himself, something like eight years old, might have been a casting problem. However, a straight-play adaptation of another Kid-hero comic strip from the *Herald*, *Buster Brown* (1905), had starred a performer billed as Master Gabriel, and he played Nemo. A genuine spectacle, the show was drawn almost entirely from episodes in McCay's artwork, including "The Land of the Fairies of St. Valentine," "The Weather Factory in Cloudland," and an island of savages, host to yet another of those incorrigible coon songs, "The Cannibal Barbecue." There were echoes of *Babes in Toyland*: "March of the Valentines" has the same structure as "March of the Toys," and "In Happy Slumberland" is a waltzy counterpart to "Toyland." But *Little Nemo* focuses far more than the earlier show on the attitudes of children: the Princess' "I Want To Be a Naughty Little Girl (and a scrappy little girl, but a happy little girl)"; a duet for Nemo and the Princess, "Won't You Be My Playmate?"; "If I Could Teach My Teddy Bear To Dance (like the bear I saw in the show)"; and Nemo's confession of embarrassing grownups with his honesty, "I Guess I Talk Too Much."

Quite incidentally, *Little Nemo* gives us a snapshot of the musical's design technology, for most musicals of 1908 limited their action to a single set per act. This was a disaster for the book writer: everything had to occur in one particular place for an hour or so, and then everything else had to occur in another place—even if, logically, the plot needed to ramble through a slew of places.

One way around this was to insert a short scene "in one" (that is, far downstage in front of a traveler curtain) between two major scenes. The short scenes kept the plot running while stagehands readied the next big set behind the traveler—but now the book writer had to find *something* for his characters to do "in one" that was in some way relevant to the action. Old-fashioned extravaganza, so greedy for specialty numbers, thought nothing of cutting in an extraneous but entertaining turn at this point— Montgomery and Stone in a crazy boat singing "Hurrah For Baffin's Bay" or suited up for "Football" in *The Wizard of Oz*, as we know.

Victor Herbert, however, was unwilling to stretch the borders of fairy-land that far. The equivalent moment in *Babes in Toyland* is a jump in the first act between two big sets. The first is Contrary Mary's Garden and the other the ghoulish Spider's Forest. There was no way to glide from the one to the other in those days, so the traveler closed and then reopened on a small set, "A Wall Back of the Garden." Here Toyland's boys and girls (all played by chorus women) sat atop the wall while title babes Jane and Alan, below them, led the gang in "I Can't Do the Sum." If you've ever seen a photograph of the original 1903 *Babes in Toyland*, you've probably seen this number. It's a tasty visual, and the song itself, burlesquing math problems ("If a woman had an English pug, ten children, and a cat . . ."), is tuneful, distinguished by the kids tapping on their slates during the chorus.

Still, "I Can't Do the Sum" is extraneous. *Little Nemo*, with even more sets than *Babes*, managed the scene transitions with greater dexterity, either through those scenes in one or by slipping back to Little Nemo's bedroom, the capital city of Little Nemo country. It's odd to see history made in the outdated form of extravaganza, but then Herbert made history in everything he did, because he brought classical technique to popular forms. Of Fred Astaire and Ginger Rogers, Katharine Hepburn famously said, "He gives her class and she gives him sex." Comparably, Victor Herbert made musical comedy classical and musical comedy made Victor Herbert sexy.

True, we don't think of Herbert as a musical-comedy man. That's George M. Cohan. And Herbert's best known scores aren't musical comedies. They're operettas, as we call them now. Like *Sweethearts* (1913), billed as a "comic opera," with an odd little blurb in the program about a fifteenth-century Princess Jeanne of Naples, smuggled off when a newborn to Bruges, found in a tulip garden by "Mother Goose," a local laundress of the Gilbert and Sullivan Katisha type, and raised with her six daughters. A princess laboring in a laundry!

Here we go again: comic opera. But *Sweethearts* is another of those shows, like *Maytime* and *Apple Blossoms*, that anticipates the twenties model in the ultra-romantic musical. Like those two titles, *Sweethearts* was set in modern times (*Maytime* spans the latter half of the nineteenth century), but in picturesque Europe, where a laundress may be wooed by a handsome stranger who is—*Spoiler Alert!*—a prince traveling incognito. The princess, Sylvia, already has a betrothed, but he's a faithless flirt. He's also a military man, which brings in the marches and uniforms without which no operetta could be called complete.

This is the stuff of twenties shows, with the "Deep In My Heart, Dear" and "Stouthearted Men." Thus, *Sweethearts* is what happened to comic opera after Broadway blew operetta fairy dust on it, and, along with *Naughty*

Marietta, it is the Herbert work most associated with America's operetta repertory, bound by Jeanette MacDonald–Nelson Eddy movies, summer nights at the St. Louis Municipal Muny,* and campy references to "Indian Love Call" on television variety shows. Musicals have a sweet tooth for ill-suited romantic leads—the bickering Curly and Laurey of *Oklahoma!*, *Guys and Dolls'* gambler and Salvation Army firebrand, *West Side Story's* American boy and immigrant girl, *Hello, Dolly!'s* grouch and yenta. But it is operetta that made a fetish of such couples with the menace of class distinction, in *The Student Prince's* waitress and royal or the plebian and the lady of the ancien régime in *The Vagabond King* and *The New Moon*.

And that's *Sweethearts*. *The Red Mill* tempered its romance with the musical-comedy ruses of Montgomery and Stone. But *Sweethearts*, though it does include the usual comic-opera comedian—in this case a representative of Princess Sylvia's native land, Zilania—is a truly emotional work. Sylvia and her prince enjoy back-to-back establishing numbers, hers the waltzy title song with a nearly two-octave range and his the dashing "Every Lover Must Meet His Fate." And note that, while comic-opera heroines tend to be little more than love dolls, Herbert preceded Oscar Hammerstein in favoring the tempestuous heroine who truly believes in something— Rose-Marie, Margot (of *The Desert Song*), Marianne (of *The New Moon*), not to mention Laurey and Mrs. Anna. *Sweethearts'* book, by the inevitable Harry B. Smith and (Ms.) Fred De Gresac, and *Sweethearts'* lyrics, by Harry's brother Robert B. Smith, present in Sylvia a mercurial sprite who cuts loose in a second-act rouser with the girls' chorus, "In the Convent They Never Taught Me That." When old-timers went gooey reminiscing about Great Portrayals, Christie MacDonald's Sylvia was invariably paragraphed with Hazel Dawn's Pink Lady and Fritzi Scheff's Mlle. Modiste. One reason is the stunning simplicity that Christie brought to "The Angelus," a shockingly pious piece for a form as profane as the musical. It's virtually a prayer, as Sylvia meditates and the Prince, looking on, reprises "Every Lover" while the bell tolls and an offstage chorus sings "Ave Maria."

Of course, *Sweethearts'* authors gave the two leads a second-act duet— the *Music Man* "Till There Was You" spot, one might say. But "The Cricket on the Hearth" is a very odd piece, almost revolutionary in the way the music reflects the shifting tones of the lovers' discourse. These two hardly know each other; she hesitantly feels her way through the scene while he, the typical royal, commands. "A princess you shall be, my pretty village

---

*Technically the St. Louis Municipal Theatre Association, an outdoor venue seating ten thousand with an annual season devoted especially to operettas, including the less famous ones.

belle!" he announces, and Herbert follows her insecurity and his confidence, jumping back and forth as, only now, she learns how their love will affect her life. She fears it, and, suddenly sensitive to her view of things, he asks what future she would wish for. Mind you, all this is sung, and now we go into *Tempo di Valse Lente*, for her "I'd like to go to some land far away . . ." Lo, she persuades him to see it her way, and now they join in the "Cricket on the Hearth" music proper, playful but *Molto moderato*, capped by a "pantomimic dance." It's a remarkable scene, challenging genre while reinventing, perfecting genre. But Herbert never gets credit for this because he appeared too early in the history. All the attention goes to Kern, Berlin, and the other Golden Agers.

Except in this book. If anything, Herbert is the animating figure who urged the Kerns and Berlins to launch their own reinventions, to turn musical storytelling into something realistic, intricate, vivid. If *Little Nemo* is Herbert in musical comedy and *Sweethearts* his matrix for twenties operetta, his very little known *The Madcap Duchess* (1913) gives us Herbert the master of dramatic technique—unfortunately in a melodically underperforming score. The scene is France in 1720, and the title role is another of those tempestuous heroines, for Seraphina (Ann Swinburne) is less madcap than intrepid—a horsewoman, a mistress of swordplay, and resourceful enough to join a commedia dell'arte troupe to keep things lively in the second act. The book and lyrics, by David Stevens and Justin Huntly McCarthy, adhered to the "Zounds!" school, as Seraphina impulsively tries to save a marquise from marriage to a prince and ends up falling for him herself. Okay, we were expecting that—but Herbert lavished upon this tale a meticulous musical narration, filled with vocal acrobatics, turns on a dime, and special effects tied to the physical action onstage. Thus, the capocomico of the commedia players has an exhibition number, "That Is Art," in which he demonstrates how a true thespian never really leaves the stage: life is a performance, as when he takes a pinch of snuff and resists the urge to sneeze. Herbert seizes the moment: in the music, you can hear the sneeze trying to burst forth and the actor blithely shutting it down.

Literally no other Broadway composer in 1913 was capable of such niche evocations, and *The Madcap Duchess* was replete with delicious touches. But somehow Herbert failed to plumb his well of melody as he did in *The Red Mill* and *Sweethearts*. Even *The Madcap Duchess*' designated hit tune, "Love Is a Story That's Old," plugged throughout the evening, is third division. After damagingly "respectful" reviews, a decent run of 71 performances, and the usual tour, *The Madcap Duchess* faded away while *The Red Mill*'s "The Streets of New York" and *Sweethearts*' clippety-clopping "Jeannette and

Her Little Wooden Shoes" became wallpaper in the living room of popular song. The two shows even enjoyed smash-hit revivals in the 1940s.

In the end, Herbert not only led American theatre music but defined it; the very sound of the man was everywhere, from the opera house to the summer park bandshell. Herbert was his generation: that was the problem. As we're about to see, it was the older generation. By Herbert's death, in 1924, every single major voice of the Third Age—the Golden Age, from about 1920 to about 1980—had made it to Broadway. Their music did not sweep Herbert away, no—at least, not for two generations. Still, in the 1920s, everybody could be divided into two groups. One was hot. The other was geeky. The geeky group believed in minding your parents, avoiding sex before marriage, and listening to Victor Herbert.

People called the hot group "jazz."

CHAPTER 6

༄

The New Music

One of the most influential creators of the American musical was neither a writer, a performer, a director, a choreographer, or a producer, and he is seldom mentioned in the dispatches. His name was Max Dreyfus and he was a music publisher, the head of T. B. Harms, which managed the careers of every important songwriting source except the samizdat Irving Berlin and George M. Cohan, the latter of whom went with various secondary firms and, occasionally, his own imprint with his partner, Sam H. Harris. Harms, which eventually underwent one of those business conversions into Chappell, published Jerome Kern, Cole Porter, the Gershwins, Rodgers and Hart, Vincent Youmans, Sigmund Romberg, Rudolf Friml, De Sylva, Brown, and Henderson, Harold Arlen, Kurt Weill, E. Y. Harburg, Rodgers and Hammerstein, Lerner and Loewe . . . in other words: Broadway, period.

Kern owned part of Harms himself, which tells us how connected he was in the very history of the musical: he writes great songs, he publishes great songs, he wants to know who else will write great songs. Kern becomes American music. Meanwhile, invisible to all but those in the music-publishing concern, Max Dreyfus "orchestrates" American music. He brings composers and lyricists together. He recommends them to producers. He packages in the orchestrator, the dance arranger. He is Dreyfus the auteur of the Broadway sound. He auditions and makes judgments—for instance, that the young Richard Rodgers had "nothing of value" to offer, even in the number that, when it was finally heard, gave Rodgers and Hart their boost. This was "Manhattan," with its cornucopia of impish rhymes ("Tell me what street" is linked to "compares with Mott Street") and insouciantly swinging little tune.

So Rodgers himself recalled, in his autobiography. And when Dreyfus turned you down, you were virtually out. Harms was Broadway and Broadway was Harms. When Rodgers and Hart—and "Manhattan"—finally got their first effective booking, in *The Garrick Gaieties* (1925), the publisher was the Edward B. Marks Company.

But the *Gaieties*, a semi-amateur revue put on by Theatre Guild subordinates at the Guild's soon-to-be-vacated old playhouse, the Garrick, down in Herald Square, was a surprise smash. And now, slowly, Max Dreyfus turns, step by step. Dreyfus signs Rodgers and Hart. Dreyfus offers his advice on whom Rodgers and Hart should write shows with. Dreyfus tells Rodgers about orchestrations and sheet music sales. And Dreyfus asks Rodgers why he didn't offer Dreyfus *The Garrick Gaieties* in the first place. Rodgers, a tough customer himself, says something like, "I did, and you said there was nothing of value in it."

Never mind: they got on fine after that. Nearly every Golden Age name got on fine with Max Dreyfus, because he loved being their music man. As Rodgers put it, "His copyrights were his children." Dreyfus not only tapped composers for glorification but maintained a music production assembly line made of not journeymen but artists. Entrenched publishers like Witmark and Schirmer were instantly rendered old hat while the innovative Harms drew a line: everything before and during Victor Herbert is nothing. Everything after is the future of American music.

Three events of 1914 fix this upheaval for us—though, we must note, the Harms imprint was involved with only one of them, the Broadway production of the Sidney Jones-Paul Rubens English show *The Girl From Utah*. A thin storyline involved a heroine (Julia Sanderson) aided in her flight from marriage to a Mormon by a handsome actor (Donald Brian) and—this is the comic role—a butcher (Joseph Cawthorn). As always, producer Charles Frohman sought to juice up the score with American interpolations, and, as often before, Frohman applied for them to Jerome Kern, working with Harry B. Smith.

Business as usual. But something bizarre happened this time: Kern turned out, all of a sudden, to have become the master of the New Music, and his contributions to *The Girl From Utah*—a substantial portion of its American score—are where scholars locate the starting point of the Golden Age. Above all, they single out "They Didn't Believe Me" (written with lyricist M. E. Rourke), an expansive ballad with the bittersweet sting of a diminished supertonic seventh chord on "[be]lieve me." In fact, the other Kern *Utah* numbers are just as entrancing—the wistful barcarolle "Alice In Wonderland"; an irresistibly dancy one-step, "Same Sort Of Girl"; "The Land Of 'Let's Pretend,'" highlighting two qualities that Kern more or less introduced into popular songwriting, the use of major sevenths and ninths in the vocal line and little fill-in figures in the accompaniment that extend melody from the voice to the orchestra and back in tiny concertos. Other writers made donations to the American *Girl From Utah*—"Florrie the Flapper," "Gilbert the Filbert." And in "At Our Tango Tea," by Worton David and Bert Lee, Joseph Cawthorn got a droll patter number about the misadventures overtaking games and party turns, the entire piece couched in not tango tempo but quasi-religioso recitative. Nevertheless, the cognoscenti heard the Kerns above all, and when the Victor Light Opera Company released its *Girl From Utah* medley—the standard recording platform for the dissemination of theatre music—it was almost entirely devoted to the Kern insert numbers.

The second epochal event of 1914 was Irving Berlin's first Broadway score, *Watch Your Step*. Bustling about the theatre world in his customary way, Harry B. Smith collaborated on this one, too, his all but plotless book relating the adventures of young people out to see the sights of New York while two of them stand to inherit a fortune and the others try to keep them from it. Producer Charles Dillingham gave the piece a lavish production designed by artists of *Vogue* magazine, and dance—the latest fad in American middle-class leisure—filled the stage. Those courtiers of the ballroom Vernon and Irene Castle were in the cast, and in "The Dancing Teacher," Vernon confessed that he used to get around in "crosstown trolleys" with the plebes till he took up the status of leadership on the dance floor. And "Now I know how it feels to ride in automobiles," he crowed, "for I'm a dancing teacher now!"

Indeed, *Watch Your Step* anticipated the era of Agnes de Mille, Jerome Robbins, and Bob Fosse: the show was obsessed with dance. The attorney who announces the terms of the will is a "tango lawyer," and his high-fashion chambers are a "law office de danse." Other numbers were "Show Us How To Do the Fox Trot," The Syncopated Walk," "The Minstrel Parade," and "(Won't you play a) Simple Melody," not a dance number but a quodlibet whose strains oppose a soothing ballad to a snazzy rag. The two strains are then sung simultaneously, in a form Irving Berlin virtually made his own, but the point is that the gentle tune emphasizes by comparison the ragged tune—irresistibly terpsichorean, less an invitation to the dance than a command. As they put it in a coeval Kern number, "I've Got To Dance": "Get up and walk!"

Our third innovative show of 1914 is, startling as this may sound, a Victor Herbert title, *The Only Girl*, "a musical farcical comedy." It was one of Herbert's biggest hits, but a Herbert hit was supposed to leave behind a beloved score. Think of "Ah! Sweet Mystery of Life," "I'm Falling In

Love With Someone," "Italian Street Song," "'Neath the Southern Moon," "Tramp! Tramp! Tramp!," and "Naughty Marietta," to cite a single show's classic titles.

The Only Girl had but one hit, "When You're Away," and the rest of the music was standard enjoyable Herbert, no more. It was not the score but the concept of the show itself that made *The Only Girl* one of the most influential musicals of all time. Somehow, Herbert and his librettist, Henry Blossom, came up with the idea of a play with songs—more precisely, a musical that smashes the handbook. One, they used a small cast without chorus, and, two, all the numbers leaped up out of the plot continuity without a single diversion. The setting for all three acts was an apartment in Manhattan, and there wasn't a trace of the legacy-with-a-catch or stolen-jewels premise that powered up so many modern-dress shows. *The Only Girl* even skipped the opening number, relying on a bit of teasy curtain music, *Allegretto scherzando*—and there were no act finalettos. For perhaps the first time, an entire score worked submissively within the storyline: four bachelors swear to remain single, then three of them marry while the fourth, a playwright, collaborates with a woman composer on a musical very like *The Only Girl*. These last two intend to keep it platonic: "Just two machines and nothing more!" they sing:

HE: I'll write the book!
SHE: I'll write the score!

Of course, nothing's platonic in a musical farcical comedy. The playwright has fallen in love: with the composer's music—specifically with a 'cello theme that becomes the "When You're Away" refrain. And then he falls in love with her, and she with him. They kiss. They go into "You're the Only Girl For Me." The rest of the cast pours in for a last reprise of "When You're Away." And the curtain falls.

The show was a sensation for its very simplicity. Its logic. There was one slightly extraneous element, an actress character named Patsy (Adele Rowland) whose purpose was to enliven the action with songs about show business—"Personality" and "You Have To Have a Part To Make a Hit." Otherwise, *The Only Girl* was not just integrated but naturalistic; no other musical was. Its intimacy, too, had appeal, giving it a snug fit in the 699-seat Thirty-Ninth Street Theatre, though rave reviews led the Shuberts to invite producer Joe Weber to move his production to the Lyric—almost twice as big—just two weeks into its 240-performance run.

And then, one year later, the series known as the Princess Theatre musicals set up shop, ironically just across the road from the Thirty-Ninth Street at an even smaller house, for the Princess held just 299 spectators. Historians invariably make an extended port of call of the Princess shows and their small-scaled, lightly realistic contemporary pieces, usually based on recently produced comedies and set in or around New York City. Much credit is given to agent Elisabeth Marbury and the Princess managers, F. Ray Comstock, William Elliott, and Morris Gest. But the Princess formula used *The Only Girl* as its model, observing differences of emphasis, not of kind: every single Princess title was an offshoot of Herbert and Blossom's invention. But then, as Roseanne Barr puts it, "Imitation is the sincerest form of show business."

Except—and it's a vast except—*The Only Girl* offered more of that Old Music of marches, 6/8 hippety-hop, and ballads for the parlor musicale, while the Princess showcased the New Music. The series lasted from 1915 through 1919, when the last title, *Zip! Goes a Million*, closed in tryout. But those five years produced the first set of revivable classics, in *Very Good Eddie* (1915), *Have A Heart* (1917), *Oh, Boy!* (1917), *Leave It To Jane* (1917), and *Oh, Lady! Lady!!* (1918), all with music by Jerome Kern and book by Guy Bolton and, starting with *Have a Heart*, book collaboration and all the lyrics by P. G. Wodehouse. To some writers, the very sound of "Kern, Bolton, and Wodehouse" is a summoning term for the true beginnings of The Musical As We Know It. To them, everything before this trio is just so much genealogy.

Yet if the Princess shows made a revolution, it was a daffy one, because every storyline was contentless farce. In *Leave It To Jane*, the college vamp beguiles a football ace into playing for the home team. *Oh, Boy!* and *Oh, Lady! Lady!!* track the threatening of an engagement by eccentric interlopers. Moreover, line by line the scripts aren't especially funny, though they do play well, moving faster than most musical-comedy books and banning the self-contained shtick scenes that infested star-comic shows. A typical moment, from *Oh, Boy!*, as a prospective mother-in-law grills her daughter's sweetheart:

MRS. CARTER: Can you support a family?
GEORGE: How many of you are there?

Then, too, the song cues often have the air of a public announcement, as when *Oh, Boy!*'s girl of the Second Couple is about to breeze into her credo of dating many men, each for his unique qualities, "Rolled Into One":

JACKY: Give a man a smile and he thinks that hands him the right to scowl at every other creature on your visiting list.

At that, a few numbers in every Princess show were inserts, especially in the characteristic second-act trio in reminiscence of some historical figure. *Leave It To Jane* had "Sir Galahad" and *Oh, Boy!* had "Flubby-Dub, the Caveman." The song cues were so blatant they could be heard on the Jersey Flats:

GEORGE: I wish we were back in the golden age—
JACKIE: Or the Bronze Age—
JIM: Or the Stone Age. I'm strong for the Stone Age. Think, Jackie, you'd be the seductive Tanglefoot, and I would be Flubby-Dub, your burly companion . . .

Guy Bolton is an unlikely candidate for revolution in the first place. Born in England of American parentage, he wrote books for Broadway and West End musicals for fifty years, starting in 1915. He worked with the Gershwins, Rodgers and Hart, and Cole Porter, and his shows were, mostly, hits. One of them, *Follow the Girls* (1944), closed as the longest-running book musical in Broadway history, though it was immediately overtaken by *Carousel*. (And *Oklahoma!* ultimately outran them both.) Yet Bolton was essentially a hack, notable for his faults. A Bolton book was an assembly of more or less autonomous parts—the charming crook, the silly-ass Brit, the helter-skelter disguise as someone bizarre, such as a Quaker aunt (in *Oh, Boy!*), a Slavic Lorelei (in *Sally*), or the maid (in *Oh, Kay!*). If Guy Bolton had taught Bookwriting 101, the blackboard would have read, "When your second act runs thin—and it will—have someone steal the jewels."

Further, the Princess format's famous intimacy is a legend; most of the shows opened at or were moved to larger theatres. (*Oh, Boy!* played most of its run at the Casino, more than four times the Princess' size.) So the series was not remotely as innovative as it is often said to be. Yet even in their brief heyday, the shows struck some commentators as an important breakaway. Why was that?

The scores. Those Kern-Wodehouse songs were not only New Music but New Lyrics, for Wodehouse lavished upon the Princess' weightlessly superficial characters the gravity of wit, surprise, and poetry. A transplanted Englishman who had already embarked on the all but endless stream of short humorous novels that would occupy a unique and beloved corner of twentieth-century lit, Wodehouse singlehandedly enlarged the lyricist's vocabulary, and vastly. He peppered his lines with slang (some of which he simply invented), got off so many jokes that some of them turned up in love songs, and individualized his singers with a novelist's ear for character. He even constructed conversations in the verses as they ramped up to the refrain. Here's a sample of the first verse of *Oh, Boy!*'s "Words Are Not Needed," as Lou Ellen explains to the chorus gentlemen how sweethearts know they're in love:

LOU ELLEN: A girl in love does not need words
To say so to a man.
For love has a language of its own—
MEN: Can she learn it?
LOU ELLEN: She can.
MEN: Would he understand it?
LOU ELLEN: Who?
MEN: Why, the chap she's talking to . . .

Most individually, Wodehouse introduced a highly useful conceit, to be adopted by everyone from Cole Porter to Lorenz Hart: treating history in modern terms. Consider *Leave It To Jane*'s "Cleopatterer":

In days of old beside the Nile,
A famous queen there dwelt.
Her clothes were few, but full of style;
Her figure slim and svelte.
On every man that wandered by
She pulled the Theda Bara eye;
And everyone observed with awe
That her work was swift, but never raw . . .

As the music was usually written first and the lyrics then tacked onto them, the number was conceived around a bare premise—wallflower dreams of turning vamp, using Cleopatra as a reference point—and "Egyptian" effects in the accompaniment. Tiny fanfares launch verse and chorus, with the squealy havoc we associate with "prayer" hands under a slithery chin and the suggestion of drums being pounded. Then, after Wodehouse set the music to words, so to say, the fantasy was complete: a girl of today merges with Cleopatra, pastiche as characterization.

This sort of thing was utterly new to the musical, and Kern matched Wodehouse with innovations of his own. One of *Leave It To Jane*'s ballads, "There It Is Again," centers on the hero's romanticizing of a particular melody, and Kern starts the A strains with that tune, no words. Yes, "There it is again," the hero cries in response. And the work's hit title, "The Siren's Song," was originally a duet sung against the girls' chorus imitating the plinking of a banjo.

The Princess was a music box—a zealous one, stacking its melodies. Borodin and Tchaikofsky make guest appearances in *Oh, Boy!*'s score, and while Kern and Wodehouse created the obligatory college song for *Leave It To Jane*, "Good Old Atwater," Kern included a medley of real-life college songs for atmosphere—or, let's say, accuracy. Perhaps he was growing impatient with the flimsy realism of musicals in general and wanted to authenticate them, substantiate them. Certainly, as we're about to see, his music became more expansive after this, as if to swell the frivolous storylines with a *musical* realism, haunting and emotional, humanism embedded in not what the story did but how the characters might feel in an *important* story.

Still, the Princess did run dramaturgical experiments as well. For instance, *Oh, Lady! Lady!!*—like *The Only Girl* before it—raised its curtain on a bit of music but no vocal of any kind. *The Only Girl* then programmed a rousing number after the first book scene, "The More I See of Others, Dear, The Better I Like You." Sung by the vivacious actress character, Patsy, marked *Animato*, and hustled along with rumbles and syncopations in the accompaniment, it was designed to enthuse the public, sock its energy level up to that of the actors.

Oh, Lady! Lady!!, however, followed its book scene with a gentle charm song, "Bill." It was a bold defiance of protocol and one of the best songs anyone ever wrote: and it failed, because it baffled the audience. Sung by the heroine, Mollie (Vivienne Segal), "Bill" catalogued the personal faults of her boy friend in an amusing way. "Whenever he dances," she tells us, "his partner takes chances." But she's to marry him that afternoon; it's an odd attitude for a bride, especially given that Bill was played by Carl Randall, winning in every way but especially noted for his dancing. True, Wodehouse could simply have replaced the couplet; Oscar Hammerstein did exactly that when the number was slipped into *Show Boat*, nine years later. Still, the problem lay not in a stray line or two but in the very idea of the song, so confessional, even disloyal. Anyway, in 1918, the First Number was never a ballad. By the 1930s, audiences were more sophisticated, so *Flying High* (1930) gives its heroine the winsome "I'll Know Him" before anything else is sung; *Anything Goes* (1934) let Ethel Merman follow the overture and the subsequent book scene with "I Get a Kick Out Of You"; and the first song in *Babes in Arms* (1937) is "Where or When," not only a ballad but one of Rodgers and Hart's most elusive conceptions, on déja vu. In 1918, however, inaugurating the musical program with a sweet number proved mystifying, and even the stubborn Kern was forced to pull "Bill" from *Oh, Lady! Lady!!* after it repeatedly died in tryouts.

Princess style's transparent anatomy made imitation irresistibly easy. After all, these shows were not unconventional They simply invented new conventions—that trio in the last act, for instance, or the exclamation of a show's title as the last spoken line before the reprise finale:

LOU ELLEN: I see, George, I'll have to be a little firm with you.
GEORGE: A little firm? Good! Let's incorporate right now.
(They kiss.)
A PASSING WAITER: Oh, boy!
EVERYONE ON STAGE: (One last chorus of "Till the Clouds Roll By")
CURTAIN

Thus, the Princess could bring in an outside team for *Go To It* (1916), a flop because of its subject, centered on a funeral. Alternatively, Bolton and Wodehouse could be married to an outside composer, Louis Hirsch, for the much merrier *Oh, My Dear!* (1918), in which the typical Princess screwballs complicate the heretofore blameless life of a health-farm director.

Princess usage took hold elsewhere on Broadway. *Going Up* (1917) flourished the Princess virtues in a piece about an aviation "expert" who can't—yet is forced to—pilot a plane. (Amusing to report, he was played by Frank Craven, later the original Stage Manager in *Our Town.*) *Irene* (1919) borrowed *Going Up*'s heroine, Edith Day, for a Cinderella tale à la Princess, about an Irish lass from Manhattan's Hell's Kitchen who crashes Society with two sidekicks and ends up taking the heir. Like *Going Up*, *Irene* was drawn from a play, a Princess practice also dating back to *The Only Girl*: because then the new script could follow the old script and stay on plot track, avoiding the tangent of the inserted vaudeville sketch, that curse of the Musical Before *Oklahoma!*. *Irene*'s book, by James Montgomery, came from his play *Irene O'Dare*, which had closed in tryouts in 1916. So the heroine's name, carried over in the musical, characterizes her even before she appears on stage as one who dares—takes chances, seizes opportunity. The American musical dotes on achievers, especially when they're young and cute. And of course Irene was Irish—not because Irish characters gave writers a stock of images and jokes to play with, but because the Irish were engaged at the time in democratic scuffling with New York's Italian and Jewish communities over the sharing of political power.

Irene was one of several shows to converse with the public on the effects of immigration, as various minority groups began to assert themselves in urban American culture. Harrigan and Hart did the surveying, and George M. Cohan laid the paving stones. But only now, moving into the 1920s, was the way cleared for a multitude of first-generation Americans to take stage—as the stars of shows but also as the people the shows were about.

Then, too, *Irene*'s score, by Harry Tierney and Joseph McCarthy, was even better integrated than most Princess scores. Tierney was no Kern, true. Still, his and McCarthy's intentions toward the plot were honorable, from the gleefully scampering "We're Getting Away With It" to the gently ragging "The Last Part of Every Party." And the hit tune, "Alice Blue Gown," was as Princess as "Bill" or "Till the Clouds Roll By": pure music on one very basic idea pulled right out of the script—I love my beau despite his faults; I'll stay till it stops raining and by the way I like you; My one good dress was secondhand but my joy in wearing it made it mine. The darkly exotic-looking Edith Day, a vibrant soprano, became a major star in *Irene*, which broke the long-run record at 670 performances. It triumphed in London as well, and even returned to Broadway (albeit in vast revision), with Debbie Reynolds, in 1973.

Musicals with one-word woman's-name titles began to trend, and *Mary* (1920), a more modest hit, was yet another of these New Musicals. This time, the driver of the action was not the heroine (Janet Velie) but the hero (Jack McGowan), who dreams of changing the world by building inexpensive, pre-fabricated houses for working people. George M. Cohan produced, directed, and "Cohanized" the piece, filling it with dance, though this, too, was a Princess convention: *Oh, Lady! Lady!!* included a dance after virtually every number except the love songs. *Mary* did make room for the New Dance Sensation, the "Tom Tom Toddle," which defied the Princess rules of engagement. Kern must have thought they were silly, for his twelve twenties shows in New York (there were three others in London), almost entirely ignored a song genre that utterly colonized Broadway throughout the decade— "Scandal Walk," "Black Bottom," "The Forty-Second Street Strut," "The Jijibo," "The Monkey Doodle Doo," "The Marathon Step," "The Varsity Drag."

Princess influence was most concentrated in Kern's contribution, for some of the most enduring composers of the day spoke of making repeated visits to the Princess just to collect the music. True, we don't "hear" Kern in Rodgers or Gershwin, two of his most ardent devotees; the impact was more an inspiration than a matrix. Yet one composer did imitate Kern with the humility of an acolyte: Louis Hirsch. Utterly forgot today, though, prolific and successful, Hirsch was a Kern intimate but impressionable also in general. Scarcely had the Metropolitan Opera premiered Richard Strauss' *Der Rosenkavalier* when Hirsch appropriated the wistfully edgy celesta theme associated with its young lovers, slipping it into his "Marie Odile," in *Ziegfeld Follies of 1915*.

Still, it was Kern whom Hirsch emulated, and Hirsch who, after Kern, most popularized Princess style. Three of the shows cited directly above— the at-the-Princess *Oh, My Dear!*, along with *Going Up* and *Mary*—were composed by Hirsch, and many of his tunes are so like Kern's that their mothers couldn't have told them apart. *Oh, My Dear!*'s "City Of Dreams" has the jingly Kern fill-in bits between the vocal phrases. The title song of another Hirsch show, *See-Saw* (1919), has not only the fill-in bits but the "long" melodic cell rising to a major seventh, so much a Kern invention, as I've said, that it could have been copyrighted.

Still, it was Hirsch's *The Rainbow Girl* (1918), a smash hit, that most surely emulated the Princess Kern, albeit in the huge New Amsterdam. Based on Jerome K. Jerome's play *The New Lady Bantock*, *The Rainbow Girl* retold that fantasy beloved of English musicals, wherein a musical-comedy star weds a lord. Unfortunately, this musical-comedy star turns out to be related to all the servants at her new husband's ancestral mansion. Rennold Wolf wrote the book and lyrics, and he and Hirsch devised an unusual way to start the action: in a theatre's green room, as the heroine, unseen in the wings, sings "My Rainbow Girl" on that theatre's stage: a First Number belonging, in effect, to another show.

The Rainbow Girl's score as a whole was state of the art for 1918: ballads for the heroine and her spouse, Lord Wetherell; "Alimony Blues" for the lord's sidekick, "blues" being a twenties buzz term in song titles; a "jazz" rouser about the Bacchic intensity of the latest dance rhythms for the heroine's sidekick, "Mister Drummer!"; duets for the usual Second Couple, "I'll Think of You (and maybe you will think of me)" and "Soon We'll Be Seen Upon the Screen"; the lord's fake flirtation number with the chorus girls, "In a Month or Two"; and the elaborate scene finales, notably one in which the heroine's relations scold her in chorus. "You're awful in your ways, Lady Wetherell," they sing, to a dancing one-step. In all, this is the form that the Golden Age score would take (until Rodgers and Hammerstein recentered the use of song to focus on character rather than blues, jazz, and fake flirtations).

So the New Music was creating the New Musical even before the 1920s, rationalizing it, clearing out debris. Once, authors sent a protagonist into exotic geography filled with magic jewels, floods, comically hostile peoples. Now they married you to a Fancy Dan whose butler is your uncle. More important, the score grew more focused yet more varied, engaging with the narrative even as it sought more expansive formatting. Kern led the way, for instance in developing trio sections to break up the monotony of the verse-chorus-second verse-chorus layout that had locked songs into

stagnant repetition.* Kern also varied the structure of his numbers, creating flowing musical continuity rather than a chain of end-stopped songs.
True, these "musical scenes" had been long established in the finaletto used
at the end of all acts but the final one; the finaletto predates Gilbert and
Sullivan and Offenbach and was still in use everywhere in the West. But
Kern was innovative in employing the finaletto's combination of song,
arioso (a more vocalized recitative), and underscored dialogue anywhere in
a show's running time. In *Good Morning, Dearie* (1921), Kern treated the
Boy Meets Girl as a tiny opera, as Boy (Oscar Shaw) courts Girl (Louise
Groody) with "Rose-Marie," as she tries to wriggle out of his dangerous seduction in dialogue while the music plays underneath, tempting her,
touching her heart. Still she resists, snatching at a chaste topic: the innocence of youth. Boy responds. A duet: "Didn't You Believe (that the bears
would catch the naughty children?)," recalling the credulous little era of the
tooth fairy and Santa Claus. A bouncy piece with a slight tug of wistfulness,
it's designed to tame him—but instead the two bond; and Boy will Get Girl.

   As the Princess shows bring us more or less within ten years of Kern's
monumental achievement, *Show Boat* (1927), historians look for the transitions that graduate Kern from Princess charm to *Show Boat* power. The
most frequently cited titles, both from 1924, are *Sitting Pretty*, in the Princess style, reunited with Bolton and Wodehouse; and *Dear Sir* (to a book by
Edgar Selwyn and lyrics by Howard Dietz). The pair flopped because of poor
casting; *Dear Sir*'s three leads were, in fact, uncertain or terrible singers, an
odd occurrence for an experimental lyrical score.

   However, another Kern show, overlooked by all, demonstrates his bur-
geoning powers, despite its antiquated genre. In the wake of their stupendous success in *The Wizard of Oz*, Montgomery and Stone went into the
extravaganza business with producer Charles Dillingham, each new production celebrated for a spectacular mounting, fresh-corn comedy, and
music by the brand names. Victor Herbert composed their Cinderella show,
The Lady Of the Slipper (1912). Ivan Caryll stepped in for an Aladdin piece,
Chin-Chin (1914), and, for Stone by himself after Montgomery's death, *Jack
O'Lantern* (1917) and *Tip Top* (1920). Note the gaps between the shows:
these were huge hits, with big runs in New York and lengthy tours. Caryll,

---

* "Trio" here refers not to music for three voices, but rather to the middle section of
the minuet (later scherzo) movement of the early symphony, which composers habitually scored for three instruments. The term *trio* was then used for any middle section.
For example, in *Camelot*'s "I Wonder What the King Is Doing Tonight," the verse ("I know
what my people . . .") leads into the chorus (at the song's title words), but then veers
into a somewhat different area of discussion for the trio ("You mean that a king who
fought a dragon . . . "), thereby quickening the number's dramatic pulse.

however, was running out of punch, and Dillingham had become interested in the New Music. Remember, it was he who produced Irving Berlin's *Watch Your Step*, the first of the New Musicals with its binge dancing, and Dillingham had put on four Kern shows (including *Good Morning, Dearie*) when he invited the composer to take on the Fred Stone franchise with *The Stepping Stones* (1923), in which Stone would work with not only his wife (as always) but his seventeen-year-old daughter, Dorothy. The subject was, very loosely, Little Red Ridinghood.

This happened when Kern was, so to say, "between" lyricists: after P. G. Wodehouse and before Oscar Hammerstein. Kern's collaborator in this time for both book and lyrics was Anne Caldwell, possibly the most underrated of all the musical's wordsmiths.* Together, Kern and Caldwell gave Broadway a work as newly minted in its approach as it was ancient in its genre. A fairy waves her wand, magical things happen . . . yes, all that. But this entry hit all the marks of a *now* musical, with ten sets—from "The Sweet Shop" and "The Garden Of Roses" to "The Dolls' Village" and "The Palace of Prince Silvio." In essence, the plot found Otto De Wolfe (Oscar Ragland) menacing Rougette Hood (Dorothy Stone) till Peter Plug (Fred Stone) saves her for a happy ending with Prince Silvio (Roy Hoyer).

But the plot was always a shadowy element in extravaganza. This was the genre of the sweetheart and the clown, of the set and costume designers, and—especially now, in the 1920s—the songwriters. Build roads, and folks buy cars. Erect a library, and everybody reads. Write great songs, and theatregoers demand more of them. And as the Victor Herbert generation seems to be replaced by Kern, Berlin, Youmans, Gershwin, Cole Porter, Rodgers and Hart, and De Sylva, Brown, and Henderson virtually overnight (it actually took something like fifteen years), the public will start to discriminate among great scores, good scores, and lesser scores.

The Stepping Stones is a great score, even though none of it is ever heard today; the title itself means nothing even to most aficionados. Yet the work is outstanding for its effortless narrative fidelity: the story lives in the music and the music bears the wonder and silliness that storybook extravaganza was made of. But more: for the first time in his career, Kern set out to write more than just a brace of songs with a couple of musical scenes. This score is rangy yet unified, with plenty of trio sections to let the action

---

*Caldwell at her best is deft and delightful, but her hit tunes—"Ka-lu-a," "I Know That You Know" (written with Vincent Youmans)—faded early on, and none of her shows achieved classic status. Then, too, it took one generation after Caldwell for the veteran Dorothy Fields and the newcomer Betty Comden to promote the notion of women writers in the musical who were as adept as men.

breathe and some gala ensemble scenes. Back at the Princess, the chorus did little more than egg events along every so often; in *The Stepping Stones*, the singers and dancers helped create the atmosphere of a marvelous little world in which even the villains are sort of cute.

Stone and his daughter did this most momentously in "Raggedy Ann," costumed as Johnny Gruelle's beloved children's book figures, but the chorus got into the act as well, as when the Tiller Girls (synchronized dancers antedating Radio City Music Hall's Rockettes) appeared as wood nymphs and, later, "mystic hussars," or when Act One ended with "Our Lovely Rose" and a medley of famous Rose Songs. (Echoing his friend Louis Hirsch, Kern tucked a tiny quotation of the final duet from *Der Rosenkavalier* into the verse of "Our Lovely Rose.") Of course, the use of "Ma Blushin' Rosie" and such others in a piece set in fairyland could be thought disruptive. But Kern obsessively interpolated pre-existing music into his scores—those college songs into *Leave It To Jane*, oldtime favorites as an overture to *Sweet Adeline*. Then, too, keeping the contemporary and the faraway simultaneously in play was elemental in extravaganza, where castles and magic shared the stage with jokes about Charlie Chaplin and the speakeasy. Similarly, "Raggedy Ann," for all its childlike quaintness, is contoured in rag, but the main ballad, "Once in a Blue Moon," has a Neverland feeling, tender and a bit wounded, like a valentine you offer to a sweetheart you're unsure of. Further, the extensive dance music is closely allied to the vocal pieces, as variations on them or in wacky counter-melodies. When Fred and Dorothy dueted on "Wonderful Dad," a fox trot with syncopations and blue harmony, they followed their vocal with a dance to slithery strains suggestive of a skeleton doing a cakewalk.*

Kern must have been unusually proud of *The Stepping Stones*, because it was his only title between the Princess shows and *Show Boat* that he brought out in a full American vocal score. Remember, Kern was not only Max Dreyfus' favorite composer: Kern was a partner in T. B. Harms, and thus could publish his music any way he wanted to. Then, too, *The Stepping Stones* got a beautiful production from Charles Dillingham, something to rival even the great Ziegfeld, incidentally Dillingham's crony, sometime

---

*The dance arranger was one of the musical's secrets at this time. Victor Herbert and a few others composed their own dances, but the musicians who arranged them for other songwriters—along with various incidental bits as called for—did not get billing till the mid-1940s, when the Big Ballet of the 1930s had become essential to the prestige musical. We don't know who composed *The Stepping Stones'* dances, but Kern's hand is all over them, for instance in the transformation of another Fred and Dorothy duet, "Dear Little Peter Pan," into a one-step raveup long before the song itself is heard, in the pantomimed prologue customary in extravaganza.

business partner, and major irritation. To ice the cake, Dillingham gave young Dorothy Stone the greatest coming-out party in history: Broadway stardom. Out of town, she had had featured billing, below the title. But audience response to her first scene at the New York premiere was so intense that, while the show played on, Dillingham had his electrician put Dorothy's name in lights right next to her dad's.

Well, that was the story that Dillingham sent out through the PR circuits, anyway. But the show was, unquestionably, one of the decade's biggest in every sense. With tickets starting at a very high $5.50 top and going up to $7.70 when it started selling out, *The Stepping Stones* ran 241 performances, closed only by the second Equity Strike, in 1924. When it was settled, Dillingham sent the company out for the tour, and they didn't return for two years.

And just as Offenbach rose through *opéra bouffe* to *The Tales Of Hoffmann*— a piece so abundantly creative that we still haven't caught up with it—Kern would leave Princess farce behind him. Once you exalt the musical power of a "light" form, it will get serious, and the master of the music was now on his way to *Show Boat*.

CHAPTER 7

✧

The Variety Show

Of all the musical's forms no longer in operation, none has been quite so eradicated as revue. Pantomime died out, true: but it had never been an important form in the United States. Burlesque was subsumed by musical comedy, so its spirit lives on, and fairy-tale extravaganza grew closer and closer to musical comedy till the last big one, *Simple Simon* (1930), Ziegfeld's Ed Wynn romp with a Rodgers and Hart score, was essentially a musical comedy with Rapunzel and Bo-Peep in it.

However, the revue was at one time as sovereign a genre as any other. It had one outstanding decade, the 1920s, remained imposing in the 1930s and 1940s, and became endangered in the 1950s, when television appropriated revue's mixed-grill format of song, dance, and sketch comedy. By the 1960s, variety revue was all but dead.

In America, the genre dates back to *The Passing Show* (1894), and, as the word "revue" (spelled "review" at the time) suggests, the concept was a look at events of the previous year. There were sequels, but revue as such was not firmly established till Florenz Ziegfeld Jr. unveiled *Follies of 1907*, the first in a line that would last almost annually through 1931. After Ziegfeld's death, in 1932, others took over the brand, the last so-called *Follies* playing Broadway as late as 1957.

The earliest *Follies* were not typical *Follies*, because Ziegfeld didn't yet know what he wanted from revue as a form. Eventually he hit upon an extremely odd program to emphasize the musical's most ancient elements: once again, the sweetheart and the clown. Thus, his showgirls were American beauties, whether wearing little more than lighting or costumed to the nth as milkmaids, princesses, the contents of a salad, or as impressions of classical melodies from Schubert to Massenet. But Ziegfeld's comics were exotic: Irish and Jewish and working in unapologetic ethnic humor that some of the public must have found baffling. Unprecedentedly, Ziegfeld filled out his *Follies* lineup with Bert Williams, the first black to break out of what was known as the "black time" and headline on the "white time"— and at the top at that: the *Follies*. The "big time." Nor was Williams a *Follies* novelty. Ziegfeld kept him on for eight editions and would have extended the welcome but for Williams' illness and untimely death.

Williams didn't headline in the *Follies*: nobody did. Ziegfeld's plan was to stuff his revue with stars and superb supporting talent while giving billing to no one. The star was the *Follies*. The star was Ziegfeld. The star was, even, the audience, smart and hip enough to attend: it was bragging by irony. The *Follies* regulars included, besides Williams, Fanny Brice,* Eddie Cantor, W. C. Fields, cowboy Will Rogers, Leon Errol (who played black-guy-out-smarts-white-guy comedy with Williams), dancer Ann Pennington, talent-less beauty Lillian Lorraine, singing act (Gus) Van and (Joe) Schenck, and a host of lovelies as likely to be called Drucilla Strain or Gladys Glad as plain old Marion Davies or even Betty Brown.

The notion of combining Nordic beauties with ethnic jesters was very, very ahead of the curve. Yes, there is a bit of this in the Weber and Fields burlesques, but only by happenstance. Ziegfeld made it a fetish. We can call it bizarre—but all of the *Follies* was bizarre: sophisticated, worldly, exhibitionistic, silly, crazy, cute, shocking. One thing the *Follies* never was: ordinary. Two things the *Follies* often was: dazzling and classy. For example, the gentleman in tails who sang the salutes to the girls on parade was John Steel, a tenor who in timbre, diction, and phrasing sounded exactly like John McCormack, arguably the most popular but also prestigious tenor after Enrico Caruso. With his extraordinarily sweet sound, Steel lovingly presented the girls while teaching the art of pear-shaped vowels. "A Pretty Girl Is Like a Melody" begins, in the Steel version, "I have an ear for myuzeeeek . . ." And the *Follies* was cultural, a bourgeois notion of art but also, from something like 1911—the year in which Ziegfeld first put his name on his creation as the *Ziegfeld Follies*—a way of defining oneself socially. To attend was to join the elite—or so it appeared, for Ziegfeld was a master of PR technique and *Follies* opening nights were the first in Broadway history to count as Celebrated New York Events, with hyperbolic newspaper coverage, mounted police, and surging crowds framing the arrival of the rank and fashion of the town.

---

*One sometimes sees Brice's Christian name as "Fannie." She herself started the confusion, using both spellings interchangeably. As her biographer Barbara Grossman tells us, "Sometimes, both versions appeared in the course of one article or the same playbill."

Who was Ziegfeld? A Chicago-born child of cultured immigrants from central Europe, he was a spendthrift and dangerous-stakes gambler, a plunger betting it all on the turn of a card. And that's how Ziegfeld produced his shows, playing everything he had on his stable of talent and beauty: silken soigné grandeur cut by orders of hot comedy to go. They spoke of the "Ziegfeld touch," as if he waved a wand. In fact, each *Follies* was conceived, rehearsed, and even performed in utter chaos, for Ziegfeld lived in a state of intensely decisive changes of mind, and his art was like his life. Harry B. Smith, who helped Ziegfeld fashion the first few *Follies*, shares in his memoirs an illustration of just how unreliable—or perhaps resourceful— Ziegfeld could be. In Monte Carlo with a friend, Ziegfeld chanced their every last sou at the casino and won a fortune, which he entrusted to his friend.

"No matter what happens," Ziegfeld told him, "don't let me have it"— because sooner or later the gambler loses it all.

Not too much later, Ziegfeld asked for their mutual winnings. No: demanded the money, for it was madness to desert a winning streak. The friend yielded, and Ziegfeld gave it up at the gaming table, right down to the last chip. The pair wouldn't even be able to order breakfast. But then the friend, strolling through their hotel, caught Ziegfeld in the dining room, hosting a fabulous supper. Joining the party, the friend whispered to Ziegfeld, "Where did you get the money?"

"Cabled your father," Ziegfeld replied.

He couldn't be trusted (especially in paying writers their due royalties). Yet he laid down rules that show business obeys to this day: One, You never get anywhere hustling the midway, so always go big; Two, You can't go big on a tight budget, so buy your talent retail, hiring the best, from stars to chorus; and, Three, Make a lot of noise about everything you do, even if you have to invent your publicity stories. It isn't lying. It's performing: because all the world's a stage.

So Ziegfeld hustled: but he hustled Broadway, most notably in the *Follies*, at its height by 1915, bursting with talent and decorated by America's most striking sets (by Joseph Urban) and costumes (by, most notably, the English couturière and sinking-of-the-Titanic survivor Lady Duff-Gordon, billed mononymously as Lucile). Urban's art was gigantic paintings in many styles, with banks of flowers, city skylines, or exotic geography in pointillistic detail; and the sight of Ziegfeld's famously "glorified" girls walking the Ziegfeld Walk (proud, grand, emotionless) across the stage in one of Lucile's concoctions astonished the public as if no one had seen a beautiful girl cross a stage before. And no one had: not like this. Ziegfeld was waving his wand.

Behind all the talent and expertise lay Ziegfeld's ingenious publicity machine. P. T. Barnum started but Ziegfeld perfected it: the art of getting everyone to talk about you. "The one thing that counts in America," Lady Duff-Gordon observed in her memoirs, "is self-advancenent of the most blatant sort." Still—in that time, though not ours—it only worked if you were *worth* talking about, especially if you flattered the public's self-image as tastemakers. To hear recordings of John Steel today is to visit a tinkly puppet show of the nevermore. In his day, however, Steel was the classy guy singing classy music while Ziegfeld's elect descended the Ziegfeld staircase of Beauty Is Truth.

And yet Ziegfeld's comics projected a truth as well, one of new art, immigrant art. When Fanny Brice offered *Follies* routines on first-generation American girls befuddled by life beyond the ghetto (as in "Becky Is Back in the Ballet"), she was giving good show biz—but she was also treating a sociological issue. It was boutique art, yes, but it had resonance. Comparably, Bert Williams' theme song, "Nobody" (introduced in vaudeville, but sung in a number of *Follies* editions), the lament of an eternal victim, could be looked at as a position paper on racism. "I ain't never done nothin' to nobody," Williams explains. So why is everyone so down on him?

Ethnic integration is elemental in show business today; it was unheard of when Ziegfeld launched the *Follies*. More than unheard of: impractical. Forbidden by unwritten law. As the buddy of powerful millionaires like the at the time New York–based William Randolph Hearst, Ziegfeld could defy orthodoxy. Still, his ecumenical appreciation of first-division talent was literally wonderful. Where did it come from? There had been a very few black musicals before the *Follies*, but they were *black musicals*, produced in "white time" venues yet separate from the rest of Broadway. Later, in the 1920s, an entire cycle of black musicals emerged, most famously Noble Sissle and Eubie Blake's *Shuffle Along* (1921); its sequel, *Runnin' Wild* (1923), which introduced an immortal New Dance Sensation in "Charleston"; and a revue, *Blackbirds of 1928*, whose score (by white Jimmy McHugh and Dorothy Fields) included another undying number in "I Can't Give You Anything But Love (baby)." But it was Ziegfeld who integrated Broadway, when he hired Bert Williams for *Follies of 1910*.

It's hard to see this as anything less than a political act, yet it also true that Ziegfeld was especially attracted to versatile talent that, like Williams, shone in music and comedy alike. One of the most influential aspects of the *Follies* was the way it unified a series of unrelated sequences. The original idea of "reviewing" the previous year's fancies and scandals was dropped early on; to bond his entertainment, Ziegfeld used Williams, Brice, Cantor, and the others in various ways throughout the evening. Even Will Rogers, really known only for his ironic monologues on the day's politics (delivered in full cowboy regalia while performing rope tricks), took part in sketches and sometimes even a musical number, seeming to wander in on the spur of the moment.

That was another *Follies* quality—the spontaneity. Ziegfeld's people were adept at improvisation, a lost art today. The last time I saw anything substantial of the kind was in Bert Lahr's final musical, *Foxy* (1964), wherein much of Lahr's role unfolded with an air of "Let me try this and see how it goes over." One gets this occasionally on *Saturday Night Live*, and at certain moments in awards shows. Still, the freewheeling nature of the comedy in musical comedy, free in the truest sense in the nineteenth century, when audiences and actors found themselves locked in a fragile embrace, now loving and now noisily vexed, enjoyed its last hurrah in the *Follies*.

Ziegfeld sometimes built this unpredictability into the script. At one point in *Follies of 1907*—right at the series' start—someone ran into the auditorium during a takeoff on Salome's Dance of the Seven Veils shouting that the cops were raiding the theatre. Sure enough, a squad of New York's Finest came pouring down the aisle, only to leap onto the stage and join Salome in a cancan: for the policemen were part of the show. Then, too, the 1912 *Follies* began as audience members started arguing about what sort of entertainment they hoped for; of course, these, too, were cast members.

One element of Ziegfeld's format became lodged in the revue generally, lasting as long as revue itself did: a big set piece for the first-act finale. In the 1919 *Follies*—often cited as the best of the entire line—Ziegfeld had his four male singing leads offer a close-harmony medley of old southland numbers in front of the traveler curtain. It was an odd quartet: three of them were comic in spirit (Eddie Dowling, Van and Schenck) while the other was that superhero of suave John Steel. Then the traveler parted on a fabulous tiered set of pink, silver, and white, the company attired to match in traditional minstrel-show grouping, with Eddie Cantor and Bert Williams as Tambo and Bones and George LeMaire as the Interlocutor. Each of the stars then took stage for a specialty. Van and Schenck revived an old Irving Berlin number that had gone nowhere under the title "Sterling Silver Moon," capped by Marilyn Miller's song-and-dance rendition in her unique combination of midcult soprano and playful tap. Now called "Mandy," the song went Top 40 (so to say) and even became the informal theme song of nearly every minstrel resuscitation from then on.

As for the music of the *Follies*, the early scores were grab bags by all and sundry. In the 1912 edition, however, composer Dave Stamper and lyricist

Gene Buck joined up to become the *Follies* house songwriters through the very last entry that Ziegfeld produced, in 1931, one year before his death. Mindful of the public's growing interest in being serenaded by the brand names of the day, Ziegfeld took interpolations from Victor Herbert, Jerome Kern, Rudolf Friml, and Louis Hirsch, featuring Irving Berlin most prominently, in 1919, 1920, and 1927. Nevertheless, it was Stamper and Buck who articulated *Follies* song style, to be imitated by other *Follies* songwriters. There was, first of all, what we might call the Roscoe Number—after the tenor of Stephen Sondheim's *Follies*, who Brings on the Beautiful Girls. In the later show, the subjects simply parade into view in party dress; in Ziegfeld's *Follies*, they were costumed to fit the theme of a song (another of Ziegfeld's many inventions). Thus, in 1915, Louis Hirsch, with Channing Pollock and Rennold Wolf, came up with "A Girl for Each Month in the Year," so Ziegfeld's harem could slither in, one by one, timed to the lyrics in weather dress:

> I want a January merry maid for New Year,
> And when the February flurry melts away,
> I want a breezy girl and arch,
> To worship me through March,
> A shower girl for April and a flower girl for May.

There were as well the au courant songs, spoofing events of cultural interest. The Ballets Russes visits New York in 1916: and that year's *Follies* offers "Nijinski," capping an extended ballet spoof with Fanny Brice once again offering the viewpoint of a girl from the neighborhood exposed to the exotic. Or, a year later, the English extravaganza *Chu Chin Chow* is about to open when the *Follies* offers a preview in the ragtime craze-up "(Beware of) Chu-Chin-Chow." In 1920, "Mary and Doug" saluted Hollywood's favorite marriage, of Mary Pickford and Douglas Fairbanks, and 1921 included a goof on the trademark catchphrase of the tumultuous drag queen Bert Savoy, "You Must Come Over." Kern wrote it with B. G. De Sylva, and while the number makes no attempt to reflect Savoy's hissy brinkmanship, still, "You should never miss a chance like this," Girl tells Boy: "For if you're clever you can steal a kiss."

The *Follies* treated history, too. Prohibition got a major look in, in 1919, with "When the Moon Shines on the Moonshine," "You Cannot Make Your Shimmy Shake on Tea," and "A Syncopated Cocktail." Even the opening of the first transcontinental telephone hook-up inspired a number. The 1915 *Follies*' "Hello, Frisco! (I Called You Up To Say 'Hello')," by Louis Hirsch and Gene Buck, pictured a young man in New York trying to reach his girl in San

Francisco (coincidentally hosting a world's fair), the second refrain decorated by little asides between the main strains:

SHE: Hello, New York, hello!
HE: How do you do, my dear, I only wish that you were here.
SHE: Hello, New York, hello!
HE: How is the fair out there, they tell me that it is a bear.

Revue's great appeal to songwriters was its greed for autonymous
numbers. In a book show, one had to tend the plot motion with love songs,
character songs, and the like. There was a lot of housekeeping to be done. In
a revue, however, one wrote about anything that struck one's fancy. Thus,
Fanny Brice and Eddie Cantor could sing, respectively, "Second Hand Rose"
and "I've Got My Captain Working For Me Now" simply because they suited
Brice and Cantor as performance pieces, she once again crushed by the limits
of working-class consumerism and he getting back at the bully. Or let the
nation be seized by a fascination with Hawaiian music, and 1916 presents "I
Left Her on the Beach at Honolulu." Rags were all over the Follies—"The Midnight Frolic Rag" (after the late-night cabaret that Ziegfeld produced on the
roof theatre of the Follies' official house, the New Amsterdam), "There's Ragtime in the Air," "Raggedy Rag," and of course a New Dance Sensation, the
"Ziegfeld Follies Rag." As always, the lyrics provide as little instruction as
possible. "You grab your gal and you start in a-walking," it suggests, "and
then you just do a sort of drag." Well, I'm all set; how about you?

In all, the Follies seemed an ideal proposition because, unlike story shows,
it had extra helpings of the good parts, especially star turns and visual spectacle. Ziegfeld had launched his Broadway career in story shows—all his
Anna Held titles, from the 1896 revival of A Parlor Match already spoken of
to Miss Innocence (1908), were book musicals, and he put on others at the
time. But anyone could produce such shows, if without Ziegfeld's unique
formal alterations; the Follies was Ziegfeld's invention. True, French revue
of the Folies Bergère sort inspired it. But from the very first edition it was
thoroughly Americanized, Broadwayized, Ziegfeldized. Then, too, the Follies
eventually became a national institution, for after playing more or less half
a year in New York the production toured with—at Ziegfeld's insistence—
all of the original stars and featured players. "The Ziegfeld Follies"* remains

---

* The first four Follies were billed by the noun and year only, as Follies of 1907, and so
on. As I've said, not till 1911 did Ziegfeld attach his name to the title, asserting artistic
copyright in the Ziegfeld Follies—and only in 1912 did the shows move into a proscenium house (almost invariably the New Amsterdam) instead of the more informal roof
theatres they started in.

a summoning term to this day, because it was so special yet, paradoxically, so generic—comics and girls, spectacle and surprise—that everyone in the country was familiar with it and there was nothing else like it.

Or, rather, there was a great deal like it, because the *Follies'* stupendous success was bound to provoke imitation. But no one ever figured out how to go Ziegfeld with style—for style was Ziegfeld's secret ingredient, the intangible element in the recipe. The revue annuals proliferated nonetheless: the folksy revue, from our old friend Raymond Hitchcock, *Hitchy Koo* (1917–1920). The arty revue: *Greenwich Village Follies* (1919–1925, 1928), on the small scale, but imaginative and distingué. The smutty revue: *Earl Carroll's Vanities* (1923–1926, 1928, 1930–1932, 1940), which not only coarsened Ziegfeld's eroticism but featured the lamest scores (even though Carroll had started as a composer-lyricist). And of course there would be the fumbly, cheap revue from the Shuberts: *The Passing Show* (1912–1919, 1921–1924), along with *Artists and Models* (1923–1925, 1927, 1930), which title at least sounded edgy and daring. Two of the revue annuals managed to imitate Ziegfeld without imitating him—that is, adopting his form with significant modifications. One was *George White's Scandals* (1919–1926, 1928–1929, 1931, 1935, 1939), very high-energy and emphasizing the latest in dance; and the ultra-classy *Music Box Revue* (1921–1924), launching the playhouse built by Irving Berlin and producer Sam H. Harris.

Everyone was using Ziegfeld's format, but, except for Earl Carroll and the Shuberts, everyone was twisting it toward different emphases. Hitchcock, for instance, left out the showgirls. George White sought the best in music, first using George Gershwin with lyricist B. G. De Sylva and then adding De Sylva to the team of Ray Henderson and Lew Brown for extra tang. Typical of this new byline of De Sylva, Brown, and Henderson was "Black Bottom," from the 1926 *Scandals* and the most athletic of New Dance Sensations. With a pastiche quotation of "Old Folks At Home," the slow-moving verse explains the title as a reference to the Swanee's muddy riverbed, and the chorus, *Allegretto giocoso*, breaks into the twisty syncopation that White's dancers would pound into a frenzy.

The *Music Box Revues* hewed closely to Ziegfeld, especially in their capitalization. The first edition cost what a *Follies* cost—$187,613, enough money, in 1921, to put on a handful of good-sized story shows. Much of the material in all four *Music Box* entries was Ziegfeldian, too—Roscoe Numbers with John Steel himself, special-effects numbers (in "Crinoline Days," Grace LaRue, another Ziegfeld alumna, rose on an elevator as her hoopskirt grew ever larger till it filled the stage), spoof numbers (as in a sextet setting of "Yes, We Have No Bananas," drawing on famous operatic melodies, with the singers dressed for the Met, from Radames to Tosca).

In the end, Ziegfeld's most influential coup was to reaffirm the growing acceptance of Broadway as the pinnacle of American theatre. As late as the turn of the century, the stage was truly a national construction. It was centered on Broadway, but there was much creative activity in other regions; Chicago had almost as many theatres as New York. However, the expansion of theatre—more playhouses, new producers to fill them with software, larger audiences attracted by the hoopla—in the 1910s and 1920s made New York more than the center of activity: the source of it. The regions grew ever more dependent on touring packages "direct from Broadway," and Ziegfeld, with his spectacular budgets and star-loaded *Follies*, arrived at just the right time to position revue as, in effect, a Statement that only Broadway could make. The *Follies'* post-Broadway tour became an Experience to be collected, like the sight of the President as his train passed through town, or being present at one's offspring's college graduation ceremony, accepting the family's first diploma. After the *Follies*, we can speak of the concept of Big Broadway, in which imposing powers combine not just to entertain but impress the public, urge on the art. The original *Porgy and Bess* is an instance, as are Gertrude Lawrence's unique turn in *Lady in the Dark*, Rodgers and Hammerstein's *Oklahoma!*-topping *Carousel*, *My Fair Lady*, *Hello, Dolly!* . . . shows, we might say, with a pack-leader mentality. Florenz Ziegfeld Jr. was the inventor of not only revue as such but an idea of show biz that had the brilliance of American know-how with the variety of its emerging new ethnic subcultures that were to enrich the musical in particular.

PART THREE

The Third Age

CHAPTER 8

꿍

The Structure of Twenties Musical Comedy

As the Golden Age begins, in something like 1920, the score—not merely a pleasant but an interesting one—is securely in place as one of the musical's most essential elements. But if the composer and lyricist have arrived, the bookwriter of quality is rare. That will change within the 1920s. Still, one technical problem will hobble the musical till the 1930s, one that we have already touched on: set design.

Eventually, the revolving stage and the use of mobile "wagons" enabled the substitution of one full-stage set for another during a blackout while the orchestra quoted from the score, beguiling the public only to fade out as the lights came up again. Starting in the 1940s (with *Around the World*, *Allegro*, and then *South Pacific*), directors spiced a show's theatrical flavor by "dissolving" scenes cinematically, bringing each next set and its players into view as the previous set and players moved off. This procedure, still experimental in the 1950s, was not wholly in use till the 1960s.

In the 1920s, none of this was possible. As in the early days of Victor Herbert, shows kept to one set per act, or alternated each big scene with those aforementioned short scenes in one (while the stagehands, out of sight, changed the decor), and so on. Revue and extravaganza were more generous, but most musicals held to one or two main locations per act. To emphasize what I've said before, this was a disaster for the musical as drama: everything in the storyline had to occur in just a few places—even if, say, "Living Room of Betty's Apartment" would have to play host to quite a congregation of people just to keep the plot in motion. How, then, to introduce the dancing chorus, so necessary in topping off the livelier numbers? Are they friends of Betty's? What, all of them? And how did they get into her apartment?

Veteran librettists used a work-around, constructing a dramatis personae in which almost everybody already knew everybody else. In *Babes in Toyland*, Glen MacDonough filled the stage with the inhabitants of a Mother Goose book, presumably a coterie of intimates. (If Tommy Tucker doesn't know Miss Muffet, he doesn't know anyone.) The only outsiders were the evil uncle and his henchmen and his niece and nephew, all of whom quickly made themselves at home. Amusingly, the show began with a surprise. Just as *The Phantom of the Opera* starts with not a burst of music but a book scene, *Babes in Toyland* raised its curtain on a modest little set whose action warned the audience of the uncle's designs on the children's fortune. This then gave way to the spectacle everyone expected: "Electric Storm At Sea and Wreck of the Galleon." Thereafter, big scenes ("Country Fete in Contrary Mary's Garden") alternated with scenes in one (such as the aforementioned Garden Wall set with its "I Can't Do the Sum" number), followed by another big scene ("Spider's Forest").

Still, one set per act made everything easier, especially in three-act pieces. The classic thus is *No, No, Nanette* (1925), with a score composed by Vincent Youmans to the lyrics of Irving Caesar and Otto Harbach and a book by Harbach and Frank Mandel. A farce about a Bible publisher who is keeping three penniless young ladies in separate dens, *No, No, Nanette* filled out the story with the publisher's family, friends, and professional associates, to facilitate comings and goings—and the chorus people were all friends of the titular heroine. The question is: has the Bible man— engaged in holy work, after all—been intimate with his charities, or is he purely philanthropic? The show never tells, but a cut number, the gleeful "(Oh I wish that I could be a) Santa Claus," provides a clue: "Santa Claus" was period slang for "old lecher."*

Harbach, Caesar, and Mandel were all stalwarts of the era, Harbach being especially notable as Oscar Hammerstein's mentor. However, *No, No, Nanette's* major name is composer Youmans. Extremely gifted but eventually sidelined by tuberculosis, Youmans enjoyed little more than a decade of stage work, including two huge hits, *Wildflower* (1923) and *Hit the Deck!* (1927). Still, *No, No, Nanette* remains one of the two or three essential

---

*We get another reference in Victor Herbert's *It Happened in Nordland* (1904):

PRINCESS ALINE: Doctor Popoff is a gentleman. I know it because he didn't try to kiss me till the *second* time he saw me.

DUKE OF TOXEN: Why, Doctor, you're a naughty old Santa Claus!

twenties musical comedies, with an ingenuously tuneful score (peaking in "Tea For Two" and "I Want To Be Happy") and that silly plot about the "does he or doesn't he?" Biblemaker. Yet the book has some thematic content, for young Nanette is trying to break out of genderist confines, and almost everyone else is scheming to make or spend money—even Pauline, the maid. The show is so twenties that Sandy Wilson used it as his template for a nostalgic English piece, *The Boy Friend* (London, 1953; New York, 1954), with an all-pastiche score. *Nanette's* "Flappers Are We" became "Perfect Young Ladies," the jagged outline of *Nanette's* "The Call of the Sea" informed *The Boy Friend's* "Sur la Plage," and so on. (Just to make it interesting, Wilson slipped over to a Rodgers and Hart song, "Blue Ocean Blues," from *Present Arms* (1928), for *The Boy Friend's* "'You Don't Want To Play With Me' Blues," a brand-new composition in dazzlingly observed recreation.)

Speaking of Rodgers and Hart, *Dearest Enemy* (1925) was another three-act work, though it used one set twice. Herbert Fields' book drew loosely—very loosely, as the heroine made her entrance apparently nude inside a barrel—on a real-life incident in the Revolutionary War. A gracious Anglophile hostess detains the British so our forces can retreat strategically; her barrel-wearing niece (Helen Ford) supplies the romance, with an English captain.

A pretty production, with lavish costuming amid the simple set plan, *Dearest Enemy* was in fact a sophisticated piece, reifying the musical's time-honored wish to play chicken with the received pieties, especially about sex. In fact, Herbert Fields was the unofficial leader of a group of book writers who, just at this time, infused musical comedy with blue material. Rodgers and Hart were in synch, for "(What do all) The Hermits (do in springtime?)" and "Old Enough To Love" are frank discussions of the erotic appetite, unthinkable in Victor Herbert—whose last work, *The Dream Girl*, debuted (posthumously) just a year before *Dearest Enemy*.

Rodgers and Hart stood right at the center of a number of revolutions, for their first shows reveal how speedily set-change technology was developing. *Peggy-Ann*, only a year after *Dearest Enemy* and still with Herbert Fields, was almost entirely a dream, and dreams do rather ramble about. Helen Ford was again the heroine, a small-town girl arguing and then making up with her boy friend (Lester Cole) in a scenario that had no more plot than that yet was stuffed with crazy nonsense: the dream. It appears that the authors wanted to spoof the expressionism trending at the time, in Eugene O'Neill and others of Broadway's artier precincts. In expressionism, everything is exaggerated and distorted, so Peggy-Ann's dream is a riot of the bizarre. She visits the big city (New York, of course), goes yachting, gets shipwrecked, then ritzes it up at the races in Havana, mapping around using scenes in one to facilitate the trip. Along the way she meets cops with pink mustaches, a talking fish (with an English accent, no less), relatives turning up in odd identities (her aunt takes stage in Havana as a kind of Texas Guinan, with a number drawn from speakeasy proprietor Guinan's famed book of personal idioms, "Give This Little Girl a Hand").

Peggy-Ann has become famous for its lack of convention, for instance starting with some music from the pit as the curtain rose but then going into an expository book scene before the chorus trooped on for the first number, "Hello." However, we've already seen Princess shows trying this out. All the same, Rodgers and Hart were genuine innovators, deconstructing the score of *Chee-Chee* (1928), yet another show for Helen Ford, till it had almost as many little bitty songlets running through it as *The Beggar's Opera*, or introducing "rhythmic dialogue" (in effect, lyrics spoken rather than sung) in most of their Hollywood films. What made *Peggy-Ann* a hit, at 333 performances, was its novelty, yes. But what made Rodgers and Hart's far less ambitious *The Girl Friend* (1926), *A Connecticut Yankee* (1927), *Present Arms* (1928), and *Heads Up!* (1929) hits were the songs: "The Blue Room," "Thou Swell," "You Took Advantage of Me," "A Ship Without a Sail." It was slang and poetry, heart and jazz, and all of it was—though the word itself is tired—fresh.

Historians become obsessed with the notion that Jerome Kern's "They Didn't Believe Me" turned the first page of the Golden Age Songbook. But one could say as much for the moment in Rodgers and Hart's small-scaled benefit revue for the Theatre Guild, *The Garrick Gaieties* (1925), when Sterling Holloway and June Cochrane launched into the refrain of the aforementioned "Manhattan." Word instantly went out, and the cognoscenti flocked to the old Garrick on Herald Square to sample the Newer Music. After struggling for five years to be heard, Rodgers and Hart were made. Dick was focused and eager while Larry was always sneaking off to drink and party: a bad marriage. But Rodgers couldn't divorce a wit as keen as Hart's. Only Cole Porter was as sharp—and, as both Hart and Porter were gay, their worldview commanded a rich perspective. Later, with Oscar Hammerstein, Rodgers would turn love songs into hymns: Boy meets Nun. With Hart, Rodgers worked a worried and less stable idea of romance. To cite one of *Peggy-Ann*'s numbers, "Where's That Rainbow (you hear about?)."

In other words, the *fresh*-sounding score was now one of the musical's essentials. Once, a show's authors wrote the core numbers while specialists zoomed in to write the interpolations. That's not a score: that's an open house. Now, in the 1920s, the authors were the specialists, and they wrote the whole score themselves.

Thus, the new producing team of Alex A. Aarons and Vinton Freedley based a series of musicals on the combination of, one, top stars, and, two, a top score in ultra-contemporary sound. Aarons and Freedley produced two shows with Rodgers and Hart, but their house songwriting team was George and Ira Gershwin, primary symbols of the newer music. Lyricist Ira, the older brother, was saucy and cultured—but all the major lyricists were by now. It was really composer George who made the brand unique, for his fidgety rhythmic pulse and harmonic mischief centered twenties jazz as a component of Broadway style.

Famous for hogging the piano at show-biz parties—and dazzling everyone with his explosive dexterity—Gershwin wrote the keyboard into his autograph. His shows featured duo-pianists in the pit, giving his music a profile to match the sexy trumpet and clarinet solos one heard in the recordings of black bands, just then breaking wide in American culture. Consider: Victor Herbert's instrument was the 'cello—waves of tone, classical in usage, something beloved. The heroine of *The Only Girl*—Herbert's "modern" play with songs that led to the Princess shows—is not just a composer but a 'cellist, and we hear her playing throughout the show, rich as cream. Gershwin countered Herbert with jazz, sly as sex. Jazz was the age and the attitude; it was how youth expressed "Sex, drugs, rock and roll" before Elvis came along. It's notable that all the other major twenties composers emphasized the foxtrotting two-step, in 4/4 time, while Gershwin held onto the outdated but faster one-step, in 2/4 time. Musical comedy, he might have said, is *motion*.

Then, too, because George and Ira wrote so often for Aarons and Freedley, Gershwin songs became associated with the racy, wacky, absolutely twenties Aarons-Freedley worldview, with its fortune-hunting and rumrunning and mistaken identity. It's a zany world—almost Offenbachian. Let someone produce a pair of handcuffs and two foes will get locked up together for most of an act; or a taxi pulls up in Arizona and out steps a New Yorker. (His fare is $742.30.)

Most twenties musical comedies are so forgot today that some smash hits—*Good Morning, Dearie*; *Tangerine*; *Queen High*—are unknown even to the buffs. Yet many Gershwin titles have ring: *Lady, Be Good!* (1924), *Oh, Kay!* (1926), *Funny Face* (1927), *Strike Up the Band* (closed in tryout, 1927; 1930), *Girl Crazy* (1930), *Of Thee I Sing* (1931). The standards take in "Fascinating Rhythm," "Someone To Watch Over Me," "Embraceable You," and even a cut number, "The Man I Love"—but the scores were *wholly* melodious entities, for Gershwin never ham-and-egged his way through a song. As more and more shows experimented with those little scenes in one, songwriters covered the set change with throwaway music, but not George. *Lady, Be Good!*'s first-act change moves from a street scene to a Society party, a soirée being the best way to assemble the principals without insulting plot realism. The street scene concerns the apartment eviction of Fred and Adele Astaire, "because the rent is a mere eighteen months overdue," she notes. Fred will save them through marriage to the party's hostess, though he loves another.

Now comes the transition, set outside the Society mansion. George revs up audience anticipation with a dashing yet piquant ritornello, music the orchestra repeats between the vocal sections, as the ensemble surges in to cover the ruckus of stagehands behind the traveler with "A Wonderful Party." A bit of spoken material and some dancing shtick for the Astaires will follow—but the purpose of this interlude is to move from outside the party to inside it, using a servant to usher in the guests. "Sounds like our entrance cue," the chorus exclaims, heading inside. Though "A Wonderful Party" never caught on in the hit-tune manner—unpublished, it wasn't even recorded till sixty-eight years later—it is delightful and smart and keeps the show's energy level up between the first scene (the exposition) and the party (the development and crisis).

The Princess-show alumnus Guy Bolton wrote the book to many an Aarons-Freedley title, often with Fred Thompson, as here on *Lady, Be Good!*. But Bolton did his best work with the other Princess wordsmith, P. G. Wodehouse, on *Oh, Kay!*, as when Kay (Gertrude Lawrence) complains to the comic (Victor Moore) that her sweetheart is marrying another of those Society stuckups:

LAWRENCE: That girl won't make him happy.
MOORE: How do you know?
LAWRENCE: Because she won't get the chance!

Still, in the end, the breakaway twenties librettist was, once again, Herbert Fields, a historical figure also as the son of Lew of Weber and Fields and brother to playwrighting siblings, Joseph and Dorothy (who was also one of the musical' s best lyricists). Fields was especially adept at accommodating the limitations of the "not enough sets per act" platform, and he had a sharp sense of humor. Some critics found his jesting uncomfortably bawdy. Fields' book for the aforementioned *Chee-Chee* was not just an experiment in how much leeway the dialogue can give the songs: it was also the tale of a man fleeing his duties as the soon-to-be Grand Eunuch of China.

As I've said, Fields made his early history with Rodgers and Hart, and very much in the Kern-Bolton-Wodehouse manner: a trio engaged *simultaneously* in developing continuity. I emphasize the closeness of their collaboration because, too often at this time, the songs and the script were created at a remove from each other, the two separate forces working off a plot outline. When at last music and dialogue were combined, they would suffer misfit glitches: a number would disrupt a book scene, or characters were given songs they didn't need.

This explains how Oscar Hammerstein emerged as the most influential of the musical's wordsmiths: working on both book and lyrics, he could monitor the consistency of the storytelling, effecting a rapprochement between what the plot was doing and what the music was saying. Harry B. Smith was the musical's first important librettist-lyricist, but Hammerstein was its first great one.

More greatness: the 1920s is the first decade boasting performers we of today have some knowledge of, through their films. Fred Astaire is most pertinent here, though on Broadway he was thought the lesser half of a double act with his sister, Adele. Her adorably squeaky soprano and nutso expressions made her a delightfully offbeat heroine, and the choreography Fred laid out for them tended to the eccentric. In fact, their trademark move was a goof, capping a dance by running as if joined at the hip in ever widening circles till they reached the wings and vanished. They introduced this maneuver in *The Love Letter* (1921), but they punched out into fame in *For Goodness Sake* (1922) as the always useful Second Couple, playing a romance opposite each other in that innocent time. *For Goodness Sake* was a typically empty-headed piece. Trouble begins—as *TV Guide* might phrase it—when a wife wrongly thinks her husband has cheated, and so on. But there was something interesting about this show: it apparently marked an attempt to fabricate a Gershwin musical. Alex Aarons produced it and Vinton Freedley was in it. But more: even the music was "Gershwin." *For Goodness Sake* was co-composed, by William Daly and Paul Lannin (to Arthur Jackson's lyrics), and both Daly and Lannin were Gershwin intimates, as orchestrators and conductors. Daly's two main numbers in *For Goodness Sake*, "Every Day" and "Oh Gee, Oh Gosh," are precise imitations of what George was writing at the time—and George and Ira added two songs to the score themselves. Then, too, a Daly-Lannin-Jackson number called "The Whichness of the Whatness (and the whereness of the who!)" is so loaded with Ira-like wordplay that one assumes he must have had a hand in it. It was a typical Astaire duet, the song's kinky bliss finding reflection in the immediately ensuing dance, topped of course by the "runaround" exit.

For Goodness Sake went to London renamed *Stop Flirting*, the first of three Broadway shows the Astaires took to England. It's a measure of how broad their appeal was, for few American stars dared the British public, while the Astaires—as they put it today—killed. Their other two lend-lease titles were authentic Gershwin shows, *Lady, Be Good!* and *Funny Face*, and now the Astaires were playing the leads and having their romances with other characters. *Lady* and *Funny Face* were Aarons-Freedly productions, so each was organized around these two sibling pairs, the Gershwins for music and the Astaires for sport, as everyone else on stage took up whatever space was left. The problem with this extremely popular recipe is that the talent came before the story, creating superb yet contentless entertainment. And that is why the Aarons-Freedley method became moribund in the 1940s: after *Cabin in the Sky, Pal Joey, Lady in the Dark*, and *Oklahoma!*, a solid story became as essential as the stars and the score.

In the 1920s, however, the public took in their stars neat, unencumbered by verismo, thematic development, or character psychology. When Florenz Ziegfeld planned an Ossa-on-Pelion show incorporating both Marilyn Miller and the Astaires, he started with not a narrative but opportunities for his headliners. So Miller would be an orphan again and the Astaires would be screwball Society wastrels. They could learn humility or something, and Miller would play a Salvation Army lass, a real honey in that military drag they wear. She was raised from a tot by Allied soldiers in the Great War for that touch of hokum, and must now redeem a crass world with her radiance, her tap solo, and her matchless smiles. Oh, wait . . . *Smiles* is her name, and *Smiles* (1930) is the show!

Only something was missing: a story. No one, from Ziegfeld on down, had any idea what exactly was going to happen, and *Smiles* ended as one of Ziegfeld's few disasters. Worse, he had neglected to include an element he thought fundamental in musical comedy: a star comic. Theatre, to Ziegfeld, gave the public what it couldn't get from real life: glamor, style, and, above all, fun.

It was an age of star comics, because musical comedy's loose structure lent them all the room their shtick comedy required. Joe Cook, for instance, had his love of uniforms, his inevitable rambling monologue about the four Hywoyans (Hawaiians), and his insanely detailed contraptions. In *The Great Clowns of Broadway*, Stanley Green describes one for us, used in *Rain or Shine* (1928): "Joe pulled a lever which started a whirling buzzsaw which goosed a man holding a soda-water siphon which squirted a man whose gyrations turned a Ferris Wheel whose five passengers took turns bopping [Cook's official stooge] Dave Chasen on the head with their violins." This caused Chasen to hit a triangle to accompany Cook's trumpet rendition of "Three O'Clock in the Morning." Ed Wynn, who reveled in being known as "the perfect fool," introduced tidier contraptions, such as a device for eating corn on the cob as one works a typewriter; he also liked to emcee revues so he could wander on stage during the acts and kibitz. ("Aren't they wonderful?" he might ask of the audience, of a ballroom duo running through its act. If the public failed to respond, Wynn would say, "No?," and, mock-sternly, add, "After Saturday, it's back to Mr. Orpheum [head of the famous vaudeville circuit] with them!") Jimmy Durante's kit included a rough New York accent, an ideal delivery agent for his outbursts of paranoia. "Everybody wants ta get inta de act!" he'd cry, slamming his arms against his sides. Or, of an impedient assistant: "I don't know what I'd do wit'out him, but I'd *rather!*" Bobby Clark, with painted-on glasses and cigar, was the smutty one, forever getting involved with chorus lovelies on very short acquaintance while making hubba-hubba faces at the house.

These were not comic performers of the kind we have now, such as Nathan Lane or Danny Burstein, basically actors with a jester's gifts. Third Age comics couldn't act in any real sense (though a very few of them eventually took on the challenge in works from Aristophanes through Molière and Restoration comedy to Samuel Beckett). Rather, they were professional toons, improvisational rather than script-driven and autonymous rather than members of an ensemble.

None of them could sing, but as long as they avoided operetta (which didn't host star clowns in any case), that was never a problem. Songwriters gave them musical chatter; Jimmy Durante even wrote his own. And Bert Lahr had voice enough to spoof opera and the kitsch singer, with his meticulous diction and clueless confidence in jejune material. Lahr could get so much out of these mockups that he spawned a genre, which we might call the Fatuous Loser's Exhibition Piece, most famously delineated as "If I Were King of the Forest" by Lahr's Lion in MGM's *The Wizard of Oz.*

It should be noted, though, that musical-comedy performers generally were versed in the comic arts, because no matter how good the score, a show had to kid around or it failed. For instance, in a college setting, a big, angry football fullback—his name is Beef—combs the campus on the hunt for his treacherous girl friend, Babe:

BABE: Worried about Beef? Me? I'm not worried.
(Beef enters, eyeing Babe murderously)
SOMEONE ELSE ON STAGE: Hello, Beef
BABE: Well, I'm a little worried.

Not long after, Beef, enraged, tries to strangle her.

BABE (choking): You can't win me with flattery.

This is from *Good News!* (1927), one of the decade's biggest hits and one of its non-operetta titles to live on as a classic. Released for stock and amateur production in 1932, it remained perhaps the single most popular show among high school dramatic clubs into the early 1960s, and its appeal is easy to assess. *Good News!* has a lot of lead roles to go around, is inexpensive to stage, avoids the bawdry of the Herbert Fields school, and is rich in hit tunes, with five standards. Further, the show has a rah-rah attitude highschoolers could relate to; in 1927, the ushers wore football jerseys, and George Olsen's band, in the pit, launched the overture with a home-team cheer.

Laurence Schwab and B. G. De Sylva wrote the book and De Sylva, Brown, and Henderson the songs, and, once again we have a location—the Tait College campus—that allows any student, teacher, or football-team associate to appear at will, so the limited number of sets doesn't hobble the narration. The plot itself is remarkably concise for the day: Tait can't win the Big Game unless Girl (Mary Lawlor) tutors Boy (John Price Jones) in astronomy—but, if he wins, he must marry Other Girl (Shirley Vernon). The usual comic Second Couple, Babe (Inez Courtney) and a new flame, the hapless Bobby (Gus Shy), provide zip and sarcasm, as when Babe makes mischief in Bobby's room:

BABE: Wouldn't it be funny if Beef came in now?
BOBBY: You should tell your jokes in graveyards.

And the students major in school spirit and haze the freshmen.

With so little story, the authors filled the book with virtually self-contained sketch comedy, as when Beef methodically dismantles Bobby's automobile, or when Bobby pretends to be immune to Other Girl's charms while trying to scam a kiss off her. Set changes were executed with a traveler curtain and music, a throwaway number such as "On the Campus," because De Sylva, Brown, and Henderson had a policy of rationing their inspiration. Melody reigned in the romance, as in the Heroine's Wanting Song, "Just Imagine (that he loves me dearly)," or the big love number, "The Best Things in Life Are Free," or a sorority waltz, "The Girl of the Pi Beta Phi." Not untypically for the 1920s, there was only one character song, Babe's "Flaming Youth," a dynamite number that has strangely disappeared from all of *Good News!*'s film and revival adaptations.

In fact, *Good News!* is not only a typical twenties musical comedy but a strenuously conventional one: it does absolutely nothing original from overture to finale. Betty Comden and Adolph Green used to perform an operetta spoof, *The Baroness Bazooka*, that began with an opening chorus of "peasants gamboling on the green." It managed to be insipid and idiotic at the same time—but so is *Good News!*'s opening chorus, beginning "Students are we of dear old Tait College." Act One ends with the customary reprise (of "Lucky in Love," another of the show's charting titles) and plot-suspense curtain (Girl faints, Boy catches her, Other Girl fumes). And Act Two starts with a "we're singing because Act Two always starts with singing" number, the "Pi Beta Phi" tune.

This is by-the-numbers writing. At another point, four students enter, and one of them heaps scorn on booklearning. Why study history when you can *make* it . . . with a New Dance Sensation? *Yes!* And that's how "The Varsity Drag" gets into *Good News!*: by contrivance, even trickery. Yet the songs themselves were so engaging that the score in effect relates to the book even when the book fails to relate to the score.

Thus musical comedy. But another form of twenties musical was integrated almost as a rule, because, in this genre, the score controlled the narrative. In musical comedy, the script told the story and the score enhanced it in various ways. But in operetta, the music told the story and the script went along for the ride.

CHAPTER 9

❧

The Structure of Twenties Operetta

You know you're at an operetta when the setting is Europe and the era is historical—Sigmund Romberg's *Blossom Time* (1921), for instance, using the life and music of Franz Schubert. Or Romberg's *The Student Prince* (1924), set in 1860, when young Karl Franz matriculates at Heidelberg and loves a waitress. But he is royal, so alas my love we must part. *Blossom Time* is stuffed with some of Schubert's loveliest melodies (including the famous theme from the Unfinished Symphony, debauched as a sing-songy operetta waltz). Still, it was *The Student Prince* that gave operetta its essential toasting number, "Drink, Drink, Drink."

Or you know you're at an operetta when, even in the New World, the atmosphere is exotically ethnic, as in *The New Moon* (1928), set in and around New Orleans at the time of the French Revolution, with a Romberg-Hammerstein score. *Rose-Marie* (1924) is even more exotic, in a mixture of strains from Indian and French to Canadian Mountie. *Rose-Marie* was co-composed by Rudolf Friml and Herbert Stothart, to the lyrics (and book) of Otto Harbach and Hammerstein again—and they all felt they had created such a unity of song and story that they declined to provide the usual complete list of songs in the playbill. Nevertheless, the popular numbers were easily extracted for recording and radio play, and while *The New Moon* gave operetta its essential Marching Anthem, "Stouthearted Men," *Rose-Marie* produced the unrivaled Future Campy Romance Duet, "Indian Love Call."

And of course you know you're at an operetta if all or most of the males are in uniform, as in Romberg's *My Maryland* (1927), set during the Civil War. A huge hit that broke a long-run record in Philadelphia on its tryout, *My Maryland* is one of the has-been titles in this line, for hit twenties operettas became classics almost as a rule, and with a score best described as incomparably adequate, *My Maryland* did not survive its day. It did have a "Stouthearted Men" of its own, "Your Land and My Land," which closes with a clever pastiche twist on "The Battle Hymn of the Republic."

But you really know you're at an operetta when only one or two characters in the entire cast ever do anything funny. Twenties operettas weren't musical comedies with grander music; twenties operettas were musical plays—some were literally billed as such—with all the comedy compartmentalized in a subsidiary character or two. At that, the jokes were often so feeble that the critics routinely complained about the jokers as if they had written their own roles. Of *Blossom Time*'s William Danforth, lumbered with "old souse" banter, the *Telegraph*'s Alan Dale said, "Let loose to do his worst."

But the writers who could toss off real fun tended to work in musical comedy. Operetta books were the province of more lavish personalities, literary people. Harry B. Smith's memoirs recall the difficulties of Bernard Gorcey when appearing in an operetta "in which additional comedy was a desideratum." During rehearsals, the librettist added in what he assured Gorcey was a surefire jest: "I come from a country where they get furs from fir trees and eggs from eggplant."

This was when puns were starting to seem *so* nineteenth century, and Gorcey didn't think the line would fly. The author insisted, and Gorcey obediently gave it a shot at the first public performance.

Smith tells us there was a "deadly silence." Then someone at the back of the house let out "a loud guffaw."

At intermission, the writer caught Gorcey backstage with "I told you it would be a laugh."

And Gorcey responded, "Yes, I know, old boy. But you may not be here every night."

Still, in the right hands—Hammerstein's, for instance—the system worked. In *The Desert Song* (1926), a Romberg show that Hammerstein co-wrote with Otto Harbach and Frank Mandel, the comic is Benjamin Kidd, an English reporter more or less trapped in the Moroccan desert when the French Foreign Legion is confronting an uprising of the local Rif (spelled "Riff" in the show) tribe. Bennie, created by Eddie Buzzell, represents a type very popular at the time, basically a gay heterosexual: of unclear appetite, somewhat effeminate in demeanor, and leery of women though unofficially engaged to his opposite, usually a secretary, nurse, or comparable partner. The character was forever being bullied by bad guys and vamped by exotics. Eddie Cantor made this the content of a star turn, but all the other such specialists were supporting players—and, in operetta, they did provide relief from the plot's relentlessly lofty occasions.

The Desert Song's authors wasted no time in putting Bennie to work. No sooner have the Riffs and their leader, the Red Shadow, sung the curtain up than the captive Bennie has a scene with two murderous Riffs. Bennie insists that he's harmless, a mere "Society correspondent":

> BENNIE: You know, parties, dances . . . (Looking at the glowering Hassi) No, you wouldn't know. (To the more pacific-looking Sid) You might, (To Hassi) but you wouldn't.

The Riffs don't like correspondents. They ask too many questions. But that last correspondent they dealt with won't be asking any questions now:

> BENNIE: (Fainting) I don't think I feel very well.
> HASSI: (Grasping his knife) When I see a spy, I want blood.
> BENNIE: Don't look at me, I'm anemic.

Bennie had been horseback riding with his friend Pierre when Bennie's horse ran off with him:

> BENNIE: You can imagine how I felt. (To Hassi) No. You couldn't imagine. (To Sid) But *you* might imagine. (To Hassi) But you couldn't.

Hassi and Sid find this dork too pathetic to be worth killing. He's such a "shrimp":

> HASSI: Are there no *big* men born in England?
> BENNIE: No, only babies are born in England.

The Desert Song claims the most interesting story of all the famous operettas, for the Red Shadow and Pierre are the same person (Robert Halliday), absurdly mild-mannered with his fellow French but, masked, a ruthless fighter for the Riffs. And he loves Margot (Vivienne Segal), but she loves . . . romance! It's the central conceit of operetta, of course, and she defines it for us in her establishing number, called, with a certain logic, "Romance." It turns out to be many things—"a playboy," "a flame," "a prince who tells a country maid, '"I love you.'" That last simile could be the motto of all operetta, expressing its obsession with social mésalliance, as with the student prince and his waitress or *The New Moon*'s bondservant and highborn lady.

One sometimes feels that Hammerstein made a pitch sheet for each work before he started writing, concisely stating its theme like a Hollywood log line. For example, here's *Hello, Dolly!*: a life-loving matchmaker finds a bride for a grouchy half-a-millionaire . . . herself. Thus, you know the driveline of your material from the start. Operettas of course had love plots. But too often they had no driveline—no *content*. *The Desert Song* looks at what a woman wants her man to be—companion or hero? Lover or tyrant? The lover, surely—but what if love *is* tyranny? Log line: Margot longs for love . . . until she's in it. Note that, in a different setting, Hammerstein would return to this in *The King and I*, in a vastly more fulfilled consideration—indeed, in one of the best books ever written for a musical.

Let's get closer to twenties operetta in one classic title, Rudolf Friml's *The Vagabond King* (1925). Though more or less completely benched by now, it was a viable property for over a generation, and was filmed more than once.* It threw off several hit tunes, from the merrily ripsnorting "Song of the Vagabonds" to the foxtrotting "Only a Rose (I gi-i-ive you)," and left so potent an impression that the former number's last line, "And to hell with Burgundy!," was spoofed in two fifties shows, *Make a Wish* and *Once Upon a Mattress*. Amusingly, each uses "Burgundy" to mean something different—the wine, the province, and, in the original show, the duke by that name, the villain of the piece.

That's because *The Vagabond King* is set in fifteenth-century France, when that Duke of Burgundy intended to take Paris and the French throne for himself. *The Vagabond King*'s source was *If I Were King* (1901), a play by Justin Huntly McCarthy (our *Madcap Duchess* collaborator, four chapters ago) that E. H. Sothern made the centerpiece of his career for fifteen years. Sothern played François Villon, a lusty knave, as legend tells, but of course a poet as well. When Friml and his lyricist, Brian Hooker, gave Villon music, they had something novel in the line of operetta heroes, for Villon first appears as a shaggy, dirty street brawler, then gets into courtly raiment

---

*Rose-Marie and *The Desert Song* went Hollywood three times, though the former's first outing, with Joan Crawford, was a silent, and the two remakes maintained only a glancing acquaintance with the stage show's storyline. *The New Moon*, better known for the Jeanette MacDonald–Nelson Eddy remake, was first filmed with Grace Moore and Lawrence Tibbett, but the plot appears to be drawn from a 1919 Norma Talmadge silent, also called *The New Moon*. MacDonald's filmed operetta adaptations—which in fact began with a *Vagabond King*, in 1930—demonstrate this music's staying power. There were ten in ten years, and some of them reached back to Second Age titles, albeit with, once again, plot replacements. Given Hollywood's conservatively commercial business outlook, it's worth noting that even after MacDonald and her various partners moved on, Hollywood continued to pump from the operetta cistern, discovering a "new" MacDonald in Kathryn Grayson, who starred (with the shyly mononymous Oreste) in a *Vagabond King* remake as late as 1956. Finally, only one of Broadway's classic twenties operettas was never filmed at all: *Blossom Time*.

when King Louis XI makes him King For a Day. At day's end, if he has not won the heart of Lady Katherine de Vaucelles, he dies.

It's a role for Douglas Fairbanks or for John Barrymore (who played Villon in *The Beloved Rogue*, a silent clearly inspired by *The Vagabond King*), but not, surely, for the typical wooden operetta baritone. Luckily, the English émigré Dennis King had revealed a solid voice as dashing Big Jim in *Rose-Marie*, and King's English training had equipped him with Shakespearean enunciation, fencing skills, and a ton of swagger. King was John Barrymore in the operetta version—but operetta didn't really deal in stars. Only in Europe did this form create headliners, from Richard Tauber and Gitta Alpar to Evelyn Laye and Yvonne Printemps.

Anyway, poster billing didn't sell operetta. What sold it was the spectacular visuals, the opera-trained voices, the huge choruses. And operetta did have its Bennies. *The Vagabond King*'s comics were a Villon sidekick, Guy Tabarie (Herbert Corthell), and a big fat pompous courtier, Oliver Le Dain (Julian Winter). Tabarie calls Oliver "Ollie" and Oliver calls Tabarie "Tabbie," and that's about as funny as they ever get. When Tabarie is shot by an arrow in the backside, he cries, "One of the William Tells got me." Oliver asks, "Where?," and Tabarie replies, "A long way from the apple."

Yes, ha. But then, no one attended operetta for the comedy. Besides King's panache in switching from Villon the ruffian to Villon the princeling, complete with Jekyll and Hyde makeover, there was the Friml music. Operetta lyrics tended to the stodgy, but the melodies encompassed a range unknown to musical comedy. True, Jerome Kern was just then pursuing his expansion of the lyricism in the latter form. But the other composers sought the enjoyable rather than the emotional. Nothing in *Lady, Be Good!* or *Good News!*—not even in the latter's plaintive "Just Imagine"—compares to the Big Sing that operetta raised as a rule, the spell that it cast.

The Vagabond King's variety of song types is truly various—a "Drinking Song" (with a verse heard first in C Major, then c minor, the last chorus a cappella); the dreamy, elaborate choral "Nocturne" next to the grisly "Scotch Archer's Song," in celebration of hangings; or a "Serenade" for the two cutups and the heroine, mock-amorous with vocal imitations of a plucked lute, an Offenbachian touch in a score that otherwise has all the caprice of Joan of Arc. The featured woman, a prostitute named Huguette, so in love with Villon that she willingly dies protecting him from an assailant, is introduced by "Love For Sale," a mercurial piece, even a neurotic one. Its tempo keeps changing as if torn between ballad and rouser, and its orchestration is a no man's land, ruled by the harp and crowded by the strings, with woodwinds scampering about between the vocal lines.

King for a day! But Villon is noosed at the gibbet in Act Four when Lady Katherine steps forward with "I offer the hand that spares his life." In a musical comedy, we'd be at most five spoken lines from the finale. Operettas, however, often had too much to say, and it's a good three minutes before the company breaks into a last reprise of "Only a Rose." True, a foxtrot is an odd way to cap a costume piece. One half expects Fred and Adele Astaire to tap in—though operetta favored ballet as a rule. *The Vagabond King*'s big dance number is a tarantella, featuring Tarantella Girls armed with tambourines.

The classic twenties operettas, from *Blossom Time* and *The Student Prince* through *Rose-Marie* and *The Desert Song* to *The New Moon*, hold the fringes of the repertory today. But *Show Boat*—a backstager about the *Cotton Blossom*'s "floating show," its people, and what happens to them in the outside world—is always with us. So, finally, you know you're at an operetta when . . . except *Show Boat* isn't really an operetta. Its profusion of musical scenes; its generous-voiced First Couple singing the ultra-passionate "You Are Love" waltz duet; its colossal folkish anthem "Ol' Man River"; its sheer scope, in a story taking in both north and south and bridging some forty years, are all told too deep and wide for musical comedy. Then, too, *Show Boat*'s action occurs in two spheres of existence: the natural world of the Mississippi River and the artificial, man-made world of American culture. The natural world protects and comforts. The man-made world destabilizes. This is almost too deep and wide for theatre, period.

There's yet more in this almost insanely rich work: instead of the usual configuration of one romantic couple and one comic couple, *Show Boat* counts five extremely diverse couples:

Captain Andy (star comic Charles Winninger) and his wife, Parthy Ann (Edna May Oliver, a specialist in sour beldame roles). He runs the *Cotton Blossom* and she busybodies around in a frustrated fascism. "How I hate not to know things," she mutters.

Their daughter, Magnolia (soprano Norma Terris) and Gaylord Ravenal (tenor Howard Marsh, though revivals often cast a baritone). The romantic couple, she on the strong and he the flighty side. A first in the musical: he abandons her and their daughter out of shame that he can't support them.

Frank Schultz and Ellie May Chipley (Sammy White and Eva Puck, married vaudevillians). The fun couple, who do what the lovers can't: bicker, utter sarcasms, and dance.

Queenie (blackface specialist Tess Gardella, who worked as "Aunt Jemima") and her husband, Joe (baritone recitalist Jules Bledsoe).

Black *Cotton Blossom* employees, very aware of America's racial divide, yet only apolitically observant.

Julie (torch singer Helen Morgan) and Steve (Charles Ellis, the one *Show Boat* principal with no other major credit).

Another novelty: the dramatic couple, more typical of a straight play. They are forced to leave the *Cotton Blossom* because Julie is half black; when she reappears, in Act Two, Steve has vanished. We infer that this is part of Julie's tragic destiny.

So much sheer character in a form that ran on stars and stereotypes makes *Show Boat* important aside from its music. This show is stuffed with material, but then it was based on a novel (of the same title) by Edna Ferber, a visionary who spun yarns about beautiful weak men and resigned powerful women set against the grandeur of the American epic. *Cimarron*: the settling of the West. *Saratoga Trunk*: the war between aristos and upstarts in late-nineteenth-century New Orleans and New York. Ferber sang America—and Jerome Kern, struck by the novel *Show Boat*'s theatricality and emotionalism, got Oscar Hammerstein to agree to collaborate. They convinced Ferber, but she asked for a highly unusual price—one-third of the copyright of the future musical. And they invited Florenz Ziegfeld to produce it, as the second attraction of his unique Ziegfeld Theatre, a gigantic egg splashed from ceiling to sides with a thrilling mural on *The Joy of Living*, in 1927.

Here at last was the important story for the musical's two greatest writers to develop, with its social commentary but also its tremendous love of theatre as the magic that inspires but also improves us. The theatre is fantasy? *Life*, says Hammerstein, is fantasy. Theatre simply orders and explains it. Theatre mirrors life: when Julie is exiled from the show boat to an uncertain future because of Mississippi's miscegenation law, the time is the late 1880s. But that law was still in force when *Show Boat* premiered, and would remain so for a further forty years, till 1967.

"As the river goes, so time goes." Historian Geoffrey Block found this lyric in the archives: the early, discarded first line of *Show Boat*'s first love song, "Make Believe." It must derive from Hammerstein's initial thoughts, making Ravenal the show's thematic mouthpiece. Ravenal is the driver of the plot, for it is he who takes Magnolia away from her safe place into the dislocation of . . . well, you could call it the bustling anomie of American urban life or simply *Show Boat*'s second act. Captain Andy is *Show Boat*'s philosopher-king: the CEO of the art. Julie is *Show Boat*'s iconic martyr: the cry for help in a world lacking in humanist compassion. But Ravenal, Hammerstein thought—at first, apparently—is the intelligence and energy of the story.

Then Hammerstein realized that Ravenal was simply a handsome face in *Show Boat*'s panorama. He's a leisure-class charmer, a gambler by trade. Such a man wouldn't remark upon symbolic concepts like the river and time. Instead, Hammerstein found his spokesman in the *Cotton Blossom*'s deckhand, Joe, who is but lightly embedded in the plot action. Almost akin to the interlocutor of minstrel-show days, Joe has perspective. He doesn't understand time—no one does—but he does understand place: the river and its laws and people. Those who know how river life works, and who strictly observe its conventions, live safely. Julie offends convention: by being half-black and entering into marriage with a white man. So the place has its treacherous side, its oppression. Yet it is comprehensible, and, for those it favors, a safe place. It had been safe for Julie till some vicious miscreant right out of a show boat melodrama denounced her to the sheriff. Again, life is fantasy—and so Julie leaves the show boat, to her despair and, we imagine, early death. As the river goes, so time goes: but time is the river's unpredictable counterpart, the dangerous place. Suddenly, now, in 1927, Guy Bolton and his stolen jewels seemed wildly irrelevant.

Show Boat opened up the musical as D. W. Griffith's *Intolerance* opened up American moviemaking. The commanding presence of "Ol' Man River" by itself marks the score as a Big Sing beyond operetta's scope—yet, at the same time, almost all the principals play book comedy and participate in a play-within-a-play spoof, *The Parson's Bride*. Such capers are the property of pint-sized musical comedy. Most surprising, this very template of artistic revolution blithely made room for specialty acts by some of its leads. Sammy White got his dancing turn (as a scene-changer), Norma Terris did her imitations, and Tess Gardella actually revived the coon song (in two interpolations, "May Irwin's Bully Song" and "Coal Black Lady") till Kern and Hammerstein wrote her a new number during the tryout, "Hey, Feller!" This song could be said definitively to have terminated the old black stereotyping with a full-blooded character number. But more: "Hey, Feller!" moors the last scene in 1927, when the Flapper of Today throws aside Little Miss Muffett flirt games and boldly chases men.

What about all the set changes necessary in this epic picaresque? Hammerstein was ingenious in balancing full-stage scenes with little scenes, and Ziegfeld's pet designer, Joseph Urban, kept the whole thing flowing, albeit with a few stage waits while the orchestra played through a blackout or Jules Bledsoe crossed the stage with a reprise (with new lyrics) of "Ol' Man River." Still, all that scenery reminds us that *Show Boat* doesn't run out of story in Act Two, as many musicals do. (That's why they call it "second-act trouble.") No, *Show Boat* has to update us on the tragedy of Julie. Further, Ziegfeld apparently asked Kern and Hammerstein to include a sequence set at the Chicago World's Fair of 1893—a sentimental touch. His career began there, when he opened a cabaret to lure fairgoers away from such spots as the Dahomey Village, which ended up in *Show Boat* as a production number for the black ensemble—a homage, at the same time, to *In Dahomey* (1903), the first musical written and performed by blacks to be seen on Broadway.

Show Boat is filled with homages, because it is more than storytelling and storysinging. Like the first revues, *Show Boat* looks back—not at the events of the year just past but at the history of American show biz. As Hammerstein told the story, it was Kern who first saw Ferber's novel as a musical—but it was Hammerstein who had a thing about theatre. A number of Hammerstein shows are backstagers—*Sweet Adeline*, *Music in the Air*, *Very Warm For May*, *Me and Juliet*. Further, there are "performance" spots in many of the others, including, with Richard Rodgers, *South Pacific*, *The King and I*, *Pipe Dream*, and *The Sound of Music*.

Show Boat is more than a backstager, obviously. Still, it does take a look at how theatre soothes and inspires us. Later, with Rodgers on *Me and Juliet*, Hammerstein described the audience as "a big black giant" whose worldview is improved by playgoing: "You send him out a nicer giant than he was when he came in."

Above all, there is *Show Boat*'s score, known for an unprecedented wealth of melody. What today's listeners don't realize is how intensely the story flows through the songs. We take this for granted now; it was innovative in the 1920s. Most lyricists had a style all their own; Hammerstein's style changed from song to song, to suit his characters. Joe, in "Ol' Man River," uses language in a wholly different way than does Ravenal in "Till Good Luck Comes My Way," or than Frank and Ellie in "I Might Fall Back on You."

Then, too, *Show Boat* is the culmination of Kern's experiments in the New Music. At times, it seems as if the orchestra will never stop reporting, commenting, accompanying, as if all those couples and the "river" and "time" thing were too rich a meal for fasting. The immobile old song structure of the verse-chorus-verse-chorus number dissolves as we listen; Julie's cabaret rehearsal song when she reappears in Act Two, "Bill," stands out because it's in the old format, left over from *Oh, Lady! Lady!!*, as I've said. So when Magnolia and Ravenal first meet, their scene moves from one musical period to another like a movie camera: first in a close-up on the hero in a solo, "Who Cares If My Boat Goes Upstream?," then to the meeting it-self: a strangely emotional flirtation in the chorus of "Make Believe," some conversation on love and pretending in trio sections, and at last a reprise of the chorus, love at first sight. Instead of halting the narrative, the number becomes the narrative, absorbs and carries it along.

Ziegfeld billed *Show Boat* as his "all American musical comedy": a na-tional epic, with its contrasts of city and country, reality vs. playacting, white and black, tradition and novelty, all designed to scroll down through depictions of the ever-changing attitudes of popular art, from oldtime melodrama to radio and the movies.* No musical before *Show Boat* un-folded such a panorama, nor dared comment on it with such omniscient perspective. In Friedrich Schiller's terminology of "naive" and "sentimen-tal" art, musicals before *Show Boat* were naive: free of perspective. *Show Boat* is sentimental: observant. It sorts through what, in this life, is a vanity and what is worthy, consistent, natural. As the river goes, so time goes.

---

*The radio is brought in in the penultimate scene, wherein Ravenal, about to reu-nite with Magnolia after so many years, hears her singing in a broadcast. Then, in the last scene, we learn that Frank and Ellie have finally become show-biz successes—as the parents of a kid movie star. Most revivals drop these developments, especially Frank and Ellie's reappearance at the end.

CHAPTER 10

✧✦✧

Dancing in the Dark

The New Music was contagious; now everyone could write a musical-comedy score. Irving Berlin, thus far the author of specialty numbers, go-everywhere ballads, and comedy inserts, tackled his first full-scale narrative show in *Face the Music* (1932), and slipped easily into the protocol of a story score. *Watch Your Step* and *Stop! Look! Listen!*, after all, had been filled with revue numbers, and even *The Cocoanuts* (1925), a spoof of Florida land-grabbing with the Marx Brothers, had a story but not a story score. Yes, the ballads—"A Little Bungalow (an hour or so from anywhere)" and "We Should Care"—identified the love couple, and her "Family Reputation" reflected the gulf separating her social standing from his lack of Position. (Her mother was Margaret Dumont, which explains everything.) But all the rest of the music was vaudeville—the New Dance Sensation, "Monkey Doodle Doo"; a sequence starting with "Five O'clock Tea" that kept the plotless second act humming with "They're Blaming the Charleston" and "Minstrel Days"; the inevitable Zeppo Number, "Florida By the Sea," used to cover a scene change; Groucho's "Why Am I a Hit With the Ladies?"; and Chico's piano and Harpo's harp.

Suddenly, in *Face the Music*, Berlin sculpts plot and character. Moss Hart's book was, characteristically for him, a sophisticate's revelry. It told of a scam to launder police-graft boodle by producing a flop musical, and was filled with in-jokes about show biz, the newly impoverished rich, New York's ethnicity relations, and the recent real-life police-graft scandal that was to force Jimmy Walker out of the mayoralty and the passionate reformist Fiorello La Guardia into it. *Face the Music* was Big Broadway, with the book scenes directed by Hart's new writing partner, George S. Kaufman; choreography by Albertina Rasch; and production supervision by Hassard

Short, one of the professional geniuses of the day. Producer Sam H. Harris put them all into the New Amsterdam. For some reason, the show ran only 165 performances. Still, it was one of the decade's smartest attractions, from the grande-dame dithering of Mary Boland to Short's fabulous realization of "Soft Lights and Sweet Music" in front of a stageful of mirrors.

It was as well very up-to-date, not only in its subject matter but in its writing. The Herbert Fields influence, ubiquitous by this time, gave the cast a number of double meanings to toy with, and, in the name of the Higher Earthiness, Hart included "A Lady of the Evening" (so billed in the program) in the cast. (The 2007 Encores! concert revival, less delicately, called her "A Streetwalker.") Berlin gave her a twist in "Torch Song": yes, she has sold her body, but only to undergo the pain of love, to purify her art "the same as Helen Morgan."

But then the entire *Face the Music* score is twisted, as Berlin opens with a merry-villager chorus detailing the treat of celebrity spotting in "Lunching at the Automat"; as the old-time Irish Number gets a brisk makeover in "The Police of New York"; as the First Couple (operetta stalwart J. Harold Murray and Arthur Schwartz's wife, Katherine Carrington) court to a lusciously irrelevant tango, "On a Roof in Manhattan." It's a mad lark of a score, as when that Mirror Number startles on the refrain's very first note, a tonic flatted seventh.

The use of a municipal scandal in a musical comedy suggests that the hard times of the Depression had politicized the form. In fact, while the *spoken* stage reflected the social moment to a great degree—even to the Group Theatre's creation of an influential acting technique (the so-called Method), designed specifically for socially progressive drama—the musical sustained its mission as an escapist lark. Chance political jokes proliferated, yes. But there were no more than a handful of outspoken political shows.

For instance, *Strike Up the Band* brought together the Gershwins of *Lady, Be Good!* and George S. Kaufman of *The Cocoanuts* in a biting look at how the power class drags the nation into conflict. One character, a Colonel Holmes, was clearly modeled on Woodrow Wilson's shadowy adviser Colonel House, foreshadowing stage appearances in the 1930s by actors representing Hoover, Roosevelt (and his cabinet), Neville Chamberlain, Hitler, Stalin, and many other such. The action saw the United States go to war against the Swiss over cheese, and while the 1927 production got great notices in Philadelphia, the public didn't come, and, sensing a disaster, a number of the leads simply walked out. The producer, Edgar Selwyn, had no choice but to close for revisions: Morrie Ryskind rewrote Kaufman's book and the Gershwins revised the score. Reaching Broadway in 1930, the new version was a hit, leading some to deduce that it must have been 1927 watered down. It wasn't. Ryskind did alter the action to frame the Swiss war as a dream, yes—but the criticism of warmongering remains sharp. MGM turned Dorothy's Oz visit into a dream; it doesn't nullify the power of the fantasy.

In fact, the 1927 show failed because Philadelphians didn't support it. It had no headliners; the 1930 version starred Bobby Clark and Paul McCullough, at their height as a sort of demented Montgomery and Stone. Does a dream pacify the commentary if you portray industrialists and politicians putting on a war as if it were a show? "We don't know what we're fighting for," the title song carols, "but we didn't know the last time." That line is in both 1927 and 1930, and it typifies *Strike Up the Band*'s edgy worldview. In 1930 Ryskind changed the casus belli from cheese to chocolate. Is that supposed to be what saved the show?

The Gershwins, Kaufman, and Ryskind all came back for two more political satires, *Of Thee I Sing* (1931) and *Let 'Em Eat Cake* (1933), the latter a sequel in such studied recapitulation that it seemed like *Of Thee I Sing*'s third act. First, John P. Wintergreen (William Gaxton) and his stumblebum running mate, Alexander Throttlebottom (Victor Moore), gain the White House on a campaign of love. Then, having lost the re-election, Wintergreen and Throttlebottom head a revolution.

My readers may be aware of the Curse of the Sequel that created such disasters as *Bring Back Birdie* (1981), *Annie 2* (1990, closed in tryout), and even a *Phantom of the Opera 2*, in London, actually titled *Love Never Dies* (2010). It was *Let 'Em Eat Cake* that established the curse; after all, nine of the Harrigan and Hart titles were in effect sequels to *The Mulligan Guards' Picnic*, and all were successful by the standards of the day. *Let 'Em Eat Cake* tried out one novelty, building its score on a contrapuntal feeling. Scowling leftists sing "Union Square"; snoring oligarchs sing "Union League." And the show's one hit, "Mine," is a quodlibet, though both melodies are dreary. The show itself wasn't. Cruel and sour, it was a kind of Where do we go after *Of Thee I Sing*? Why didn't they write sequels to *Anything Goes*, *Brigadoon*, *My Fair Lady*? We know why: sequels don't work. *Cake*'s second act actually set poor Throttlebottom into a guillotine. True, he was reprieved, even promoted to president. But the show was irritating when it wasn't regurgitating *Of Thee I Sing*, music and all.

Face the Music and these three Gershwin titles, early in the 1930s, suggest an epoch resounding with the musical's version of punditry—as when Irving Berlin and Moss Hart tried revue, in *As Thousands Cheer* (1933). They constructed the evening out of newspaper reports, even letting Ethel Waters sing, in "Supper Time," a widow's lament to go with the headline UN-KNOWN NEGRO LYNCHED BY FRENZIED MOB. But, again, this was otherwise a cautious decade, not an experimental one. Depression economics dissolved Broadway's working capital so thoroughly that anything hewing too far from the *Lady, Be Good!* business model had all the commercial appeal of a grizzly-bear petting zoo. Above all, one might lose out on the support system of a screen sale. With sound acculturated by 1929, Hollywood went mad for musicals—nice ones, not political ones: *Roberta, Babes in Arms, Too Many Girls*.

Thus, the Gershwins wrote a musical set in Dresden, Germany, at a time when that country was roiling under the threat of a Nazi takeover. Hitler had lost the presidential election, but the victorious incumbent, the senile Paul von Hindenburg, was under pressure to bring the Nazis into government. The Gershwin show, *Pardon My English*, started rehearsals about three months before von Hindenburg in fact appointed Hitler Germany's Chancellor, and the Nazi *Machtergreifung*—the Seizure of Power—began that same day, January 30, 1933—just over a week after *Pardon My English* opened. Yet there is no mention of this in the book, by Herbert Fields and Morrie Ryskind, nor in the Gershwins' songs—"In Three-Quarter Time," "Dancing in the Streets," "Isn't It a Pity (we never met before)?," "So What?," "My Cousin in Milwaukee," and so on. No, *Pardon My English* was concerned only with the hero's split personality—shifting from nice guy to crook and back—which occurs whenever he is hit on the head.

The debonair English star Jack Buchanan played the role till he (and Ryskind) walked out during a hysterical "Change everything!" tryout that turned a wobbly show into a terrible one. Alas, the producers, Aarons and Freedley, replaced Buchanan with a nobody, though their show depended on seeing the famously suave Buchanan snarling and threatening when he turned into crook. The key scene was pure non-musical farce: in a park, Buchanan, wearing a derby and carrying a cane that sprouts an umbrella when he activates a spring, must protect his noggin from apples falling from a tree, a pesky little girl recklessly bouncing a ball within Buchanan's danger zone, and a laborer very carelessly carrying a grandfather's clock and constantly swinging it inches from Buchanan's head. He withstands all hazards, then hears a plop on his hat from a passing bird. When he doffs his hat to clean it, a birdhouse suddenly drops out of the tree. *Clonk!* Blackout.

And that, really, was the musical's focus at this time: crazy fun, not sociopolitical considerations. It was a heyday of star comics, because their shtick never failed with their large lock audiences—Bert Lahr, for instance, whose mercurial-guttersnipe persona mated perfectly with the earthy humor Herbert Fields had introduced in the late 1920s. Lahr made the otherwise pleasant De Sylva, Brown, and Henderson show *Flying High* (1930) a smash as an aviator who can't fly—perfect Lahr territory. We recall that

Going Up used the same trope thirteen years before—but *Going Up*, one of those Princess imitations, fielded a gentle hero. Lahr represented the arriving generation of ethnic talent, making theatre out of the first-generation American's frantic revision of Old World coping skills for life in a New one. Thus, Lahr's *Flying High* character, Rusty Krause, announces that he will discover the North Pole. That's been done? All right, the South Pole. That one, too? Then the West Pole. A heckler calls out, "There ain't no West Pole." Yeah, but you know why?:

LAHR: Because nobody's had the *guts* to go out and *look* for it!

One of the new thirties comics was known primarily as a singer, though all her roles into the 1940s were written as a string of gags: Ethel Merman. Arguably the greatest star the musical ever had, Merman certainly enjoyed its most momentous debut, in the Gershwins' *Girl Crazy* (1930). The show's less than plot-synchronized score is all the same very tuneful, and Merman had three numbers showing off her range, from the boozy jazz anthem "Sam and Delilah" through the immediately following rave-up "I Got Rhythm" to a second-act semi-torch spot, "Boy! What Love Has Done To Me!" Still in her early twenties, Merman stunned first-nighters with the sheer flying confidence of her talent; the critics reported numerous encores for "I Got Rhythm," though the unsigned *Times* review called Merman's vocal style "peculiar."

Merman had a role in the plot, playing "Why, you—" comedy with her inattentive husband (William Kent) and offering sympathy to the Boy (Allen Kearns) after the Girl (Ginger Rogers) humiliated him in the first-act finale. Right from the start, Merman barked out her lines as if they were all marked "loud and funny," and her excellent diction and matchless vocal power made her song spots unique. There was no one else like her, and everyone started to write her psychotronic personality into her roles.

Thus, when Cole Porter created the title song of *Anything Goes* (1934), he gave Merman a verse jumping off a downward revelation of the notes in the tonic minor on "Times have cha-anged" as a kind of musical pun on who Merman was, which could be described as A Tough Lady With a Really Big Dick.

Merman didn't play roles. She inspired them; created them. Cole Porter loved her because show biz was supposed to be about the riffraff, and that was his subject matter. Besides, she had the lung power and pronunciation to send Porter's lyrics right to the top of the Imperial Theatre's balcony. And Arthur Laurents hated her, because he knew that if he tried to abuse her she would have cut his head off, and Laurents lived to abuse and abused to live. He loved to tell the world that Merman, in *Gypsy*, wasn't acting but rather played her scenes by rote: count three, turn, shout. A bit of that is true. During the Lincoln Center revival of *Annie Get Your Gun*, sensing by peripheral vision that Jerry Orbach was interfering with her performance of "Doin' What Comes Natur'lly," Merman confronted him: What are you doing while I'm singing? Orbach said he wasn't doing anything—just reacting to what she was saying. Aha! Said Merman: "I'll make a deal with you. I won't react to you and *you* won't react to *me!*"

So Merman was limited in the sense that "acting" was taking stage without interference: they came to see me, not you. Some call it "indicating"; Merman called it "show business." You turn up every single night, you spit your lines out, you justify the music. I call it "professionalism." Most important, there was something sharp and springy in Merman's conversation that book writers slipped into their scripts, for Merman and others, creating a Merman tintype as a musical-comedy heroine. Whether as a good-time gal, an ambassadress, or as Dolly—for Jerry Herman planned the *Hello, Dolly!* score for Merman—she was the heroine who overturned the Christie MacDonald and Marilyn Miller character. They were sweethearts. Merman was a broad, capable of tenderness but ultimately self-willing and independent.

Merman's liberated woman, Herbert Fields' sexy scripts, and Cole Porter's seditiously erotic songs reveal a colorful and very nearly x-ratable Broadway. Porter's *The New Yorkers* (1930), to a Fields book, mixed blue bloods with gangsters as if Society was now less exclusive than notorious. As in *Face the Music*, a prostitute gets a number—but Berlin's was comic. Porter's was a howl of pain, so ahead of its time that, seventy years after, when The Fine Young Cannibals rocked "Love For Sale" on a Porter anthology CD, the song sounded as if it had just been written.

Porter's next show, *Gay Divorce* (1932), was less raucous than *The New Yorkers*, soothed by the English setting, mostly English characters, and the democratic suave of Fred Astaire, working without his sister for the first time and on the stage for the last. Yet an air of libertine recklessness pervades. Astaire played a novelist caught up in Claire Luce's attempt to divorce a stodgy husband through a fake adulterous act in a seaside hotel fairly shaking with lust. There were no chorus men, only women, and one sprightly beauty tells her chums that she checked the front-desk register to find out who of the male guests is married:

SECOND GIRL: Innocent—but the right instincts.
FIRST GIRL: There were six Smiths.
THIRD GIRL: How the Smiths do weekend!

FIRST GIRL: And four Browns.

FOURTH GIRL: The lost tribe. Lost on Friday . . . found on Monday.

This leads into "Why Marry Them?," one of the many Porter numbers written from a woman's point of view in a way no other lyricist ever approaches. It's a satire, of course: "As lovers they love you, as your husbands they snore," the ladies explain. Claire Luce's official co-respondent in her "adultery" is one Tonetti (Erik Rhodes). "Put on your blond wig, girls," one of our chorus ladies cries, "it's an Italian!" Latin was the new Dutch as a comic stereotype: excitable, full of mispronunciations, and strangely inconclusive in seduction. "Your wife is safe with Tonetti," his motto runs. "He prefers spaghetti." In fact, it is the unassuming Astaire who takes stage as Great Lover, using "Night and Day" and its following dance duet as a campaign so (shall we say) penetrating that for once boy really Gets girl.

Operetta, on the other hand, had no place for these sensual revolutions. Operetta dwelled in the land of romance, an entire map away from Herbert Fields' or Cole Porter's views on life as lived. Operetta was also the place where most of the artistic experimenting went on. Jerome Kern, with Otto Harbach on *The Cat and the Fiddle* (1931) and Oscar Hammerstein on *Music in the Air* (1932), created two of the most integrated scores of all time, for the former offers a score broken apart and then intricately interlocked with the book and the latter is so overrun with music that it plays as one endless musical scene.

Otherwise, the two shows don't have a lot in common. Both are set in modern-day Europe and are in part backstagers. But *The Cat and the Fiddle*, billed as "a musical love story," is really a florid musical comedy, at once lush and jiving, while *Music in the Air*, "a musical adventure," is an operetta, so fully composed that each scene is structured as a set piece—Sonata, Caprice, Humoresque, Rondo. To put it another way, *Cat* was scored (by Robert Russell Bennett) for an unusually small pit of only six strings but a wail of winds including three saxophones, three trumpets, three pianos, and a percussion battery fit for Paul Whiteman. Bennett orchestrated also *Music in the Air* for a big pit of some two dozen or so, mainly strings.

Each show treats a war between opposites, but very different wars. *Cat*'s First Couple are composers, but she (Bettina Hall) writes hot and he (Georges Metaxa) writes classy. *Music in the Air* opposes the theatre professional to the amateur in a shocking way, for, breaking the cardinal show-biz rule that the heroine goes out there a youngster but comes back a star, *Music*'s heroine (Katherine Carrington) comes back a flop. She and her boy friend (Walter Slezak, in his youthfully slim days) have traveled from their village paradise to Munich to sell a song, for he, too, is a composer.

The song is "I've Told Every Little Star," a superbly simple creation in both words and music, suggesting a folk piece. Unfortunately, Kern and Hammerstein reprised it so insistently that the audience must have left not merely humming the tune but singing it in sixteen-part harmony with soprano descants. But at least the audience heard the entire song: had it turned up in *The Cat and the Fiddle*, they would have got its verse in one scene, its first A strain in another, and the rest of it later on mixed in with something else. That's how *Cat*'s "She Didn't Say 'Yes'" is performed—a bit there and a bit there, each bit's lyrics reflecting the plot action.

Both shows were big hits, *Cat* at 395 performances and *Music* at 342, extremely strong runs in the Depression. And both were filmed. Yet somehow they never caught on as classics and are seldom seen. True, *Cat*'s book is slow and dull, and its duel of pop and classical is very thirties. It's reminiscent of a Walt Disney Silly Symphony of 1935, *Music Land*, in which the Land of Symphony faces the Isle of Jazz across the Sea of Discord. The Jazz prince loves the Symphony princess, so war breaks out, brass cannonfire against organ-pipe rockets. At the time, this was a national conversation: sweet or hot? But it's not vital after *West Side Story* and "Eleanor Rigby," for contemporary music can be sweet *and* hot.

Anyway, relatively few thirties musicals have become classics. Indeed, two of the decade's defining forms, the "little" revue and the big "theme" revue, are virtually unrevivable if only because they were filled with references to events and names of the day. Composer Arthur Schwartz and his most constant lyricist, Howard Dietz, became prominent in the intimate format: *The Little Show* (1929), *The Second Little Show* (1930), *Three's a Crowd* (1930), *Flying Colors* (1932). (There was a *Third Little Show*, written by others.) "Intimate," at the time, was a euphemism for "sophisticated," itself a euphemism for many things, from "worldly" and "tolerant" to just plain old "sexual" in all its variations. There were "intimate" talents, of esoteric appeal, such as torch singer Libby Holman and dry comic Fred Allen. There were "intimate" songs, such as *The Little Show*'s "I Guess I'll Have To Change My Plan," the lament of a man whose love has married another. In the second chorus, he decides to woo the lady anyway, which is worldly enough. But the song really shatters the Commandments in the line "Why did I buy those blue pajamas before the big affair began?"—for the very mention of bedroom wear was thought uncouth and dangerous. It conjured up visions of, you know . . . skin.

During their intimate period, Schwartz and Dietz crossed over into big revue with one of the very best, *The Band Wagon* (1931), filling the New Amsterdam with "big" talent—the Astaires, comic Frank Morgan (later the title player in MGM's *The Wizard of Oz*), tart-tongued Helen Broderick, and strange artistic lesbian ballerina Tilly Losch. *The Band Wagon* had an "intimate" side, though—intimate in its erotic connotation. In "Confession," the chorus girls revealed their apparently sinless lifestyle. "I never kissed a man before," they explained, adding, "before I knew his name." The Astaires played wicked French tots in "Hoops," spying on a grownup world populated exclusively by adulterers. And in a southern sketch called "The Pride of the Claghornes," daughter Breeze (Adele Astaire) was disinherited for being a virgin. "The proudest family in all the countryside!" thunders her daddy, the Colonel. "And now—this!"

Many of the big revues were organized around a theme, like Irving Berlin's aforementioned newspaper of a musical, *As Thousands Cheer*. Schwartz and Dietz's *At Home Abroad* (1935) took the form of a world cruise, and while it offered Eleanor Powell for dancing and Ethel Waters for singing, it gloried in its lead comic, Beatrice Lillie. Hard to cast in story shows, Lillie was a great revue personality, versatile and magnetic, with a gift for playing the maddest absurdity as if it were the very essence of logic. *At Home Abroad* found her as a geisha girl, a Parisian *Folies star*, a Russian ballet dancer who "could not face the *muzhik*," and, most memorably, an Englishwoman driving herself and three store clerks bonkers trying to order "two dozen double damask dinner napkins." Danner nipkins. Napper dinkips. No, two nuzzen mouble dazek *nanner dipniks*!

Some writers enjoyed revue's freedom, which allowed them to create songs and sketches from scratch on any notion they fancied (as opposed to working within a narrative structure). Schwartz and Dietz had such success with *The Band Wagon*'s songs that they tried to write them all over again for *Flying Colors* the following year. The Astaires' tap-happy "Sweet Music" inspired *Flying Colors*' "A Shine on Your Shoes"; "I Love Louisa," with its Germanized English, led to "Mein Kleine Akrobat"; "Dancing in the Dark, *The Band Wagon*'s haunting hit tune, introduced by the typical revue baritone (John Barker) and then danced by Tilly Losch in a "place" made of mirrors and trick lighting, showed up in *Flying Colors* as "Alone Together," haunting to a fault. Indeed, the two numbers so precisely shared a tone of worried rhapsody that critic John Mason Brown dubbed the latter title "Dancing in the Schwartz."

One advantage of Big Revue was state-of-the-art design—not just the "pretty" look associated with twenties operetta but technical experiments. *The Band Wagon*, uniquely, set all its main numbers on Albert Johnson's design platform of two revolving stages, one inside the other. Thus, "I Love Louisa" was presented on a working carousel, and for "Hoops" the Astaires gamboled around a central construction of greenery and executed their "runaround" exit almost literally on the fly. Useful in set changes, the revolves could also provide a cinematic dissolve within a number, as in "The Beggar Waltz," apparently the very first of the Dream Ballets destined to decorate—or, really, psychoanalyze—musicals of all kinds in the 1940s and 1950s. *The Band Wagon*'s choreographer, Albertina Rasch, presented beggar Fred Astaire sleeping outside a theatre which, through the revolve, turned "inside out" to reveal the stage, where Astaire triumphed in a pas de deux with a star ballerina (Losch). As his dream dissolved, the revolve took us back outside, where Losch, making her exit, paused, stared meaningfully at Astaire—*was* it a dream?—and tossed him her purse as she danced off.

We should note that Broadway's "ballet" at this time was becoming less like *Swan Lake* and more like what Fred Astaire would do when he felt ecstatic. Figures from the classical dance world were choreographing musicals—Charles Weidman, José Limón, Harry Losee, Agnes de Mille, and, most influentially in the 1930s, George Balanchine. But they were so to say compromising with show-biz dance, blending hoofing into the *entrechats* and *pas de poisson*.

Balanchine's key work in this matter was Rodgers and Hart's *On Your Toes* (1936), partly for its evening-long duel of ballet and tap but mainly for the dance that combined them, "Slaughter on Tenth Avenue." This piece stands out for its narrative drive, centering on thwarted romance in the slums: the Boy, the Girl, the Gangster. However, the big ballet spot in the next Rodgers and Hart show, *Babes in Arms* (1937), "Peter's Journey," is so plotted it's an adventure. Peter, one of the babes, has won a typical Depression pick-me-up, the local cinema's Bank Night, and now he dreams of travel. Taking off on the song "Imagine (your bills are paid)," the dance is one of the largest in the musical's history at some ten minutes, and it's worth noting that much of its narration was composed as pastiche, to place each episode as Peter travels from New York into the ocean, then on to Hollywood, the Emerald City of America.* Thus we hear Waldteufel's "Skater's Waltz" (for elegance) when Peter drops in on Radio City Music Hall, and, for the ocean, "Sailing, Sailing Over the Bounding Main" and a quick sample of Rimsky-Korsakof's *Scheherazade* sea theme (to a vast clang of the gong). A pas de deux with a mermaid gives us a lush tango version of "Imagine," and, at last, Hollywood is revered in an anthem setting of "Imagine" that almost anticipates "Climb Every Mountain."

---

*The music bears the stamp of Rodgers' style as later dances in his shows do not. (The "Carousel Waltz," an apparent exception, is a pantomime, not a dance.) We know that Rodgers composed both of *On Your Toes*' Big Ballets—"La Princesse Zenobia" along with "Slaughter on Tenth Avenue"—and I wondered if he wrote "Peter's Journey" as well. Rodgers and Hammerstein chief Ted Chapin confirmed that "Peter's Journey" was indeed the last ballet for a show that Rodgers himself composed.

Nothing so self-consciously artistic slowed the continuity of a Cole Porter show. Those Dream Ballets were so . . . psychological. Musicals were supposed to treat guiltless fun, especially as enjoyed by, one, the rich and, two, outlaws, the only two free peoples on the planet. A Porter show would give us a revivalist broad, Public Enemy Number 13, and a lawyer-turned-stowaway sailing the Atlantic with shmancy bigwigs: *Anything Goes* (1934), the classic Porter show till *Kiss Me, Kate* fourteen years later. This is Porter at his height, with the title song; the revivalist's rave-up, "Blow, Gabriel, Blow"; the Porter list song, "You're the Top"; the love number, "All Through the Night"; and perhaps the Porterest song he ever wrote, "I Get a Kick Out of You." But note that Porter's distinctive voice—a blend of slang and wit akin to his mating of toffs and gangsters—is the voice of every character in a Porter show, including the chorus. It's the opposite of Oscar Hammerstein's approach. In *The Desert Song*, in "I Want a Kiss," Hammerstein gives us a vainglorious Foreign Legion officer flirting with the heroine in words that truly suit a braggart in uniform. He's not the bad guy, but he's crowding the hero, edging him with his own sweetheart, and Hammerstein writes him to sound that way. Then, in *Music in the Air*, a village schoolteacher versifies a love song—it's "I've Told Every Little Star"—and now Hammerstein's lyric suggests a young fellow from a narrow cultural background who is hopeless in love talk. He tells his devotion to the sky, to the brook, even to his friends. "Why haven't I told you?" he asks. It's the most obvious line of all, yet with the music and the rhyme it's poetry. Or, rather, it's the rapture of a country boy revealed in the things he knows and trusts. The images come from not the author but the character.

Porter generalizes his characters; they all sound like Porter. Nonetheless, *Anything Goes* is a central thirties musical, though it's a strange concoction. It may be that, at some very early point, the plan was to treat a merry shipwreck, because this irritatingly fraudulent factoid has dogged *Anything Goes* ever since. In truth, the script, conceived by Guy Bolton and P. G. Wodehouse, included no shipwreck. Instead, there was an attempt by hero William Gaxton to thrill heroine Bettina Hall by foiling a (contrived) mad-bomber attack, leaving everyone on shipboard to fill Act Two with anxiety.* Then the *Morro Castle* exploded off the coast of New Jersey, with 134 lives lost, and the Bolton-Wodehouse text had to be freed of its bombing business. As the two authors were in Europe and rehearsals about to begin, director Howard Lindsay rewrote the book with Russel Crouse,

---

* The *original* Bolton–Wodehouse *Anything Goes* script has not survived, but Bolton's elaborate scenario, off of which the script was written, is still with us, mad bomber and all. There is no shipwreck in it.

removing the bomb subplot and, while they were at it, improving the script in general.

However, a new irritating factoid now dogs *Anything Goes*: that Lindsay and Crouse were hired to sharpen a dull script. This did not happen. Interviewed by Miles Kreuger for the liner notes to John McGlinn's restoration of the original *Anything Goes* score, in 1989, Lindsay addressed this specifically: "When the [finished Bolton-Wodehouse] script came from abroad, and the *Morro Castle* went down . . . and there was something in their book that suggested that sort of thing at sea, we knew immediately the audience would not rise to any gaiety after anything like that was mentioned. So the book had to be changed."

Nowhere in the interview does Lindsay say anything about being asked to rewrite a terrible book—though the Bolton scenario indeed previews a lifeless treatment. (Merman isn't even a revivalist in Bolton's plan—but then why did Porter give her "Blow, Gabriel, Blow"?) Either Wodehouse's participation vastly improved upon Bolton—or Lindsay and Crouse, while writing the mad bomber out of the script, revised (and improved) the entire document. However it happened, the Lindsay-Crouse text positioned *Anything Goes* as the most traditional yet up-to-date of thirties shows, fast, funny, and sophisticated, with a show-biz evangelist and a gangster—the pop-up celebs of the day—at its center. Then, too, in First Couple-Second Couple style, *Anything Goes* would cast Bettina Hall as the sweetheart and Ethel Merman as the seriocomic. Usage demands they run with separate men, but *Anything Goes* finds Merman chasing Gaxton chasing Hall, on a somewhat feminist slant. True, Hall got Gaxton—but Merman got the songs.

Most trendy of all was the show's view that celebrity creates morality, when the entire ship revels in proximity to Gaxton, who they believe is a notorious criminal. It's a Walter Winchell universe: fame is the first virtue. Porter discusses this in the title song—"Good's bad today" really means "Bad's *good*." As I've already said, *Anything Goes* starts with a book scene before the First Number, but like virtually all thirties musicals it launched its second act with an ensemble piece. This one is "Public Enemy Number One"—a salute to Gaxton for his patronage, as the presence of a major Wanted Man guarantees that the shipping line will now "be crowded on ev'ry run."

This is more of the "likeness and unlikeness to life" that Simon Trussler spoke of concerning *The Beggar's Opera*: the musical's ability to explore real social mores surrealistically. And it's more of what Offenbach revealed to us about the resources of a form half theatre and half music: the music expands the theatre.

Porter's music does so especially well because his notes are as witty as his words, and his games with rhythm and comparable devices provide an air of delicious instability. The verse of "Blow, Gabriel, Blow" and the chorus of "You're the Top" both start with wordless flourishes from the orchestra, a genuine innovation, and the title song jumps with such a greed for syncopation that it suggests hordes of faddists shoving each other out of the way as they rush to defy behavioral norms. Is it a song or an exposé? But then we have the gently rocking intro to the verse of "I Get a Kick Out of You" and its lullaby-like chorus, a melody sailing over its accompaniment—and note the *five* rhymes Porter gets into a single line in "*Fly*ing too *high* with some *guy* in the *sky* is my *i*dea of nothing to do."

In all, *Anything Goes* offered the 1930s a view of itself that runs right through dialogue and score in one sweeping motion. When Cole Porter writes a list song like "You're the Top"—"You're the nimble tread," one line runs, "of the feet of Fred Astaire"—he is breaking open the piñata of buzz-terms known to smart folks, from high art to drug-store paraphernalia; and when he gives Merman a sinner's-holiday hymn in the form of a Broadway rave-up combining heavenly rest with jazzy tooting, it's because everything in American life conduces to show business. *Anything* goes. It's a snapshot of a society taken by its severest critic and biggest booster. Porter wouldn't have been caught dead without his button-hole carnation, and his shows are like that: absolutely necessary fluff.

CHAPTER 11

ᴄᴧ᷎ᴐ

Blue Monday Blues

Hard Times are political times, and the Depression politicized the spoken theatre. But there was art within the revolution, for along with socially progressive plays came a newly naturalistic theory of acting to develop the realism in those plays—and this in turn influenced the writing of drama. "Here he comes now" transitions, staircase entrances, and thunderously operatic curtain lines became passé, the mummy dust of ancient history.

Yet the musical remained largely escapist. As with *Face the Music*, shows might indulge in social critique, but mainly for novelty. Thus, one of the decade's biggest hits, *I'd Rather Be Right* (1937), offered George M. Cohan as Franklin Delano Roosevelt, trying to balance the budget so Phil (Austin Marshall) and Peggy (Joy Hodges) can get married. The support included Roosevelt's cabinet; the Supreme Court (all made up to look like the Chief Justice, Charles Evans Hughes, an easy target because of his Victorian facial hair), and even Sara Roosevelt, the President's mother. The work was obviously political in nature, and there was plenty of remark on features of the New Deal—the relief programs, the Court's resistance to legislation, Roosevelt's fireside chats for radio broadcast. Still, the show, glowingly pro-Roosevelt, was far more a star vehicle than an exploration of the issues. George S. Kaufman and Moss Hart's book was extremely funny, and a Cohan turn as F.D.R. was a producer's dream.

The Boston tryout drew tremendous press, for Cohan hadn't appeared in a musical since he had stopped writing them, nine years earlier. A wee bit of bootleg footage survives, and in it one can see Cohan taking over a crowded stage with the lunatic jig and giddy grin of the kind of star we don't see any more—a pixie from another world who does everything *con brio.* Those Boston dispatches told of backstage acrimony, as Cohan, on his own, wrote his own lyrics to replace some of those in the big patter song, "Off the Record"—a shocking breach of performer decorum. But then Cohan did nothing to hide his contempt for the show's songwriters, Rodgers and Hart, nor even his hatred of F.D.R. In 1934, during the first year of the New Deal, Cohan published "What a Man!," a march in Roosevelt's honor. "The journey to Utopia is far," runs the verse, "without a guiding star like F.D.R." Apparently, like some others, Cohan then turned against the president for his expansion of the executive power. Yet here was Cohan, three years later, impersonating Roosevelt in a valentine of a show.

True, it was an awfully spoofy valentine. For instance, in a cabinet meeting—and, yes, they all appeared under their own names, from the Postmaster General, James A. Farley, to the Secretary of State, Cordell Hull—Farley wants "to create jobs for deserving Democrats":

> HULL: I hope I shall not be requested to place any more deserving Democrats in the State Department. Mr. Farley's last appointee did not know Brazil from brassieres. In fact, we got a good deal of trouble with Brazil on that account.
> FARLEY: All right, we all make mistakes, Cordell. Besides, it was only Brazil.

Incorrectly billed as a "musical revue," *I'd Rather Be Right* was simply an episodic book show, for there was no plot per se, only F.D.R.'s ceaseless attempt to get the country's finances in trim. But the show's structure was indeed somewhat revue-like in its succession of scenelets and songs, each relating to the central theme of the president's quest—the Wagner Act (which turns out to be a vaudeville duo, Hans and Fritz Wagner), or the Public Works Administration boys "leaning on their shovels" (as angry Republicans of the day put it) in the gleeful "Labor Is the Thing," for they're all former captains of industry who are now captains of a federal bailout.

Rodgers and Hart were not at their best for *I'd Rather Be Right*, but the combination of Cohan and the pointed humor made it one of the most entertaining shows of its day. Note, however, that "art" was so in the air in the 1930s that many sheerly lovable shows, like this one, were eager to derive prestige from an essay or two in the higher dance. *I'd Rather Be Right* actually had a Dream Ballet, choreographed by Charles Weidman, entitled "American Couple." Placed within the first minutes of Act Two, it began with the two kids and F.D.R. on stage; then the dancing corps took over, with dream counterparts for Marshall and Hodges. The ballet's scenario was the biography of a marriage (with a piquant interlude at the circus, presumably to enliven what was otherwise a sentimental presentation, for revving up the audience after the intermission was a standard feature of Third Age aesthetics). Then, in the self-referential style unique to American musical comedy (and not to the musical play or to European light opera), Cohan commented on the ballet as if he had been sitting in the Alvin Theatre's audience:

PEGGY (waking up): Have—have I been asleep?
PHIL: You certainly have.
ROOSEVELT: I should say so. You got married, and had children, and everything.

Roosevelt's notable constitutional error, his plan to "pack" the hostile Supreme Court with six new appointees, was mentioned only in passing, but there was critique of governmental waste and incompetence. Still, the cumulative effect was of a cocktail mixed of equal parts of Broadway's love of George M. Cohan and the authors' admiration of the New Deal. Like *Of Thee I Sing* (whose book George S. Kaufman also co-authored), *I'd Rather Be Right* had no wish to change the minds of its public about how the land was governed.

However, some musicals did intend to enlighten the unknowing or un-caring, to persuade them to have another think about the social contract. The revue *Pins and Needles* (1937), originally an amateur show written for and staged by the International Ladies Garment Workers Union, has biting lines here and there, not only in the sketches but in Harold Rome's songs. One number, the scathingly ironic "Four Little Angels of Peace," even set Hitler on stage. Compared with the chaotic loony-tunes revue *Hellzapoppin* (1938), with which it shared the distinction of a multi-year run, *Pins and Needles* is intensely class-conscious, especially in its view of workers' per-sonal lives. Fanny Brice's *Follies* numbers treated the attitudes of Jewish girls flummoxed by the mysteries of American culture; *Pins and Needles* naturalized this concept in "Nobody Makes a Pass at Me," transcending Brice's "Becky Is Back in the Ballet" and "Soul Saving Sadie (of Avenue A)" to listen to a young woman who has tried all the remedies, from beauty tips to literature ("I began *Gone With the Wind*") and still can't get a beau. The song is funny but also touching, the opposite of George M. Cohan's Roosevelt turn: something from the neighborhood.

Thus, we might call *Pins and Needles* a Compassion Musical, conceived to consider life among those unknown to mainstream culture, at least in honest portrayal. It brings to mind a lyric from Jule Styne's *Hazel Flagg* (1953), in which a Jimmy Walker–like mayor sings "Every Street's a Boulevard in Old New York." The mayor was played by Jack Whiting, the amiable hero of countless musical comedies since the early 1920s, variously a boxer, a Coast Guard lieutenant, a movie star, a theatrical producer, a band leader: everyman. Now, as the mayor, he declared New York "a kingdom where the people wear the crown"—and that could be a definition of the American musical.

Of the very few musicals that challenged the public with an edgy view of the issues were two by the immigrant Kurt Weill, who arrived from Nazi Germany in 1935 with his actress wife, Lotte Lenja (later Americanized to "Lenya"). Distinguishing himself in work with Bertolt Brecht, especially on *Die Dreigroschenoper* (The Threepenny Opera, 1928) and the opera *Aufstieg und Fall der Stadt Mahagonny* (Rise and Fall of Mahagonny City, 1930), both critiques of capitalism, Weill would seem pre-set to compose political musicals. However, it was not Brecht's radical politics that attracted Weill but rather Brecht's radical innovations as a playwright, for Weill disdained business-as-usual librettists. He liked creating unique shows with writers who didn't know the ropes.

Now, in America, Weill went right on collaborating with playwrights. He had come to the United States as composer of a Biblical pageant, *The Eternal Road* (1937), but while it was still in production Weill teamed up with Paul Green for *Johnny Johnson* (1936). Here is a truly edgy piece: a nice young guy enlists in World War I, loses his ideals in battlefield carnage, attempts to stop the war by drugging the fat cats directing it, is hauled off to the madhouse, and is last seen as a vagabond toymaker, selling not little soldiers but the playthings of peace.

Johnny Johnson was supposedly the most common name among American recruits in the war, and Weill and Green meant their hero (Russell Collins) as the most basic soul: gentle and sensitive, yet tough when provoked. To emphasize his isolation as a genuine idealist in a cynical world, this Boy does not get Girl—and virtually everyone he meets is an eccentric, from Army captain to psychiatrist. Weill was working with the left-wing Group Theatre, fascinated with not only socially progressive drama but also the mechanics of theatre; unfortunately, the Group actors were not singers, and the Group's director, Lee Strasberg, thought musicals were plays irritated by an orchestra. *Johnny Johnson* failed, at 68 performances, and revivals have not been able to reinstate the piece.

Even so, its final scene is one of the great conclusions in the musical's history, desolated yet vital. After many years apart, Johnny meets up with his former love, Minny Belle (Phoebe Brand). She now represents everything that Johnny lost when he comprehended the war as not a correction but a destruction. Had he respected Authority, he might have come home, married, familied, and lived through the peace till the next war, when he in his turn would urge young men to enlist. Johnny's rival in romance, the local twerp, stayed out of the war and married Minny Belle. In effect, he has taken Johnny's life. After a scene with Minny Belle's young son—the son Johnny would have had—Johnny is alone, the only one in the show who understands what has been happening. In an unpublished interview with Rhoda Wynn, Green called Johnny "defeated." Yet the show's final number, "Johnny's Song," in which he shares his understanding with the audience, has a wistful lilt with a conversational swing in the bridge, and the last bars before the curtain falls sound not defeated but decisive and hopeful. It is as if Green wrote about the wreck of his hero but Weill scored it as that hero's triumph.

Weill's next musical, *Knickerbocker Holiday* (1938), written with Maxwell Anderson, boasts a solid Boy Gets Girl, and its superb score, much more integrated than *Johnny Johnson*'s, finds music in everything, from political corruption ("The One Indispensable Man") to syphilis ("The Scars"). The setting is old Nieuw Amsterdam, and Pieter Stuyvesant (Walter Huston in a gleeful star turn complete with an apparent pegleg) arrives to take over as not just governor but despot:

> STUYVESANT: Nothing gives me more pain than the violence which I commit when I discover the least breath of opposition to my altruistic policies.

A fanatic libertarian, Anderson meant thus to portray F.D.R.'s ambitious presidency, though his public assumed he was attacking Hitler. At least Anderson proved a surprisingly deft lyricist, giving Weill the words to one of his biggest hits, "September Song," in which the aged Stuyvesant woos the Girl of the sweetheart couple. Because Stuyvesant was the non-singing Walter Huston, Anderson figured they would have to construct something modest, but Weill, with some amusement, told Anderson they would give Huston "the most romantic song ever written"—which "September Song" more or less is.

Of all the political musicals, only two dared to rip it up on the dangerous level. One was the short-lived and totally forgot revue *Parade* (1935). The attitude of this angry show might be summed up in "You Ain't So Hot," the solo of a black lady's maid (Avis Andrews), with scathing flatted notes and irritated syncopations: and "you" is the lady. "I've got a special name for you," one lyric runs, without specifying or offering a hint. (Use your imagination.) *Parade*'s songs, composed by Jerome Moross to Paul Peters and George Sklar's lyrics, attracted no attention; only two titles were published at a time when between five and eight was the norm. Interestingly, another *Parade* number, "Life Could Be So Beautiful," anticipates today's economic cross-section of the 1 percent versus the 99 percent: "If just a few didn't own everything," it laments, "and the rest of us nothing at all."

One of *Parade*'s many contributors was Marc Blitzstein, who happened to write all of the other dangerous thirties musicals. But his is still performed today, *The Cradle Will Rock* (1937). Using stereotypes to analyze the social blueprint of an imaginary American town in the throes of a labor dispute, *Cradle* is extremely confrontational, and Blitzstein must have been prepared for a failure-success, with blistering notices and a short run yet great talkabout among theatre folk and the intelligentsia.

But something else happened. Thinking the piece incendiary in flammable times, the federal government—*Cradle*'s producer through one of F.D.R.'s relief programs—closed the production before it could open. Finding Maxine Elliott's Theatre padlocked, the *Cradle* company and ticketholders marched all the way up Broadway from Thirty-Ninth Street to the empty Venice Theatre, on Fifty-Ninth Street, in the most resolute assertion of the "show must go on" ethic in thespian history. Banned from the stage by their union, the actors performed in the auditorium while Blitzstein, at an upright piano on stage, accompanied and narrated. It was an opening night in the raw: no sets, no costumes, no orchestra players, no ushers, no critics: just a play and its actors. The following year, *Cradle* went for an open run in a different house, retaining the improvisational feeling of that first performance, though now the actors were ranged in rows upstage and came forth to play their parts at stage center. Revivals almost always offer a simulacrum of this approach, though the show was in fact meant to be seen like any other musical, with a dressed stage and an orchestra.

It's an exciting tale, but there's good news and bad news. The good: Blitzstein was arguably the most acute character composer of the time, able to limn an individual in a single number. Each of his characters sounds completely different from the others; and his characters sound like nobody else's in the first place. *Cradle*'s Moll, a streetwalker, is given, in "Nickel Under the Foot," an establishing number that utterly reveals her to us in the first A section: hardened by life in a rough world, with almost all the wishfulness kicked out of her. But the bad news is that Blitzstein was no melodist. Little in *Cradle* is enjoyable as music—and Blitzstein's second show, *No For an Answer* (1941), on the growing defiance of mistreated resort workers, is the same only more so: an extremely character-conscious score of no aesthetic appeal whatsoever. For instance, "Francie," a love duet, gives Boy little more to sing than the title word and "da da da" while

Girl dialogues. It's a fascinating reinvention of genre, but not one most people would want to hear twice.

At that, *No For an Answer* never got an open run. The Ancient Arabic Order of the Nobles of the Mystic Shrine, an American version of the Free-masons, built a moorish meeting hall on Manhattan's Fifty-Fifth Street, the Mecca Temple. When the Shriners (as they were generally known) lost the building in the 1929 crash, the city took it over, hiring it out on four-walls deals with an auditorium of folding chairs. It eventually became the City Center of Music and Drama, today the home of Encores!, but in 1941 it hosted *No For an Answer* in three successive Sunday night airings. The cast consisted largely of unknowns, among them Carol Channing, well ahead of the daffy baby-doll basso she was to trademark in *Gentlemen Prefer Blondes*.

This takes us far from Broadway, where the opposite of Marc Blitzstein was Cole Porter and Rodgers and Hart, champs of melodic songwriting and attached most often to big-budget productions with glossy casting. Porter got the bigger stars: Sophie Tucker and Gaxton and Moore in *Leave It To Me!* (1938), which featured Mary Martin, debuting with "My Heart Belongs To Daddy"; Merman and Lahr in *DuBarry Was a Lady* (1939); Merman alone, with a *Time* magazine cover, in *Panama Hattie* (1940). But Rodgers and Hart got the bigger song hits: "My Romance," "Little Girl Blue," "There's a Small Hotel," "Johnny One Note," "Where or When," "The Lady Is a Tramp," "This Can't Be Love," and in the unique style of the "Rodgers Waltz," "The Most Beautiful Girl in the World" and "Falling in Love With Love (is falling for make believe)."[*]

Rodgers and Hart's best score, to *Pal Joey* (1940), did not catch on at first, though—contrary to legend—the show was a hit from the start (and, twelve years later, a smash in revival). More important, *Joey*'s seedy world of third-rate showbiz grunts, adultery, and blackmail, drawn from John O'Hara's *New Yorker* stories with a book by O'Hara himself, brought realistic dialogue into the musical. It is not that pedestrian nightclub emcee Joey (Gene Kelly) and his payer of the bills Vera (Vivienne Segal) broke new character ground. They did—but the history was more truly made by the casually blunt way in which they expressed themselves. "Blow," Joey tells Vera in their last scene together, after she cuts off his bank account; men didn't address women that way in musicals. *Pal Joey*'s score is less

---

[*] Ironically, the team's biggest hit isn't from anything. It started in Hollywood as "Oh Lord, Why Won't You Make Me a Star?" and underwent a series of new lyrics till MGM's music publisher, Jack Robbins, told them to make it simple. Like one of those Moon Songs. And Hart changed the lyric one last time: to "Blue Moon."

revolutionary, though "I Could Write a Book"; "Bewitched, Bothered and Bewildered"; the strip-tease list song "Zip"; "You Mustn't Kick It Around"; and the sinfully blasé "Den of Iniquity" match O'Hara's picture of a guiltless underworld. Vera's "Bewitched" is risqué enough to liken Joey to a laugh, and "the laugh's on me."

Compared with the political shows, *Pal Joey* seems mainstream, but it marked a bold departure in its raffish naturalism—and, indeed, something was stirring in the musical. With the Depression's end, capitalization was freed up and the ticket-buying pool enlarged, and Hollywood began paying huge amounts for the film rights to shows, even daring ones, such as *Cabin in the Sky* (1940). The first famous all-black musical comedy since *Shuffle Along* in 1921, *Cabin in the Sky* was also the first Third Age title to be staged primarily by a choreographer, George Balanchine. Dance had become not only elemental but crucial—and, make no mistake, it was *dance*: neither hoofing nor ballet exactly but the new style, movement and playwrighting at once, that had been revealed in "Slaughter on Tenth Avenue" and the many thirties Dream Ballets. Suddenly, the musical was—some said—more than entertainment: an art.

Thus, *Cabin in the Sky*, with a book by Lynn Root and a score by Vernon Duke and John Latouche, broke with the hijinks of the twenties black shows. They were frolics; this was a parable. Agents of heaven (Todd Duncan) and hell (Rex Ingram) fight over the soul of Little Joe (Dooley Wilson) as he veers between his God-fearing wife, Petunia (Ethel Waters) and the wiles of a certain Miss Georgia Brown (Katherine Dunham). A flavorsome blend of fantasy and realism, the sacred and the profane, *Cabin in the Sky* pulled together ingredients that had been flung about during the 1920s and 1930s—the folk-cultural survey (as in *The Green Pastures*), semi-abstract design (here in the sets and costumes of Boris Aronson), and of course the leadership of dance. When Ethel Waters capped the rhumba "Savannah" with a spectacular vocal slide—over five measures—from on high to very low, or when she turned her sunburst charm loose in "Taking a Chance on Love," *Cabin* was already a superb show. But Aronson's stylized sets—one scene, in hell, looked like a futuristic nightclub of fiery poles supporting a transparent plastic ceiling— gave the work distinctive look to complement Balanchine's ballet-accented footwork. Then, too, the book, with its battle between the churchly and the impious, was like nothing else on Broadway, not least when Waters, fighting fire with fire, cut loose in Act Two as a dance-hall tigress to steal Little Joe back from Miss Georgia Brown. There was even a twist ending: approaching the Pearly Gates, Petunia learns that Little Joe's wastrel life disqualifies him from immortal reward. But wait—what did Little Joe threw all his money away on? Miss Georgia Brown. And what did Miss Georgia Brown do with that money? Well, it seems she suddenly felt religion coming on and gave that money to the church. *Hallelujah!* For Little Joe has done good in the world after all, and he and Petunia enter the glorious kingdom.

Cabin was a kind of *Gesamtkunstwerk*—a piece in which all arts blend in unity. Dance permeates the action; design matches the music. Experimenting in the opposite direction, one can separate the arts—and this brings us to *Lady in the Dark* (1941), so "not a musical" that its script functions like that of a straight play. Musical librettos of the time tended to fritter about in search of comic business or cue in the next number. But *Lady in the Dark* speaks in the single-minded throughline and roomy character development of the "legit" dramatist. Nor does it have the musical's procession of discrete song spots, from the First Number through the Wanting Song to the Big Ballet and so on. *Lady in the Dark* has only one song . . . and three one-act operas: the heroine's dreams, as her psychiatrist probes her unconscious.

Thus, *Lady in the Dark*'s authors—composer Kurt Weill, lyricist Ira Gershwin, and librettist Moss Hart—segregated the musical's two basic components, the book and the music, at a time when all the other first-division authors were trying to unite them. Further, the show was a star vehicle, conceived for Katharine Cornell but then, as Weill's music penetrated Hart's program, redesigned for Gertrude Lawrence, known as much for actressy jobs in plays as for her verve in musical comedy. Her role in the "play" *Lady in the Dark*, as a mannish magazine executive, does not align with but counters her role in the "musical" *Lady in the Dark*, when she imagines herself as glamorous: the toast of the town, a movie star's bride, and the queen of the circus.

Thus the constituent parts of the musical are broken up to create a genre claiming a single title—this one. In a musical, the score runs through the action. In this work, the *book* runs through the action, leaving the score in a separate place, gazing upon the story rather than cooperating with it.

There are two unifying elements. One is the heroine's dream melody, "My Ship," an objective-correlative for her mental crisis. The other is the use of her real-life cohorts as figures in her dreams. One of the show's many surprises in 1941 was their appearance in the first dream before the audience knew who they were in Lawrence's magazine world. It was a way to actuate the fantasy—a way for Moss Hart, an obsessive of the analyst's couch, to proselytize: your imagination explains your life. And so, in the first dream, a marine marches into the nightclub where Lawrence is reigning as New York's diva to paint her portrait for the next first-class stamp.

But the picture reveals a monster, and the dream implodes in terror. (Now for a staging trick: during the tumult, Lawrence slipped offstage, leaving a double in her costume to distract the audience while Lawrence breathlessly changed into street clothes to reappear seconds after the blackout, back in the psychiatrist's office as if she had never left it.) As the narration moves on to the magazine suite, the marine now turns up in his "real life" as Lawrence's managing editor, a tough guy in a suit, and the only man who has power over her. She doesn't know it yet; she thinks of him as irritating but great at his job. After seeing what she's been dreaming, however, we know more about their relationship than she does.

Ironically, *Lady in the Dark* is both a "play with music" and one of the most *musical* plays ever put on: because, when the three main dreams were in operation, they burst with sound—not just songs but orchestral narration and through-sung narrative. True, the old act finalettos that had only recently died out often behaved that way. But they were constructed out of stock practices and were not very kinetic dramatically. *Lady in the Dark*'s first two dreams bounce surrealistically from place to place, constantly veering into surprises, as when Liza buys her wedding ring and the jeweler suddenly pulls a knife on her. (Of course it's that managing editor again.) The third dream is a combination of circus and trial: Liza is accused of the crime of Ambivalence About Everything in Her Life. But this dream diagnoses her problem, and the fourth, non-musical, dream reveals the cause: bad parenting that left her feeling inferior. Moss Hart has the cure: Girl Gets Boy, who turns out to be the managing editor, because he's the only other character who can sing "My Ship."

Partly because it was uniquely entertaining, partly because it dealt with psychiatry—trendy but very mysterious at the time—and partly because it gave the fascinating Gertrude Lawrence unlimited opportunity, *Lady in the Dark* was one of the biggest hits the musical had known. It was exceedingly well staged, too, using two adjacent revolving stages, each containing a smaller revolve, to expedite set changes leading into and out of but also during the dreams. Hassard Short, one of the go-to directors of the day, so magisterial that he often "supervised" productions utilizing separate dialogue stagers and choreographers, got the signing credit, but this was Moss Hart's project from start to end, and the casting says "Hart" all over. He had an acute sense of how theatre works—not just writing and presenting plays but what's *really* going on inside them. To put it another way, Hart knew what life was like and who's in it. He clearly created the men in Liza's world as iconic types that a woman who is confused and unhappy—in the dark, as the title tells—might see as accoutrements in her attempt to compensate for her "failings" by appearing successful in the creative life, the social life, the romantic life. In 1941, sophisticates knew that the creative life depended on the taste and smarts of gay men, and Liza's is the magazine's photographer, Russell Paxton (Danny Kaye, in the role that propelled him to stardom, not least for the tongue-twisting "Tchaikowsky"). For the social life, Liza takes a wealthy older lover, Kendall Nesbitt (greying, patrician Bert Lytell), and for the romantic life there is the movie star Randy Curtis (Victor Mature). "Girls, he's God-like!" Paxton shrieks. Hart originally wanted Buster Crabbe for the part: Hollywood's Flash Gordon, visually a Strongheart but, offscreen, frat-boy corny. Hart's point is that none of Liza's men is effective protection from her fears, and Hart would have been fitting the performers to these important subsidiary roles to project all the more interest onto the managing editor (Macdonald Carey). Hart wanted to show us what Liza cannot see: that he is the only "man" in her life after all.

Aside from its interest as drama, *Lady in the Dark* reminds us of the musical's Offenbachian ambition to reinvent the form with Extra Music. And this takes us to the 1930s' outstanding work of music theatre—though it, too, is not a musical. It's an opera. When it premiered, in 1935, the WASP establishment that ran American Music was hostile to it, for two generations of composers had tried and failed to produce the Great American Opera. Their work was European in tone and classy as a rule, with, for instance, a libretto by Edna St. Vincent Millay on a source in the fiction of George du Maurier. Giulio Gatti-Casazza, manager of the Metropolitan Opera, was keen on indigenous new work, but nothing took hold.

And then George Gershwin, with Du Bose Heyward and Ira Gershwin, came forth with *Porgy and Bess* (1935), after Heyward's 1927 play *Porgy* (co-written with his wife, Dorothy), from Heyward's novel. *Porgy and Bess* became town tidings after the theatre world's leadership class sat in on the final rehearsals—and Kurt Weill, having just fled an increasingly Nazified Europe, was there, utterly amazed that Americans were so open to minority art. But remember, it's a kingdom where the people wear the crown. *Porgy and Bess'* first public performance, at the start of the Boston tryout, was the most electric in the history of America's music theatre, with both music and drama critics sitting in on this epochal event. The New York papers sent both tiers as well to the Broadway premiere, and, as surely as courtiers hate revolution, the music men scorned the work. The theatre men were impressed but confused. Brooks Atkinson called it "glorious"—but why was there so much singing? An opera is . . . what?

Commercially, *Porgy and Bess* was a failure. In every other respect—the ones that matter—it was a smash. Its 124 performances marked tremendous public interest in an opera in the worst year of Depression theatregoing. The music was everywhere, especially in what we now call "crossover" format. You weren't a soprano if you didn't sing "Summertime"; a baritone without "I Got Plenty O' Nuttin'" was insincere. The show returned to Broadway six years after the original production had closed, lasting two-and-half years counting the tour and a return engagement. It has been revived in virtually every decade after that—at the City Center, on Broadway, at Radio City Music Hall—and is now, arguably, the *My Fair Lady* of opera.

Ironically, the whole thing started small, in one of those imitation Ziegfeld revues, *George White's Scandals of 1922*. Somehow or other, Gershwin and his then lyricist, B. G. De Sylva, convinced White to include a short opera, "a colored tragedy," as its tiny prologue phrases it, "Blue Monday Blues." Performed in blackface and musically adorned with sexy "blue" notes, hip-swiveling triplets, and the jazz harmony soon to be popularized in Gershwin's *Rhapsody in Blue*, "Blue Monday Blues" tells of a woman's intuition gone wrong. In a saloon, Joe reveals that he plans a trip to see his mother, but his jealous girl friend, Vi, thinking him unfaithful, shoots him. As he lies bleeding, Vi finds a telegram that he has just received from his sister: his mother has in fact been dead for three years. Horrified, Vi begs forgiveness as Joe sings that he will see his mother after all: in heaven.

Tawdry and sentimentalized, the piece was essentially the Frankie and Johnny meme enlivened by the Jolson vibe. The critics thought it hideous, and White pulled it from the show right after opening night. Still, we see in this ten-minute opera the first stirrings of Gershwin's wish to expand the structures of vernacular music, as Offenbach did in *The Tales of Hoffmann*. "Blue Monday Blues" makes an unlikely starting point; it even lacks good tunes. Yet its *sound* is the one that Gershwin was making his own, a chowder of whorehouse piano and Puccini, the twenties "jazz" that meant virtually anything that wasn't a waltz, a Bible study group, or a banker's top hat: again, the old term for Sex, Drugs, Rock and Roll. And "Blue Monday Blues" even anticipates *Porgy and Bess* dramaturgically, in its look at lovers who don't quite understand each other—for Porgy accepts Bess without knowing what survival skills she may have had to resort to, and Bess responds to Porgy's tenderness without realizing how powerful a figure he is. There is even a Sporting Life/Crown figure—the instruments of destiny who tear Bess from Porgy—in "Blue Monday Blues": Tom, a miscreant who first comes on to Vi and then lies to her about "the woman" Joe wants to visit.

It tells us how big a shadow Al Jolson and his minstrelsy cast that, according to Gershwin's biographer Charles Schwartz, when Jolson proposed to star (in blackface) in a *Porgy* musical to be written by a post–*Show Boat* Jerome Kern and Oscar Hammerstein, Heyward was inclined to favor them over Gershwin. And Gershwin, says Schwartz, "saw no conflict between Jolson's planned musical and his own future treatment of the work." This seems incredible. How could there be two different musical adaptations of the story of Porgy and Bess within a single generation? In any case, the Jolson project collapsed for unknown reasons, but, judging by what Gershwin finally wrote, he must have been all but fanatically inspired by the possibilities in the property: a society of very narrow culture with no material possessions, in which religion, the one thing that comes free in every clime, is an obsession. What a background for the music—not only the faith itself, but charity, healing, sharing, helping, praising, mourning. Think of the ensembles alone: the crap game that explodes in murder, Robbins' wake ("Gone, Gone, Gone") that grows into a kind of locomotive raveup ("Oh, the Train Is in the Station"), the joyful gathering for a picnic ("Oh, I Can't Sit Down") and then the drum-crazed abandon of the picnic itself ("I Ain't Got No Shame"), and of course the spiritual, most effective in the blazing rhapsody of "I'm on My Way," possibly the greatest finale ever heard on Broadway.

And at the heart of all this is that central triangle of Porgy, Bess, and Crown/Sporting Life. Throughout the work, we see Catfish Row define itself through interaction with these characters: somewhat in awe of Porgy, contemptuous of Bess (but then sympathetic when Porgy gives her his imprimatur), fearful of the homicidal Crown, and hazy about just where the flashy Sporting Life fits into their undecorated lives. At the picnic scene, they let him cap their impious revel with "It Ain't Necessarily So," an episode akin to the blasphemy of the Golden Calf. But Maria, one of Catfish Row's elders, gives us what Quakers refer to as "the intelligence of the Meeting" in "I Hates Yo' Struttin' Style," notated in *Sprechstimme*, perhaps to emphasize Maria's caustic tirade by having her "talk" her song.

The Theatre Guild, which had produced the play *Porgy*, also produced *Porgy and Bess*. Alexander Smallens conducted an orchestra of some forty players, with Todd Duncan and Anne Brown in the title parts. Rouben Mamoulian, who had staged the play, now staged the opera, and in all it was an amazing achievement, for there was no black talent pool for this kind of thing. Broadway had a black *acting* pool; the opera's Maria, Georgette Harvey, had created the role in the play. And Broadway had a black song-and-dance pool of the *Blackbirds* sort, which presumably would have supported Jolson if his *Porgy* had materialized. But Broadway did not have a black opera pool, and the Guild had to scramble in casting.

It was a beginning, but then the American musical's ever-shifting priorities include a love of restarts and innovations. *Porgy and Bess* gave the musical an opera format to work with ever after, a level of *espressivo* that had never before been even hinted at, except in "Ol' Man River." We wonder what Gershwin might have given the stage after *Porgy*, for he then went to Hollywood for movie work. In 1937, before he could return to New York, he complained of headaches and dizziness, and began to deteriorate physically. A spinal tap revealed a brain tumor, and within twenty-four hours Gershwin was dead.

CHAPTER 12

⌀

The Rodgers and Hammerstein Handbook

O f the nine stage shows Richard Rodgers and Oscar Hammerstein created between 1943 and 1959, one was an outright commercial failure, another was a succès d'estime, and two were hits but did not enter the abiding repertory. The remaining five form the most phenomenal success story in the musical's saga, making up a unique short list of eternally revivable classics and governing Broadway for a generation.

However, many of the breakthroughs credited to the Rodgers and Hammerstein (from now on R & H) canon in fact precede their partnership, especially the main one: that they integrated the musical. *The Beggar's Opera* was integrated, Gilbert and Sullivan and Offenbach were integrated, *Robin Hood*, *El Capitan*, and *The Red Mill* were integrated. Nor did R & H's emphasis on dance as a psychological instrument open a new path: we've seen plenty of Dream Ballets in the 1930s. Then, too, Rodgers himself defined a "great musical" as one in which "all the individual parts complement each other." In his words, "the orchestrations sound the way the costumes look." Rodgers expressly offered *Oklahoma!* as an example. But that first *Oklahoma!* production, in 1943, with its unprecedented five-year run and eleven-year national tour, was compromised by a tight budget, and the sets, at least, looked cheap. The orchestrations, by Robert Russell Bennett, sounded wonderful, yes: Bennett was the Beowulf of his profession. And Miles White's costumes exploited the novel western setting. However, scenery is usually the biggest expense in producing musicals, and Lemuel Ayers had to limit his geography to small side pieces against backdrops, adding overhead wires strung with baskets for the "Farmer and the Cowman" picnic party.*

No, what made the R & H musicals great was their insistence on unique characters whose interaction creates unique stories. Even that was not new; it's what attracted Kern and Hammerstein to *Show Boat*. But from *Lady, Be Good!* on—that is, for about twenty years before *Oklahoma!*—the Aarons-Freedley program reigned: begin with interesting stars and an appealing score, and when the plot thins have someone don a disguise.

R & H didn't cast stars till their fourth show; in any case, while the Aarons-Freedley format essentially creates the same piece time after time, the R & H titles are refreshingly inconsistent. We can infer a few guidelines even so. Rule One: Develop each story's community background, its culture and mores. Thus, *Oklahoma!* isn't just about the farmer and the cowman: it is imbued with their attitudes and feelings, seeking to pacify their squabbles with a bond as a society so that their territory be fit to join the union.

Conversely, *Carousel* (1945) sees in its New England setting a place divided into those with power and those without. It's not overtly expressed, yet it's ever present in the controlling force of policeman, mill owner, and such, and *Carousel*'s hero, Billy Bigelow (John Raitt), exemplifies this as a charismatic rascal who is splendid company as long as he doesn't feel crowded by authority. Interweaving the separate yet connected love plots of Billy and Julie (Jan Clayton) and the Second Couple, Carrie (Jean Darling) and Mr. Snow (Eric Mattson), R & H troubled to place them in a social context, giving their neighbors "June Is Bustin' Out All Over"; the sea chanty "Blow High, Blow Low"; "This Was a Real Nice Clambake"; and a hymn tune, "You'll Never Walk Alone": all together, enough chorale for a Passion.

Long after all this, *Pippin* (1972), with a medieval Frankish setting, a Stephen Schwartz score, and an imaginative Bob Fosse staging, proposed a hero with no ambition in life. Searching for meaning, he cried, "I know this is a musical comedy. But I want my life to mean something." Unfortunately for Pippin, Roger O. Hirson's book gave him no substance—which brings us to R & H Rule Two: Write about people whose lives have meaning. *Allegro* (1947) was the team's first original; *Oklahoma!* and *Carousel*, produced by the Theatre Guild, were drawn from Guild productions, Lynn Riggs'

---

*Almost all the stage shots of the original *Oklahoma!* are black-and-whites, hiding from us the extremely colorful clothes, favoring pastels even for the cowboys. Not till 2011, when the University of North Carolina School of the Arts staged a replica revival of the original *Oklahoma!*, did we of today get a look at Curly's mango shirt and orange tie, Ali Hakim's loud checked suit, or Ado Annie's orange-and-white layered skirt and jacket combo, the white stippled with polka dots.

Green Grow the Lilacs and Ferenc Molnár's *Liliom*, respectively. *Allegro*'s protagonist, Joseph Taylor Jr., was a doctor's son and a doctor himself, raised
in the person-scaled culture of small-town America, who sees his values
disintegrate as a big-city physician to rich idiots. A beautiful symmetry
connected his youthful innocence to his later rueful wisdom in a choral
number, "One Foot, Other Foot": first sung when little Joey stood and
walked for the first time, it closed the story when he renounced empty
prosperity to return to village life.

Allegro was arguably the strangest musical to that point in Broadway
history. The title means "lively," and R & H conceived it to be more or
less ceaselessly in motion, to reflect the discordant hubbub of modern
life. Accordingly, they promoted *Oklahoma!* and *Carousel*'s choreographer,
Agnes de Mille, to director-choreographer, to stage the show as if it were a
three-hour musical number, using back projections and small set pieces but
no full-scale scenery as such: a dancer's space.

To keep the show tripping along, de Mille used dissolves as each scene
ended, bringing on the next team of players while the previous team moved
off. In a further decomposition of format, R & H wrote a score using its
own version of those small set pieces, some barely eight bars long, and the
normal-length songs were distributed among the many principals, so no
character—not even the protagonist—was able to offer himself to the
public with the eloquence of, for instance, Curly's "Oh, What a Beautiful
Mornin'" and "The Surrey With the Fringe on Top." Curly's sweetheart,
Laurey, got a mildly feminist rebel number in "Many a New Day," but her
Allegro counterpart, Jenny Brinker, scarcely sang at all—and, while we're at
it, she tore up the sweetheart activity sheet to commit adultery. (*Pal Joey*'s
Vera sleeps around, too, but Vera's no sweetheart.)

Critics and public alike were enthralled, bemused, baffled, irritated. Was
Allegro a masterpiece (if a flawed one) or did its ambition outstrip its
power? One problem was the design. Jo Mielziner, who with Albert Johnson, Boris Aronson, and Oliver Smith comprised the musical's quartet of
Golden Age setmakers, semed unable to make the unique playing area in-
telligible. Steps cut into the flooring looked odd, the projections worked
only sometimes, and curtained openings in the wings for entrances and
exits suggested fitting rooms in Ladies' Lingerie.

Still, *Allegro* was the first musical to align its staging with its theme.
Joseph Taylor wanted his life to mean something, and the Majestic Theatre's big stage teemed with the bustle of people eager to catch hold of
something, connect, achieve. From the moment the curtain rose on a
woman in bed and a robed chorus explaining that she has just given birth
to a boy—our hero to be—the public knew it was in for something special

in the opening number alone. It was, in fact, the musical's first attempt to start with not fourth-wall realism but a collage of images, as that First Number expanded to take in other principals and the townsfolk as well, in a reality made of different locations collapsed into one.

This brings us to R & H Rule Three: Start uniquely. *Oklahoma!* started with a tiny tone poem of dawn on a golden morning, with Aunt Eller churning butter in her front yard on an otherwise empty stage. After the music died away, Curly was heard offstage launching "Oh, What a Beautiful Mornin'" a cappella, and a bit after the orchestra struck back up to accompany him, he sauntered in. This was actually very much the way *Green Grow the Lilacs* had begun, twelve years earlier (though in that production, which interpolated folk songs, Curly sang "Get Along, Little Dogies"). Still, to most of *Oklahoma!*'s public, these first minutes of stage time were a surprise, with neither the big choral opening nor the bustling book scene that virtually all musicals got into when the curtain went up.

Carousel's first minutes were shocking. Typically, a musical of the 1940s began with a lengthy overture, played in semi-darkness. As it was ending—or, after it had ended, to "curtain music," the house lights darkened all the way, as if to usher the public into the ceremony of theatre, and the curtain rose. All this emphasized the moment of contact between real life and fantasy, with its made-up characters, its attitudes, symbols, and myth. But *Carousel* had no overture. An odd, scratchy prelude suggested the winding up of the mechanism of a merry-go-round, and, after about a minute of music, the house began to dim—way ahead of the usual time, startling the audience—and the curtain then unexpectedly went up on the sight of a carnival in full cry. There was no singing, no dialogue: the story began in pantomime, and it really was *Carousel*'s story, as most of the major characters made their first appearance, the scene carefully staged to point out crucial details of the exposition: Julie and Carrie are friends, and Billy is the center of attention, especially Julie's.

And the fourth R & H show, *South Pacific* (1949), another adaptation, this time from war stories by James Michener, began with two Polynesian children singing a simple French tune, "Dites-moi." Actually, the kids are half-Polynesian (which will be an important plot point later on), but before the audience can digest the mystifying number—who are these children and what are they singing about?—the show's stars suddenly walked on: Mary Martin and Ezio Pinza.

This in itself was astonishing, as stars tended to get star entrances, usually heralded with a ramp-up. But R & H didn't write for stars even when stars were cast in their shows, a direct contradiction of the Aarons-Freedley mode, in which a star's persona created the script and score as if by dictation. The Astaires, Gertrude Lawrence, and Bert Lahr weren't just performers: they were characters, part of the fabric of the composition, even the reason that the composition existed. Without the availability of the Astaires, there never would have been a *Lady, Be Good!*. But *South Pacific* was going to be the next R & H show after *Allegro*, with or without Martin and Pinza.

South Pacific offers another departure from convention: No choreography. No dance, really, to speak of. The R & H revolution partook gluttonously of thirties "dance"—that blend of hoofing and ballet that was to inform the work of all the great masters from Jerome Robbins to Gower Champion. Then, too, *South Pacific* tested the R & H sense of community by treating the divisive notion of racism, for Pinza, as a Frenchman, was the father of the two children from the opening scene, which is why they are but half Polynesian. Martin, a southern girl, from Little Rock, lives within the unquestioned racism of her background. After so many musicals where intermissions fell just after a risible sweethearts' misunderstanding, it was unsettling that *South Pacific*'s first-act curtain fell when Martin, realizing that Pinza has cohabited with an Asian, deserted him in fear and confusion. Race becomes her crucible, her test, and we can rephrase Pippin's line as "I want my show to mean something."

Of course, all of this dramatic bravado would be worthless without first-division music and lyrics, and Rule Four is: Anchor the score with character traction. *The King and I* (1951) exemplifies this above all in a form R & H virtually made their own, the restless, searching monologue in which a character lays bare his feelings to the public, most often structured as a collection of songlets while his focus shifts from topic to topic. The outstanding such exhibit is *Carousel*'s "Soliloquy," especially arresting in its exploration of Billy's attitudes and concerns in the very words he would use to articulate them. Anticipating the birth of a son, he veers from exuberance to anxiety to confidence. What will he become? What if some "boss' daughter"—another authority figure, Billy's natural enemy—scoops him up into a loveless marriage? No—Billy can advise his boy on the boxing-ring of romance. But while he gloats over his mastery of fatherhood, a terrible thought strikes him: what if he has a daughter instead? After all—in a superb Hammerstein insight—a scapegrace like Billy instinctively understands the difference between genders. You can raise a boy rough, but a girl needs the tenderness that Billy doesn't possess. Yet as he tells us this, he *sounds* tender, feeling it more easily than he can verbalize it.

One wonders what audiences in 1945, when *Carousel* was new to them, were thinking as this masterpiece of poetic psychoanalysis unfolded.

Never before had a musical number so scrutinized a character—and *The King and I* (1951) has two such, the King's "A Puzzlement" and Anna's "Shall I Tell You What I Think of You?" These brilliant scenes situate these two—arguably the strongest characters in all R & H—as antagonists by temperament. He is all about policy and maintaining a powerful image—Yul Brynner, the original King, to the life. She is all about feelings—the trembly, easily hurt, yet fiercely independent Gertrude Lawrence, the show's original headliner. Ironically, both characters are conservatives, but of two very different worlds, his pre-industrial and hers Victorian. Their dueling behavioral norms will drive them apart just when they have most closely bonded, creating in effect a sad ending for the First Couple and offending the musical's oldest ceremony, the happy romance. After all, even *Show Boat*'s Magnolia and Ravenal were reunited (after twenty-three years), and though Porgy's departure to reclaim Bess defies reasonable expectations, the atmosphere is ecstatic. *Pal Joey* closes without a kiss panel, but that show is comically heartless throughout. It was really R & H, in *Carousel*, *Allegro*, and then *The King and I*, who saw the musical as potentially tragic or, as in *Allegro*, romantically inconclusive, freeing other writers to do the same in, among many other titles, *On the Town*, *A Tree Grows in Brooklyn*, *West Side Story*, *Milk and Honey*, *Tenderloin*, *No Strings*, *Flora, the Red Menace*, *Do I Hear a Waltz?*, and *Cabaret*.

Along with Hammerstein's lyrics, Rodgers' music, too, sought to specify character far more intensely than he had done with Lorenz Hart. *Carousel* in particular is filled with arresting touches—operatic underscoring, echo texture, telling counter melodies—and they're Rodgers' work. The R & H production associate John Fearnley told me that he was very taken with a piquant effect in "You're a Queer One, Julie Jordan," when the trio's "weaving" theme unexpectedly decorates the return of the main strain, and Fearnley once went up to Robert Russell Bennett (who had orchestrated the scene, though not *Carousel* as a whole) and complimented him on the imaginative counterpoint.

"Oh," Bennett replied, "that was all laid out in Rodgers' parts."

Rule Five is: Change your genre from show to show, and after *The King and I* the two masters of the "musical play"—more evolved dramatically and musically than musical comedy but not exotically loony like operetta—cultivated the snazzier style of show. *Me and Juliet* (1953) was a backstager with Latin accenting in the music; *Pipe Dream* (1955), a John Steinbeckian idyll with no Second Couple, had more atmosphere than plot. And *Flower Drum Song*, with pointedly jazzy orchestrations (by Robert Russell Bennett, aided by Luther Henderson Jr.'s dance arrangements) offered a very contemporary tale about Chinese-American culture in San Francisco. The last R & H work, *The Sound of Music* (1959), again with Mary Martin, was another musical play, but a simplified one, without the typical R & H elements—the very long melody-stuffed overture, the surprising opening, the musical scenes, the soliloquy (retained in *Me and Juliet*'s "It Feels Good" and *Pipe Dream*'s "Thinkin'"), the Dream Ballet.

Considering the phenomenal success of the film version, *The Sound of Music* might be the team's greatest hit, but it must be said that a certain pall hangs over the second half of the R & H output. *Variety*, crunching shows' capitalization and box-office take into the Hit or Flop category— and preserved in the Burns Mantle *Best Plays* annuals—called *Me and Juliet* a hit. Still, the piece failed to outlast its season. As with *Allegro*, its cast album quickly disappeared—a dire outcome for an R & H title, which more usually produced "If I Loved You"s and "Some Enchanted Evening"s: the bullet points of American song. And *Pipe Dream*, said *Variety*, was a flop. Further, it bears the reputation of having bowdlerized Steinbeck's wastrels and whores of the mid-California coast—of work at the canneries, cheap wine, and flophouses—as if R & H were cleaning up saucy, bawdy musical comedy in general, running off the showgirls and con men that had flavored it since the late 1920s.

"Mug shows" was the term Cy Feuer coined for this kind of musical, idealized in *Guys and Dolls*, which Feuer, with his longtime partner, Ernest H. Martin, produced. But R & H put on—and they used exactly these words—"family shows." So Hammerstein's Steinbeck lacked the novelist's earthy anarchism, the magnificent languor of California mañana culture, and—their own producers, if not always in name, from *Carousel* on—R & H may have erred in casting the Met Brünnhilde Helen Traubel as a bordello madam. The R & H musical play isn't simply more "playwritten" and musically idealized than the musical comedies of Cole Porter or, for that matter, Rodgers and Hart. It's about different things: the thrilling nationalism of *Oklahoma!*'s impending statehood, *Carousel*'s class war in New England, the life of a doctor. R & H don't do bordellos. As the Theatre Guild PR associate Helene Hanff recalled in her memoirs, *Oklahoma!* opened "with a middle-aged farm woman . . . churning butter, and from then on it got cleaner."

That is the standard measure of *Oklahoma!*: a family show on a Broadway obsessed with sex and gags, the work that no one wanted to invest in and all the wisenheimers said would flop. True enough, *Oklahoma!*'s rustic setting was startling in 1943, given the near-to-strip-burlesque riot of the typical wartime musical. "No gags, no gals, no chance" is, legendarily, the producer Mike Todd's dismissal of the show on its New

Haven tryout.* However, *Oklahoma!*'s Dream Ballet featured de Mille's depiction of Jud Fry's naughty-postcard girls doing the cancan in cut-down-to-there black fetish, and if the New Haven stay revealed glitches, the Boston tryout played very, very well.

There's too much legend in the R & H saga. We are told also that Rodgers was tough of heart and Hammerstein the softy. On the contrary, both were very experienced theatre men who knew that playmaking devolves into chaos without the muscle of ruthless leadership. One night during *Allegro*'s tryout, while singing "The Gentleman Is a Dope" way downstage, Lisa Kirk lost her footing and pitched headlong into the orchestra players. They helped her back onto the stage while she gamely kept her place in the music, and of course the audience gave her a hand. Americans love the underdog who triumphs. It's the kind of event that gives a performer talkabout in the business, and Kirk foolishly decided to repeat the stunt. Storming backstage, Hammerstein told her that if she did it again she'd be fired.

And Rodgers was no dearheart. Ask any actor—auditions before the Big Guys are the hardest in the life. They can be distant and unsympathetic, bunched up in Row J with a "Show me" face, even with major names. I played Russell Nype's audition for the role of the lawyer in the original production of *Chicago*, and I still remember how Bob Fosse troubled to come up onto the stage to shake Russell's hand and say how eager Fosse was to hear him. Compare that with Jon Cypher's close encounter with Rodgers when auditioning for the role of the Prince in the R & H television original, *Cinderella* (1957). The cast, headed by Julie Andrews a year after *My Fair Lady* opened, was to be all stars except for the hero, and Cypher, just starting out, not only sang and read well but was tall and handsome. Still, few are they who audition confidently, and Cypher told Rodgers, "I have to admit, I'm a little nervous."

And Rodgers replied, "That's your problem."

Of course, Rule Six is: Don't have rules. Yet the R & H style was readily imitable. Six months after *Oklahoma!* opened, Kurt Weill's *One Touch of Venus* (1943) included ballets by Agnes de Mille, as did *Bloomer Girl* (1944) a year after *Venus*. And if *Venus* was a conventional fun show, *Bloomer Girl* partook of the R & H community feeling, this time emphasizing suffragette feminism and protection for runaway slaves in a period piece. Harold Arlen

---

*Helene Hanff says that it was not Todd but a spy for Walter Winchell—"Winchell's Rose" is how everyone referred to her—and that her wording was "No legs, no jokes, no chance." The quotation has taken numerous forms over the years, though most historians now favor Hanff's version.

and E. Y. Harburg's score included the defiant "It Was Good Enough for Grandma (but it ain't good enough for us)," followed by de Mille's sororal ballet of women wishing for more to do than housekeeping. But de Mille's overriding contribution to *Bloomer Girl* was the "Civil War Ballet," about not the military but worrying wives and as artistic as anything in *Oklahoma!*. Further, *Bloomer Girl's* protagonist was Celeste Holm, *Oklahoma!'s* Ado Annie, and there was a tiny set-piece musical version of *Uncle Tom's Cabin*—just what R & H might have done with a mid-nineteenth-century setting, and exactly what they did do in *The King and I*, in an Asian-theatre adaptation of Stowe, "The Small House of Uncle Thomas."

The writing team most under the R & H spell was Frederick Loewe and Alan Jay Lerner, who started with other partners, then hooked up for an old-fashioned star-comic musical comedy, *What's Up?* (1943), with Jimmy Savo as a rajah getting into mischief in a girls' school. As with so many shows in the early 1940s, much of the men's chorus was in uniform, and the women were used in quasi-burlesque style. It was as far from *Oklahoma!* as one could get, though there was a Dream Ballet. And for their second show, Lerner and Loewe tried something meaningful, with strong characters (and another Dream Ballet, by Anthony Tudor). There was even a fantasy sequence in which Plato, Voltaire, and Freud (with a Jewish accent) diagnosed the heroine's problems. The surreal, remember, was an element of R & H: *Carousel*, which concluded with Billy's brief return from "Up There," had opened seven months earlier. This show was *The Day Before Spring* (1945), which anticipated *Follies* in its look at a college reunion in which Katherine (Irene Manning) and Alex (Bill Johnson) appear eager to desert their spouses and rekindle their old spark. Alex admits it openly:

> ALEX: I had to find out whether I was still in love with you or just in-fatuated with a memory.

Such *Follies*-like insights about the tantalizing Road You Didn't Take haunt the piece. As Alex's assistant tells Katherine, "Romance is never what you have. It's what you haven't."

The Day Before Spring did not succeed, possibly because Lerner's book lacked humor: this was a time when every musical, whatever else it did, was supposed to be funny. Then, too, hit tunes were key in attracting business; people would hear a song they liked and ask, "What's that from?," because the best tunes were show (or movie) tunes. *The Day Before Spring's* score is interesting, especially in the ballad "You Haven't Changed At All," actually just one segment in an extended musical scene, as "If I Loved You" is in *Carousel*. But nothing in the appealing but conventional slate of songs caught on even momentarily, for Loewe really was at his best only when a specific place and time inspired his sense of musical imagery, from gold-rushing California (*Paint Your Wagon*, 1951) to Arthurian myth (*Camelot*, 1960).

Or eighteenth-century Scotland, which provisioned Lerner and Loewe's work most fervently in the R & H style—complete with de Mille choreography—*Brigadoon* (1947). This one is a complete fantasy: a Scots village is protected from malign influences by appearing but once a century. The catch is that if any villager leaves, the spell is broken, and Brigadoon enters into endless night—and of course someone tries to do just that, for a very suspenseful intermission curtain.

This brings up R & H Rule Seven, which Hammerstein himself gave voice to on a number of occasions: The second act should last half as long as the first with twice as much action. Indeed, not all that much occurs in *Briga-doon*'s first act; it's almost all exposition, except for the driveline of the First Couple's romance. Her Wanting Song, "Waitin' For My Dearie," reaches for their first duet, "The Heather on the Hill," and, a bit later, when he breaks into "Almost Like Being in Love"'s short verse and then starts the chorus with "What a day this has been," the tune's confident swing celebrates Broadway's mastery of American popular song—the era, we might say, of What's that from?

One reason is the sheer carefree wonder with which Lerner and Loewe invest this extremely central up-tune version of a love song. The musical always made romance seem so easy; prince meets waitress and it's "Deep in My Heart, Dear." Or, at least, it is in *The Student Prince*. Yet by the mid-1940s, everything in the musical is starting to become difficult. Someone dies or is actually murdered in every R & H show from *Oklahoma!* through *The King and I*, and in *Brigadoon* as well. A bit later, death becomes almost prevalent. In Arthur Schwartz and Dorothy Fields' *A Tree Grows in Brooklyn* (1951), the hero dies. In Harold Rome's *Fanny* (1954), the comic dies. Nobody dies in Bob Merrill's *New Girl in Town* (1957), but the heroine is a prostitute, and not in a coy, happy-go-lucky way: a woman from an abusive background who has a problem dealing with men. Her bitter establishing song, "On the Farm," includes verbal pictures of a girl overpowered by rapacious male relatives—the religious hypocrite Uncle Sven, and sessions "in the barn" conducted by Uncle Jake: "If ya squeal, ya get the rake."

So *New Girl in Town* was a serious show—but one created by musical-comedy talents. George Abbott wrote the book and directed; Bob Merrill created the score, his first after years of hammering out jingles such as "How Much Is That Doggie in the Window?"; Bob Fosse choreographed; and Gwen Verdon played the lead. Yet their source was Eugene O'Neill's

Anna Christie, a contentious piece, antagonistic to rules of Boy Gets Girl. The original plan, when the musical was entitled *Pay the Piper*—a reference to the Greek-O'Neillian concept of "destiny creates character"—was to showcase Verdon in an acting role in a "musical play." Yet Verdon had stolen *Can-Can* in a "Garden of Eden" ballet and dominated *Damn Yankees* as the Lola who gets whatever Lola wants. To present her in a non-dancing role would have been absurd. It is the musical's passion to exalt its performing whizzes in their turns of strength—besides, Fosse and Verdon were a team by then, not yet married but artistically a tight unit, and their theme was dance.

This led to yet another Dream Ballet, laid out to capture Anna's horror of her past life, which she has been trying to overcome. Anna isn't simply tired of men: she's disgusted with them, including the two who spend much of the play fighting over her—her scow captain father (Cameron Prud'homme) and her sailor boy friend (George Wallace). Fosse was a sensualist and Verdon a dedicated thespian, and both believed that *New Girl in Town* gave them the right to explore the musical's long-established erotic subtext in an innovatively overt way. Lydia Thompson's burlesques alarmed authorities with what they saw as the feminist independence of the performers, and of course the *Ziegfeld Follies*, however suavely, celebrated the appetitive concerns of the men in the audience. And "Eadie Was a Lady," from *Take a Chance* (1932), gave Ethel Merman an opportunity to stop the show—not simply rouse the public but provoke such an ovation that the continuity froze for a while—with a salute to a daughter of joy who had "class with a capital K."

In *New Girl in Town*'s second act, however, coming off the torcher "If That Was Love," Verdon went into a danced flashback to her days working in a bordello, with the other girls and a customer (John Aristides), that appalled tryout audiences. Abbott wanted to cut it, but Fosse and Verdon, he says, "fought for it like tigers." In a famous story, the pair tells Abbott that their ballet is "high art" and that "people had thrown fruit at Stravinsky." Says Abbott, "The act of throwing fruit at a project [is] not in the strictest logic an absolute proof of its high art." Very funny. But Abbott was always behind the curve when his people tried something bold and unusual.

A Tree Grows in Brooklyn and *Fanny* have dream sequences, too. *Brooklyn*'s Big Ballet, set on Hallowe'en and choreographed by Herbert Ross, was less a dream than a nightmarish summary of the plot, in which a charming ne'er-do-well is overcome by his destiny: to fail at everything. *A Tree Grows in Brooklyn* is based on Betty Smith's novel about Irish-Americans at the turn of the last century, and it is very realistically drawn. The show's hero is that hapless charmer, Johnny Nolan (Johnny Johnston), but its protagonist is Johnny's wife, Katie (Marcia Van Dyke): long-suffering yet strong and proud. Katie loves Johnny because he's beautiful, and their daughter (Nomi Mitty) loves him because he's wonderful. But he dies in both novel and musical, because the R & H musical play encouraged progressive inquiry into the nature of society, and poverty breeds death. True, *Brooklyn* was a George Abbott show, and Abbott liked the fun stuff. So, besides its hero and protagonist, *Brooklyn* had a star, Shirley Booth, as Katie's Aunt Cissy. Booth's daffy line delivery and kewpie-doll vocalism, combined with a theatre-filling personal warmth, made her *Brooklyn*'s central character even though she and her live-in (Nathaniel Frey) were technically the Second Couple.

Still, the book, by Smith and Abbott, struggled to keep the novel's humanist issues in play; this was a much richer libretto than *New Girl in Town*'s. Though the work enjoyed only a passing success and is seldom revived, it counts as one of the best scores of the time. Clearly, Schwartz and Fields saw the R & H matrix as a challenge to rise to. Tender with the Nolans and cheeky with Cissy, they found numbers as well for the street life of the Williamsburg neighborhood, making this almost an inner-city *Carousel*. Fields, heretofore an engaging talent, suddenly became a brilliant one. In "Love Is the Reason," Cissy outlines the dos and don'ts of cohabitation, and a single line—"If you shut your big mouth when his relatives call"—catches the character, her ethnic culture, and a philosophy of life in a stroke.

Harold Rome was another songwriter who expanded his survey at this time, and *Fanny* is more or less operatic. One odd aspect of the R & H era is that while Rodgers himself preferred singers who could act to actors who could sing, those under his influence continued to write for theatre voices, not trained ones. Of *New Girl in Town*'s four leads, only George Wallace had a voice in any real sense, and the all but toneless Cameron Prud'homme and Thelma Ritter had to carry four numbers.

But *Fanny* employed R & H casting, with one opera singer (Ezio Pinza) and two superb "Broadway" singers for the sweethearts (Florence Henderson, William Tabbert). Even the comic, Walter Slezak, had enjoyed important roles in operettas in the 1930s. This quartet had a lot to deal with, for *Fanny*'s source, Marcel Pagnol's thirties stage-and-film trilogy—*Marius*, *Fanny*, and *César*—is stuffed with wanting. The concept of need, or hope, or wish-fulfillment, is what drives the best musicals, why their characters sing. It's so simple it's absurd: a character requires something to complete his or her existence, and, in confiding in us, draws us sympathetically into his narrative. "I Get a Kick Out of You." "If Momma Was Married." "The Music and the Mirror." "The Wizard and I." In *Fanny*, the Boy wants the sea, the Girl wants the Boy, the comic wants a son, and Ezio Pinza wants everybody to get along. If *New Girl in Town* has a pop score with some character content, and if *A Tree Grows in Brooklyn* is a very characterful pop score, *Fanny* is somewhat beyond them, too pop for opera but too rich not to be.

Interestingly, *Fanny* set its dream sequence as not a dance but in a book-and-music scene, during the Girl's wedding to the comic after the Boy has run off to sail the world. As the Girl dances lovelessly with her new husband, their gay little waltz turns dissonant, the lights dim, the chorus starts to wail, and, to a deceptively sweet reprise of the title tune—the Boy's love song to the Girl—the Boy himself appears to the Girl as everyone else freezes. "How could I ever have longed for the sea!" he cries, as they embrace. This is an early instance of what we will come to call Concept Musical thinking, in which characters with psychological access to each other can appear together on stage even when, in the story, they are actually miles apart—even, as here in *Fanny*, on other sides of the globe from each other, or, as in *Allegro*, after one or more of them has died.

Another mark of the R & H effect is the proliferation of serious shows, like this trio of *New Girl*'s haunted ex-prostitute, *Brooklyn*'s struggles of the urban poor, the Boy who so obsessively sabotages *Fanny*'s Boy Gets Girl protocol (even if he does, like *Show Boat*'s Ravenal, eventually return). However, touches of the R & H aesthetic found their way even into musical comedy. Meredith Willson's *The Music Man* (1957) is typical: a happy rather than heavy piece on the theme of the con man redeemed by love. In the title role, Robert Preston was an outstanding example of a fifties invention, the Novelty Star: someone not associated with musicals (or with singing, period) who could carry a show with a good-enough voice and dynamite charisma. Rosalind Russell in *Wonderful Town* (1953), Tony Randall in *Oh Captain!* (1958), Lucille Ball in *Wildcat* (1960), Julie Harris in *Skyscraper* (1965), and Katharine Hepburn in *Coco* (1969) demonstrate that the musical's cultural prestige now attracted even Hollywood folk or, in Harris' case, "real" actors. They also suggest that the musical's new essential of a "big" story—the direct result of the book-rich R & H titles—needed big acting talents to support it.

Certainly, Preston's music man, Harold Hill, was not a specifically singing, dancing, or comic triumph. Rather, Preston gave a bravura performance in an all-around way that star roles of the old days never provisioned. Setting *The Music Man* in his native Iowa gave Willson a chance to *detail* the show in many particulars, so that Preston seemed an authentic alien in an authentic Midwest, right down to a line about kids neglecting their chores till they forget to prime the pump and folks are "caught with the cistern empty on a Saturday night."

That lyric is from "Trouble," Willson's styling of the con man's spiel in a unique musical number—but *The Music Man*'s score is very unusual as a whole. "Piano Lesson" unites a child's finger exercises with a conversation between the heroine (Barbara Cook) and her mother (Pert Kelton). "Pickalittle" slices the ladies' gossip brigade into a quodlibet with a barbershop quartet. "Seventy-Six Trombones" and "Goodnight, My Someone"—a march and a waltz—are the same melody in alternate conformations. Most amusing is the Library Number, wherein Preston tries to break the ice with Cook, the town librarian. Strictly business, she tells him he can select a book and leave:

COOK: What do you want to take out?
PRESTON: The librarian.

Whereupon the orchestra launches a slithery boogie-woogie bass, and Preston, producing a little drawstring bag, sings the first word of "Marian the Librarian." Then:

PRESTON: Marbles. Six steelies, eight aggies, a dozen peewees and one big glassie with an American flag in the middle. I think I'll drop 'em.
COOK: No!

He proceeds with the song, which then erupts into a full-scale ballet in arranger Laurence Rosenthal's ingenious variations on the main tune and its insinuating rhythm. Choreographer Onna White gave the dance a cute blackout cap when Cook tried to slap Preston and accidentally got one of the kids—but note that Cook and Preston took part in a ballet that, in the 1940s, would have been set exclusively for dancers. It wasn't Alfred Drake, Joan Roberts, or Howard da Silva who appeared in *Oklahoma!*'s "Laurey Makes Up Her Mind," but Marc Platt, Katharine Sergava, and George Church dressed as Drake, Roberts, and Church. But by the 1950s, dance was embedded too acutely into a show's dramatic continuity for these personnel substitutions. Even essentially non-dancing leads now had to act their way through the most elaborate dances, even Dream Ballets—as Johnny Johnston did in *A Tree Grows in Brooklyn*'s Hallowe'en sequence.

Clearly, R & H all but reinvented the musical. *Oklahoma!* and *Carousel* weren't more integrated than musicals had been: they were more influential. Yet many successful shows ignored some or all of the new handbook. Cole Porter's *Mexican Hayride* (1944) was strictly, merrily, even recklessly pre-*Oklahoma!* in every way, a lavish fiesta of Girls and Gags. To start with, there was no story, just a filmy premise concerning a crooked lottery and centered on three Americans in Mexico: a con man (Bobby Clark), a woman bullfighter (June Havoc, the real-life, grownup Baby June of *Gypsy*), and a diplomat for Havoc's love interest (Wilbur Evans). This was a book-heavy show with a lot of dance but a short score (four numbers were cut in Boston without replacement), and Porter came to feel that he had been robbed. All the same, the show was a smash, partly because the producer, Michael Todd, raised up an eye-filling production and also because the Herbert and Dorothy Fields script was made almost entirely of comedy, sometimes using out-of-story gags that no truly integrated musical would allow:

EVANS: (To Clark) You're wanted in four states.
CLARK'S WIFE: Five states!
CLARK: Four.
CLARK'S WIFE: *Five!* You forgot Oklahoma.
CLARK: I couldn't get tickets.

Clark, as always, gamed with the public, another R & H no-no. Read the next joke carefully, for it hides a slippery pun:

CLARK (speaking to the lead soprano about her weight): You know,
    I could get that off you.
SOPRANO: You mean diet?
CLARK: No, I'm sure it's the right color. (Turning to the audience, who
    are slow to get the gag) I want a bigger response. I'll wait.

In fact, *Mexican Hayride* is a storyless story carried along by self-contained sketches with musical interludes. Sketch Number One: Clark and a vampy Russian woman. Sketch Number Two: an American couple fumbling around in bad Spanish. Sketch Number Six: a Saks Fifth Avenue buyer haggling over jewelry. Sketch Number Eight: Clark trying to pick up a girl and tossing the word "retroactive" at her:

GIRL: What in the world is that?
CLARK: You'll be retro, and I'll be active!

Unfortunately for Porter, most of the songs that remained after the Boston housecleaning were third-rate. The aforementioned lead soprano, Corinna Mura, had two sumptuous numbers in Porter's Latin style, each topped by a high C. (This must have been at Todd's insistence, for Porter couldn't stand operatic sopranos in musicals.) There was one hit, "I Love

You," whose distinction lies in a descending minor seventh on the refrain's first two pitches. Still, after the lack of enthusiasm for the music of Porter's previous title, *Something For the Boys* (1943), even with Ethel Merman introducing most of the songs, *Mexican Hayride* seemed to affirm a slide from popularity that afflicted Porter till he pulled off his biggest hit near the end of the 1940s, as we'll presently see.

Another big hit we can't associate with the R & H matrix was produced by R & H themselves, though Irving Berlin wrote the score, to another book by the Fieldses. This was as well another Ethel Merman show, *Annie Get Your Gun* (1946), with Merman as Annie Oakley, so formidable a shot that she outguns—really, emasculates—her man, Frank Butler (Ray Middleton). This created a genuine problem in the love plot, a psychological problem (as in *Oklahoma!* and *Carousel*) rather than the contrived misunderstandings that temporarily divided sweethearts in earlier shows. Nevertheless, *Annie Get Your Gun* is pure musical comedy—but a purified one, unlike *Mexican Hayride*. And isn't Irving Berlin suddenly eager to do what Dick and Oscar do, in a parade of character songs (such as her "You Can't Get a Man With a Gun" and his "The Girl That I Marry") that place these two for us right at the core of their problem? Berlin even retired his generical specialties—the quodlibet, the first-act finaletto (here reduced to a single sung line), the "love-to hate you" duet. How often Berlin had written that last number for a couple that had just met yet could fluently itemize everything they abhorred about each other, from dress to manners. *Annie Get Your Gun* was too rational for that; instead, Berlin saved it for Annie and Frank's last number, "Anything You Can Do (I can do better)." It's an eleven o'clock song, one so wedged into the plot that it isn't thought of as one, because the eleven o'clock number is a party piece for the star or star duo, like *DuBarry Was a Lady*'s "Friendship" or *Bells Are Ringing*'s "I'm Going Back": unnecessary fun. "Anything You Can Do" is, on the contrary, the point to which *Annie Get Your Gun* has been pressing since *he* realized that *she* can outshoot him. It marked another way in which R & H reeducated format even in shows that resisted the very notion of a "musical play."

Like Berlin, Cole Porter found R & H a bracing challenge—not to write *their* kind of musical but to incorporate the character power of their songs in *his* kind. Reclaiming his old flash, he gave *Kiss Me, Kate* (1948) the patina of operetta, schmaltzy and classy, but not excluding the wicked wit that kept his projects sounding as up-to-date as a newsreel. *Kate*, set during the tryout of a production of *The Taming of the Shrew*, necessitated the creation of two scores, one for the show's characters and the other for the *Shrew* scenes they were playing in, and Porter bent his very musicianly talents— so often obscured in his Ethel Merman scores—into suffusing the *Shrew* songs with an Italianate feeling in the music and impish Shakespearean gestures in the lyrics. We hear the tarantella and gavotte and lashings of Elizabethan text, even a soupçon of Verdi when the brass instruments toot out the last bit of "We Open in Venice" with two measures of the "Miserere" from *Il Trovatore*. Meanwhile, the backstage scenes revel in slang and low-down rhythm. Yet Porter bonds the two worlds here and there, creating the exquisite "So in Love" for the real-life romance, quoting the Decadent English poet Ernest Dowson in the swinging "Always True To You in My Fashion," and jamming smuttily during the *Shrew* in the coda to "Tom, Dick and Harry," where it turns out that "dick" has another meaning.

This marriage of art and jive informed the casting as well. As the First Couple, Alfred Drake abandoned cowboy Curly for a hammy "Shakespearean" side that he nourished for the rest of his career, while Patricia Morison fielded a combination belt-cum-soprano, even if Porter kept her music from getting too *Desert Song*. The Second Couple was pure pop in Harold Lang and Lisa Kirk, though like everyone else they still had to navigate through Shakespearean text in the onstage scenes.

We can identify the R & H revolution by comparing the Couples in the four most influential R & H titles with *Kate*'s quartet. For one thing, all the R & H First Couples are socially dissonant. Laurey and Curly are the farmer and cowman who must learn democratic compromise in order for their territory to be granted statehood. *Carousel*'s Billy and Julie are separated by his hostility to authority of any kind; though the "Soliloquy" reveals how tenderly he views the arrival of a daughter, he is essentially anti-bourgeois, even an outlaw. Emile and Nellie are obviously ill-suited from the moment they appear. As she puts it in their "Twin Soliloquies," he's "a cultured Frenchman" while she's "a little hick" from the American south. More important, they are far apart in age—nearly twenty-two years stood between Martin and Pinza when *South Pacific* opened. And then there's the aforementioned racial complication. Anna and the King are yet more opposed, for her background forbids any personal relating beyond business casual. She is the schoolmarm and he is . . . the barbarian.

All that content gave the R & H shows more drama than any musical had ever had before, including even *Show Boat*, which offers cultural rather than character development. *Kiss Me, Kate*'s First Couple give us figures familiar from Hollywood's thirties romantic comedies, separated and bickering but still in love. *Kate*'s Second Couple, too, are show-biz clichés: he's reckless but lovable and she likes to party. Although his gambling I.O.U. sets *Kate*'s plot in motion—the gangsters who come to collect think Drake is the debtor—after that, Lang and Kirk have nothing to do but dance and sing.

Consider how much more an R & H Second Couple can contribute to the action. *Carousel*'s Carrie and Mr. Snow may seem at first like the standard comic duo, like *Good News!*'s Babe and Bobby or *Show Boat*'s Ellie and Frank. Bobby tells the football-team trainer that he takes a cold bath every morning. When did that start? "This morning." Bobby's entire role is like that, as is Babe's: being silly is how they live. And Carrie is the flighty sort, though "Mister Snow" reveals a dearly romantic soul. Snow himself, though amusingly awkward, is a bourgeois with intense upward-mobility ambitions: the exact opposite of Julie's anarchistic Billy. As *Carousel* proceeds, we see how differently the lives of Julie and Carrie turn out, as most people would view it, for Julie is a penniless widow and Carrie a bride of capitalism. Yet Julie has given and received love, while Carrie's emotional life has been stifled by the pompous Snow.

Nevertheless, the public seemed to see R & H as strong in, above all, their scores. So the excellence of Cole Porter's *Kate* numbers set him up as a, so to say, son of the revolution. Before *Kate* opened, Porter's stock sold so low that the show had to accept a booking at the New Century Theatre, the former Jolson's Fifty-Ninth Street, much too far from the theatre district's epicenter, on Forty-Fourth Street. Then reports from out of town told the smart money that a heavy hit was coming in; and the reviews were ecstatic. *Kiss Me, Kate* jump-started Porter's career all over again, and he was in superb form for the succeeding *Out of This World* (1950), another musical-comedy operetta, and *Can-Can* (1953), pure musical comedy with a hit-studded score—"I Love Paris"; "It's All Right With Me"; "C'est Magnifique"; "Allez-vous-en"; "Come Along With Me," marked *Tempo di Gavotte* but another of Porter's erotically elusive merengues; the ultra-Porter salute to liberty, "Live and Let Live," an anthem urged on by brass fanfares; and the richly ambivalent "I Am in Love." Porter was back on top, even if *Silk Stockings* (1955), based on the Ernst Lubitsch film *Ninotchka*—this time, Garbo sings!—marked a slight setback. Still, the show itself was a hit, complete with its musical Garbo, the German actress Hildegarde Knef, whose voice seemed to sound even lower than that of her vis-à-vis, Don Ameche. For once, *she* was the muscle and *he* the romantic: in dueling solos, Porter pitted her scientific dismissal of love ("It's a Chemical Reaction, That's All") against his valentine ("All of You").

Long thought too sophisticated for national popularity, Porter was by now as commercial as R & H or Irving Berlin. So when television commissioned original musicals to hype them as once-in-a-lifetime events, the first was R & H's *Cinderella* (1957), but the second was Porter's *Aladdin* (1958). In truth, there were countless television musicals, both originals and adaptations of Broadway—*Kiss Me, Kate*, to name one, and starring Drake and

Morison. However, a new Cole Porter score was headline news (and of course no one knew that, after finishing it, he would write nothing more till his death, six years later). Unfortunately, *Aladdin* was not as impressive as Cinderella. Locked into crowded little sets and cast largely from the B list, the show lacked *Cinderella*'s glamor, with Edith Adams' living doll of a fairy godmother and two of Broadway's sharpest comics, Kaye Ballard and Alice Ghostley, as the sisters. Cyril Ritchard played *Aladdin*'s villain with his usual giggly preening, Sal Mineo and Anna Maria Alberghetti made pallid lovers, and much of the rest was constructed of incompatible odds and ends, though the use of a baby elephant was refreshing. This being live TV, there was an amusing mishap when, at the end of "No Wonder Taxes Are High," Ritchard, hoist on some choristers, nearly took a tumble.

What matters here is how central Broadway and its music had become to the culture at large. The musical's infrastructure included not only a major profile on the home screen (taking in tastes of the latest hits on *The Ed Sullivan Show* and heavy plugs on everything from sitcoms to variety hours) but that sine qua non of the middle-class household, the cast album. Today, Broadway discs are niche commerce, but Columbia's *My Fair Lady* was the biggest-selling LP of the 1950s. Of course R & H would be asked to write *Cinderella*: this was their age, and given their "family show" reputation, the ideal project. But it's interesting, even arresting, that Porter was chosen for *Aladdin*, given his background in the other side of the musical, with lowlife characters and erotic subtexts. Indeed, for *Aladdin* he was on his best behavior, so subdued that Ritchard's list song, "Come To the Supermarket (In Old Peking)," sounds like an expurgated version of itself.

Of other established songwriters, only one nourished a vision of music theatre so individual that he was beyond the inspiration of R & H and their musical play: Kurt Weill. He died young, in 1950, but two of his last works, *Street Scene* (1947) and *Love Life* (1948), stand among the most influential shows in history, the former for its opera-with-dialogue genre and the latter for its story-with-analysis structure. *Street Scene*, from Elmer Rice's play of 1929, represents the musical's ability to transcend itself in number structures too large and expressive to be thought of as "songs." *A Tree Grows in Brooklyn*, which like *Street Scene* treats New York working-class life, has songs. *Street Scene* has musical scenes, encompassing the dreams and despairs of people trapped in a narrow culture that gives them little room for hope. All his life, Weill sought to bring the theatre's edgy realism into opera and opera's intense vocalism to the theatre—and he believed that he did so most conclusively in *Street Scene*. Some of its score suggests the attitudes typical of the forties musical play—the bluesy "I Got a Marble and a Star"; the sex-hustling "Wouldn't You Like To Be on Broadway"; a mother's touching address of her young school-bound son (in their last moments together, as she will be murdered shortly thereafter); the sweethearts' "We'll Go Away Together." But some of the score clearly belongs to—as Weill termed it—"An American Opera": "Somehow I Never Could Believe (Aria)": "Ice Cream Sextet"; "There'll Be Trouble (Trio)." And one title, "The Woman Who Lived Up There," an elegy for the mother, stands among the very best of the decade, mixed of song and speech, covering plot action (a crowd gathers outside a brownstone as the mother is brought out on a stretcher and her daughter tries to talk to her), and at last breaking into a full-throated ensemble even as a police siren goes off: the noise of the glowering city cutting into every event, every emotion.

Weill wrote *Love Life* with Alan Jay Lerner on a startling idea, even a fantastical one. Like *Kiss Me, Kate*, *Love Life* contains two scores—one for Sam (Ray Middleton) and Susan (Nanette Fabray) Cooper as they live agelessly from 1791 to 1948, and the other for a kind of vaudeville troupe that pops up between the story scenes in commentative insert numbers. If *Allegro* was the first Concept Musical, *Love Life*—the second—was the one that anticipated the modern Concept shows with out-of-story numbers remarking on the action in the style later popularized by *Cabaret*. The story: the Cooper marriage, established in "Here I'll Stay (with you)," gets into community spirit (in "Green-Up Time"), weathers feminist ruction ("Women's Club Blues"), wobbles into divorce (Susan's "Is It Him Or Is It Me?"), then explodes in a minstrel show discussing possibilities for the Coopers' future. The vaudeville: the culture moves from the farm to industry (the soft-shoeing "Progress"), hard times set in ("Economics"), feminism is viewed more personally (a waltzing kids' trio, "Mother's Getting Nervous"), why is marriage so difficult (a hobo's wondering "Love Song")?, marriage goes to court (a Big Ballet, "Punch and Judy Get a Divorce").

It's a brilliant notion, as innovative as any show to this date. But Lerner ran out of plot in Act Two, and the production did not clearly mark the bizarre chronology for a baffled public. Then, too, the minstrel sequence feels like the real-life self-defense of the eventually much-married Lerner. "If he's not perfect," Sam cries, sarcastically, "fire him! If he has worries and doesn't understand you every minute of the day, throw him out!" He asks the chorus women if any of them has found Mr. Right; they all say no. Which is realer, marriage or divorce? And the interlocutor explains, "We're selling illusions."

A lavish staging at the University of Michigan, in 1987, used surtitles to support the chronology, and made the vaudeville more "readable" with two capocomicos, who led the acts with managerial flourish. It worked very well, but that saggy second act has kept *Love Life* from reclaiming its historical rights as a founding title of one of the musical's most theatrical genres. Still, it is worth emphasizing that both *Street Scene* and *Love Life* owed nothing to the R & H model.

Two other shows of the time were similarly independent. *Finian's Rainbow* (1947) was a traditional musical comedy with a fantasy plot, Irish stereotype comedy, a couple of self-contained comic sketches, and very pointed choreography (by Michael Kidd). Yet the piece was innovative as well, in its multicultural look at southern sharecroppers oppressed by the "good old boy" network. We've seen plenty of black shows, and black performers headlining in otherwise white shows—and Duke Ellington's *Beggar's Holiday* (1946), which opened just two weeks before *Finian's Rainbow*, offered mixed-race principals and even a miscegenative romance. But *Finian's Rainbow*'s chorus was half-white and half-black in a physically integrated ensemble, and this was unheard of at the time. The show was focused on its principals, of course: sweethearts Sharon (Ella Logan) and Woody (Donald Richards); Sharon's Irish flahooley-filled father (Albert Sharpe), who has stolen the leprechauns' wish-granting pot of gold; a leprechaun (David Wayne) chasing after the gold; and Woody's mute sister (Anita Alvarez), who communicates in angry, frustrated dance steps. Still, *Finian's* librettists, E. Y. Harburg and Fred Saidy, appear to have conceived *Finian* to address southern racism, along with American consumer capitalism, which led to an astonishing first-act finale, "That Great Come-and-Get-It Day," which blends *Porgy and Bess*-like spiritual with the buy-now-pay-later ecstasy of folks who have just discovered the notion of credit. After the intermission and a costume change, they reappear in iconic "star" outfits as love goddess, big-game hunter, and the like for "When the Idle Poor Become the Idle Rich."

We should note *Finian's* score in general. Composed with Harburg by Burton Lane, it is one of the great ones, made of pure song. There are no soliloquies, even a paucity of verses and trio sections. The Irish and black themes control some of the numbers, but almost all of them sing very happily out of story context, as in the typical "boy and girl have clicked" spot, "If This Isn't Love," or the leprechaun's "When I'm Not Near the Girl I Love," his realization that he must finally have turned mortal because he feels sexually promiscuous. Interestingly, Ella Logan, a swing singer, made no attempt to harmonize her style with the straiter Broadway sound, blithely singing across bar lines and around notes as if jamming in a cabaret. This absolutely defied the rules. When pop singers went Broadway— Gertrude Niesen in *Follow the Girls* (1944), for instance—they were expected to adopt a more "correct" delivery. Yet *Finian's Rainbow* is so bizarre that Logan fit in as another charming oddity in the Harburgian universe.

The other outstanding non-R & H musical comedy of the 1940s is Leonard Bernstein, Betty Comden and Adolph Green, and Jerome Robbins' *On the Town* (1944), a paradox of a piece with the flimsiest bit of storyline that gradually multiplies its emotional insights till it seems as epic and moving as *Carousel* or *The King and I*. *On the Town* bonds warring elements: the songs are pop but the abundant dance music is classical, of the modern, dissonant kind—"that Prokofyef stuff," the show's director, George Abbott, called it. And the script is wholly comic while the situation, really, is sad: three sailors with twenty-four hours' leave meet three girls, then ship off to war.

How do these anatagonistic materials merge? For one thing, Adolph Green, an opera buff, loved slipping allusions and even whole snatches of opera into his shows, and some *On the Town* numbers have a spoof-opera feeling, to connect with the dance music, especially when genuine singers tackle them. The most obvious such is "I Understand," almost "Ridi, Pagliaccio" in tone. But the legit zinger is "Carried Away," the confessions of a pair of over-the-top personalities: opera characters, in short. As for the heavy dance quotient, this is a carryover from the show's source, Bernstein and Robbins' ballet *Fancy Free* (which, interestingly, contains a vocal number itself but does not in any way anticipate the musical's score and, further, characterizes its three sailors as competitors rather than *On the Town*'s true-blue buddies). Robbins used *On the Town*'s ballets to pursue storytelling through means other than dialogue and song: to narrate through dance. Yes, *Oklahoma!* did that in "Laurey Makes Up Her Mind." But *Oklahoma!*'s other dances discuss changing times, women's sensitivity, community spirit. *On the Town*'s dances are locked into its plot continuity. For instance, *On the Town* honors the cliché of the sailor eager to get lucky, but only two of its three seamen score in real life. The third connects with his Dream Girl in a Dream Ballet, "The Great Lover": when the work rips away social protections to reveal its beating heart.

As for the script, it is not only genuinely funny but filled with coincidences that would have shamed Guy Bolton. People turn up in the oddest places, especially when the show's villain, Madame Dilly, has to serve as the plot's deus ex machina. A voice teacher, Maude P. Dilly is a heartless, money-grubbing drunk, albeit an amusing one:

MADAME DILLY: Sex and art don't mix. If they did, I'd have gone right to the top.

Gabey (John Battles) is our hero, smitten with a photograph of Miss Turnstiles (Sono Osato). He and his two pals (Adolph Green, Cris Alexander) break up to search for her, and Gabey succeeds. He and Miss Turnstiles agree to meet later, but Madame Dilly wrecks it, even as Gabey's chums have picked up their dates, an anthropologist (Betty Comden) and a cab driver (Nancy Walker). Gabey is heartbroken.

The Boy Gets Girl, essential as far back as *The Black Crook*, is often just another piece of furniture in the musical's living room. Yet one of *On the Town's* paradoxes is that, suddenly, it really matters, amid the crazy fun, that a young man in wartime service to his country Get the Girl—that he fulfill the romantic idyll so basic to the musical. So *On the Town* really *must* bring Gabey and Miss Turnstiles together, and the script simply plonks Madame Dilly in front of Gabey—it doesn't matter how—and she tells him where to locate his ideal: Coney Island. With the twenty-four-hour leave all but over, Gabey speeds off, his friends in pursuit.

What protects the show's silliness is the looming sadness in the happy ending. Yes, Gabey gets Miss Turnstiles—in his Dream Ballet and then, in real time, for a moment only, as he and his friends must return to their ship. Comden and Green were perhaps the daffiest of the musical's word-smiths, not as witty as some yet with a love of the sublimely ridiculous that made their work unique. Except for *A Doll's Life* (1982), an unappreciated look at what happens after Ibsen's *A Doll's House*, Comden and Green never ventured out of the arena of the absurd, especially the subvenue of New York eccentrics. Again with Bernstein on *Wonderful Town* (1953), they conjured up a place where the secret of success is to get in touch with one's inner zany. "One Hundred Easy Ways (to lose a man)," "Pass the Football," "Conversation Piece," "Conga!," and "Swing" consider whether to conform or rebel. The hit tune, "Ohio," offers a trio section on the babbitry of small-town life. The merry-villagers opening, "Christopher Street," set in a Manhattan village—Greenwich—repeatedly halts for tiny book scenes introducing unorthodox town "characters." And even the eleven o'clock number, "The Wrong Note Rag," develops this. A Comden and Green personality is a wrong-note personality, like Judy Holliday's switchboard operator in *Bells Are Ringing* (1956), who does "wrong" when trying to do right, getting involved with clients to solve their personal problems. Indeed, Green himself was a cutup: late in life, Green was ailing and under care, and one night his son, helping Green to bed, said, "Take my hand"—and Green immediately started singing Borodin on the words "I'm a stranger in Samarkand."* Yet even within their devilry, Comden and Green could write as

---

*The joke turns on *Kismet's* "Stranger in Paradise." Note that Green, ever the craftsman, tidied up the rhyme scheme for a match with "hand."

sentimentally as any, and for *On the Town* they created the arrestingly tender "Some Other Time." A quartet for Gabey's two partners and their girls, it reminds us that, for all the show's farcical picaresque, real feelings are at stake as the sailors' leave time counts down to zero.

One odd note: in the 1920s, the classic shows tend to be operettas. In the 1930s, besides the obvious exception of *Porgy and Bess*, the classics tend to be musical comedies—*Of Thee I Sing, Anything Goes, Babes in Arms, The Boys From Syracuse*. In the 1940s, both genres attain posterity, the musical play (essentially operetta's modernization) in the R & H atelier and musical comedy in *Annie Get Your Gun, Finian's Rainbow, Kiss Me, Kate* . . . and *On the Town*. It has been revived three times in New York; in Europe, it is treated as a key American title. In 2005, the English National Opera staged it in high style with a sharp cast led by the American Aaron Lazar as Gabey.

The director, Jude Kelly, emphasized the wartime background, for instance in a newspaper kiosk advertising the headline THREE SHIPS HIT, 561 DEAD, and choreographer Stephen Mears sensualized the "Lonely Town" dance, traditionally an expression of Gabey's longing but here a massing up of civilian men hot to rendezvous with Miss Turnstiles, just as Gabey is. The show's musical-comedy attitudes were solidly in place in Gabey's pals, raucous Tim Howar and softy Adam Garcia, and their dates, an amusingly grand Lucy Schaufer and the expertly comic Caroline O'Connor. And the music was very well sung, as befits an opera troupe. But the ENO production was at its best in its wedding of the work's halves of musical comedy and ballet—its sex and art, so to say. One reason that *On the Town* has become an evergreen classic is this tension of elements: a sensitive piece hiding inside a hellzapoppin.

Of course, *On the Town* really *is* a farce. But the dances expand it into musical-play power. When Gabey at last meets his idol in the aforementioned Dream Ballet, Bernstein brings together the leitmotifs associated with Gabey and Miss Turnstiles, and European *On the Town*s often stage this erotically, with a dream Gabey and his love nearly naked in passionate embrace. The ENO, however, presented instead that singular fear of wartime: the warrior who doesn't return. In this "Great Lover," Aaron Lazar, sleeping on the subway ride (realized as a construction girder), visualizes his marriage to and fatherhood with Miss Turnstiles. He and other sailors march off to war, Miss Turnstiles rocks her "baby" . . . but then she dashes through a column of sailors, looking for Gabey. She can't find him, and we understand that he has been killed. As the ballet ends, Lazar awakens and speeds off to find Miss Turnstiles—not for his devoutly wished-for date but to reassure her that he is alive: a real-life person in a Dream Ballet world.

A fusion of the satiric and the romantic into one organic whole, *On the Town* was the opposite of R & H, wherein the ingredients are homogenized. In Comden and Green's world, two women office workers keep showing up, discussing a problem boss, one incessantly asking, "So what did *he* say?," and the other insistently replying, "So *I* said . . ." It's more of that New York eccentricity; there are no eccentrics in R & H. Nor is any Prokofyef stuff, or anything like the boogie-woogie brawl of the cab driver's "I Can Cook, Too," a list song of food-sex double meanings. ("My seafood's the best in the town.") The R & H shows are about art, but musical comedy, from its burlesque days with Lydia Thompson, has always been about sex. *On the Town* is the musical comedy in which sex and art mixed.

CHAPTER 13

✣

Something to Dance About

The 1950s was the musical's most confident decade, when everyone seemed to know how to write a dramatic score while creating hit tunes: "Wish You Were Here," "Hey, There," "Standing on the Corner," "Goodnight, My Someone," "Namely You," "Tonight." Cast albums were middle-class status holders, and hit shows ran about twice as long as hit shows in the 1940s.

There was one immediate structural loss: television killed off the revue. The form turned up persistently throughout the 1950s, but the last bunch of *successful* ones arrived early in the decade, led by two star shows, *Two on the Aisle* (1951), with Bert Lahr and Dolores Gray, and *Two's Company* (1952), with Bette Davis. Yes, that Bette Davis. Still, as we recall from the 1930s, revue as a form depended on great songwriting; virtually every major composer except Kurt Weill and lyricist except Oscar Hammerstein tried revue at least once in the years between, say, 1915 and 1955. *Two on the Aisle's* composer was Jule Styne, in his first collaboration with Comden and Green, while *Two's Company's* music man was Vernon Duke, working mostly with Ogden Nash.

The Styne-Comden-Green teaming was essential to the age, for Styne had only just hit Broadway (after seven years in Hollywood) in two nostalgia shows, *High Button Shoes* (1947) and *Gentlemen Prefer Blondes* (1949). He was to work constantly with Comden and Green, from the Mary Martin *Peter Pan* (1954) and our Judy Holliday vehicle *Bells Are Ringing* (1956) to the Carol Burnett movie spoof *Fade Out Fade In* (1964) and a study of American race relations in Concept Musical format, *Hallelujah, Baby!* (1967). For *Two on the Aisle*, the authors put together a string of ballads for Dolores Gray and sketches for Bert Lahr, but Gray was deft enough to take on the playlets as well and Lahr had a musical solo, "The Clown," a medley of party turns on such as Rudolph Valentino and Queen Victoria ("You must obey my vhims!"), tailored to his stars-in-eyes grandiosity, operatic vibrato, and good old-fashioned paranoid hysteria.

Early revue doted on self-contained song spots. But by the 1930s the numbers were often framed within sketches or dance scenes to give them narrative power. So Gray's "Hold Me Tight" found her as a coquette entertaining various suitors, and she sang "If You Hadn't, But You Did" after shooting a treacherous boy friend. To close Act One, the two stars were in matching loud checked outfits as vaudevillians saved from retirement by Rudolf Bing's new regime at the Metropolitan Opera House. Bing was famous for giving the old barn a taste of show biz with English-language performances and a *Fledermaus* for which Danny Kaye was invited to play Frosch, the comic jailer in Act Three, who repeatedly takes a fall down a trick staircase. (Jack Gilford ultimately got the role.) The act's finale found Lahr and Gray "onstage" as Siegfried and Brünnhilde in fractured German, Lahr attacking the dragon with a seltzer bottle. The cleverest of the sketches was "Triangle," in which the stars and Elliott Reid tried an adultery scenario in three styles—burlesque, T. S. Eliot (for pleasure, they read the fun parts of Spengler's *The Decline of the West*), and Cole Porterian musical comedy. However, the funniest of the sketches, "Space Brigade," proposed Lahr as Captain Universe in a takeoff on children's television sci-fi shows like *Captain Video*. On the planet Venus, Universe and his men encounter aliens, and, fearing an attack, they defend themselves:

LAHR: Use your disintegrator guns.
MAN 1: No effect, Captain.
LAHR: Try your paralizerifles. (They fail.) The superatomizers!
MAN 2: Captain, what do we do now?
LAHR: Run like hell!

Thus, *Two on the Aisle* made the most of its stars' fortes. *Two's Company*, however, had first to establish exactly what a "Bette Davis musical" could be; the notion itself is not unlike a Passion Play starring Ricky Gervais. Then, too, Vernon Duke, though a brilliant composer with an outstandingly resourceful harmonic palette, usually suffered abject failures. Three of his shows had closed in tryout; two more were to do so. But if anyone could figure out what "Bette Davis music" must sound like, it was Duke. Too often, when writing for a non-singer, a composer invests in ditties with a three-note range, as André Previn did for Katharine Hepburn in *Coco* (1969). It's star insurance, but it isn't music. Davis and Duke might have chosen that option, but, on the contrary, he gave her real music that she could really navigate, and Davis, refusing to ham-and-egg her way through the challenge of carrying a big musical, threw herself into the doings.

At least she was helped by an extremely solid group of young vocalists—Peter Kelley, Bill Callahan (who also danced, in the Harold Lang-*Pal Joey* manner), Sue Hight, and especially Ellen Hanley, who had perhaps the loveliest soprano on Broadway. The rousing opening, "Theatre Is a Lady," the carefree waltz "Out of a Clear Blue Sky," and Hanley's "Haunted Hot Spot" (the tale of a stripper caught between a drummer and a "hot-dog pianist") set Broadway's revues apart from the ones on TV in the quality of the writing and performing alike. And while a TV spot might follow a torch vocal like "Haunted Hot Spot" with a dance interpretation of the story told in the lyrics, only *Two's Company* could offer Nora Kaye's stripper, Callahan's drummer, and Buzz Miller's pianist, in choreography by Jerome Robbins.

But the public came for Davis—and it did come, for the show was still doing terrific business after 90 performances, when Davis, as always when on stage, suddenly developed a case of that rare medical complaint Shut up I'm quitting, and the production closed. Naturally, the New York smartypants opinion was that Davis was hopelessly out of her league as a musical-comedy star, but Davis' scenes focused on her possibilities rather than on her limitations. She was a hoot as Sadie Thompson in an overstated replica of Jeanne Eagels' *Rain* costume, from parasol to spats, and then went country with blackened teeth and Mammy Yokum pipe for "Purple Rose," a spoof of those Romeo-and-Juliet sagas of thwarted love in the hills. Against an intricate arrangement filled with choral twangs and fiddly keening, Davis held her own—because, again, Vernon Duke was musician enough to invent a Davis style in song. She even performed an eleven o'clock number, "Just Like a Man." True, it's awfully talky—but it actually came from one of Duke's out-of-town disasters, *Sweet Bye and Bye*, where it was sung by Dolores Gray.

New Faces of 1952 played without headliners by its very mission statement as the introduction of unknown talent, though in the long run Paul Lynde, Eartha Kitt, Alice Ghostley, Ronny Graham, and the underused Carol Lawrence all went on to stardom. The producer, Leonard Sillman, had been thus introducing his unknowns since the 1930s and would go on doing so through the 1960s, but this was the only *New Faces* edition to leave a memory. The second reason was a very tuneful score, but the first was a daffy attitude that ran through the evening, from a *commère* (Virginia de Luce) whose theme song ("He Takes Me Off His Income Tax") keeps getting stopped by an offstage voice to a closing parody of Gian Carlo Menotti's opera *The Medium*. In between was sheer craziness—riffs on Restoration comedy, canasta, Comden and Green (in a duet they might have written for themselves, "Take Off the Mask"), Truman Capote (played by Graham lolling in a hammock), big-game hunting, Johnny Ray, and an indescribable Scots bit, "Nanty Puts Her Hair Up." As with the *Ziegfeld Follies*, only an informed public would catch all the allusions, as in Mel Brooks' sketch "Of Fathers and Sons," an Arthur Miller smackdown with Lynde as the criminal father of goody-goody son Graham, in a baseball uniform. "You're well liked!" Lynde cried in despair, staggering offstage as Ghostley, playing Graham's mother, shouted, "You're killing that man!" The entire show found its center in a sketch whose title ran longer than its playing time: "Whither America? (Another Revival?); or, The Energy Contained in a Glass of Water Would Drive an Ocean Liner?" Little happened: a snake charmer entered an office and went into his act, beguiling the switchboard operator into a mesmerized dance. Then the snake charmer packed up and left. The stenographer, who had been typing away through all this, now piped up with "You know, he was late today." Blackout.

Two on the Aisle's and *New Faces*' choreographers were, respectively, the little known Ted Cappy and Richard Barstow. But *Two's Company*'s Jerome Robbins links us to the 1950s' salient identification as the first decade in which a brace of star choreographers became the musical's newest "authors." Irving Berlin's *Call Me Madam* (1950) was a Gimmick Musical: Ethel Merman as a fictional copy of Perle Mesta, a noted Washington, D.C., hostess who served as our ambassador to Luxembourg. Of course Berlin programmed typical Merman numbers, such as her establishing song, "The Hostess With the Mostes' on the Ball," swinging with syncopation and *pow*! top notes. But Berlin programmed also numbers to provide a dance platform for, again, Jerome Robbins, as in "The Washington Square Dance"; a piece celebrating the odd little wind instrument that later became so strategic in the *Legend of Zelda* video games, "The Ocarina"; or "Something To Dance About." Even a simple Boy-Girl duet, for Russell Nype and Galina Talva, "It's a Lovely Day Today," erupted in a full-scale production number, with the chorus singers offering a free arrangement of the tune while the dancers reveled in romance.

In the old-time musical, the Boy and Girl themselves would have provided a bit of hoofing after the vocal to cap the song. Now, unless a star dancer like Gwen Verdon or a jigging clodhopper like Eddie Foy Jr. was in charge, the ensemble would constantly swarm the stage for the dance sequence. True, there were as well smaller dance constructions. Here are two from Bob Fosse: the trio of Carol Haney, Peter Gennaro, and Buzz Miller in tuxedos topped with derbies for *The Pajama Game*'s "Steam Heat" or the "Shoeless Joe from Hannibal, Mo." dance in *Damn Yankees* (1955), based on the tobacco-chewing strut of the classic baseball player, in which bowed legs pump forward while the torso swings from side to side.

Long before, dance was either hoofing or ballet; now there were *styles* of dance, as in Michael Kidd's stomping country folk in *Li'l Abner* (1956) or Agnes de Mille's period evocations in *Goldilocks* (1958), on the early silent-film era. And when the best choreographers become directors, an entire show could be defined in its staging as much as in its writing. Exhibit A is *Redhead* (1959), a murder mystery set in Edwardian London but, mainly, Bob Fosse's valentine to Gwen Verdon. Constantly sending the sets into the flies to clear the stage, Fosse created a show that was one big dance number interrupted by book scenes. Or consider Joe Layton's staging of Richard Rodgers' *No Strings* (1962) as a fashion magazine layout come to life, with haughty beauties posing *en chic* and lighting units turned this way and that—because the heroine was a model. *No Strings* could be typed as Rodgers' first show after Hammerstein, because he wrote his own lyrics; or one of the first shows after *Beggar's Holiday* to feature an interracial romance (here between Richard Kiley and Diahann Carroll). However, in its day, *No Strings* was above all a unique staging triumph.

This was as well the era in which the musical asserted an Offenbachian right to expand the size and power of the score. Such espressivo had long belonged to operetta, and sure enough, Robert Wright and George Forrest's *Kismet* (1953), "a musical Arabian night" using themes—as we know—from Alyeksandr Borodin, held to the exotic locale (in this case, ancient Bagdad) and the legit voices that were always written into operetta's activity sheet. However, another operetta, Sigmund Romberg's *The Girl in Pink Tights* (1954), based on events leading up to the production of *The Black Crook*, was at times close to opera in its vocal arrangements. *Kismet*'s score presented a quartet, "And This Is My Beloved," but *Pink Tights*' quartet, "You've Got To Be a Little Crazy (to want to produce a play)," is *really* a quartet, with contrapuntal part writing and block harmony calling for voices of opera weight. Further, the choral writing, generally intricate, seemed determined to end each number with vast chords pushing the sopranos to a top C.

More important, certain titles were now, like *Porgy and Bess* and *Street Scene*, moving into full-blown operatic territory, whether using pop formations, going quite classical, or fusing the two. *The Golden Apple* (1954), Jerome Moross and John Latouche's through-sung updating of Homer, was "popular" opera, a kind of spoof of musicals even as it went where no musical had ever gone before. It's an indescribable piece, idealistic yet mischievous, irreverent yet still romantic: something that brilliant college kids might have dreamed up for the annual show. Ulysses (Stephen Douglass) is a hero of heroes and Penelope (Priscilla Gillette) a wife of wives, as in the Greek text—but Helen (Kaye Ballard), originally a princess, is now the neighborhood trollop, and Hector (Jack Whiting), the Trojan prince, has become the corrupt mayor of nighttown, oozing with filthy charisma. After the (Trojan) war, the *Odyssey* is enacted as a vaudeville of destruction in which act after act employs tropes of modern life—space exploration, stock-market trading, and such—to kill off Ulysses' comrades. To authenticate the bill, Moross and Latouche wrote a parody of a famous *Ziegfeld Follies* number, "Mister Gallagher and Mister Shean," and the rest of the olio similarly nodded at old song forms. Note, then, that—like *Show Boat* and *Love Life* (and, later, *Follies*)—*The Golden Apple* used show biz as a metaphor for American life, as if a people so wrapped up in dreams of stardom can be analyzed only through depictions drawn from the performing arts.

Frank Loesser's music-rich *The Most Happy Fella* of course belongs in this company, but Leonard Bernstein's *Candide* (1956) takes us into the classical arena—and it was a book musical rather than an opera. Both these shows were adaptations, though Loesser greatly simplified Sidney Howard's play *They Knew What They Wanted* to aim his music at the romantic triangle of the older man, the younger man, and the girl. To fill the stage, Loesser supported them with the atmosphere of an Italian immigrant's vineyard, a kind of extended family made of "the neighbors and all the neighbors' neighbors," as a Loesser lyric puts it. *Candide* used more of its source, Voltaire's picaresque novelette, which piles atrocity upon enormity in scathingly deadpan narrative tone as his people stagger through the Western world, killing and dying and rising up again. Slaughter on the grand scale becomes as central to *Candide* as candy in a child's daydream—the thing that makes life worth living, by Voltaire's sarcastic analysis. Yet none of his characters wishes for a way out. On the contrary, Voltaire's idiot savant (in the most literal sense), Dr. Pangloss, keeps telling them they live in utopia. And they believe him, bcause they're puppets, which made a musical *Candide* quite a challenge for Bernstein, his librettist, Lillian Hellman, and some five lyricists, mainly Richard Wilbur.

Loesser's *Happy Fella* principals, on the other hand, are flesh-and-blood characters, aching with longing—which, as I said in my Introduction, made them ideal for musicalization. The setting of the California wine country also gave Loesser ideas to work with, allowing him to vary his musical textures—Italian pastiche for Tony (the title part) and his workers; Top 40 for Herman, the easygoing ranchhand of the Second Couple; smoky sensuality for Joe, Tony's foreman and the troublesome hunk who threatens the stability of the First Couple's intergenerational romance. Loesser's casting, too, emphasized needy lyricism, with a Met baritone (Robert Weede) as Tony, a "Broadway" soprano (Jo Sullivan) as his Rosabella, a lush-voiced pop baritone (Art Lund) as Joe, two extremely able pop singers (Shorty Long, Susan Johnson) as the Second Couple, and an ensemble that counted a mixture of pop and legit voices. It was a *Carousel* cast, a *Fanny* cast.

Candide, however, drew almost entirely on the opera-singing pool, along with one Broadway ingenue (Barbara Cook, shockingly adept in her coloratura) and, as Dr. Pangloss, a non-singing British thespian, Max Adrian. His brittle, consonant-clipped *Sprechstimme* was presumably designed to distance the audience from *Candide's* disturbing fantasies about war, political oppression (an auto-da-fé was conducted as if it were an HUAC hearing), and the general sociopathic solipsism of the human race. For further "alienation," the fourth lead was Irra Petina, another Met singer but, strangely enough, a natural comic with a heavy Russian accent (her surname was pronounced *Pye*-tina) whose role had a puckish, even gay edge of a kind seldom seen on Broadway at that time.

In other words, *The Most Happy Fella* used singing actors and one acting singer, Weede, while *Candide* utilized almost Brechtian casting, distractingly heterogeneous. But then, *Candide* was torn between dramatizing its story and matching Voltaire's whimsical misanthropy with musical card tricks. Irony. Spoof. Parody. Camp. Then, in the final scene, the eighteenth-century characters appeared in modern rags, as if they had just stepped out of a bomb shelter, to sing the all but sinfully eloquent "Make Our Garden Grow." It's a line right out of Voltaire—*Candide's* last sentence, *"Il faut cultiver son jardin"*—but it demands our sympathy and wonder after an evening of mostly heartless frolic. Surviving failed revivals in countless revisions, *Candide* made its way into the opera house, where consistent narrating is less important than good musicmaking; and there *Candide* has thrived.

The 1950s hosted not only an expansion of musical power but a juggling of the formal conventions. I've spoken of *Wonderful Town's* opening, eccentric and clever, but, on a very basic level, another of those time-honored "opening choruses." However, the show's second act started not with the usual "get the public back into a musical groove" ensemble number but a book scene, to create a situation—pretty girl in jail charms cops—that could give way to a bit of Irish pastiche, "My Darlin' Eileen."

Conversely, Lerner and Loewe's *Paint Your Wagon* (1951), another piece of R & H Americana with Agnes de Mille choreography—this one on the California gold rush—started with a book scene in which gold is discovered during a makeshift funeral. Then came the First Number, "I'm On My Way," like *Wonderful Town's* "Christopher Street" a cross-section, here of prospectors flocking to the site. Yet *Paint Your Wagon's* second-act curtain rose on the usual irrelevant rouser, "Hand Me Down That Can O' Beans."

Wonderful Town was a musical comedy and *Paint Your Wagon* a musical play, so we are not surprised to find the latter more serious in tone, treating the loneliness of the prospectors and including a kangaroo court culminating in a lynching. But serious themes were edging into musical comedy. *The Pajama Game's* hero, John Raitt, had a notable establishing song, "A New Town Is a Blue Town," that mixed self-belief and defiance so freely that one suspects Frank Loesser, mentor (and publisher) of *The Pajama Game's* songwriters, Adler and Ross, might have had a hand in it. Another example: the good-versus-evil ethos of Harold Rome's western *Destry Rides Again* (1959) led to a drastic first-act curtain when the pacifist hero (Andy Griffith) gave a spectacular shooting display as the chorus intoned the dire "Ballad of the Gun."

For that matter, *Do Re Mi* (1960), another Styne-Comden-Green collaboration, came off as something of a serious musical comedy. Not a musical play: a funny, crazy show that nevertheless dealt with the life of a loser. Hubie Cram (Phil Silvers), only marginally law-abiding and always looking for "an angle," spent the show working a con in the jukebox business that was to turn him into a "biggie": intimate with celebs, sitting at ringside tables, worshiped by the other losers. With Nancy Walker as Cram's wife, *Do Re Mi* had two star comics. Yet it cut the amusement with Walker's nagging and Silvers' unsavory business partners—not the genial crooks Jimmy Durante used to play, but genuine hoods. The show's last number, Silvers' "All of My Life," was the opposite of an eleven o'clock song, the bitter, beaten epitaph of a living corpse. Meanwhile, the sweetheart couple, a recording executive (John Reardon) and Cram's folk-singer discovery (Nancy Dussault), carried on as if in a standard make-happy show, he shamelessly oversinging the ballads (including a hit, "Make Someone Happy") with his velvety opera baritone and she running through "Cry Like the Wind" as a Broadway Joan Baez till she zoomed up to a climax on the B and A just below the top C.

Styne and Comden and Green were known for, essentially, farces, so *Do Re Mi* was an odd item. But then the 1950s was the first decade in which highly original musicals became common. Three more titles from 1959 would have been all but impossible only ten years before: *Once Upon a Mattress*, *Fiorello!*, and *The Nervous Set*. *Mattress*, which introduced a second-generation composer in Richard Rodgers' daughter Mary, revived nineteenth-century burlesque if only in its plot premise, a spoof of "The Princess and the Pea." Given the medieval setting, the chorus women were dressed from neck to toe, an amusing violation of the musical's formal etiquette, as burlesque and its pretties in tights were the reason people of the 1870s spoke of "the wicked stage," and the showgirl was still a key element in musicals in the 1950s. *Mattress* was notable for the zest and wit with which it addressed its subject, and for giving Carol Burnett, as Winifred the Woebegone, her platform for stardom.

Biographical musicals have become common, but they were unusual in the 1950s, so *Fiorello!* was outstanding enough to win the Pulitzer Prize.* Incredibly, the director, George Abbott, found someone who resembled New York's short, barrel-shaped reformist mayor, Tom Bosley, and the Jerry Bock–Sheldon Harnick score breached the gulf between then and now with a bit of pastiche (in a demobilization march, "Home Again"; a Bowery waltz, "Politics and Poker"; the ironic soft shoe "Little Tin Box"; and "Gentleman Jimmy," a charleston devoted to Fiorello La Guardia's predecessor, Jimmy Walker) but mainly in character songs of a sweet and wistful nature. State of the art in its revolving-stage scene changes, *Fiorello!* nevertheless maintained an air of the antique in its tone—an authenticity, perhaps. "On the Side of the Angels" was the ideal First Number, setting up the show's placetime while describing its hero—who played his role almost entirely in book scenes—in how his colleagues, and his beneficiaries, and the world saw him. It was an odd way to write a musical, perhaps: but La Guardia was an odd character.

The Nervous Set was the ultimate contemporary show. Jules Feiffer, the *Village Voice* cartoonist associated with urban angst, drew the show's poster art, which told everyone what to expect: a look at Manhattan's maverick community. "Man, We're Beat" was the First Number, and the Tommy Wolf–Fran Landesman score dipped here and there into riffs of modern jazz—the pit was a quartet of piano, electric guitar, bass, and drums. Still, most of the music wouldn't have been out of place in other shows, and the lyrics only occasionally defied Broadway with downtown patter. "New York" found two Villagers (Richard Hayes, Thomas [later Tom] Aldredge) ragging on the city's "phoneys" and "squares." Some of the public must have been startled when "The Waldorf's really draggy" continued to "But the Plaza's not so faggy"—certainly the first time the last word turned up in a musical's lyric. It was all the more ironic in that the Plaza's bar was a notorious gay hunting ground at the time.

Star vehicles remained a staple, though the 1950s most unexpectedly hosted three Big Broadway titles for black headliners, till then integrated

---

* Only two musicals preceded *Fiorello!* thus, *Of Thee I Sing* and *South Pacific*. In 1944, the year the Prize went to Thornton Wilder's absurdist play *The Skin of Our Teeth*, *Oklahoma!* was given a special award by the Pulitzer committee.

into otherwise white shows or sidelined in productions of modest importance. Pearl Bailey got *House of Flowers* (1954), with a Harold Arlen–Truman Capote score that was a glory of the age. Just the notion of the chic literary artisan Capote's collaboration on a musical spurred major interest, and the West Indies setting, realized by the English designer Oliver Messel, filled the eye. Unfortunately, World War III broke out during the Philadelphia tryout, and the show hit New York a lush ruin. Sammy Davis Jr. had better luck in *Mr. Wonderful* (1956), essentially a conventional white musical with a black First Couple. (Olga James played Davis' sweetheart.) Lena Horne's *Jamaica* (1957), despite a feeble book, proved the smash of these three titles for its rich feast of song, again by Arlen, now with his more accustomed partner, E. Y. Harburg, and some wonderfully exotic choreography by Jack Cole.

Lehman Engel, who conducted *Jamaica*, believed it was the first instance of a performer's being body-miked, for Horne's tiny instrument couldn't cut through *Jamaica's* brassy pit unaided. The vast Center Theatre had introduced footlight miking in the 1930s, and a few shows in regular Broadway houses adopted the system, starting in the 1939–1940 season. By the 1950s it was commonplace; Richard Rodgers famously stated that *Carousel* was his last show not to use microphones. As live-performance tapes of the day reveal, even then a performer's simply turning to speak to a fellow actor instead of facing front caused the audience to miss lines and lyrics, for this relatively primitive miking amounted to, as they put it then, a mere "sweetening" of the sound, not today's high-tech processing that renders everything jumbled up in canned polyphony. Again referring to those live tapes, one can hear "space" around the different sections of the orchestra, so that the strings sound contrapuntally against the winds, the piano or harp sings out as a favorite son, and the percussion bombs in from alien territory. However, as the sound became more and more engineered, the Broadway pit—which once came off as a cross between a swing band and a symphony orchestra—ceased to be, in any real sense, "live."

The miking of Lena Horne did not lead directly to the mass body-miking of the millennium. It took time: the next known assisted performer after Horne was Anna Maria Alberghetti in *Carnival!*, four years later. However, John Fearnley, the aforementioned R & H team member, told me that Helen Traubel was personally miked in *Pipe Dream*. It seems amazing, for she had sung Brünnhilde in a Met *Ring* cycle only four years earlier and Isolde—the Hippodrome of soprano roles—two seasons after that. It was not Traubel's singing that needed a boost, but her dialogue. She had never had to speak in her opera career, and after leaving the Met she worked in

Hollywood and nightclubs, where everything is miked. Traubel, Fearnley said, was not willing to project her lines into the three cavernous Shubert Theatres that *Pipe Dream* played, in New Haven, Boston, and New York. Fearnley didn't specifically state that Traubel was body-miked; and there was a way of setting her apparatus into the scenery. However it was done, this is the earliest example I know of in which an actor was individually amplified.

Above all, the 1950s is known for a cornucopia of classic titles that are infinitely revivable without revision. They rewrite *Show Boat*, *Anything Goes*, *Pal Joey*, *Annie Get Your Gun*. But many fifties shows are so singular that they seem permanently fresh. Frank Loesser's *Guys and Dolls* (1950) is one such, with its raffish crew of Damon Runyon gamblers and broads speaking their peculiar English—"Big Jule, you cannot interpolate Chicago dice into a New York crap game"—and living entirely within a five-minute radius of the George M. Cohan statue at Forty-Sixth and Broadway. Though not unconventional in structure, *Guys and Dolls* employs the First and Second Couples so synergistically that it isn't clear which of them *is* the First. Most Third Age musicals use the Couples at least somewhat divergently; in extreme cases the lower pair are all but extraneous, begging to be written out in the first revision—which is exactly what happened to them when *Annie Get Your Gun* was revived for Ethel Merman at Lincoln Center in 1966.

But *Guys and Dolls'* Nathan Detroit (Sam Levene) and Miss Adelaide (Vivian Blaine) are inextricably linked with Sky Masterson (Robert Alda, father of actor Alan) and Sarah (Isabel Bigley), in a macguffin: Nathan bets Sky that he can't date Sarah, not a Runyonland broad but a warrior of the Salvation Army, at once savior and mortal enemy of sinner Sky. In Abe Burrows' very funny but also expertly organized book, the first scene established the milieu—from a pantomime of the Times Square hurlyburly through three touts' "Fugue for Tinhorns" to the Bible-thumping "Follow the Fold"—then Nathan and Sky made their wager, and the show followed the consequences for both Couples as inexorably as a Calvinist preacher tracking the elect.

So *Guys and Dolls* was in no danger of suffering the second-act trouble of too little plot development, because Sky spends the second act desperately trying to redeem himself with Sarah, who wrongly thinks he dated her as a ruse to enable his fellow sinners to hold their crap game in her mission. At the same time, the romance of Nathan and Adelaide is reaching crisis level, and, in a wonderful surprise, Sarah and Adelaide—the "nice" girl and the "naughty" girl—meet for the first time and, in a slinky duet, "Marry the Man Today," bond as soul-saving sisters with a novel mission. Yes, they'll reform their men, but not with religion: with the grail of bourgeois regeneration, from golf to galoshes.

Along with the unique Runyon *tinta*, *Guys and Dolls* derives vitality from Loesser's use of classical touches in a score sung almost wholly by society's outcasts. For his Broadway debut, *Where's Charley* (1948), Loesser wrote largely in the standard popular vein favored in Hollywood, where he had worked, for the most part as lyricist only, for some ten years. Still, a few of the *Charley* numbers were rooted in situation and character, as if Loesser was venturing into genuine music theatre, and *Guys and Dolls* is shockingly well integrated, its only pop tunes being the floor numbers at Adelaide's club, the Hot Box, "A Bushel and a Peck" and a striptease special that itemizes the inventory as it loses it, "Take Back Your Mink." As if working his way into the downright operatic structures of his following show, *The Most Happy Fella*, Loesser created for *Guys and Dolls* a musical oxymoron: his pariahs sing recitative in place of the usual melodic verse, in "Adelaide's Lament" and the title number. It's the La Scala version. That "Fugue for Tinhorns" is actually a simple canon, not a fugue—but the suggestion of High Art in the show's first vocal sequence establishes the fantasy of an outlaw crew that will charm rather than menace us.

Loesser went a step further—a step, one might say, closer to *The Most Happy Fella*—in Sky's "My Time of Day," in praise of "the dark time: a couple of deals before dawn." It's a one-of-a-kind solo, almost through-composed (denoting unstructured music that glides along without repeating or developing its melodic cells), and it is *Guys and Dolls'* most personal number, even though it is followed by "I've Never Been in Love Before," obviously personal in that it seals the Sky and Sarah romance with a vow. Nevertheless, "My Time of Day" is central, not only to Sky but to all his raffish cohort, as it uses the empty panorama of late-night Manhattan as a metaphor for the liberty Sky lives in. It tells us why these gamblers have no use for golf or galoshes—why your "outlaw" is their "free soul."

And just as *The King and I*'s "Shall We Dance" draws Anna and the King close just before the event—the punishment of Tuptim—that will destroy their relationship, the "My Time of Day"/"I've Never Been in Love Before" scene occurs just before the police raid the mission crap game. This creates a very believable Boy Loses Girl, with one of the musical's great first-act curtain lines. It gave Burrows and the show's director, George S. Kaufman, a lot of trouble. Kaufman's daughter, Anne, vividly recalls sitting in while Burrows and her father tried to work through the scene, stalled as they were at Sky's asking the angry Sarah, "What the hell kind of dame are you?"

Anne said she thought the line incorrect for the character, and her irascible father asked, in the sarcastic tone he usually saved for impedient minor functionaries from cab drivers to drugstore clerks, what Anne thought Sky should say instead.

"'What kind of *doll* are you?'" Anne replied—and Burrows, realizing that she was right, asked what Sarah should reply.

And Anne said, for Sarah, "'I'm a mission doll!'"

Curtain.

My Fair Lady (1956), like *Guys and Dolls* a perfect show, became the buzz term for the Great American Musical, though it is English not only in the casting of its crucial roles (Rex Harrison, Julie Andrews, Stanley Holloway) but of course in its source, Shaw's play *Pygmalion* (and its physical expansion in his screenplay for the 1938 movie). Its very Englishness tips us to one of its many unique qualities: elegance. We've seen numerous masterpieces thus far, from *Show Boat* to *Brigadoon*, *Porgy and Bess* to *South Pacific*. But we haven't seen anything this luxurious—in the lofty I.Q. of its Shavian dialogue, its Cecil Beaton costumes for the Ascot racing scene and the Embassy Ball, the Viennese waltz suite for the latter, even for set designer Oliver Smith's spectacular effect when the revolving stage turned the view from the Embassy promenade into the ballroom itself. And just as Frederick Loewe composed highland flings for *Brigadoon* and western uproar for *Paint Your Wagon*, he once again stamped his passport, for an Anglophile tour. Much earlier, I mentioned how much pastiche informs *My Fair Lady*'s score; for now, consider as well the twee polka of "Why Can't the English?," the soft-shoe ease of "I'm an Ordinary Man," which suggests an old music-hall song and dance. Even Al Hirschfeld's poster logo art of a heavenly Shaw working the strings of a Rex Harrison puppet working the strings of a Julie Andrews puppet, the two stars in costume as Henry Higgins and Eliza Doolittle, aligned with the show's prevailing air of wit and grace.

It's worth noting that the musical's imperishable older partnerships are, by common usage, Rodgers and Hammerstein, George and Ira Gershwin, Rodgers and Hart, and perhaps Kern and Hammerstein (if only for *Show Boat*), to which we might add the bachelors Irving Berlin and Cole Porter. It's not clear exactly where in that list the billing of "Book and lyrics by Alan Jay Lerner, music by Frederick Loewe" belongs—yet it is they who wrote what is still regarded by the public at large (if not the historians and aficionados) as the greatest of the great musicals. Or is it just the greatest hit in the history of hits? The saga began among show folk even before the Philadelphia tryout and went wide directly after the ecstatic New York reviews. (The *World-Telegram & Sun*: "A legendary evening.") The music was literally everywhere; the difficulty of obtaining tickets was a national joke. And when it closed, it had broken *Oklahoma!*'s long-run record at 2,717 performances—at that with a production that was much more expensive to maintain.

Yet when Gabriel Pascal, who had produced a number of movie versions of Shaw's plays (including that 1938 *Pygmalion*), first offered the work for musical transformation, virtually every writer thought it couldn't be done. According to historian Stanley Green, Pascal approached Noël Coward, Cole Porter, E. Y. Harburg, Arthur Schwartz and Howard Dietz; and they all said no. Rodgers and Hammerstein tried it for a year before abandoning the work as hopelessly unmusical. What would Henry Higgins sing about? Elocution? Where do the ballads go? Even Alan Jay Lerner at first balked— not because he couldn't hear music in it, but because there was no Second Couple and therefore a shortage of narrative.

But then Lerner realized that Eliza's bumptious father provided a way to thicken the score with what we might term "working-class point-of-view numbers in infectious dance rhythm," which ultimately became "With a Little Bit of Luck" and "Get Me To the Church on Time." These of course help define Shaw's intense analysis of how class creates destiny. They behave like insert numbers whose only purpose is to raise up a joyful noise, yet they all the same help run the work's thematic machinery.

And then there was Freddy Eynsford-Hill—the young man who becomes besotted with Eliza at Ascot. Lerner and Loewe saw the possibility for a love song in that, yet from the very first public performance, in New Haven, the number they wrote was dying. Lerner himself tells how Loewe and their director, Moss Hart, wanted to cut it, though surely Loewe must have been proud of the pretty melody. The lyrics were a problem, for unlike the rest of *My Fair Lady*'s songs, so contextual in their Englishisms and character warfare, this one was a ballad that any ardent fellow might sing in any time or place. The verse was perfunctory ("There's the tree she rushes under when it starts to rain . . .") and the lines of the refrain seemed to belong to some other show. Lerner insisted the song remain till he figured out why the audience rejected it, and at last it hit him: they didn't know who was singing it, and while they were wondering, they weren't listening.

Here's why: the scene followed the Ascot sequences, and while Cecil Beaton's Ascot design dressed each woman individually, the men were in regulation gray. Further to confuse: the Freddy, John Michael King, had been cast precisely because he looked pleasantly nondescript and thus wasn't registering with the audience. Who was this guy in the Ascot outfit? Nothing in the lyric connected him to his captivated dialogue with Eliza at Ascot, and the tricky thing about musicals is that music emphasizes everything. The character must land for the song to land. If not, you will mystify and even irritate the audience. So Lerner and Loewe wrote a completely different verse, to precede the refrain with images tied to the Ascot scene ("When she mentioned how her aunt bit off the spoon . . ."). Now the public knew who Freddy was, and the house could luxuriate in the music as he broke into the chorus with "I have often walked down this street before . . ." And the number of course became the show's biggest hit, "On the Street Where You Live."* The successful resolution of the "Freddy ballad" problem drew a choice summation from Moss Hart, quoted by Lerner: "Every show makes you feel like an amateur."

Yet Hart was at his best directing the show, which became one of the most memorable productions of its time—a spectacle, to be sure, but also because Hart made a fetish out of the cast's body language. Scenes involving the proletariat looked and moved differently from those for the gentry: the "knees up" abandon of the chorus work in "A Little Bit of Luck" compared dissonantly with the rigid comportment of the Ascot folk. Hart was adept, too, at taming the irritable Harrison and privately coaching Andrews, a former child singing prodigy and the heroine of Sandy Wilson's *The Boy Friend* in its Broadway visit but still only twenty years old and in difficulty as Eliza. Andrews' struggle in evolving from the Cockney guttersnipe to the debutante may be why the role ended as one of the great voice killers, because she was asked to work in warring vocal registers to portray Eliza's transformation by the very pitches she sings. Her first solos lie in low keys, but the later ones veer into a "ladylike" soprano range, with "I Could Have Danced All Night" and "Show Me" both ending on a top G. Then Eliza's last solo, "Without You," moves her back into the lower range, perhaps because she is finally confronting her abusive mentor and doesn't need to play well-bred with him. Wrenching the voice from belt to soprano and back eight times a week has created problems for more than one Eliza, though Andrews played the show for two years in New York and another sixteen months in London, both times in very big houses. Note, too, that Eliza Doolittle and Henry Higgins are more of those powerful characters that R & H made essential. Before *Oklahoma!*, few musicals—even *Show*

---

*One other *My Fair Lady* number fails also to match the pointed lyrics of the rest of the score, Higgins' "I've Grown Accustomed To Her Face." However, the chorus gives way to a trio section on Higgins' revenge fantasy that refits the solo to Higgins' way of speaking. Incidentally, the discarded "Street Where You Live" verse left an echo in the score, for a bit of it (on the line "This street is like a garden and her door a garden gate"), transformed into a sweeping romantic phrase, is heard in the underscoring when Eliza returns briefly to Covent Garden and finds that she herself has been so transformed that her old friends don't recognize her. Then, too, when the song was published as a single sheet, the original verse came along, with the words slightly restyled for popular performance.

The Star Turn

George M. Cohan as President Franklin Delano Roosevelt in *I'd Rather Be Right* was the outstanding headliner musical of the 1930s. *Above*, Cohan treats the show's sweethearts (Austin Marshall, Joy Hodges) to a snack in Central Park. ROOSEVELT: This is the way I like to eat ice cream. At the White House, we have to have [Vice-President John Nance] Garner with it.

Two views of *Anything Goes*. First, Ethel Merman leads the cast *(above)* in "Blow, Gabriel, Blow." (Note "Gabriel" tooting at rear.) Then Merman's replacement, Benay Venuta, poses for photographers *(below)* with her "angels" as they board for a midnight sailing to England.

Above, the incoherent *Jamaica* was a hit because of New York's love affair with Lena Horne (*right*, with Josephine Premice and Ossie Davis). Before Alfred Drake (from the 1940s on) and Robert Preston (from the 1950s), the musical's male stars were comics. One exception was the singing Shakespearean Dennis King. Playing the beggar-poet François Villon in *The Vagabond King,* he has been bathed, groomed, and perfumed for presentation at court (*right*, with pompous courtier Julian Winter).

The Star Comic

Above, Irish-accented Bobby Gaylor sings "On a Pay Night Evening" in the title role of *The Wizard of Oz,* way back in 1903. *Right,* Big Rosie and Jimmy Durante in *Jumbo,* in 1935. By then, minority-group stereotype humor was losing traction; Durante's persona, as a proletarian Noo Yawk rogue, was social rather than ethnic.

The First Couple

Above, Boy Meets Girl in *Bells Are Ringing* (Judy Holliday, Sydney Chaplin). *Below left*, Boy Loses Girl in *Little Nellie Kelly*, as snobbish aunt (Georgia Caine) turns Society scion (Barrett Greenwood) against the heroine, a proud daughter of the working class. But Boy Gets Girl *(right)* in *Seventeen* (Kenneth Nelson, Ann Crowley) as the cast reprises the big ballad, "After All, It's Spring."

The Second Couple

While sweethearts romance, professional cutups dance, bicker, and pass sarcastic remarks. *Above,* Albert Von Tilzer's *Honey Girl*, in 1920, lays it out for us in blueprint, with First Couple Lynne Overman and Edna Bates mooning and Second Couple George McKay and Louise Myers ready for mischief. Most shows of the classic era use the two couples, some observing variations. Thus, *opposite above,* Harry Tierney's *Irene*, in 1919, offers as Second Couple the heroine's pals (Eva Puck and Gladys Miller), here enchanting Society scions in *Little Nellie Kelly* style.

I Married an Angel's Second Couple (Walter Slezak, Vivienne Segal, *above*) is truly offbeat, as soigné cutups of Budapest. They're old flames reunited. SLEZAK: You've been waiting for me for fifteen years? . . . Didn't you get married? SEGAL: A little. Only four times.

The Ambitious Score

Historians date the rise of important American show music to 1914, when Jerome Kern interpolated "They Didn't Believe Me" into an English import, *The Girl From Utah;* other Kern *Utah* numbers included "Alice in Wonderland" *(above),* Julia Sanderson, center. Kern's pure-toned yet quirky melody mentored a generation of composers, and his *Show Boat* is the musical's first official masterpiece. *Opposite above,* the first-act finale, as Parthy Ann Hawks discovers her incipient son-in-law is a murderer. Left to right, boat captain Charles Winninger, fiancés Howard Marsh and Norma Terris, Second Couple Sammy White and Eva Puck again, a pointing Edna May Oliver, sheriff Thomas Gunn, evil whistleblower Bert Chapman. Note the error above; it should be "Hawks' Cotton Blossom."

Below, after *Show Boat,* there was nowhere to go but opera, in George Gershwin's *Porgy and Bess,* seen as Catfish Row departs for the picnic on Kittiwah Island in "Oh, I Can't Sit Down." First Couple Todd Duncan and Anne Brown at far right.

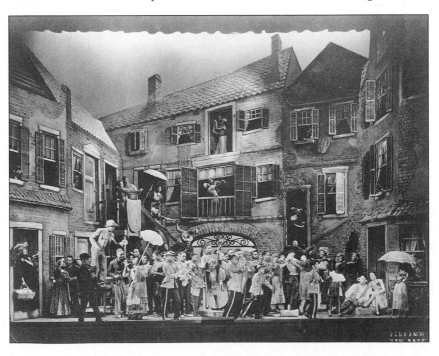

The First Number

Oldtime musicals didn't necessarily begin with a chorus: many shows took off on a book scene. By the 1950s, this was standard, to establish a situation that could then be developed in music. So it's best to speak of a First Number rather than an opening number. *Above,* here's another look at *Seventeen,* as the boys, having dialogued some plot and character information, celebrate their parish rendezvous in "Weatherbee's Drug Store."

The Heroine's Wanting Song

We usually hear this early in Act One—"Just Imagine" (in *Good News!*), "Everybody's Got a Home But Me" (in *Pipe Dream*), "The Simple Joys of Maidenhood" (in *Camelot*). *Above,* in a bemusing twist on the genre, Elaine Stritch sings *Goldilocks'* "Give the Little Lady (a great big hand)" because she *has* what she wants: to leave the theatre for married life. But Elaine Stritch was a bemusing twist on the heroine in the first place.

Design

Before economic woes cut back on the size of everything from cast to orchestra, lavish visuals were very common, especially in operetta. *The New Moon* had a cast of ninety-nine, and the sets of Donald Oenslager and the costumes of Charles LeMaire were almost as potent as the Sigmund Romberg–Oscar Hammerstein score. In "An Interrupted Love Song," *above,* Evelyn Herbert listens to interfering Other Man Edward Nell Jr. while the real hero kibitzes impediently offstage.

Left, note the detail in Ethel Merman's Wild West finery in *Annie Get Your Gun.* Some girls want shoes to match the bag; Merman's got boots to match the rifle. That's class. *Below,* shockingly high-cut beachwear sets off the dance ensemble in Cole Porter's naughtiest show, *Jubilee.*

Dance

In the 1930s, a slithery combination of hoofing and ballet became common, and by the 1940s it was essential. *Above*, we have Dance as a Set Piece, in *Sing Out, Sweet Land!*'s "Jesse James," choreographed by Charles Weidman (and dropped shortly after the opening). A book show using folk motifs and folk music, *Sing Out, Sweet Land!* typifies the period-Americana meme popular during World War II and after, in *Oklahoma!, Bloomer Girl, Carousel, Up in Central Park, Memphis Bound!, St. Louis Woman, Annie Get Your Gun, High Button Shoes, Miss Liberty*. So artists from the "legit" dance world, like Weidman, Helen Tamiris, Jerome Robbins, and especially Agnes de Mille, were as influential in creating a national style in movement as composers of the legit music world were in creating a national soundscape. This "Jesse James" ballet, though little known, is directly comparable to Aaron Copland's *Appalachian Spring*, from the same year as *Sing Out, Sweet Land!*, 1944.

Above, Kurt Weill's *Love Life* offers Dance as Commentary, in "Punch and Judy Get a Divorce," as the sweethearts' bond dissolves and the dancers take over in an "abstract" of the plot. Their wooden slats are the "slapsticks," sliced at one end, that make a sharp report when used as weapons, in the Punch and Judy tradition. (Choreography by Michael Kidd.) The commentary ballet was the least useful of the dance genres, as it observed a show's contents from a certain distance, disturbing the narrative purity beloved of forties musicals. The truly integrated show drew dance into its continuity organically, as in the two most popular of the ballet formats (on the following page), one developing plot and the other analyzing character. . .

. . . First, Dance as Narrative, in *A Tree Grows in Brooklyn. Right,* Lou Wills Jr. and bordello girls haunt cowering Johnny Johnston on Halloween. (Choreography by Herbert Ross.) *Below,* more *Goldilocks* in a Dream Ballet by Agnes de Mille: Pat Stanley separates Princesses from Prince Charmings in "Lady in Waiting," because she wants a hunk, too. After all, it's spring.

Boat—could boast of such arresting leads (though *Porgy and Bess*, as always, is an exception).

West Side Story (1957) rivals *My Fair Lady* as the title we paste onto the concept of the Perfect Musical, and some might prefer *West Side Story* if only because Leonard Bernstein, his lyricist, Stephen Sondheim, their bookwriter, Arthur Laurents, and the director, Jerome Robbins, had more to perfect. *My Fair Lady* is, essentially, *Pygmalion* with songs. *West Side Story*, based on no more than the outline of *Romeo and Juliet*, is an original show, and one developed to go where no show had gone before. Its heavy reliance on dance as an abstraction of the narrative reflects exactly the use of dance in Bernstein and Robbins' *On the Town*. Otherwise, however, *West Side Story* was unique. Musicals were still being cast at the time with a combination of mainly singers, mainly dancers, and actors who hardly (or not at all) sang or danced. *West Side Story* had four of those actors, playing the grownups. But the Jets and Sharks gangs and their girls were cast as much as possible by singer-actors, thus inventing a new subject of integration: the performers. A year later, *Flower Drum Song*'s Dream Ballet used dancing doubles for Myoshi Umeki and Pat Suzuki, just as Dream Ballets had often done since *I'd Rather Be Right* and *Oklahoma!*. But *West Side Story*'s Dream Ballet, built around the song "Somewhere," used the performers playing Tony (Larry Kert), Maria (Carol Lawrence), the by then murdered Riff (Mickey Calin), and the others, thereby substantiating the show's realism even when the action had become most fantastical.

And of course that crossroads of naturalism and romance is precisely where the show's creative team had long been headed. Keeping a log through the work's gestation, from 1949 (when Robbins conceived of the gang-war *Romeo and Juliet*, though the hostile gangs were originally Catholic versus Jewish) to 1957 (at the tryout's first night), Bernstein noted the show's "fine line between opera and Broadway, between realism and poetry." *On the Town*, after all, had been one thing primarily—musical comedy. *West Side Story*'s format was airier, almost mysteriously liquid, with its turf-war ballets, its lyrical violence. It wasn't a musical comedy, yet it didn't seem much like a musical play, either: musical plays balanced the elements of song and dance with a lot of book (as with *Oklahoma!*, *Brigadoon*, and *My Fair Lady*) or de-emphasized dance (as with *South Pacific*, *Lost in the Stars*, and *Candide*). In *West Side Story*, Bernstein noted, the line between the art and the entertainment "is there, but it's very fine, and [it] sometimes takes a lot of peering around to discern it."

Then, too, the action seemed to move almost entirely (two exceptions being the "One Hand, One Heart" scene in the bridal shop and the post-rumble comic relief of the "Gee, Officer Krupke" number) from one expanse of the stage to another, with different decoration, a novelty first adopted in *Allegro*. In a Dramatists Guild panel on the work, Sondheim said that, before *West Side Story*, "shows had been staged fairly stodgily." He was referring to the use of the scene-changing periods in one that we discussed back in the 1910s as the instrument that liberated writers to move their stories from place to place within an act. Over the decades, it had settled into an almost invariable ritual, as Sondheim explained it: "a scene in three [that is, the full stage] . . . then there'd be a scene in one, and then a scene in three, and so forth." *West Side Story* used the full stage almost from start to finish.

There is as well the novelty of Bernstein's use of modern jazz in the score. *The Nervous Set* slipped jazz in as atmospheric tinkle; Bernstein thrust it front and center in the very first notes, accompanying a dance establishing the Jets' and Sharks' conflict. The melodies are unsettling, angular, stretching over nervy intervals, riffs rather than a tune. (Oddly, all of that music had been written to be sung, in a bizarre reimposition of the merry villagers' opening chorus. The lyrics were dropped because Robbins could realize the ethnic antagonism better through dance.) This was, truly, new music on Broadway. There had never been anything resembling, for example, "Cool," with its anxious Jekyll and Hyde of the smooth and the rough, using musical practices better known in honky tonks. All of Bernstein's Broadway scores are very "composed"—even *Wonderful Town*, his only conventional musical comedy. Still, his other shows offer music a middle-class public could have heard elsewhere at the time, if in more classical venues. But *West Side Story* truly was, in every sense, different.

Some historians see *West Side Story* as a revolutionary item in the R & H era, the first sixties show, even the inauguration of the Sondheim-Prince works of the 1970s. It is certainly true that the last really famous musical in the R & H style—famous the way *South Pacific* and *The King and I* are famous—came along only a bit after *West Side Story*, in 1960. This was Lerner and Loewe's *Camelot*, based on T. H. White's novel *The Once and Future King*. As in R & H's best work, the story derives its power from a troubling character relationship; *Camelot*'s is that of Arthur and Lancelot, the king and his noblest, most fearsome, most wonderful knight. It's an excellent partnership in Arthur's attempt to invent democracy in a "might makes right" age, save for Lancelot's love of Arthur's queen. Worse, she reciprocates, because among this generation of men, Arthur is the greatest but Lancelot is the best. *Camelot* made this unmissable in a musical scene called "The Jousts," in which Lancelot stands in combat against three sturdy fighters, one after the other, and all goaded into action by the queen, who apparently hates Lancelot's arrogance but in fact fears that he will overwhelm Arthur and his fragile democracy. Lancelot not only defeats the knights but kills the third—and promptly revives him through prayer. Thus, Lancelot is beyond invincible: a superman, elect of heaven. He is also very, very pretty. In director Moss Hart's finely shaded moment, you could actually see Julie Andrews falling in love with Robert Goulet on the spot.

The Matter of Arthur, as it is called, has inspired so many retellings because it collects so many of the constituent parts of Western mythology—the magical wound, the sorcerer-mentor, the holy quest, the death of a king as the death of an entire people. T. H. White's vast novel, a romance written by a misanthrope with a tickling sense of humor, gave Lerner and Loewe too much to work with, which may have led to its abiding flaw, a first act that is musical play with comedy and a second act that is only musical play, even a deadly one—worse, a corny one. However, when it was announced, *Camelot* struck everyone as just more *My Fair Lady*, with much of the same production crew, with another Novelty Star leading man—Richard Burton opposite Andrews—with the English setting, albeit "A long time ago," as the script states it, rather than Shaw's Edwardian England. And even with the strangely short overture but very long entr'acte, a reversal of the usual practice of the time.

Had R & H tackled White's novel, they might have come up with something very like *Camelot*, with its profusion of character songs ("I Wonder What the King Is Doing Tonight," "The Simple Joys of Maidenhood," "C'est Moi," "The Seven Deadly Virtues"), its community festival number ("The Lusty Month of May," which does almost exactly what "June Is Bustin' Out All Over" does in *Carousel*, right down to the sexual observations), even the three-note theme that runs through the score as a geographical calling card (the pitches heard on the title words of the title song, directly comparable to *South Pacific*'s three-note *ur*-theme on the title words of "Bali Ha'i"). *Camelot*'s was a big score—dangerously so, as some of both critics and public have trouble absorbing "too much" music. However, the cultural hegemony of the Big Broadway cast album, at its height in 1960, after *My Fair Lady* and before the *Sgt. Pepper* rock revolution, meant that most show scores would be heard repeatedly more or less in their original theatre context outside the theatre, at home. This affected composition, because reprises based on not dramatic necessity but a wish to popularize a melody were no longer required. On the contrary, the *dramatically revised* reprise began to flower as a new element of integration.

Thus, *Camelot*'s title song, the second vocal number, is heard throughout the work, its lyrics repointed in meaning—for example, to cap the scene in which Arthur conceives of the round table ("We'll send the heralds riding through the country . . ."), but now as a duet for king and queen, showing us how close they have grown. Then, immediately after, it serves as a lead-in to Lancelot's "C'est Moi," demonstrating the enthusiasm that Arthur's idealism generates in noble hearts. Conversely, Lerner and Loewe could waste one of their best numbers, the diaphanous "Follow Me," in plot action and underscored dialogue, knowing that Columbia's Goddard Lieberson would record it with all the talking deleted, as a purely musical experience.

Camelot was a big show in every way. Even as Lerner stripped White's morose fantasy down to the central triangle, Arthur's vision of his city on a hill, and a bit of magic in the smallish roles of Merlyn and Morgan Le Fay, the evening suffered from dimension-itis, with a grand and gala score but a somewhat ordinary book. The subject is Biblical, Shakespearean—but the feeling, between the numbers, is too often earthbound.

They were frantically fixing it in tryout when Hart was felled with a heart attack, and, upon his recovery, they continued to fix it in New York after it opened, cutting two numbers. And they're fixing it yet today. Like *Show Boat* and *Follies, Camelot* is seldom performed the same way twice. Ever since *Oklahoma!* opened at London's Drury Lane, in 1947, American musicals bowed in the West End in replica stagings, but—typically—when *Camelot* went to Drury Lane, in 1964, it was in an entirely new production with the two cut numbers reinstated and some dialogue revisions. (For one thing, the finale, in which Arthur knights a lad named Tom with the mission to spread the legend of Camelot, now identified the boy by his full name: Thomas Malory, who of course went on, albeit something like a thousand years later, to write *Le Morte D'Arthur*, not the earliest but the fullest source for Arthurian adaptations.)

In truth, most *Camelot*s nowadays are very poorly brought off, with none of the spectacle the original raised up and with superannuated stars clomping through Arthur's role as if playing the bull in Noël Coward's china shop. No: Arthur is a shy and insecure princeling who becomes possessed by the wish—and the power—to reinvent the world. No wonder President John Kennedy singled the show out as a favorite; it is why the show's title is inextricably linked with him. In 1960 (though not in an unhappy, much later tour), Richard Burton spit out Arthur's lines as a man struck by lightning. Shocking as it sounds, his Arthur was even better than his Hamlet. Andrews and Goulet, too, were excellent. But that *Camelot* is as vanished as the real one. Revivals cartoon the piece; it is now customary to play the villain, Arthur's bastard son, Mordred, as a *Bwa-ha-ha!* Snidely Whiplash, though in 1960 Roddy McDowall portrayed him as ascetic, quietly simmering with his evil plans, and thus all the more likely to seduce the Round Table knights away from Arthur's visionary prescriptions.

This is not to say that the musical cannot accommodate the epic. *Show Boat* did so—though they ceaselessly try to tidy up *Show Boat*, too. Rather, the musical had to find a new way to encompass big stories, perhaps in shows written *and staged* to rise above realistic linear narration, to leap through time and space in fantastical interlockings of naturalism and fantasy, and to analyze those powerful character relationships even while enacting them.

CHAPTER 14

༷

After *West Side Story*

Richard Bissell's 1953 novel about life in a pajama factory, *7½ Cents*, became *The Pajama Game*, a standard-make George Abbott musical—fast and funny, with a weakening of plot concentration in Act Two beefed up by a performance piece, in this case the aforementioned "Steam Heat," presented as entertainment at a union rally. Bissell himself collaborated on the script with Abbott, and the novelist then got a novel out of the experience of putting on a musical. The amiably tough-as-bullets Abbott was irresistible as a model for one Richard Hackett, "the great man of the theater," but otherwise Bissell invented his characters. Certainly, *The Pajama Game*'s songwriters, Richard Adler and Jerry Ross, were nothing like Rudy Lorraine, the frantically womanizing songwriter of Bissell's novel, obsessed with the concoction of simplistic hit tunes for Bissell's fictional show, *The Girl From Indiana*.

Bissell called his book *Say, Darling*, and this, too, was adapted for Broadway, as not a musical but a spoken comedy with songs and incidental musical bits. However, those songs were by Jule Styne and Betty Comden and Adolph Green, who were not known for incidental bits. RCA Victor decided to give *Say, Darling* a cast album, expanding the musical spots as full-out numbers and jumping the sound from the two-piano accompaniment used in the theatre to a complete orchestration by Victor's house arranger, Sid Ramin. And, says Steven Suskin in *The Sound of Broadway Music*, from the moment Styne heard Ramin's *Say, Darling* overture, he was flabbergasted. Ramin (assisted, says Suskin, by an unbilled Robert Ginzler) seemed to throw every instrument into the mix all at once, starting with a brass fanfare and going on to standout moments for xylophone, snare drum, a brass choir, and banjo leading into the first tune, the rollicking march

"Something's Always Happening on the River." The strings didn't come into major play till the second tune, the slow waltz "Dance Only With Me," and for the transition into the third tune, "The Husking Bee," Ramin brought in the brass "triangle."* Now, none of this was entirely new to Styne's ears. The Lena Horne show *Jamaica*, just the year before, exploded with brass tricks, especially in the overture, and Styne's *Gentlemen Prefer Blondes*, scored by Don Walker, has a very imaginative overture, using the brass triangle most excitingly in its coda. Nevertheless, something about all that brass resolve in Ramin's *Say, Darling* charts thrilled Styne. Perhaps it was because the *Say, Darling* music, a mere accessory in the theatre, suddenly sounded like a string of hit tunes. What matters here is that Styne may well have heard in "Ramin's *Say, Darling*" the template for how Styne's next musical should sound. That musical was *Gypsy* (1959), and with *Gypsy* we seem to move away from the strings-dominated R & H score to the brass-dominated scores of the 1960s and after.

Gypsy has long held pride of place even on the short list of perfect shows, because, compared with, say, *Brigadoon* or *Hello, Dolly!*, the character relationships are so sternly yet so richly drawn. It was billed as "a musical fable"—The Tale of the Hungry Woman and the Children She Destroyed Together, one might say. But it's really an intimate drama about three people. And if Rose is the stage mother from hell, she is also very much loved by both daughter Louise and consort Herbie. Louise even likes Rose, which is almost impossible with mothers. For her part, Rose needs Herbie—a little—and when he walks out on her, she is devastated even as she knows she'll get past it: because she has just realized that Louise is actually good for something after all: stripping in burlesque.

Ironically, while the very title of *Gypsy* has become as much a summoning term as "Oklahoma!" or "My Fair Lady"—that is, so embedded in the musical's history that it stands beyond criticism, "Gypsy" is more a thrilling noise than a description, because the show isn't about Gypsy—or Louise, as she is called for most of the action. It's about her mother.

According to Stanley Green, the idea for the show came from David Merrick's having read the first chapter of Gypsy Rose Lee's memoirs. Seeing the tale's potential as a musical, Merrick snapped up the rights, no doubt sensing, in that "musical fable" to be, a panorama of old show biz, with its

---

*This special practice calls for three brass instruments—three trumpets, say. The first hits a note and holds it, then the second hits a higher note and holds it, then the third does the same—but then the first hits a yet higher note, and so on. The effect is that of brilliant pitches chiming inside of an echo chamber, and there's literally nothing else like it in the science of orchestration.

desperate wannabes battling their way out of tanktown vaudeville into the big time—the way, for example, Fred and Adele Astaire and Marilyn Miller made stardom.* And Merrick must also have realized what a titanic vehicle this would make for Ethel Merman. Once the writing team was assembled—Arthur Laurents for the book and Jule Styne and Stephen Sondheim for the score—Laurents was the one who contacted Merman, warning her that, this time, she couldn't Merman her way through the evening on voice and personality. Now she would have to act.

In one of Merman's two autobiographies, she recalls telling Laurents that she was eager to, and his asking her, "How far are you willing to go?"

"As far as you want me to," she replied.

Did she balk at carrying a show whose title singled out another character? Since *Panama Hattie* and Merman's *Time* cover, she'd been the sole headliner on every show. Nevertheless, Gypsy Rose Lee, who gave the *Gypsy* gang a free hand, did attach one condition: their show must bear the same title as her memoirs: *Gypsy.*

So the title character is what the ancient Greeks called the "second actor," Rose being the protagonist—the "first actor," so to say. To let Louise function in the narrative, she has key scenes without Rose—in other words, during Merman's rest periods. But these are crucial scenes. Louise's "Little Lamb" has the air of a Heroine's Wanting Song, but that slot is filled by Rose's driving, almost maddened "Some People." Still, the lost and tender "Little Lamb" does establish Louise. Louise is developed further in her one extended scene with her sister, June (the real-life June Havoc), which leads into "If Momma Was Married." It's the only time we get any sense of how Louise and June regard their family relationship. June sees it as penal servitude:

> JUNE (cold anger): It's a terrible act and I hate it! I've hated it from the beginning and I hate it more now!

Then, as the famous *Gypsy* placards at the sides of the stage read "Dreams of Glory," Louise got another scene and song, now with one of the boys in the act, Tulsa, this one leading into "All I Need Is the Girl."

---

*In fact, *Gypsy*'s director, Jerome Robbins, had it in mind to spice the production with the participation of vaudevillians of various kinds—in scene-change crossovers, story bits, and a strange opening vignette between a mother and daughter that was designed to startle the audience till it figured out that this was a playlet of the kind often seen in vaudeville houses. All of this was eventually dropped, though a few of the variety artistes were still in the company when tryouts began.

Here *Gypsy* breaks a cardinal rule: Never give a character number to a nobody. But then, it's not Tulsa's solo as much as it is Louise's second duet. "Momma" placed her alienation from show biz. "All I Need" reveals her longing, as she shyly tries to engage with Tulsa by getting into his act—and, we notice, he has a good one, romantic yet snazzy, very openly modeled on Fred Astaire but correctly so, inspiringly so. Tulsa is all set on how he'll look, what "she" will do, how they'll fit together. It's an expert act, traditional yet fresh. So Tulsa knows more than Rose does, with her idiotic scenarios, irrelevant flag-waving, and June's forced intimacy with the audience. ("My name is June, what's *yours*?") Is Rose's flaw not her ruthlessness but simply her coarse taste in art?

Besides, if Rose is such a powerhouse, why didn't she go on the stage herself? It has to be asked—and Rose herself answers, in the turbulent monologue that cues up the show's last number, "Rose's Turn." It is offered as a solo of solos, with Rose all alone on a stage emptied of everything but, the script says, "a few stacked flats of scenery used earlier in the big production numbers"—as if, in Concept Musical style, the real life of the "fable" has given way to out-of-story commentary. The piled-up scenery of the previous scenes is like a record of Rose's life, not as she truly lived it but as it has been presented to us in the previous two-and-a-half hours. To put it another way, it is as if the authors have suddenly decided that the foregoing action was a play-within-the-play, and only now are they giving us the play itself. So far, we have seen a divertissement entitled *Gypsy*. Now comes the truth about a human being named Rose, performing on "stage" with the scenery of her life just as "Rose's Turn" reprises snatches of her music. For five minutes, *Gypsy* becomes a meta-musical, so now we get Rose's explanation of why she didn't get into show biz as a performer:

> ROSE: Because I was born too soon and started too late, that's why! With what I have in me, I could have been better than any of you!

Yet Rose seems exactly like the Nora Bayeses and Sophie Tuckers of her own day. Couldn't she have done what they did? Show biz then was teeming, with room for nearly everyone who applied. And of course Rose is a great singing lead, which pushes the character even closer to those early-twentieth century women stage pioneers. Rose knows how much sheer nerve creates stardom, as when she dismisses those who long for the uniquely American sainthood of entertainment-industry success but don't pursue it. "Some people sit on their butts," she observes. "Got the dream, yeah, but not the guts"—perhaps the greatest single character lyric ever heard.

Or is *Gypsy*'s great secret asset all the information that is left to be discovered in between the lines the performers actually utter? *Gypsy* is a show we return to over and over because it isn't just wonderful: it's mysterious. R & H spend, in their shows, more time on the details, rounding off their characters and their dilemmas with specifics. *Gypsy* races through its narrative, leaving few clues about its people's various backstories or their day-to-day. It was the first great musical written this way, so perhaps it really is a fable: the outline of a saga, using symbols and signifiers—Rose's love of animals (instead of children, such as hers) and Chinese food as opposed to home cooking, because she doesn't want a home—to explain something about the nature of life. *Show Boat* and *Follies* are epics. *Gypsy* is a small world.

None of the other star shows of the time rivals it. Some major names took beatings—Alfred Drake in Wright and Forrest's *Kean* (1961) and Mary Martin in Schwartz and Dietz's *Jennie* (1963), each playing real-life actors of yore, Edmund Kean and Laurette Taylor. Drake needed a show like this badly, because as an operetta ham he didn't have a wide choice of jobs. But Martin was thought protean, capable of playing almost anything. Countless shows were offered to her, from *My Fair Lady* to *Funny Girl*, but she did pick a winner in Harvey Schmidt and Tom Jones' *I Do! I Do!* (1966) opposite Robert Preston in an imaginative Gower Champion staging that somehow came off as sumptuous though Martin and Preston were the entire cast. Its close-fisted producer, David Merrick, utterly loved it, with only two salaries to pay and no sets, just pieces flown in. Preston, too, needed the show badly, for he seldom had a hit after *The Music Man*, despite his winning stage presence and ability to play, like Martin, virtually anything. In the title role of *Ben Franklin in Paris* (1964), he even got a show with a splendid book (by Sidney Michaels). Yet the piece failed; and two others of Preston's shows closed out of town. In Bob Merrill's *The Prince of Grand Street* (1978), Preston appeared as the leading actor of New York's old Yiddish theatre, not exactly a tight fit for this actor. When the production folded, in Philadelphia, Preston's vis-à-vis, Neva Small, was heartbroken. How she had believed in the piece! How she loved the music, so much more lyrical and dramatic than Merrill was known for! Thus agonized, Small told Preston she was going to accept her boy friend's proposal and give up the stage altogether.

"Kid," Preston told her, "never get married off a flop."

Some of the sixties failures puzzle us, because nothing went wrong. Back in 1948, Sid Caesar led the cast of a smash revue, *Make Mine Manhattan*, with takeoffs on everything from the United Nations to *Allegro*, then became an outstanding television comic in a revue-like format. Thus, his playing of seven crazy roles in *Little Me* (1962) should have created another smash, with a very funny Neil Simon book and Bob Fosse's choreography.

Moreover, Caesar applied his TV trick of playing diverse parts—a cantankerous old miser in a wheelchair, a European monarch on his deathbed, a Maurice Chevalier type—while varying his body English but not his characterizations, even when, in costume-change sleight-of-hand, he morphed from one part to another and back in an exit and re-entrance in, at most, four seconds. Cy Coleman's *Little Me* music (to Carolyn Leigh's lyrics) was ideal for musical comedy, with a spoofy undercurrent that struck the correct chords while gaming with the very notion of a musical-comedy romance, a musical-comedy war, even a musical-comedy sinking of the Gigantic, with the stage floor tilting precariously. And except for the idiotic *Times* critic, Howard Taubman, the reviews were raves. Yet the show lasted only 257 performances. In the 1920s, 100 performances marked a success, 200 a hit. But 257 was now the tally of a flop.

At that, Bock and Harnick's *The Apple Tree* failed, at 463 performances—a fourteen months' run. This tryptich of one-acts on the concept of Eve the tempter gave headline billing to Barbara Harris, Alan Alda, and Larry Blyden, but it was Harris who had the star turn, touching as Eve herself, sexually devouring as the heathen Bar*bara*, and both plaintive and paramount as a chimney-sweep who is magically transformed into a movie star. Broadway had seen great musical-comedy heroines in great roles—Marilyn Miller in *Sally*, Mary Martin in *South Pacific*, impish and fey but at times very moving. Still, there had never been anything as dimensioned as Harris in these three-in-one parts. Fourteen months is a good run—or, rather, *was* a good run. By the 1960s, 500 performances was the new 50.

It was the hit star shows that defined the 1960s. Such works as Frank Loesser's *How To Succeed in Business Without Really Trying* (1961), with Robert Morse as the deviously ingratiating J. Pierrepont Finch, or *Mame* (1966), with Angela Lansbury, were colorful, savvy, up-to-the-minute productions. *Succeed* was cartoony in its look and behavior, almost a combination of Jules Feiffer and Walt Disney, and it boasted the return of Rudy Vallee, whose signature mode of vigorously attentive vapidity perfected his role as a Captain of Industry. *Mame* offered a very sixties reading of the nonconformist, and it, too, boasted—not of a return but of the rehabilitation of Angela Lansbury after participation in another piece on nonconformity, Sondheim's one-week failure *Anyone Can Whistle* (1966). They made Lansbury audition for *Mame* four times, torn between her image (slim, quixotic, intelligent) and that of Dolores Gray (heavy, blunt, domineering). Considering how difficult Gray could be, it seems absurd that *Mame*'s producers took so long to settle on Lansbury, especially given the fabulous success she ultimately enjoyed in the part. Moss Hart was right: every show really does make you feel like an amateur.

Some of the hit star shows were more extraordinary, out of the general run of sixties style. *A Funny Thing Happened on the Way To the Forum* (1962), known in its day for its gaggle of comics led by Zero Mostel, is now known as the occasion when the public first heard a score composed (as opposed to simply lyricked) by Stephen Sondheim. But there is something odd about *Forum*. As with *How To Succeed*, its love plot is the least interesting thing in it. Instead, the driveline is the protagonist's quest: Robert Morse's climb to power and Mostel's manumission. But *How To Succeed*, like other sixties musical comedies, is essentially a funny story spiked with jokes. *Forum* has no story; rather, it has a premise run amok to the point that—as bookwriters Burt Shevelove and Larry Gelbart spun it out—the jokes became the show. Further, *Forum*'s songs are as relentlessly zany as *Forum*'s book. "Tragedy tomorrow," Mostel promised the audience during *Forum*'s opening, "Comedy Tonight," and, indeed, this first of the Sondheim scores to be performed on Broadway must be the drollest ever written. Even the number that establishes the romance, "Love, I Hear," culminates in a jest, on "Today I woke too weak to walk."

On the other hand, Charles Strouse and Lee Adams' *Golden Boy* (1964), from Clifford Odets' 1937 play about a young boxer on the rise, is astonishingly dark for the era. Except for Sammy Davis Jr. as the boxer, Joe Wellington (he was Joe Bonaparte in Odets' play, and white) and Billy Daniels as a crooked promoter, *Golden Boy* was cast mainly with actors rather than singers. This accommodated the intense dramatic challenges in the book, started by Odets and finished by William Gibson after Odets' death. Its dialogue is at once naturalistic and poetic, dire and honest. The romance, with Lorna Moon (Paula Wayne) was interracial; early on, in the story, three white punks attacked Davis with "Hands offa the lady, nigger!," and after they were chased away, Davis flinched when he accidentally touched Wayne:

LORNA: Three at one blow and girls scare you?
JOE (his voice low): White girls.

Golden Boy's score, like *Forum*'s, exactly matched its book in a different way, catching the anxiety of a dramatis personae all ceaselessly on edge. Some of the music gave the piece a much needed lift, as in Joe's "Night Song," one of the most notable establishing numbers ever written for a star. Setting Joe alone on a tenement rooftop, solitary and isolated, it gave the character a sharp profile while letting Davis' voice soothe it in his unique style of thrusting lyricism.

Once, star shows were "vehicles" in the parlance, hobby horses for the charismatic personality to ride in his or her trademark fun. Shows written for Marie Cahill, Al Jolson, or the Marx Brothers had no validity without them. But after *Oklahoma*! led writers to strong stories, the nature of the vehicle changed. *Gypsy* especially but also *Golden Boy* and, say, *Ben Franklin in Paris* typify the new kind of star show, still composed around the central performer yet worthy art in its own right, almost as if the star had been cast coincidentally. And even when a musical catered to the gifts of an upcoming star, with all the shepherding and spotlighting that suggests, and even when the book of such a show might be underpowered, the musical characterization could be quite high. It was as if there will always be a problem getting a brilliant script but there will always be brilliant songwriters whose work supersedes the script, even takes over for it. Thus, whether the show itself succeeds or fails, the cast album will be a smash, as with Meredith Willson's *The Unsinkable Molly Brown* (1960), Jule Styne and Bob Merrill's *Funny Girl* (1964), and John Kander and Fred Ebb's *Flora, the Red Menace* (1965). Here are three title roles, two based on real-life figures, and offering stars so varied in their show-biz standing that *Molly Brown*'s Tammy Grimes won a Tony for Best *Supporting* Actress (on a ridiculous technicality involving her poster billing), that *Funny Girl*'s Barbra Streisand was named *Cue* magazine's Entertainer of the Year while the show was in rehearsal, and that *Flora*'s Liza Minnelli was the only one making her Broadway debut despite having been born in an extremely famous show-biz trunk.

This trio headed very different kinds of shows as well. True, all three works were old-fashioned period narratives with a "quest" theme using the wagons-and-backdrops design common at the time, when big set changes could be made—in full view of the audience or in blackout—in seconds. But the quests were odd: Molly Brown hoped to crash an unworthy Society. The funny girl, Fanny Brice, was a Ziegfeld comic seeking redemption as a beauty, the better to be loved. And Flora, hunting for self-fulfillment, was temporarily lured by the Communist Party. The leading men varied as well, from *Molly Brown*'s opera-weight baritone (Harve Presnell) through Brice's cake-decoration husband (Sydney Chaplin) to Flora's flighty Party mentor (Bob Dishy).

It was the music that made these shows. *Molly Brown*'s score could not compare to Willson's *Music Man* games with song form, but it was inventive all the same—and Tammy Grimes' throaty belt was just the sound for her socially unconventional character. Streisand and Minnelli, more typically Top 40 vocalists, gave their shows real presence, playing youngsters on the upswing in songs as fitted as ever Porter's were for Ethel Merman. Streisand's "The Music That Makes Me Dance" and Minnelli's "All I Need (Is One Good Break)" were the equivalent of the "I Got "Rhythm" and "Eadie Was a

Lady" that placed the young Merman as the next musical phenomenon. But more: *Funny Girl* enjoyed that brassy glister (orchestrated by Ralph Burns) that Styne had so loved in the *Say, Darling* charts—the *Funny Girl* overture rivals *Gypsy*'s—and *Flora*, the first show with a Kander and Ebb score, unveiled their "If I can make it here" anthem genre, ideal for the show's Depression setting. Thus, the curtain rose on a breadline, which gave way to a high-school graduation ceremony and a rousing student chorus led by the blazing Minnelli, "Unafraid." Shaking off their fear of hard times, the kids reached the last chord in block harmony of joyous determination as the orchestra transformed the "breadline" theme into a triumphant fanfare.

In short, the musical-comedy format had been altered completely since the Princess shows of the 1910s, the Guy Bolton or Herbert Fields farces of the 1920s, and the Ethel Merman–Cole Porter model of the 1930s. From the 1940s on—and especially by the 1960s—each musical comedy was its own musical comedy. Further, the rise of the director-choreographer enabled that individual to conceive a work uniquely, "authoring" how it would look and sound as if he were writing it.

Such a work would be, for example, Bob Fosse's *Sweet Charity* (1966), based on Federico Fellini's film *Le Notti di Cabiria*. Today, the musical is flooded with renenactments of screenplays with songs added, but Fosse and his librettist, Neil Simon, and his songwriters, Cy Coleman and Dorothy Fields, truly reimagined Fellini's tale of a prostitute eternally crushed by life yet ever bouncing back. Cabiria (played by Giulietta Masina, Fellini's wife) is naive to a fault, giving her money to "fiancés" who then abandon her, getting picked up by a movie star—it's the high life!—only to be locked in the bathroom all night while he enjoys a liaison, being used by a magician who hypnotizes her, exposing her to ridicule, and so on. It's virtually a disaster film, and Fellini leaves her—robbed and abandoned once more—trudging alone along a roadway, so betrayed that we sense that this time she realizes how hopeless her life is. And yet. Out of nowhere, a group of young people surround her, serenading her on guitar and harmonica. As they all walk along together, their music and high spirits tease her despair. And she almost, sort of, smiles.

Fosse saw *The Nights of Cabiria* as a splendid showcase for *his* wife, Gwen Verdon, though he seems to have envisioned a darker show than the one he ended up with, mainly because Neil Simon saw the tale as inspiring rather than depressing and persuaded Fosse not to take Fellini out of context. At that, the collaborators were very adroit in their adaptation, retaining many of the film's episodes while realigning them with musical-theatre technique. The magician sequence was omitted, but, amusingly, Cabiria's visit to the Sanctuary of the Madonna of Divine Love was transmogrified into a look at an "American sixties" cult church, the Rhythm of Life, with the Madonna (surely too pure an icon for Fosse) changed to a Daddy, a word whose sexual connotation suited both Charity's world and the Fosse style.

In the end, *Sweet Charity* was lighter than *Cabiria*, airy and fleet. At the same time, it is more erotic, even if Cabiria and her pals were changed from prostitutes to dance-hall girls. True, it's a euphemism. "Who dances?" one of the girls explains. "We defend ourselves to music." Fosse's staging of "Big Spender," with the girls lined up behind (and draped on top of) a horizontal bar, calling out to prospective partners like exotic birds in some lowdown aviary, marked the sublime and the bawdy at once, and Coleman got as many double meanings out of the music as Fields did in her lyrics.

It was a bawdy show generally, the opposite of the kind of thing Gower Champion looked for in his projects. Rodgers and Hammerstein are famous for the "family show," but they occasionally flirt with the erotic, and the menace level—from villains in *Oklahoma!* and *Carousel*, for starters—can be high. It was Champion, really, who maintained a "respectable" establishment in show after show, and Fosse who, from *New Girl in Town* on, kept edging into uncharted arenas of sex and snuff. *Redhead* actually began with a thrill killing, of an actress by a maniac fondling the strangle scarf he then used to murder her—and *Redhead* was a comic show. *Sweet Charity* avoided the violence, but it did get off one smutty pun so subtle that audiences may have missed it. During "There's Gotta Be Something Better Than This," as Charity and her two sidekicks dream of more bourgeois jobs, Nickie (Helen Gallagher) outlines becoming a receptionist "in one of those big glass office buildings." She'll have a desk and typewriter . . . (and here's the pun): "Underwood!" "What else?" says Helene (Thelma Oliver), with a knowing shrug.

Above all, *Sweet Charity* seemed absolutely contempo, the latest musical comedy, wired into the Zeitgeist. Though it feels all but archeological in *Charity* revivals, the "Rich Man's Frug" came off in 1966 as reportorial: a look at Madonnaesque voguing before its time, the cigarette-puffing dancers' posture presenting their upper half as tortured mannequin and lower half as spider, all to a throbbing electric guitar. As with *Funny Girl*, orchestrator Ralph Burns was one of the show's central collaborators, with a highly fastidious percussion section, outfitting the two players with timpani and six other kinds of drum and moving on to chimes, pop gun, whip, siren, ratchet, bell tree, anvil, castanets, and twelve more.

Fosse made the piece, but Gwen Verdon *was* the piece, because, quite aside from her spectacular ability in dance, she was fabulous company.

The musical's great stars aren't just great talents: they're great eccentrics, visitors from Mars. Verdon came to prominence as a dancer, yes; her break-out part, in *Can-Can*, gave her very little dialogue and, most inappropriately, a quasi-soprano tessitura for her one number (with the ensemble), "If You Loved Me Truly." By *Damn Yankees*, her first starring role, she was established—in part through Fosse's choreography—as a dancing comic-*cum*-romantic lead, and in *New Girl in Town* (based on Eugene O'Neill, remember), she had an acting part expanded by dancing. Then, in *Redhead* (1959), Verdon was carrying the show, and one doesn't carry a hit to the first Tony sweep in the musical's history on one gift alone.

It's hard to know what to call Verdon—charming, versatile, enchanting, bizarre? Above all, she was Fosse's instrument, unique in the world of the director-choreographer in how centrally she inhabited his style. George Balanchine had such avatars in the ballet world, but on Broadway neither de Mille nor Robbins—or any of their colleagues—claimed so essential and starry an exponent. The very first "shot" of *Sweet Charity*—the heroine posed in her trademark black dress, heels, and bag, her body tilted against itself, a broken toy ineptly mended—is the Fosse physique. Was there a de Mille, a Robbins physique?

This is not to say that they were limited. De Mille probably worked in the widest range of them all. She could fill *Goldilocks* (1958) with everything from vaudeville hoofing (in the onstage opening number, "Lazy Moon") and period ballroom (in the "Town House Maxixe") to ragtime raveup (in the New Dance Sensation, "The Pussy Foot") and Dream Ballet (after "Lady in Waiting," in which the Second Couple heroine chased romantic icons from dragoon to princeling). De Mille could mix modes: for *Allegro*'s freshman dance, she set a pas de deux for Harrison Muller and Annabelle Lyon, he popping off in tap shoes and she *en pointe*, in ballet style.

Yet it was Fosse who, around the time of *Redhead*, seemed to have utterly taken charge of the look and motion of musicals, if only because the Fosse plastique was so readily identifiable. And the dazzling Verdon, figurehead on the Fosse craft, affected the writing of shows by tilting roles, Verdonizing them. As with Ethel Merman, Mary Martin, and Robert Preston, authors hoping to attract the top players tailored scripts, ready to wear, to their talents.

For example, couldn't Rose in *Bye Bye Birdie* (1960) have been a Verdon part, if she had expressed interest? Chita Rivera played the role, as Rose Alvarez, but librettist Michael Stewart had originally typed her as a Polish-American; Carol Haney (who lost her singing voice on the day of her audition) and Eydie Gormé (who got pregnant) were the first casting choices. Stewart easily switched ethnicities for Rivera, because the character's particular tribe didn't affect the show's main action, a spoof of rock-and-roll idolatry set mainly in the Midwest.

In any case, *Birdie's* casting was secondary to its formal structure, an invention of its director-choreographer, Gower Champion. A Champion musical consists of short dialogue scenes hurtling toward the next song, the next dance, as if magnetically drawn to music. This runs exactly counter to the book-heavy R & H program, in which the script, at some length, defines situation as it leads up to a song that expresses character. R & H create musical *plays*: dramas in music. Champion created *musicals*. And of course Verdon couldn't really have played Rose, for by 1960 she worked in Fosse musicals only. Fosse might have taken over the *Birdie* production, perhaps, but, as I've said, he wasn't willing to treat the ethos of happy families and teen dating etiquette in places like *Birdie's* Sweet Apple, Ohio. Ironically, Fosse did take on a somewhat comparable project a year later, without Verdon, in *The Conquering Hero* (1961), based on one of Preston Sturges' mid-American film comedies. Fosse left the show during its disastrous tryout, but it's too easy to call it a bad match of the sensualist Fosse and homespun material. On the contrary, Fosse apparently saw the show as an ironic study of American heroism, and was particularly intrigued by the chance to lay out a battlefield ballet. Rather, *The Conquering Hero* was poorly written and the cast the one thing a musical-comedy troupe cannot be: nondescript.

Birdie, on the other hand, is filled with lovable rogues, as Rivera and her vis-à-vis, Dick Van Dyke, coped with the publicity attendant upon an Elvis Presley-like draftee—Van Dyke's protégé—entering the army. On one hand there was Van Dyke's mother, Kay Medford as a Lady Macbeth of the Bronx, relentlessly chopping away at Rivera. "This is Rose?" she cries. "I can't believe it. She looks like Margo when they took her out of Shangri-la." On the other hand was Paul Lynde, as a Sweet Apple "at my age I hate everything" father. "I didn't know what puberty was," he spits out in his signature tone of sarcastic rue, "till I was almost past it." It was Champion material to the nth: winsome, spirited, funny. *Innocent*. Its most memorable scene was "The Telephone Hour," a stack of colorful cubicles in which teenagers dissected their set's latest headline: another couple Going Steady.

We last saw Charles Strouse and Lee Adams working out the intricacies of racial identity in *Golden Boy's* impassioned score, but *Bye Bye Birdie* was the show that introduced them, and while the later show is not only a musical play but a tragic one, *Birdie* is the essence of merry insanity expertly crafted. *Birdie's* first-act ensemble "Normal American Boy" is at once a plot number (as the teen idol greets the press before entraining to Ohio for a televised farewell kiss), a character number (Van Dyke is confused while Rivera has the brains of the outfit, and the idol himself, an inarticulate redneck, doesn't utter a word, for PR safety's sake), a satire (on how celebrity is manufactured with fake backstories and staged adoration), a clever helping of suspense (the idol's silence intrigues us: why isn't this king of the jukebox at least singing?), and very, very funny. It is as well fast-moving, to satisfy Gower Champion's stopwatch pacing, which doesn't merely move the story along. It moves the entire show along, pausing here and there for the ballads ("One Boy," "Baby, Talk To Me"), but above all playing tag with the zippy numbers, especially "Kids," Lynde's scathing rejection of the younger generation, a song that naturally rejects rock and roll for *his* music. The charleston.

Of course, the idol did eventually sing. The actor cast in the role, Dick Gautier—perhaps the first of the Elvis impersonators—not only looked but sounded authentic. His Presley-ready performance pieces, "Honestly Sincere" and "One Last Kiss," were the first of their kind to invade the musical. Then, after *Golden Boy*, Strouse and Adams' *It's a Bird It's a Plane It's Superman* (1966) further tasted of the latest pop styles, not just in some of what Strouse composed but in the orchestrations of Eddie Sauter. Snarly brass "flutters" and a xylophone running amok in the overture seemed to herald the show's battle of good versus evil—and Superman really flew! Bob Holiday, already known to the producer-director, Hal Prince, from *Fiorello!*, should have been a shoo-in: a handsome hunk standing six feet four with a valid baritone. But for some reason Prince insisted on auditioning half of Broadway before casting Holiday. Though the show failed, it was nobody's fault, for the work trod that vast yet tiny line between spoof and camp, balancing the sturdy Holiday with the flamboyant Jack Cassidy as a Walter Winchellesque columnist in league with Michael O'Sullivan's mad scientist: dramatic conflict as a pie fight. Years later, an interviewer asked Holiday how he managed his dual-personalities of Clark Kent and *Übermensch*. Was there nuance in the portrayal?

And Holiday replied, "One was Jewish."

Eddie Sauter's contribution emphasized the craft with which *Superman* tackled an apparently artless subject. Consider the show's best number, the bossa nova "You've Got Possibilities." Sung by Linda Lavin (as Cassidy's secretary) to Clark Kent, the number reminds us of Jerome Robbins' eternal question whenever he heard collaborators play him a new song—"But what is she doing?" In other words: "How do I stage it?" What Lavin is doing is fiddling with Clark's tie and undoing his shirt buttons, thus imperiling his secret identity as the famous red, blue, and yellow suit starts to appear. Sauter rose to the occasion with a captivating scoring, giving each A of the number to a different combination: first, clarinets and a thumping string bass, then sustained lower strings (the pit had no violins), then drums. And

Lavin made a banquet of the vocal, building very gradually from a baby voice to a nobody-gets-out-of-here-alive belt, goofing with the words and even—just once—spinning one with vibrato.

While Broadway was, in a gingerly way, tasting the new sounds of non-theatrical pop, the off-Broadway musical proved conservative, concentrating on "intimate" revues with a kind of thirties swank, new works with old-fashioned music, and revivals. Cole Porter, the Gershwins, and Rodgers and Hart were favored; and Hugh Martin and Ralph Blane's *Best Foot Forward* (1941), in 1963, gave Liza Minnelli her first break and a new number by the original authors, "You Are For Loving."*

Off-Broadway's musical wing was launched by a revival, in fact—the long-running Theatre De Lys staging of *The Threepenny Opera* with, almost thirty years after the Berlin premiere, the original Jenny, Lotte Lenya. Those old-fashioned new works I just cited were often musicalizations of ancient plays, from Molière through Restoration Comedy to Oscar Wilde, and the campy events included Rick Besoyan's operetta spoof *Little Mary Sunshine* (1959) and a realization for the stage of the Warner Bros. Depression backstager as *Dames at Sea* (1968), complete with Ruby, Dick, and Joan. An all-pastiche score cleverly revived the Harry Warren–Al Dubin song forms with impudent replicas: the list song ("It's You"), the "Man I Love" solo ("That Mister Man of Mine"), the "this would be a production number if Busby Berkeley were in charge" torcher ("Raining in My Heart"), and even goofs on "Shanghai Lil" (as "Singapore Sue") and "Shuffle Off To Buffalo" ("Choo-Choo Honeymoon").

As for the off-Broadway revue, here was where the variety show that was more or less founded in the *Ziegfeld Follies* ended its career, for the audience—even for the smarter, streamlined revue format developed in the 1930s—had simply vanished. And yet producers were tempted, because with Broadway costs running at $400,000, one could put on a little something on off-Broadway for $30,000, and even less for the bare-stage revue.

---

* The song was published as the joint effort of Martin and Blane, like the rest of the *Best Foot Forward* score. However, late in life Martin revealed that he and Blane did not collaborate but wrote their songs separately. One can pick out the Martin sound, especially in the numbers with a swinging punch to them (like "Three Men on a Date" or "The Three B's") or those with wild choral improvs built in (like "Wish I May"), for Martin was famous for his vocal arrangements, from the jiving girl-group trio of "Sing For Your Supper" in Rodgers and Hart's *The Boys From Syracuse* to the big choral note- and wordplay that became all but de rigueur in the late 1940s and early 1950s. In any case, Martin and Blane broke up their partnership after MGM's *Meet Me in St. Louis* (which Martin says he wrote entirely by himself). So "You Are For Loving" is "contractually" by Martin and Blane but probably Martin's alone.

Jerry Herman's *Parade* (1960) was typical, with a cast of two comics (Dody Goodman, Charles Nelson Reilly), two singers (Lester James, Fia Karin), and a dancer (Richard Tone). The singers handled the melody (including a bemusing anticipation of *Hello, Dolly!*'s "Ribbons Down My Back" in "Your Good Morning") while the comics kidded the Rockefellers, the demolition of the Women's House of Detention, Maria Callas playing the Palace (Mimì gets hit with a custard pie), and the many deaths in recent Broadway shows, from *The Andersonville Trial* to *J.B.* and *Rashoman*. Note the emphasis on local subject matter. From its inception in the 1910s, the Golden Age American musical was essentially a validation of the style and content of New York.

There are of course countless exceptions to this, perhaps none more so than the most famous of off-Broadway musicals, Harvey Schmidt and Tom Jones' fable-esque *The Fantasticks* (1960). Even on Broadway, in *110 in the Shade* (1963), *I Do! I Do!*, or the mythopoetic *Celebration* (1969), Schmidt and Jones treated rural or placeless scenarios. Indeed, *110 in the Shade* recalls the folksy side of R & H as well as their creation of unique lead roles for singing actors. The two Boys of the show, the exhibitionistic rainmaker Starbuck (Robert Horton) and the repressed Sheriff File (Stephen Douglass), are not all that unusual; for all his flamboyance, Starbuck is something of a cowboy Harold Hill. But the Girl, Lizzie, gave Inga Swenson a major opportunity— which she seized—as the woman too smart for her time and her town and the men in it. In the R & H manner, Schmidt and Jones gave her a titanic soliloquy, "Old Maid," to bring down the first-act curtain.

But then, the dramatic-challenge part is one of the identifying qualities of the post-*Oklahoma!* musical, and it seemed to summon into being the emergence of high-powered actors who would have been wasted trying to build careers in the 1920s and 1930s. Imagine, say, Alfred Drake in *Good News!*, Barbara Cook in *Leave It To Me!* This new kind of musical star might take a showy role or blend into an ensemble, as Cook did in Bock and Harnick's *She Loves Me* (1963), albeit as the show's pivotal character. By contrast, Mitch Leigh and Joe Darion's *Man of La Mancha* (1965) was built around two stand-out turns, Richard Kiley's Cervantes/Quixote and Joan Diener's Aldonza—and here, too, are exceptions to the New York flavor of the musical (though Irving Jacobson's Jewish-inflected Sancho Panza was almost an homage to Weber and Fields). Both shows are European in subject, if very different in tone, *She Loves Me* a luscious candybox of First and Second Couple courtship rites and *La Mancha* dedicated to the sublime madness of the individual defying the Fascist state. Their design plans separated them, too, for William and Jean Eckart placed *She Loves Me* on a revolve that "opened up" the central playing area, the boutique in which the lead characters work. *La Mancha*, performed in Howard Bay's unit set, had a comparable design effect, a forbidding one: a stairway-drawbridge that was the Inquisition's victims' only communication with the world outside their prison.

Musicals were now taking on visual plans that differed radically from the fifties format of backdrops with front pieces on wagons. Thus, Sherman Edwards' *1776* (1969) took place almost entirely in another unit set, this one so unobtrusive that *its* special design feature was a little calendar upstage whose pages turned, inexorably yet suspensefully, toward the first date every American school kid learns. At length came the settling of the Continental Congress' contentions, the arrival of "July 4" on the calendar, the tolling of the Liberty Bell as the delegates rose to sign the Declaration of Independence, the freezing of the action in a replica of the famous John Trumbull painting . . . and then, most thrillingly, a scrim came down, hiding the stage behind the bottom half of the document with its signatures. And the curtain fell.

In this age of director-choreographers, there were bound to be superproductions to validate the High Maestro's eminence, and two stand out, *Hello, Dolly!* and *Fiddler on the Roof.* They have much in common—both appeared in 1964; both were written, not only staged, by major practitioners; both featured an admired star performance; both enjoyed a huge run, a large-scale Hollywood adaptation, and constant revivals in recreations of the original production. However, the pair represent two very different strains of showmaking: *Dolly!* is a song-and-dance show, *Fiddler* a musical play. To put it another way, *Dolly!* supposes a charmed existence in a life without villains: a fantasy. *Fiddler* recalls a way of life plagued by poverty and pogroms. The worst person in *Dolly!* is not much more than a spoilsport, and by the show's end even he comes around. By *Fiddler*'s end, its way of life is all but over.

Dolly!'s director-choreographer, Gower Champion, had begun to fashion shows with a distinctive look, as with *I Do! I Do!*'s bare-stage-*cum*-props or *The Happy Time*'s photographic projections. Bob Merrill's *Carnival!* (1961), Champion's follow-up to *Bye Bye Birdie*, was notable for its unit set of an empty field in which the carnival itself—little more than a few wagons and some streamers—was set up by the cast during the First Number, "Direct From Vienna." Further, the audience was treated at times as a real-life carnival audience, with balloon and candy sellers in the aisles and a volunteer drawn up onstage for a magic trick. Then, for *Dolly!*, Champion's set designer, Oliver Smith, hung a series of period lithographs as backdrops to free-standing pieces that could appear to be moved into place by the actors, all this fronted by a crescent runway to highlight

Dolly's little chats with her late husband. The costumes, by Freddy Wittop, raved in blazing color against the black-and-white lithos, and "Put on Your Sunday Clothes" featured a train, with almost the entire cast filling the theatre with traditional musical-comedy rhapsody at the prospect of a visit to New York.

This is the ethos of The Adventure in an Exotic Place, as old as the American musical itself. *The Black Crook* is an adventure, as are *Babes in Toyland* and *The Wizard of Oz*, *Watch Your Step* and *The Gingham Girl* (in both of which the exotic place is Manhattan), *The Stepping Stones* and *Peggy-Ann*, *Leave It To Me!* and *One Touch of Venus*, even *The Book of Mormon*. And of course the *Dolly!* adventure takes in a troupe of screwballs, though the so to say tour guide (Carol Channing) is less an eccentric than a businesswoman with an eccentric facade. What she really is is a performance artist living by verbal sleight of hand, as here when trying to discourage the spoilsport, Horace Vandergelder (David Burns)—"the well-known half-a-millionaire"— from his intended bride. Dolly recommends instead a certain Ernestina Money:

> DOLLY: Age, nineteen; weight, one hundred and two; waist, forty-
>   seven . . .
> VANDERGELDER: Forty-seven?
> DOLLY: That's with the money belt.

As for Vandergelder's original choice:

> DOLLY: I for one never believed the rumors. . . . It's just that he went
>   so sudden, that's all. A few spoons of chowder she made special for
>   him, and poof! . . . Just one word of advice, Mr. Vandergelder.
>   Eeeeeeat. Oooooout.

Michael Stewart's libretto is filled with such moments, a joke book always leading on to more music. And Jerry Herman's score was ideal for Champion's zippy storytelling, for each song seizes the narrative very precisely. It isn't so much in the lyrics as in the way the music cuts into the action, as when "Put on Your Sunday Clothes" starts with a love-starved male (Charles Nelson Reilly) crying, to the punctuation of brass chords, "Out there!": for this is the place he has suddenly realized he needs to get to to find fulfillment. As the verse builds in intensity, it impulsively breaks off on a joyful vamp leading to the chorus, and we have been, in effect, thrilled into having the adventure along with him. Comparably, when we meet his vis-à-vis (Eileen Brennan), her establishing song skips the verse to zoom in on a kind of close-up, and to a harp with woods and strings she sings, "I'll be wearing ribbons down my back this summer"—and in that instant the show reminds us that musical comedy is about cute youngsters having fun while the star clown watches over, and we realize that she's the Girl and "Out there!," however awkward and unromantic he may be, is the Boy.

Fiddler's book, by Joseph Stein, the opposite of *Dolly!'s*, something of a spoken drama that, every so often, pauses for lyrical expansion, by Bock and Harnick. Hearing the *Dolly!* cast album, one wants to get up and dance; hearing *Fiddler*, one wants to meet the characters. Jerome Robbins choreographed two of the greatest dance musicals of all time in *On the Town* and *West Side Story*. But on *Fiddler* he was less a choreographer than a director—though, when the action broke into dance, it captured to the very nth that way of life in what we have to call genius moments. Consider the sudden switch from reality into fantasy in "The Tailor, Motel Kamzoil" (also called "Tevye's Dream"), when musicians casually rose up from behind the headboard of Tevye's bed as his nightmare took shape; or, in the ensuing wedding, when four men danced balancing bottles on their heads, the coordination, at one point, of a leggy step with a surge of music creating a hair-raising grandeur.

Like Channing's Dolly, Zero Mostel's Tevye was a bigger-than-life guide to the action, though the *Fiddler* company, unlike *Dolly!'s*, formed an indissoluble ensemble, befitting the community of Anatevka. Bock and Harnick troubled to open the show with a number, that, by synecdoche, pictured the folk spirit that holds the village together, "We've Never Missed a Sabbath Yet," as Tevye's wife (Maria Karnilova) and their five daughters prepared the week's one full-scale dinner before the setting sun forbade further labor.

But Robbins wasn't satisfied. In a Dramatists Guild panel on the show, Bock and Harnick recalled that Robbins kept prodding everybody to tell him what *Fiddler* was about, as *On the Town* is about the quest for beauty and *West Side Story* about the futility of clannishness. Finally, someone said *Fiddler* was about "the dissolution of a way of life." And Robbins then demanded a new First Number, showing "the traditions that are going to change." Said Robbins, this new song will serve as "a tapestry against which the entire show will play." One musical theme of the "Sabbath" number, at the line "Somehow the house will be clean," was developed into *Fiddler's* hit tune, "Matchmaker, Matchmaker," and another strain, at "There's noodles to make and chicken to be plucked," became one of the four melodies of the new opening, "Tradition."

Each of these four introduces a segment of Anatevka—the fathers, the mothers, the sons, the daughters—for this is a segmented society, the genders somewhat segregated: scandal rocks a wedding when men and women start to dance together, for Tradition says no. At *Hello, Dolly!*'s final curtain, everything is rounded out, even the hierarchy of the performers, as Champion staged a curtain call to build musically to Carol Channing's appearance in dazzling white after spending the evening in a riot of colors. But *Fiddler's* final curtain, following the forced dispersal of Anatevka's population, raised a question: what happens to tradition when the culture that nourished it is destroyed?

Hello, Dolly! ran seven years and *Fiddler* eight, surpassing *My Fair Lady* (though *Grease* [1972] then surpassed all three, and other musicals have since surpassed them). Still, the outstanding sixties super-production was *Cabaret* (1966), though it was the work of a director (Hal Prince) and a choreographer (Ron Field) rather than a single staging Maestro. *Dolly!* came from Thornton Wilder's *The Matchmaker* and *Fiddler* from Sholem Aleichem's stories. *Cabaret*, too, was an adaptation, though Christopher Isherwood's two books about Weimar Berlin and John Van Druten's play version, *I Am a Camera*, give no hint of *Cabaret's* power.

The new show wasn't simply a musical expansion of the material, but a metatheatrical transformation. Isherwood and Van Druten told of the social loop coalescing around the English nightclub singer Sally Bowles: nineteen, talentless, oddly nice-looking, impulsive, unreliable, amoral, and utterly enchanting. "I always told you I was a bit mad, didn't I?" she remarks to narrator Isherwood near the end of her section of *Goodbye To Berlin*. There's nothing mad about Van Druten's orderly single-set, seven-character play—but the musical is quite mad, for now we see Sally's workplace, the Kit Kat Klub, in its uproar of edgy buffoonery. Isherwood and Van Druten dealt to an extent with the rise of the Nazis, but only *Cabaret* confronts at once the barbarians and the onlookers who, through inaction, allow them to take power.

Greeting the public with an open stage dominated by a huge mirror, *Cabaret* turned the Broadway audience into the audience at the Kit Kat Klub in Weimar Germany, thus to treat the spectator to two shows simultaneously. One is the Sally Bowles story, and the other is a brace of cabaret numbers commenting on the story, as if explaining the basics of the social contract, from sexuality (in "Two Ladies") to racial tolerance (in "If You Could See Her Through My Eyes"). The cabaret-as-metaphor plan interlocks with the action through a logic so sensible—yet so bizarre—that the two shows merge, making it impossible to tell where *Cabaret* ends and the cabaret begins.

So *Cabaret* reached back to *Allegro* and *Love Life* to formulate the matrix for the modern Concept Musical. The term has come to mean many things.

When new, in the 1960s and 1970s, however, it usually denoted this sort of non-realistic show that depended as much on how it was presented as on the development of its story and characters. *Allegro* was a Concept Musical because it was a parable more than a narrative, because its "Greek" chorus mediated between the actors and the public, and because its cast could appear in scenes when they were meant to be emotionally but not physically present, as when, at the heart of the protagonist's despair at the false path he has chosen, his late mother appeared with his hometown folk, many miles away but in the audience's field of vision, to sing "Come Home" to him. And *Love Life* was a Concept Musical because it programmed a slate of commentary numbers between the story scenes, and because its two leading characters never aged as they lived through one hundred fifty years of American history.

Oddly, *Cabaret's* tight coordination of contents and staging style evolved more or less accidentally. In another of those Dramatists Guild panels, *Cabaret's* authors, Joe Masteroff, John Kander, and Fred Ebb, recalled that the show was originally to start with "a mélange of songs taking place all over Berlin." Ebb mentioned one about "Herman the German" and one "in a radio station." Kander remembered "a Chinese song." And one of the set was "Willkommen," the only one finally used, as the opening number. At some point, said Masteroff, "We decided to insert [these numbers] in between the book scenes," at first "in a rather random fashion," and then, somehow, with purpose.

In *Love Life*, the commentative numbers were all delivered by chorus members. *Cabaret*, however, assigned them to the Emcee, his cabaret ensemble—and Sally Bowles, bridging the gap between *Cabaret* the metaphor and *Cabaret* the story. As the show proceeds, the two *Cabaret*s start to merge, and, finally, when Sally sings the title song, it is impossible to tell whether it is her character number celebrating reckless hedonism or *the show*'s ironic jeremiad *against* reckless hedonism. In 1966, the number began onstage in the cabaret, but during the trio section ("I used to have a girl friend known as Elsie . . ."), as the song's message began to resonate—to Sally or to us?—she moved downstage. As she was about to take up the refrain again, a curtain of streamers dropped to the floor behind her, cutting her off from the cabaret and its layers of meaning, leaving the playing area naked but for this one performer and her symbolic statement: "Life is a cabaret."

Sally is *Cabaret*'s central role, though some rate the Emcee as more crucial, as he clearly is managing the action, at that in a showy turn. Joel Grey won acclaim in it, but everyone does. Sally is harder to pull off, and a lack of appreciation for Jill Haworth's in fact very fetching Sally in 1966 warns us that only when the role is turned inside out to appear as baroque as the Emcee (as it was in Bob Fosse's movie version, for Liza Minnelli) do Sallys disarm criticism. At least *Cabaret* did bring Lotte Lenya back to Broadway (after twenty-one years), as the hero's landlady, opposite Jack Gilford as a Jewish grocer who is utterly blind to the Nazi menace. *Cabaret*'s hero, an Americanized Isherwood named Clifford Bradshaw (Bert Convy), is almost as problematical as Sally, for he is the narrator and *Cabaret* is his adventure—yet he mustn't overpower this morality tale. Because it's not his story. It's ours.

CHAPTER 15

✑

The Sondheim Handbook

This one's easy. Rule One: Write about disillusioned or conflicted characters, preferably middle-aged and, if possible, having suffered a long prison stay for a crime they didn't commit, which will turn them into deranged serial killers. Rule Two: Marry smart lyrics to tuneless music, and if Jerry Herman complains, tell him, "My art's longer than your art." Rule Three: Hide your lack of joy in life behind those deceptive Concept Productions filled with narrators, ghosts, and Bernadette Peters. Rule Four: End your shows without an ending, frustrating those in the audience who haven't already walked out. Does Boy get Girl? Don't let them know. If Sondheim had written *Oklahoma!*, the farmer and the cowman would still be fighting.

Of course, that isn't the Sondheim Handbook. Rather, that's how some section of the public viewed his shows *at first*, when, in collaboration with Hal Prince, Sondheim unveiled five masterpieces in a row, the only body of work to rival the Big Five of early Rodgers and Hammerstein: *Company* (1970), *Follies* (1971), *A Little Night Music* (1973), *Pacific Overtures* (1976), and *Sweeney Todd, the Demon Barber of Fleet Street* (1979). Indeed, many Sondheim characters are disillusioned or conflicted. That's the stuff of drama. In a much later Sondheim show, *Passion*, the married Clara tells her adulterous lover, "I often wondered how much you would love me if I were free." Some may wonder if Sondheim would love the musical if it were still fancy-free musical comedy. Does he *like* complicated situations? Yes. So did Sophocles, Shakespeare, Ibsen, O'Neill, Williams, Miller, Albee. As for the impression that his lyrics outshone his music, this was soon enough unmasked as the quack opinion of those who can't hear music beyond the compositional level of "Tea for Two." Not everyone has an ear for music.

(There is as well the distracting brilliance of the lyrics, for in Sondheim's shows the continuity doesn't pause for the songs but proceeds through them, forcing one to concentrate on the words just to learn what is happening, thus missing, at first hearing, the melody.) Further, those Concept Productions do not hide anything; on the contrary, the freedom of the form allows them to break past the confines of realism to show more than realistic musicals are able to. And about those Sondheim endings: a few are ambiguous—*Company*, for example. But most are conclusive. The welling up in the orchestra of "Send in the Clowns" as *Night Music's* First Couple embraces, united at last, is not only a thoroughly happy ending but one of the most romantic moments the musical has ever known.

Still, Sondheim shows are very intensely about choices, just as the R & H shows are—another reason their musical play was a breakaway in its time. Looking back on the more adult musicals before *Oklahoma!*, we don't find a great many characters living in a state of discerning freedom. *Show Boat's* folk seem to roll along just like Ol' Man River. The people of Catfish Row are too oppressed to create their existence; only Sporting Life floats freely in his self-made habitat of pushing and pimping. *Pal Joey* presented a new realism in characterization, yet its characters let social class do their choosing for them. *Lady in the Dark's* heroine's problem is that she *fears* choice: the Circus Dream puts her on trial because she "cannot make up her mind."

But *Oklahoma!*'s Big Ballet, remember, is "Laurey Makes Up Her Mind," and R & H is stuffed with characters who try to shape their own destiny— Nellie's struggle with her intolerant background; Anna and the King's contest of wills; Maria's abandoning the cloister to be wife and mother. *Allegro* offers the most startling choice, as a man who has let others make his decisions for him suddenly rejects his successful, glamorous but wasteful life for a wholly different existence: simple and even self-sacrificing but important to *him*. And of course Oscar Hammerstein was Sondheim's mentor, and *Allegro*, the first Concept Musical, directly informed the presentational aspect of the Sondheim shows—for example, in the Liebeslieder Singers who slip into and out of *A Little Night Music* somewhat as the Greek Chorus did in *Allegro*, or in the Kabuki stylistics of *Pacific Overtures*, a work in which an entire nation faces the choice between modernization or conservatism. The English producer Cameron Macintosh once told Sondheim, "Steve, you've spent your entire life trying to fix the second act of *Allegro*."

And just as *Allegro* divided the public between enthusiasm and disappointment, the Sondheim shows of the 1970s divided audiences, now between the enthralled and the irritated. These reactions could only have been intensified by the Prince stagings, with their distinctive look that—to detractors—appeared arrogant and perverse, as if not merely exploring their individuality but vaunting it. Yet this was what made them so theatrical—intelligent and full of content, yes, but more: spectacular experiences in what design, choreography, and overall direction could do now.

Take *Company*: a look at a bachelor named Robert (Dean Jones) and his social loop of married couples. Beyond that, it was an insight into the folkways of upscale Manhattan, from dieting and going sober to sleeping around and divorce. So Prince cast not musical-comedy people and not even theatre people but *people* people. The actors of the ensemble actually looked (and danced, and even, for the most part, sang) like upscale Manhattanites, and the unit set, designed (like all Sondheim-Prince through *Sweeney Todd*) by Boris Aronson, looked like upscale Manhattan. When one character likened Robert to "the Seagram building" (presumably because it looks so open on the outside yet is in fact impenetrable without Superman's x-ray vision), he was uniting the smartiboots tone of George Furth's book, the relentless observing viewpoint of Sondheim's score, and the behavior of these newfangled musicals with their gnomic remarks, cutting observations, and wondering ambivalence. Thinking back to Richard Rodgers' defining integration in the way *Oklahoma!*'s set matched its orchestrations, we can say that it was *Company* that truly integrated the musical for the first time.*

Another invention we owe to Sondheim-Prince is the necessary redefinition of the terms "hit" and "flop." They were already becoming unstable in the 1960s, when production capitalization costs began to rise so incessantly that shows with good reviews and word-of-mouth, an appreciated score with a hit tune or two, and a full year's run actually lost money. In the case of Sondheim-Prince, we speak of works that eventually joined the core repertory along with *Show Boat*, *My Fair Lady*, and so on. Yet some of them were only somewhat profitable or didn't—at least at first—pay off.

---

*On *Company*'s national tour, the role of David—the guy who makes the crack about the Seagram building—was played by George Wallace, who fielded a strong baritone. Dropping in on the show, Prince gave Wallace a note: "George, you're singing too well." In other words, he didn't sound natural any more. He sounded like someone in a musical. On the other hand, all musicals need, in some role or other, the burnishing of genuine vocal tone. The New York production had Elaine Stritch, who gave the ensemble a kind of live "guide vocal" and, at last, enjoyed a solo, "The Ladies Who Lunch." A combination blueprint and epitaph for a fabled New York type, it is that rarity, a piece utterly unlike anything else ever written. When a writer asked Sondheim if, completing the composition, he realized that it was a great song bound to become a standard—not to mention expert sociology—Sondheim replied, "No, I just thought it was a good number for Elaine."

Follies is an ideal example, because no work is more admired, more analyzed. Its leading women, Sally and Phyllis, have started to rival *Gypsy*'s Rose as jobs to thrill the diva, and few shows give the director more scope. Indeed, *Follies*' problem is not its failure to generate vast profits. Rather, the "fault" lies in James Goldman's book, a nuanced stream-of-consciousness fantasia of themes so tightly expounded that it is almost a non-book, confusing spectators used to linear narratives and conventional dialogue. Worse, revivals reduce the original or amend it, making mysteries or overstatements of what was, in 1971, brilliantly underwritten.

There is another problem as well: the failure of all later stagings to match the kaleidoscopic vivacity of the 1971 original, co-directed by Prince and Michael Bennett. The physical setting is a show-biz reunion party in a theatre literally on the eve of its demolition, but the metaphorical setting is Golden Age musical comedy, once so central in American life and now on the eve of its own demolition. The leads are two couples on the edge of forty, but the leads are also the same four a generation ago. Sally (Dorothy Collins, Marti Rolph) wanted Ben (John McMartin, Kurt Peterson), who married Phyllis (Alexis Smith, Virginia Sandifur), so Sally married Buddy (Gene Nelson, Harvey Evans). But Sally still wants Ben, and she has come to the party to collect him.* The score is half pastiche, of Golden Age song genres, and half new-minted character numbers; the last quarter of the score is character numbers in pastiche style. As if that were not enough, the party is haunted: the present by the past, the age of Sondheim by the age of Jerome Kern and Cole Porter, the central quartet by the realization that they all experienced absolute free will yet are miserable, and the Prince-Bennett staging by spooks, moving and parading and stalking through the action. And all of the above can be difficult to assimilate and organize. A Kennedy Center *Follies* in 2011 did relatively little with the ghosts, starting with a view of spectral showgirls swishing along a catwalk. The 1971 *Follies* opened with disparate groupings of a miscellany of show-biz ghosts running through their old numbers, all out of synch with one another, a deliberately jarring asymmetry of incongruent agendas. Which of course gave us a first taste of what *Follies* is about: loss of purpose.

---

*Even while pretending to eulogize her hateful life with Buddy, in the number "In Buddy's Eyes," Sally sings a key line: "Nothing dies." That includes her love for Ben, her belief that only *his* love makes her wonderful. Yet she has never understood that she was too unsophisticated for the honcho-kingdom life Ben intended to lead. The first rule of the Higher Hetero Leadership Class is: A man with an inappropriate wife is an inappropriate man.

One arresting moment of that Kennedy Center *Follies* came at the very end, when the present-day leads departed the now-empty theatre. (In 1971, at this point, a section of the building's rear wall was gone, as if the wrecking crane was already at work.) At the last moment, one of the showgirl ghosts left along with them, slamming the door behind her: because Ben and Sally are still haunted by—as one *Follies* number puts it, "The Road You Didn't Take." Would they have been happy if they had married each other, instead of Phyllis and Buddy? They'll never stop being spooked by the thought: so the ghost came, too.

Yet *Follies* is obviously more than the story of four people. It's the story of what happened to American art: it got serious. Folks reach a certain age and don't like anything new. "They're not writing them the way they used to," they complain. *Follies* tells why: they were writing them sappy and unrealistic. *Anything Goes* is great fun, but *Carousel* is enlightening, a much more useful quality. Musical comedy becomes "the musical," because the prestigious shows aren't silly any more.

Paradoxically, *Follies*' old-style numbers are not at all the empty vessels of melody and ditz that their predecessors were, for in the show's context they actually help narrate. Thus, "Broadway Baby" places the ambitions of show folk for whom professional success is a personal matter, something they take pride in, reminding us that Sally and Phyllis regard show biz as nothing more than a pay-the-rent. Later, "One More Kiss (before we part)," the waltz of an apparently vapid ex-operetta star, warns us by its placement very late in the continuity that Sally's dream is about to explode. As of old, she and Ben will separate, as if they were the waitress and the royal in *The Student Prince*.

One thing that sets the Sondheim-Prince shows apart from R & H is the variety of Sondheim's music. *Company*'s score builds a steel-bright facade hiding an approach-avoidance mentality—just as its characters do. *Follies*, when not singing the songs they're not writing any more, is more lyrical in spots, and even its hard-edged numbers aren't as slashingly contemporary in sound as those in *Company*. Phyllis' "Could I Leave You?" is acid, but dear old waltzy acid; *Company*'s "Another Hundred People (just got off of the train)" was 1970's newest tune, as bright and hard as a coin out of the mint.

And then came *A Little Night Music*. Noël Coward wrote the operetta *Bitter Sweet* (1929) because he feared the (English) musical had lost its sense of romance—the military march, the gypsy strain, the nostalgic number, and above all the waltz. It's as if Sondheim thought the same thing after *Follies*, for *Night Music*, from Ingmar Bergman's *Smiles of a Summer Night*, revived not the sound but the spirit of operetta. There's so much singing that even the overture is vocal, and while the hit tune, "Send in the

Clowns," was written for the essentially non-singing Glynis Johns, it was quickly taken up by, among others, the opera soprano Renata Scotto. She actually brought the published sheet music, with its people-in-a-tree blue logo cover, out onstage at a song recital, in the encore segment.

A Little Night Music is famously the "waltz" musical, and much of the score uses the three-quarter enchantment melody that used to be called "sweeping," in the "Night Waltz" and "You Must Meet My Wife," though another waltz, "Remember?," is nervous and uncertain. Further, much of the rest of the score adopts other dance rhythms. The solo of the grand old lady (Hermione Gingold) who surveys the vacillating lovers of the Berg-manesque night with disdain and epigrams, "Liaisons," is a sarabande, and Johns' establishing number, "The Glamorous Life" (whose refrain, amus-ingly, allows not a single rhyme) is marked "Tempo di Mazurca." Perhaps *Night Music* is less a waltz score than simply one of the most lyrical pieces of music ever written for Broadway. Certainly, it marked a turn in Sondheim's fortunes, because theatregoers who had had trouble absorbing his melody— elusively various as it is—were now acclimatized to and rhapsodic about it.

But they balked at *Pacific Overtures*, because here the Concept Musical was raised to the highest power, fusing the composition and its presenta-tion so brilliantly that average theatregoers found the show difficult to digest. The subject was history—the forced opening of Japan to Western trade in the mid-nineteenth century. Thus, the libretto would have a great deal of political developments to cover, whereas *Company* covered only marriage, *Follies* show biz, and *A Little Night Music* romance.

Further, the decision to reenact these events in Kabuki style tilted the work toward a certain oblique and epigrammatic approach, as if *Pacific Overtures* were a gigantic haiku. Once again, we refer to Richard Rodgers' theory about sets and orchestrations matching, for Boris Aronson's de-signs and Jonathan Tunick's scoring blended precisely with John Weidman and Hugh Wheeler's book and the Sondheim songs—restrained and styl-ized, yet sharply etched. To this day, *Pacific Overtures* is the most "unlike" musical ever seen, though it retains Sondheim's interest in the so to say crossroads of decision making. Here it is not the protagonist who is faced with a choice, but, as I've said already, an entire nation: is Japan to resist Westernization or, to quote one of its lyrics, to "accommodate the times as one lives them"?

Personalizing this, the action centered on two figures, a Samurai (Isao Sato) and a nobody named Manjiro (Sab Shimono). Close friends through their shared management of the trauma created by American gunboat di-plomacy, they make opposing choices. The samurai becomes cosmopolitan while Manjiro turns nativist, joining the war against foreign influence.

"A Bowler Hat," a highly original number in this most original of shows, is their character duet, though only the samurai sings. His estranged friend mimes, in a demonstration of the traditional tea ceremony. As the music moves along, Kabuki practice manages the action: a narrator records the events of Japan's Westernization while stagehands, "unseen" in black, scurry about, tending to the props and even applying aging lines to the two men's faces. The tea ceremony, at stage left, was almost immobile in its contemplation of the power of the Old Ways; at stage right, the samurai's low table and kneeling mat yielded to a desk and swivel chair. A French painting appeared behind him. His lyrics—again, in spare, isolated phrases—related historical developments as his own personal program, uniting his life with Japan's just as the entire show united the writing of theatre with its presentation.

It was too artisanal for some to collect at a single viewing. The fans can be fickle; take away the ghosts and Elaine Stritch and they grow resentful. Some shows are too disturbing for their own good: Sondheim's *Assassins* (1991), inquiring into the motives of president killers. Some are too depressing: Marc Blitzstein's *Juno* (1959), from Sean O'Casey at his most tragic. *Pacific Overtures* was too smart for its good: it outstripped the public's comprehension.

My allusion to Renata Scotto was not fortuitous, because, more and more, Sondheim has been edging into the espressivo of opera—and *Sweeney Todd* is one, even if its original cast of Len Cariou, Angela Lansbury, Victor Garber, and Sarah Rice scarcely fielded a genuine instrument among them. That they were all the same very effective reminds us of Kurt Weill's achievement, in *Street Scene*, of bonding the theatrical and the musical in one artistic organism. And this of course is a reminder of how incessantly the musical has elaborated its musical grammar; long before the 1970s, the form had all the potential it needed to function as an American form of opera.

So of course someone had to throw a wrench into the action. In the 1960s, hall monitors among the intellectual class insisted that the musical needed to change its tune: to rock. The vast success of the Beatles *Sgt. Pepper's Lonely Hearts Club Band* and the "White Album" (whose actual title is *The Beatles*) promised that rock was capable of artistic expansion—though one had to wonder why intellectuals, who generally scorned the musical as corny, were passing laws about how it should sound.

In response we got *Hair* (1967; revised for Broadway 1968), the "American Tribal Love-Rock" show, and the "rock musical" was born. In fact, *Hair*'s score, composed by Galt MacDermot with lyrics by Gerome Ragni and James Rado, was more contemporary pop with rock infusions. Still, its

subject was hippie culture, especially in its mellow and anti-war formations. This made it a Zeitgeist Musical; and the music of the Zeitgeist was
rock. *Hair*'s phenomenal international popularity inspired American producers to seek out more Zeitgeist Musicals, in such aspects as rock science-
fiction (*Via Galactica*, 1972), rock *Hair* sequel (*Dude*, 1972), rock *Molière*
(*Tricks*, 1973), rock Shakespeare (*Rockabye Hamlet*, 1975), and rock Other
Famous Elizabethan Playwright (*Marlowe*, 1981). All were not just failures
but ghastly bombs, and it was the English who devised the first lasting
rock-musical recipe, in Andrew Lloyd Webber and Tim Rice's *Jesus Christ
Superstar* (recorded song cycle, 1969; New York, 1971), which introduced
the genre loosely termed "pop opera."

Broadway had already hosted pop operas, of course. But this newly
coined term denoted something racier than, say, *The Golden Apple*. No, pop
opera would be a mishmash of musical styles with contrarian social attitudes and, when needed, a touch of Concept Musical flexibility. Thus, in
Lloyd Webber and Rice's *Evita* (recorded song cycle, 1976; London, 1978;
New York, 1979), a character named simply Che wanders through the action passing remarks even though he is more a superego than a character.
Then, too, pop opera doted on not only larger-than-life characters but performers charismatic enough to play them. The star-making role in *Jesus
Christ Superstar*, ironically, is Judas, which gave Ben Vereen his punchout
job, and New York's Evita and Che were Patti LuPone and Mandy Patinkin,
two of the biggest talents of the age, she catching Eva Perón's giddy sense
of entitlement and he as scathing as Jeremiah. Hal Prince's staging found a
way to dramatize what had been written as a disjunct set of numbers, for
instance capturing the rivalry of army generals in a game of musical chairs,
or presenting the upper class as a frieze of pantywaists traveling across the
stage, noses in the air with almost imperceptible footwork. (Patinkin joined
them at one point, in Che's revolutionary fatigues, aping their pose with
lavish contempt.)

Pop operas continued to be huge hits: Lloyd Webber's *Cats* (1981; 1982)
and an English staging of Claude-Michel Schönberg's *Les Misérables* (1985;
1987) racked up a combined New York run of 14,165 performances. But the
jewel in the crown was—is, for it continues strong at this writing, after
some twenty-five years—Lloyd Webber's *The Phantom of the Opera* (1987;
1988). *Phantom* demonstrates the frailties and vigor of the form, for while
it is of one of the most engrossing and spectacular of entertainments, it
bears with its fellows the defects of the pop in opera. These include a tendency to doggerel lyrics, obsessed with monosyllabic end-rhymes and lacking in wordplay. There is also the incoherent mixing of musical styles, as
when some of *Phantom*'s "onstage" opera pastiche sounds authentic while

the soprano's debut solo, "Think of Me," which draws cheers from her "audience," does not remotely suggest music available to an opera company in *Phantom*'s time zone, 1881. Worse, the title song is a disco number.

Phantom's strengths, however, tell why it deserved to be a hit of hits—the unbelievable amount of Maria Björnson's scenery kept in rotation on stage, for example, from the pastiche opera *Hannibal*, complete with elephant (which is turned around to reveal two stagehands playing cards inside it) to the mirror transformed into a magic portal to the Phantom's grotto. A trompe l'oeil effect using doubles simulates the trip through the Opéra's catacombs until a gondola bearing the Phantom and his love glides past a "lake" of burning candles. Or a rehearsal room appears, where singers balk at their difficult Phantom-composed music till a bewitched piano sets them all off singing like robots in flawless atonality. The show's music, at its best, is enthralling, and the roles are elegantly turned, even the support—Judy Kaye won a Tony as the termagant diva Carlotta, not least for her high E, one half-step past *Candide*'s Cunegonde.

Indeed, when the critic Ken Mandelbaum first heard that Andrew Lloyd Webber would compose and Hal Prince direct an adaptation of Gustave Leroux's old novel, he predicted, "That show will run forever": because the combination of Lloyd Webber's big music and Prince's theatricality was bound to realize all the flamboyance and eerie beauty latent in the story. No doubt the lyrics would have been better if death had not taken Alan Jay Lerner off the project. But even with the less able wordsmiths who followed Tim Rice in this genre, *Phantom* provides an electrifying evening of music theatre. Too, for all its flaws, it largely avoids the unbridled screamo vocalism that has marred so many of these exhibits—and, worse, other kinds of musicals. Pop opera can even raise up a kind of quiet screamo with overladen pianissimo, as in Jean Valjean's tortured solo in *Les Misérables*, "Bring Him Home," whose first line addresses "God on high." Gerard Alessandrini's modern-day Weber and Fields, *Forbidden Broadway*, gave this number a gleeful sendup as "God, It's High (this song's too high)."

On the other hand, detractors have made too much of pop opera's visual gimmicks—*Cats'* tire rising to the Heaviside Layer or the helicopter of *Miss Saigon* (1989; 1991). *Phantom*, of course, has a chandelier, dragged off the stage and hiked to the top of the proscenium center and then daintily let fall at the end of Act One. It's a misfire. The tire was a hoot and the helicopter actually an impressive bit of stagecraft, but not till the 2004 *Phantom* movie did we see what happens when an opera-house chandelier plummets, as vast tyings burst, the audience panics, and it looks as if the very auditorium must fly apart.

Amid the influx of these new sounds, older songwriters went on cre-
ating utterly free of their influence—Richard Rodgers in *Two By Two* (1970),
Rex (1976), and *I Remember Mama* (1979), all star vehicles, respectively for
Danny Kaye as Noah, Nicol Williamson as Henry VIII, and Liv Ullmann.
Rex had some nice moments, but Rodgers was no longer working at par.
Leonard Bernstein, with Alan Jay Lerner, wrote marvelous music for an
incoherent book in *1600 Pennsylvania Avenue* (1976), in which Ken Howard
and Patricia Routledge enacted a century of presidents and first ladies, with
a showstopper for Routledge as Mrs. Rutherford B. Hayes *and* Mrs. Ulysses
S. Grant at the 1877 inauguration in "Duet For One." The outgoing Mrs. Grant
was catty and the incoming Mrs. Hayes was on top of the world as their
dueling solos recounted the history of the tangled presidential election of
1876, Routledge switching back and forth between the two by flipping her
bonnet and changing voice from yowl to La Scala. "Duet For One" was the
sort of number that no contemporary-pop musical with its pounding
beat, or pop opera with its goofy lyrics, could have duplicated, and it's why
authors continued to write in traditional style—Bock and Harnick in *The
Rothschilds* (1970), their last outing together; Cy Coleman with Comden
and Green at their most prankish in *On the Twentieth Century* (1978), a
faux-operetta art nouveau train fest. Charles Strouse and Lee Adams
worked some pop flavoring into *Applause* (1970), with Novelty Star Lauren
Bacall in Bette Davis' role in *All About Eve*; "One of a Kind" sang in the
restless riffing of modern jazz, and "Backstage Babble" recalled the breezy
Bach of the Swingles Singers.

Yet, later in the 1970s, working with Martin Charnin, Strouse composed one of the most conservative of scores for *Annie* (1977), almost a
parody of the old genres—not quite pastiche, in the *Follies* manner, but
redolent, let us say, of the old attitudes. There was an angry cakewalk for
the Depression homeless in "We'd Like To Thank You, Herbert Hoover," a
sort of Twentieth Century Fox Shirley Temple chorus for "I Think I'm
Gonna Like It Here," a blues for "Easy Street," and, at "Tempo di Ted Lewis,"
"You're Never Fully Dressed Without a Smile." That last title revealed the
backstage of a radio show complete with ventriloquist and dummy, a
"singing sisters" trio, "the only masked announcer on radio," and a sound-
effects man supplying the clacking of the host's tap breaks. This sequence
was then repeated by Annie's little friends back at the orphanage, with one
tyke imitating the typical upper mordent vocal decoration so popular in
the old days. Using two treadmills to bring scenery (and sometimes people)
on and off, with plenty of backdrops, the designer, David Mitchell, kept the
action fluid even as it raced from the orphanage to a Hooverville, a presidential cabinet meeting, and so on. Further, even while smoothing out the

unapologetically right-wing worldview of Harold Gray's *Little Orphan Annie* comic strip, Thomas Meehan's book offered a few zingers:

DADDY WARBUCKS: I was ruthless with those I had to climb over. . . .
 You don't have to be nice to the people you meet on the way up if
 you're not coming back down again.

Best of all, *Annie* had a superb comic villain in Dorothy Loudon, the monster mistress of the orphanage. "Did I hear happiness in here?" she snarled, barging in on her charges' laughter. Her solo, "Little Girls," is marked "Plain Mean"; it catches her malevolence in a tune in the minor, harping on the second tone of the scale, the musical equivalent of smoldering rage.

Jerry Herman, arguably the most traditional of all the songwriters, suffered respectable failures with *Mack and Mabel* (1974) and *The Grand Tour* (1979). Then he shifted gears for his last new show, not in his song style but in the show's content. *La Cage aux Folles* (1983), from the French play by Jean Poiret that became a globally popular film, was a most conventional yet daring work. Consider: Jean-Michel, the affianced young son of Georges (Gene Barry), is bringing the in-laws to meet his parents, and he plans to move his estranged mother back in with his father. Georges resists:

JEAN-MICHEL: But how will it look if she doesn't sleep in your room?
GEORGES: Like any couple married twenty years.

It's exactly the sort of joke that Abe Burrows might have written for virtually any fifties or sixties musical comedy. But note that *La Cage*'s librettist was the very out Harvey Fierstein, and Georges—as all of my readers surely know already—isn't living with his wife because he's living with his male partner, Albin (George Hearn).

Georges runs a drag club on the Riviera, and Albin—or Zaza, his user name—is the star attraction. Meanwhile, Jean-Michel's father-in-law-to-be is a homophobic reactionary. But when Albin learns that the boy he raised wants to cut him out of *les noces*, and that Georges is going along with it, he rips the theatre apart with "I Am What I Am," virtually a gay anthem. Throwing off his drag wig—firing it, in fact, like an explosive shell in Georges' face—Hearn then stormed off the stage as the curtain fell, a most memorable first-act suspense effect.

And this was Big Broadway, too, not a show making a quaint ruckus downtown. The show's billing emphasized this: "*La Cage aux Folles*, The Broadway Musical," and it got a grand production with excellent choreography (by

Scott Salmon) for the drag performers.* Further, the big ballad, "Song on the Sand," went to Georges and Albin; the heterosexual sweethearts were the Second Couple, taking part in the score in only a here and there way. The Boy got "With Anne on My Arm," and the two then had a dance about it; and she sang in ensembles only.

There had been overtly gay characters in musicals at least since Danny Kaye's flaming photographer in *Lady in the Dark*, and a gay partner couple hosted a party for two hetero couples in the short-lived *Sextet* (1974), strictly Little Broadway in the small-scaled Bijou Theatre. But just as Bert Williams, *Shuffle Along*, and Ethel Waters opened up possibilities for black performers and shows, *La Cage aux Folles* changed the gay experience from the love that dare not speak its name to the love that would not stop singing—in the continued use of gay characters and themes to, shall we say?, enrich the curriculum and, yet more educationally, in such works as William Finn's *Falsettos* (1992), consisting of the previously produced *March of the Falsettos* and *Falsettoland*.

This is because the musical has long been an instrument of American culture in reflecting and satirizing whatever was stirring in the nation at large. One could argue that Lydia Thompson and her "dangerous" burlesque appeared in response to the early rumbles of the feminist movement, that the concentration of minority-group participation in the *Ziegfeld Follies* was a response to the increasing visibility of immigrant cultures in daily life. The Florida real-estate bubble of the 1920s, golf, aviation, and psychiatry all got their very own musicals when they were novelties. Even a blithely entertaining musical comedy such as *Li'l Abner* (1956) had a satiric edge. Conceived as part of the cycle of Hollywood's rustic musicals launched by *Can't Help Singing* (1944) and *The Harvey Girls* (1946) and reenergized by *Seven Brides for Seven Brothers* (1954), *Li'l Abner* was to have been a film for Burton Lane and Alan Jay Lerner, but instead started on Broadway with a score by *Seven Brides'* songwriters, Gene de Paul and Johnny Mercer. Its source, Al Capp's comic-strip saga of dumb Abner and winsome Daisy Mae, was already satiric, and the musical quite naturally matched it. Just a step or two behind the romance was a menu of contemporary talking points: fear of nuclear war, the danger of scientists controlling our sloppy but free way of life, physical fitness, Congressional ineptitude, and, above all, the corruption of government by corporate money bosses. Though a smash hit, *Li'l Abner* made no important history, because the public

---

*An amusing touch: at the curtain calls, a little cart rolled from stage right to left as the twelve "Cagelles" doffed their drag outfits to reveal what few if any in the house could have guessed while they were in their drag finery: two of them were women.

expected musical comedy to treat current events just as it expected the musical play to be timeless.

Structural elements that had been habilitated over the course of the musical's development were still in place in the 1970s—except one, the easy recruitment of new songwriting talent. It was not the rock shows that interfered with the musical's survival: it was rock itself, reinforming the national ear and weaning it off its music-making traditions. Production costs, always gradually rising, now rose almost exponentially, and Broadway began to lose the commercially marginal projects that used to introduce new authors. *The Body Beautiful* (1958) on the boxing game, came and went without note, but it gave Jerry Bock and Sheldon Harnick their calling card, and while everyone thought *The Fantasticks* would close—as a line from Kander and Ebb's *Curtains* (2007) put it—"before the audience opened their playbills," it not only ran for nearly forty years but introduced Harvey Schmidt and Tom Jones.

Other shows seemed to lead to nowhere. *Grease* (1972), entirely by Jim Jacobs and Warren Casey, was not only set in a fifties high school milieu but imbued with it, so that nearly every number revived classic rock and roll. "Those Magic Changes" began as a riff calling out the chords of a standard harmonic progression, from C to a minor through F to G⁷; "Mooning" and "Beauty School Dropout" recalled the slow grind of the ensemble dance known as "the stroll"; and "doo wop" and "shuda bop bop" were lingua franca.

A hugely popular show with a hugely popular film version, *Grease* was all the same a dead end, a one-off—as was *Over Here!* (1974), this one a resuscitation of the 1940s wartime movie. Using a primitive musical vocabulary comparable to that of *Grease*, songwriters Richard M. and Robert B. Sherman came up with reasonable facsimiles of the some of the least interesting genres of American song, but they enjoyed the kiss of authenticity from the show's stars, two of the three original Andrews Sisters, who were often in those wartime movies. The mostly very youthful cast (Ann Reinking, Marilu Henner, Treat Williams, John Travolta) assisted in the tale of a German spy (Janie Sell), unmasked because she knows all the verses to the "Star-Spangled Banner," whereas no true Amerian can get through even one. Both *Grease* and *Over Here!* demonstrated the perils of building an entire score out of pastiche: as every song is a simulation, they move beyond creating helpful references and varying the musical texture, overwhelming dramatization with interference. How are we to care about characters whose reality is invented entirely by nostalgia? Strong helpings of pastiche do give *My Fair Lady* its unique *tinta*, but its two leads are musicalized in an entirely original style. And *Chicago*—as we'll presently see—uses its evening-long pastiche in a satiric way, deliberately cartooning its characters.

Similarly, *The Wiz* (1974), a slick Harlem Oz, turned itself into a one-joke event, although Charlie Smalls' score reminds us how much variety lives in the term "rhythm and blues." On one hand is the irresistibly exuberant "Ease on Down the Road," with Oz's famous yellow-brick highway portrayed by four men in gold tailcoats bearing staves to mark the physics of travel; on the other is the bad witch's rave-up, "Don't Nobody Bring Me No Bad News." At the center of the doings was young Stephanie Mills as Dorothy, a little bundle of vivacity in her white tutu and hose, scampering about the stage or tracing the contours of soul coloratura. A sensation with a four-year run, *The Wiz* had a secret: its content was very out there, even heavy-handed, yet performed with a certain delicacy. Thus, a loud, ungainly revival in 1984 lasted but two weeks, even with Mills' Dorothy and the same choreographer (George Faison) and costume-designer-*cum*-director (Geoffrey Holder), because of a coarse and ungainly staging. "Screechers, mumblers, and pointers" was the *Times'* Frank Rich's rating of the cast, in a "trunkload of marked-down, damaged goods."

While *The Wiz* combined two alien tones—L. Frank Baum's fantasy world with the earthy urban black style—*Big River* (1985) created the logical marriage of Mark Twain's *The Adventures of Huckleberry Finn* with country music. As in the novel, Huck himself narrated, and William Hauptman's *Big River* libretto was extraordinarily faithful to Twain, focusing on the story's major events, from Huck's faking his own murder and his escape with the runaway slave Jim to their meeting up with the "Duke" and the "King" and the attempt to swindle the Wilkses out of their inheritance. Much of the novel's charm lies in Twain's juggling of the lingos of the lower Mississippi—in his own words "The Missouri negro dialect; the extremest form of the backwoods South-Western dialect; the ordinary 'Pike-County' dialect; and the modified varieties of this last." Roger Miller's *Big River* songs could be viewed as the musical equivalent: a pride of communications locked in the very sound of the folk they represent—a splendid First Number with a schoolmarmish kick in "Do Ya Wanna Go To Heaven"; the rousing "Muddy Water," a breezy two-step complement to "Ol' Man River"; moments of both white and black gospel; and quixotic specialties like "(Dad gum) Guv'ment" for Huck's evil father.

A solid hit at a two-and-a-half-year stay, *Big River* wasn't a one-off, as Robert Waldman's *The Robber Bridegroom* (1976), Adam Guettel's *Floyd Collins* (1996), and Jeanine Tesori's *Violet* (1997) also employed country style, albeit more or less expansively. However, *Big River* is unique in its day for mating a classic form of American music with a classic work of American literature—a rebellious one at that. The musical has always "protected" nonconformists of various kinds—the orphan waif determined to dance in the *Follies*, the pacifist in wartime, the feminist in bloomers, the stage mother making show biz through force majeure, the novelist defying the Spanish Inquisition, the pointillistic painter ahead of the curve, the Creole drawn to forbidden music, the Witch at war with the Wizard. And Huckleberry Finn is one of America's greatest rebels, as much a runaway (from being "sivilized") as Jim is. We never do find out what happens to Huck in the end, for in Twain's last paragraph Huck is set to "light out for the [western] Territory" to avoid having to live within the captivity of middle-class cautions. And Hauptman reaches the end of his script with Twain's very last line, as *Big River*'s lights faded to black: "I been there already."

Grease, The Wiz, and *Big River* were linear narratives staged more or less realistically. By the mid-1970s, however, the figure of the director-choreographer preferred shows staged in a fantastical way. A musical is not realistic. A musical is a musical, not only performed but about performing. And Bob Fosse had the ideal project: Maurine Watkins' 1926 comedy-drama *Chicago*, about the trial of a murderess—the Gwen Verdon part, obviously. However, Watkins was now alienated from the cynical tone of the scripts and screenplays she wrote in youth, and she declined. After her death, her estate negotiated, and the Fosse-Verdon *Chicago* (1975) could be said to have ushered in a new era in the sub-history of the director-choreographer production: usually in a unit set; utilizing the Concept Musical's imaginary convergence of different times and places; and the stagemaster himself collaborating in the writing of the show.

Thus, *Chicago* played in a space without sets (though the actors were realistically costumed), the various locales defined by the action rather than by a visual map. So Verdon, as Roxie Hart, sang "Funny Honey" atop a Helen Morgan–style upright piano, the lyrics cut into a dialogue scene in which her husband is interrogated by a cop after the murder. Further to Conceptualize the scene, the conductor, Stanley Lebowsky, played announcer for the song ("For her first number . . ."), and, after the scene, one of the ensemble appeared to announce the next "act": "And now, the six merry murderesses of the Cook County jail in their rendition of the 'Cell Block Tango.'"

Billed as "a musical vaudeville," *Chicago* amounted to a deconstruction of traditional musical-comedy staging—and of its writing, for Fosse was listed as a co-author of the book with Fred Ebb.* Fosse had conceived

---

*Nine years before, Fosse had written *Sweet Charity*'s book by himself, taking the sobriquet of "Bert Lewis" (a play on his given names, Robert Louis). Realizing that he needed experienced help, he called in Neil Simon, giving Simon sole credit, but this occurred so late in the show's gestation that the first song sheets came out with the Bert Lewis billing.

Chicago as a kind of blueprint for a narrative rather than the narrative itself. *Allegro*, three decades earlier, had desegregated some of the musical's essentials—but *Allegro's* score flowed through the story all the same. *Chicago's* score (by Ebb with, of course, John Kander) stood apart from the story in a series of performance pieces—thus the announcements before the songs. Further, most of the numbers were pointedly modeled on specialties out of the show-biz past. *Follies* revived old song genres. *Chicago* revived old singers—not only Helen Morgan but Sophie Tucker, Ted Lewis, Bert Williams, Eddie Cantor, and Marilyn Miller. Besides Verdon were Chita Rivera as the chief other murderess, Jerry Orbach as their lawyer, Mary McCarty as the Sophie Tuckeresque jailer, Barney Martin as Verdon's woeful husband, and M. O'Haughey as a sob-sister reporter. The "M." stood for Michael, hidden from view because he played in drag for a twisty conclusion to Verdon's trial, when Orbach ended his summation with "Things are not always what they appear to be," pulled off O'Haughey's wig and dress, and cried, "The defense rests!"

Chicago was, in all, an evening of unprecedented theatricality, a musical about how musicals work while, so to say, "unworking" them. Further, this musical had a point to make—that show biz has so permeated American life that everything in it is an "act," and morality is a performance. Not till O. J. Simpson's acquittal in a double-murder trial did we see how observant *Chicago* had been—which may well explain the spectacular success of the 1996 Encores! concert version, which, moved to Broadway, became the longest-running revival in history, still playing at this writing.

Chicago was a hit, to be sure, but it was overshadowed by the simultaneous appearance of another High Maestro piece, Michael Bennett's *A Chorus Line*. Actually, the latter opened first, but downtown, at the New York Shakespeare Festival's Newman Theatre, to make its way to Broadway seven weeks after. *A Chorus Line's* famously innovative gestation, arising from audiotapes of performers' autobiographical recollections followed by an improvisational workshop period—not to mention the show's very origin in Joseph Papp's experimental outfit—inspired encomiums from writers who normally ignored theatre as subject matter and, it may be, seldom if ever even saw a show. It was like the attacks on the musical's Golden Age traditions that we heard in the 1960s, another uprising from outside the shareholder community. Too corny! What kitsch! And now the same outsiders sought to use off-Broadway and Joe Papp as a stick with which to beat the Big Broadway of *Chicago* and Fosse, along with all that *Oklahoma!* stuff and revivals of . . . didn't they just do *No, No, Nanette* with, like . . . Ruby Keeler?

However, despite its unorthodox incubation and the lack of apparent glamor in its nearly bare stage (there were mirrors against the back wall, used in important ways) and more or less unknown cast, *A Chorus Line* was no off-Broadway musical. Indeed, that very genre, of the campy homages and quirky subject matter, was all but over; by 1975, the "off-Broadway musical" was simply a Broadway musical having its tryout in another part of town. More important, Michael Bennett—as he would have been quick to tell you—was not an off-Broadway talent. In MGM's *For Me and My Gal*, Judy Garland berates Gene Kelly with "You'll never make the big time because you're small time in your heart!" Bennett reversed the image: he never did anything small time because he was Big Broadway from top to toe, with all the flash and dazzle that the term "Broadway musical" conveys.

Thus, despite *A Chorus Line*'s simple decor and lack of narrative (other than: who will get hired for that titular line?), Bennett's staging was eye-filling and rich in character development. The opening sequence is now all but immortal: we are hurled into the audition's elimination round, with an air of utter authenticity, the dancers struggling to master the combination as Zach, the Michael Bennett figure (Robert LuPone, brother of Patti) calls out the moves. "Turn, turn, out, in, touch, step" and "Step, kick, kick, leap, kick, touch, got it?" Already, Bennett has launched the characterization of his principals: Morales (Priscilla Lopez) is apologetic, used to being picked on, and Sheila (Carole Bishop) is insolent. During the jazz set, Zach moves her from the front row to the back, where she fudges part of the set:

ZACH: Sheila, do you know the combination?
SHEILA: I knew it when I was in front.

The pace is racy even when the music gives way to underscored dialogue and the pack is culled down. The best First Numbers bring us immediately into the story, but this sequence is so masterly in its comprehensiveness that we are handicapping the outcome, judging the talent just as Zach does. Then his assistant organizes the iconic "line," clutching their picture-and-résumés. As they spread out, he lets off a charming "There you go!" gesture, his right fist sawing leftward through the air, and he walks off as the line strides forward—but now the mirrors turn, creating a blackout, and when the lights come up again the line is downstage, holding their headshots in front of their faces.

Beyond its brilliant staging, *A Chorus Line* was unique in maintaining story suspense without a story. Rather, it contained many little "stories" in the personal revelations of the auditioners, and there was even a love plot, between Zach and his ex-girl friend (Donna McKechnie), trying for a mere job after an inconclusive spell in glamor work. There were no Concept Musical touches; this was pure fourth-wall realism. Yet there was a metaphorical feeling about the show, as if the audition was not for a musical but for life. Bennett's next show, *Ballroom* (1978), comparably saw the regeneration of a lonely widow (Dorothy Loudon) in a romance with her dancing partner (Vincent Gardenia) in terms of the equation [good performance = good life]. And the following Bennett show, *Dreamgirls* (1981), about the rise of a group not unlike the Supremes, expanded this with Bennett's most exhaustive look yet at how success in show biz creates success in how one feels about oneself.

In all, *A Chorus Line* was the work of a showman steeped in the intoxicating belief that the fabled American Dream really consists of participation in the greatest art this nation has produced: a big fat smash Broadway show. Michael Bennett didn't know what Franklin Delano Roosevelt or John Steinbeck or Mickey Mantle knew. But he knew that theatre folk enrich us with joy and enlightenment and, in payment, receive the ego gratification of owning a piece of the spectacular live performance of something unique. *A Chorus Line*'s hit tune, "What I Did for Love," was, it is generally admitted, added to the score so composer Marvin Hamlisch and lyricist Ed Kleban could get a moment of their own in An Evening With Michael Bennett. The song is not as articulate as it might have been, however: actors do it not for love. They do it for pride, in the expertise that makes them special. Ironically, the Bennett musicals used performing symbolically—yet what made them special was their high quality of performing, period.

So the director-choreographer became the musical's new captain of command; no wonder all choreographers wanted to direct. Sometimes they lent their talents to dizzy musical comedy, as Michael Kidd did in *Li'l Abner*. Sometimes they worked in the musical play, as Jerome Robbins did in *Gypsy*. Still, hovering over the High Maestro app, so to say, was the *Allegro-Love Life* model of the Concept Musical, aiming at a unique work with some reading of the nature of life. After all, these weren't just staging experiments: *Allegro* warned against letting outside demands compromise one's integrity, and *Love Life* preceded *Company* in worrying over the claustrophobic isolation of marriage. They reveled in the chance to let dance seep through the action, as *Allegro* did, or to slip intrusive numbers into the continuity, as *Love Life* did. They loved the ending to end all endings, as in *Allegro*'s ecstatic finale, as the protagonist stepped forth into the life he was meant to lead just as a little boy walks for the first time; or in *Love Life*'s alienated couple trying to reach each other at opposite ends of a tightrope, because intimacy isn't easy and—as Alan Jay Lerner might have told his eight wives—you never know your spouse till you're divorced.

But Joe Layton's bio musical *Barnum* (1980) was a dizzy musical comedy. Layton had already High Maestroed his way through a George M. Cohan bio in *George M!* (1968), using an ensemble to trade off parts while dancing, jumping, and cavorting around Joel Grey's Cohan as they all raced through his life. *George M!* was a frolic, and—aside from some deeply felt romantic moments—so was *Barnum*. Here the more and more inevitable unit set suggested the big top, and the ensemble, when not playing parts, served as circus folk. The central figure was Jim Dale, seldom offstage as he pulled off stunts and tricks, changed outfits from burgher and clown to ringmaster, resplendent in red tails, white tights, and black boots, and "humbugged" his way through the doings of Phineas T. Barnum, husband to Chairy (Glenn Close) but lover of opera star Jenny Lind (Marianne Tatum). The show's structure observed the Gower Champion plan of short dialogue scenes rushing headlong to the next musical number, the real meat of the meal. Oddly, Champion's ace librettist, Michael Stewart, was *Barnum*'s lyricist, to Cy Coleman's music. (Mark Bramble wrote the book.) The atmosphere was dashing, funny, and thrilling, like Barnum's circus itself: a flimsy piece substantiated by its staging.

But Tommy Tune's *Nine* (1982), one of the most admired works in the entire High Maestro series, returns us to serious consideration. An adaptation of Federico Fellini's movie *8½*, *Nine* deals with the mid-life crisis of a genius who can't enjoy his life because he . . . what? Neither film nor musical can tell us, because there is no answer; some people are too interesting to be happy. Fellini's protagonist was Marcello Mastroianni: attractive, smart, sly, sensitive, distracted—and one of those movie stars who always withholds a percentage of his portrayal for himself, so that one never quite collects him. Perfect: because that's true as well of the character, a kind of Fellini, whom the world sees as a savior. Hire me! Make me famous! Film my story and explain my life!

Critics have anointed *8½* as a remarkable film since its release, in 1963. Fittingly, *Nine* is a remarkable musical, in an adaptation very free in its details yet faithful in spirit, and Tune's production, sweeping of gesture yet intricate in insight, was Exhibit A in the argument favoring the director-choreographer as the musical's new owner. Most arresting is the way *Nine moved* onstage—not so much danced as swayed and shuddered—and the way Tune directed Arthur Kopit's book and Maury Yeston's score to flow together so organically that it was hard to believe that this material had ever before appeared in a different form.

The unit set presented a vaguely spa-like place. There were small seat-like risers and, at the rear, the skyline of Venice seen from far off in the lagoon, as if on the Lido. Exploiting the physical layout from the start,

Tune launched the show with a crowd of women variously uttering odd statements to the protagonist, Guido Contini (Raul Julia). As the women then settled on their seats, Guido, with a baton, vigorously conducted them in a most unusual overture—a vocal one, like that to *A Little Night Music* (though in *Night Music* the singers used the words of each song, while *Nine*'s ladies sang simply "La la la"). But more: the entire overture was a single movement, an Allegro in $\frac{2}{4}$, so that the four songs quoted swam past the ear without the slightest break or change in tempo. The four amounted to a CliffsNotes of *Nine*'s action: "My Husband Makes Movies," the establishing solo of Guido's wife, Luisa (Karen Akers); "Only With You," Guido's romantic duet with his adulterous light of love, Claudia (Shelly Burch); "Nine," sung to and about a younger Guido (Cameron Johann); and "I Can't Make This Movie," Guido's admission that his life has come to a dead end.

Thus, the overture presented, respectively, Guido the artist, Guido the lover, Guido in his platonic essence, and Guido in breakdown. In the show itself, the number that followed "I Can't Make This Movie," Guido's duet with his younger self, "Getting Tall," gently brought him back to a reconciliation with his destiny. But the ideal overture states only the problem, not its solution,* and as "I Can't Make This Movie" terminated, the show proper began, as Guido interacted with his harem, especially Luisa and Claudia; Carla (Anita Morris), a second adulterous partner, but a purely physical one; his mother (Taina Elg); and his producer (Liliane Montevecchi), a dreary old man in *8½* but, here, a flamboyant ex-showgirl. Montevecchi got her own number, "Folies Bergères," complete with an amiably vicious movie critic (Stephanie Cotsirilos) with her own solo bit ("The trouble with Contini . . ."), which the two then sang together, in quodlibet style, heating up the pressure on the protagonist while invigorating *Nine*'s showmanship.

In fact, *Nine*'s first act consisted almost entirely of a series of blazing showstoppers for the women, costumed in William Ivey Long's array of black outfits from fashionable to bizarre—Cotsirilos wore a hat that looked like something Don Basilio refused to wear in a Euro-trash staging of *The Barber of Seville*. *Nine*'s second act dealt with the film Guido was apparently going to make, a *Casanova* (which Fellini himself did film, in 1976, with the unlikely Donald Sutherland), in an extended musical sequence that emphasized *Nine*'s sophistication of elements: a phantasmagoria on the

---

*Opera buffs will point out that the most famous of the four overtures that Beethoven wrote for his one opera, *Fidelio*, the so-called *Leonore Number Three*, states both problem and solution. Beethoven, however, is always exceptional, the genius who perfects rules by breaking them.

themes of Venice and the Great Lover, a distillation of 8½'s view of a magical man in a magicless world, and a Baroque, so to say, of what Fellini could do in film and Tune could do on stage.

The musical started as a low entertainment for the masses, but by the 1920s it was the smartest Americans who were making the best musicals, and, by the 1980s, after R & H and Sondheim-Prince, the smartest musicals were very smart, and not everyone could come along with them. *Nine* got mixed reviews, but it ran two years, telling us that smart hadn't yet lost its place. And with *Nine*'s women changed into white for Luisa's return to the errant Guido and a flock of doves set off into the auditorium, *Nine* even offered a conventional happy ending. Yeston's brilliant score was filled with music that seeks beauty even in the direst situations, as in the first-act finale, "The Bells of Saint Sebastian," which unites Fellini's habitual crises of religion and sex in Guido's blending of Kyries and guilt. It was an astonishing piece, all the more so because Raul Julia could not invariably secure the song's exposed high notes. Even when he could, they sounded torn from him, which is surely what Yeston had in mind for this charming but tortured being. He was wicked, too—when Carla phoned him for sex talk, Guido told his wife it's the Vatican calling. "Go on, monsignore," he said into the receiver.

Julia's Guido remains one of the great singing-acting portrayals, along with Ethel Merman's Rose, Robert Weede's Tony, Angela Lansbury's Mame, a number of Sweeney Todds, and too many others to enumerate here. Moreover, Guido is a marathon part; except for sections of the Casanova sequence, he seemed never to leave the stage and never to try to wing his way through the action, an intense performance in the best sense. Producers had been wanting to get Julia into a musical for some time; in an unguarded moment, he agreed to play the title role in Circle-in-the Square's 1974 revival of *Where's Charley*, for which he was spectacularly unsuited: comic nonsense with a drag bit. Julia was never a nonsense actor, which is why his Guido was so electric. The musical, ontologically a nonsense form from *The Beggar's Opera* on, has gone through so many permutations that, at the time of *Nine*, near the end of the Third Age, it isn't nonsense any more, is it? It continues to offer once-over-lightly storytelling here or there. But more and more, its presence as sheer theatre has become very imposing.

Critics of the director-choreographer model claimed that the writing of musicals was being swamped by the staging of them, as when Bob Fosse's *Dancin'* (1978) dispensed with the idea of a libretto to revue its way through old music and his *Big Deal* (1986) marked a degradation even of the director-choreographer show in an ugly unit set, a boring book (by

Fosse), and a score made of old songs. Was the High Maestro out of control or simply heedless of the writing quotient in the creative process?

Michael Gore and Dean Pitchford's *Carrie* (1988) seemed to suggest both at once, in director Terry Hands' staging, a non-realistic depiction of high-school life, from Stephen King's novel, set in the big white box favored by modernist revivals of classic theatre. Produced by Great Britain's Royal Shakespeare Company, *Carrie* originated in Stratford-on-Avon, where Barbara Cook, playing Carrie's religion-fascist mother, was dismayed by Hands' lack of interest in fixing the show's many problems. Some of the score excelled; but some of it was terrible. The narrative varied from clear to opaque. And the special effects—relating to Carrie's paranormal powers—varied from incorrect to lame. Having played in shows in the charge of such expert directors as Morton da Costa, Herbert Ross, and Hal Prince, Cook knew how a musical is fitted up, and left the project before it arrived in New York, its second booking, to be replaced by Betty Buckley. A colossal failure—the classic analysis of flop musicals, Ken Mandelbaum's, is entitled, with a logic that crushes all before it, from *Ankles Aweigh* to *Kelly, Not Since Carrie*— *Carrie* managed to become a cult favorite even without a cast album, which is like becoming sangria without wine. The piece finally resurfaced, in 2012, in a cutdown off-Broadway revision, now with Marin Mazzie's mother unfortunately naturalized down from psycho to someone you might have known in summer camp. Still, the show may ultimately succeed in this new form: rescued from its director and given back to its writers.

PART FOUR

The Fourth Age

CHAPTER 16

࿇

Devolution

When Broadway needs to re-employ old music in show after show, it is reaching senility. In the past, authors quoted their hits as acts of desperation: a snatch of *HMS Pinafore* in Gilbert and Sullivan's largely uninspired *Utopia, Ltd.*; reprises of the *Of Thee I Sing* score in the woebegone *Let 'Em Eat Cake*; the interpolation of "Never on Sunday," from the film of the same title, into the film's extremely rotten adaptation, *Illya, Darling* (1967).

By the 1970s, however, Broadway was quoting entire old scores in what has become a genre all its own: the revival. Some are at least relatively faithful to the original work (and some to the original staging as well) and some are heavily rewritten, in a form termed the "revisal." Yet all revivals in effect admit that worthy new work has become so hard to find—or hard to sell to the public—that, to keep theatres open, old standbys must be refitted, one way or another.

The obsession with revivals is relatively new. In the First Age, there were few revivals. Rather, productions would tour interminably, so that each New York stand was no more than a reappearance. A few very famous titles got rebooted from time to time, mainly *The Black Crook*, whose notoriety alone sold tickets. However, the habilitation of sharper writing in the Second Age, and the arrival of the great songwriters in the Third Age, made reviving old shows largely unnecessary.

In the 1940s, suddenly, shows started coming back—*Porgy and Bess, A Connecticut Yankee* (in a wartime revisal counting the last songs ever written by Rodgers and Hart before the latter's death), *The Red Mill* (a huge hit), *Sweethearts* (starring Bobby Clark), *Show Boat* (rewritten by the authors to suppress its musical-comedy elements in favor of an R & H musical-play tone), and *Music in the Air* (now set in Switzerland, to avoid Nazi reverberations). These were all Big Broadway, but in the 1950s and 1960s, the City Center's annual spring season of authentic restagings of classics, along with off-Broadway's delight in small-scaled reairings of titles, from *Leave It To Jane* to *Gay Divorce*, took over most of the revival franchise.

Then came the aforementioned 1971 *No, No, Nanette*, with its all-star has-beens Ruby Keeler and Patsy Kelly (succeeded by Martha Raye), a smash of grand proportion. The original's twenties quirkiness was regenerated into an up-to-date camp nostalgia, emphasized in Raoul Pène du Bois' costuming: art deco sweaters, Technicolor swimming togs, plus-fours over Argyle socks, and a derby for Helen Gallagher to sport for her torch song with the boys. Though the production was billed as being "supervised" by Busby Berkeley in his return to stage work after some forty years in Hollywood, Burt Shevelove, adapting and directing, was really in charge, creating not only new life for *Nanette* but a new event in the Broadway Olympics, the has-been hit.

Nanette's producers, Harry Rigby and Cyma Rubin, sundered their partnership. She went on to an *Oh, Kay!* that closed in tryout, but he came up with another knockout in *Irene*, in 1973, starring Debbie Reynolds (succeeded by Jane Powell, and both in their Broadway debuts). For some strange reason, John Gielgud was hired to direct; perhaps Mao Tse-tung and Lawrence of Arabia weren't available. Gower Champion was, however, and after a calamitous tryout he was rushed into action. Indeed, he saved the show—and, that same year, Hal Prince also had a hit in the latest of the various attempts to fix *Candide*, mounted in Brooklyn. Prince's employed a very young cast in an environmental playing area in which house and actors intermingled; at one performance, that madcap Katharine Hepburn threw herself onto a nearby prop bed. Moved to Broadway in 1974, this *Candide* did seem to reclaim the piece for the first time. But it was vocally weak, and Voltaire's crafty Jeremiad had been turned into Duck, Duck, Goose.

Nevertheless, the age of revivals had dawned, unfortunately with the mission to revise shows that needed little more than a book touch-up and, perhaps, the replacement of a dull number or two. Was it because a 1971 *On the Town* was extremely faithful to the text yet flopped? As the original choreography was lost, Ron Field created new dances, but the words and music were heard just as in 1944. Perhaps the male leads were weak. As that English National Opera *On the Town* underlined, Gabey is the Dorothy of the piece, winning in every way; everyone else is a Scarecrow or Tin Woodman, lovable but bizarre. Bernadette Peters, Field's Hildy, was perfect, a very embodiment of the raucous, strutting city.

Certainly, it became the fashion to "fix" unbroken shows, often radically. Harry Rigby put on a *Good News!* in 1974 that adulterated the original with the De Sylva, Brown, and Henderson songbook. Pursuing his wish to *Cocoon* Hollywood retirees, Rigby starred Alice Faye and John Payne (who dropped out after a year's tour just as the production arrived in New York). It was an article of faith among almost everyone that these old titles needed reorganization; to an extent, that is true. But reorganization began to oppress even younger shows—*Little Me*, for instance, which returned in 1982 with its salient gag of one man pranking through seven parts now distributed between James Coco and Victor Garber, neither of whom was amusing in the first place.

Most of the classics, at least, remained unscathed—*Gypsy, Porgy and Bess* again (slightly cut but unmolested till a later revival diddled it unforgivably), *Fiddler on the Roof, The King and I, Man of La Mancha, Hello, Dolly!, Mame*. Some starred their original leads or returned with the original choreography. *My Fair Lady* even came back with—so it was said—its entire original staging. However, it is all but impossible to get a genuine performance out of a company tied to a previous director's playbook. The art comes out canned—as in this *My Fair Lady*, in 1981.

Still, the notion of "fidelity" was in the air, as if to combat that other notion of "revision is good for you." Even a thirties title, *On Your Toes*, returned, in 1983, in its original text (with a tiny tweak here and there). Better, *On Your Toes* pulled off a casting coup: Natalia Makarova as the ballet star. True, the role always went to ballerinas; Tamara Geva and Vera Zorina preceded Makarova, in 1936 and 1954. But Geva and Zorina appeared in other musicals. Geva even played sketch comedy in revues. Makarova was a one-off, and, in her thick Russian accent and slithery Black Swan plastique, an adorably peculiar personality. In a time when stars were becoming as naturalized as the ensemble in *Company*, Makarova radiated a unique glamor.

At that, the revival of a work nearly fifty years old was rare. The even older *No, No, Nanette* and *Good News!* were very exceptional. It was amazing, then, that the New York Shakespeare festival pulled from the historical file a title one century old, *The Pirates of Penzance*, in 1981. True, Gilbert and Sullivan have never fallen out of fashion the way, say, *Robin Hood* and *Evangeline* have. And Wilford Leach's staging, debuted in Central Park and then moved to Broadway for 787 performances, did rather "pop" the piece, with Linda Ronstadt and Rex Smith as the sweethearts and, alas, a cut-down band suggestive of Schroeder's toy piano and a mad xylophone.

One revisal was, paradoxically, so faithful to the original that it was less an alteration than a perfection: the 1987 Lincoln Center *Anything Goes*.

A previous revision, on off-Broadway in 1962, retailed an "and then he wrote" Cole Porter revueathon; at Lincoln Center, all but one of the original 1934 numbers were heard, and two dropped songs were revived. One of these, "Easy To Love," bolsters the romance at just the right moment, and the other, "There's No Cure Like Travel," creates, with "Bon Voyage," a quodlibet, for a thrilling scene change when the action moves onto the boat. Cole Porter himself was on hand to bless the proceedings, in his own recording of the title number, used to launch the overture, and in a portrait lowered from the flies during the finale. Patti LuPone, known till then for serious roles, revealed a zesty comic style in Merman's old role—and, unlike Merman, she could take part in the tap numbers that old shows always inspire in today's choreographers. But the show's star was the new book, by John Weidman and Timothy Crouse (son of Russel), a rare case of curating rather than manhandling.

So it is no wonder that Encores! *Chicago* has gone over so well. Encores! sometimes eviscerates the book—*Golden Boy* in particular comes to mind— but this time it was no more than nipped and tucked. Because Bebe Neuwirth now had Chita Rivera's old role of Velma Kelly, the production had to drop one of the original's funniest lines, after Rivera sauntered off:

ROXIE: So that's Velma Kelly.
MATRON: Yeah.
ROXIE: She sure don't look like a Kelly to me.

If *Chicago* was one of the most faithful revivals, a Roundabout *Pal Joey* in 2008, while retaining the entire 1940 score, commissioned a new book, by Richard Greenberg. Further, Joe Mantello's direction and Graciela Daniele's dances wholly reimagined a forties scenery-and-production-number entertainment as a modern piece, in a unit set with only helpings of dance. In 1940, Joey's meeting with the nice girl occurred outside a pet shop, the visual cleverly designed by Jo Mielziner with the store's lettering printed in reverse, for a trompe l'oeil effect: Joey and the "mouse," facing the audience, appeared to be looking through the store's front window. At Roundabout, this meeting spot was changed to a greasy spoon, played in a tiny inset.

Greenberg used almost none of the original John O'Hara libretto, little more than its first few lines. In 1940, Joey was introduced to us as the curtain rose, running through an audition for the small-time club manager Mike. In 2008, Joey was given a bit of backstory to underscoring: after being thrown to the floor with his suitcases in a "get out of town" vignette, he then leaped from one audition to another till he finally hooked up with

Mike. Thus, we typed him as a third-rater with a habit of agitating powerful people. Then, too, the blackmail plot that revs up the story in Act Two, comic (and easily foiled) in 1940, was now genuinely menacing—and Vera had no choice but to pay.

At that, Greenberg strengthened both Vera's interest in Joey and Joey's interest in the mouse. Originally, Vera looked on Joey as a lark and gave him up with an amused shrug; Greenberg's Vera was visibly shaken when they parted. Two lovely and all but unknown Rodgers and Hart ballads were interpolated to give the mouse romance some emotional traction, and "I'm Talking To My Pal," cut during the 1940 tryout, was reinserted, to define Joey's position just before the final curtain: he is essentially loveless. The perfect con artist, he cheats everyone and trusts none but himself. And to wrap it all up with a modernist's sensibility, Mike was gay.

In short, Greenberg revised *Pal Joey* with respect for what it represented when new. Its realism was ahead of 1940, but after nearly seventy years that realism had to be reinstructed or it would have seemed quaint. As Vera, Stockard Channing, lacking a natural singing voice, embodied the smart and acerbic but secretly tender (in Greenberg's version, not in O'Hara's) society dame so well that she simply classed her way through her music. The Joey, Matthew Risch, was promoted from the ensemble when Christian Hoff left during previews, and the critics, miffed at having to write about an understudy, reviewed their irritation rather than Risch's performance, which was stylish and expertly danced, if a bit too easily angered for a phony who's playing everyone.

The production's surprise was the Gladys, Martha Plimpton, suddenly revealed as a snazzy singer and developed in Greenberg's rewrite from O'Hara's vapid chorine into the embittered villain of the piece. She also got an extra song, for "Zip"—previously the property of a one-scene character— was now part of the floor show in Joey's new club. Plimpton pretended to need an interview from Joey while he was working at the mike:

JOEY: As you can see, I'm busy entertaining the people
GLADYS: Oh, yeah? Do the people know that?

Generally, revivals at the millennium either hewed closely to the original, like *Chicago*, or ranged widely, like *Pal Joey*. Thus, a 2009 Encores! *Finian's Rainbow*, in a Broadway transfer, gave theatregoers a reasonably faithful look at one of the last Big Broadway titles to spend an evening hawking Irish jokes, along with one of the musical's greatest scores. Again: not great in the musical-play line. Just marvelous music and extremely witty lyrics. The cast was engaging, with Cheyenne Jackson and Kate Baldwin as the sweethearts and Christopher Fitzgerald as the leprechaun. (In this production, the more mortal he became, the shorter his trousers got; by the finale, he was almost illegal.) The only disappointment was the treatment of the Susan, who communicates with her feet. Originally a stamping whirlwind, she was turned into a merry Tina the Ballerina, losing the ecstatic relief when she was magically granted the ability to speak.

How To Succeed in Business Without Really Trying came back twice, in 1995 and 2011, in more or less authentic readings and with Novelty Stars (Matthew Broderick and Daniel Radcliffe). Both were fine, but the stagings, as so often nowadays, feared letting the insanity of musical comedy permeate the evening, and characters written as spoofs ended up naturalized and on the dull side. In 1995, Miss Jones, supposedly the office termagant, was simply standoffish. In 2011, the boss' nephew, originally a delerious schemer, was a mere pouting wannabe. And the decor in both outings was drab—another problem in the revising of shows that, in their youth, were above all Technicolor eyefuls. At least 2011's director-choreographer, Rob Ashford, added something special to "Grand Old Ivy," heretofore a duet on a college fight song in a modest stand-and-deliver staging. Now the men's chorus materialized in football togs to score one for Ivy, at one point "rolling" Radcliffe overhead in slow-motion and at length disappearing by diving one by one behind a desk through a trap door, leaving Radcliffe and The Boss, John Larroquette, puffing after their workout while the audience gave them an extended cheer.

The musical play comes off better than musical comedy in this actory rationalizing, because the dramaturgy is more rational in the first place. As I've said, they've been trying to logic chop the musical comedy out of *Show Boat* ever since the Kern-Hanmerstein revision of 1946, and in 1994 Hal Prince unveiled a state-of-the-art *Show Boat* (after a season in Toronto), with an ensemble cast digging into their roles rather than toying with them in pre-*Oklahoma!* style. It worked very well in general, but certain moments—for instance, Captain Andy's one-man performance of the climax of a melodrama (taking four different parts), a tour de force for comic Andys, simply falls apart when an actor tries it. The scene is pure shtick, not properly "actable."

Cabaret returned, in 1998, in a comparable revision organized in London—and *Cabaret* is comparable to *Show Boat* as a blend of frolic and gravity. Sam Mendes' small-scaled production, with Natasha Richardson, Alan Cumming, John Benjamin Hickey, Mary Louise Wilson, and Ron Rifkin (all replaced by various notable talents over the nearly six-year run), offered twisty tweaks. One of the Nazis was gay, for instance. Still, *Cabaret* retains the glitzy mischief of musical comedy, if only in the cabaret

numbers, and, as with Hal Prince's *Show Boat*, the spirit of the original survived, at least till Mendes' "fade-out," which left us with a view of the emcee . . .
in the striped garb of a concentration-camp prisoner.

Has the revisal become the default setting? In the 2000s, there was talk
of a *Brigadoon* to be reset in the nuclear age, though the original text is one
of the soundest of the R & H era, a rare show that, in the day when New
York had seven daily newspapers, got seven raves. Even worse was a revision of Burton Lane and Alan Jay Lerner's *On a Clear Day You Can See Forever* (1965) in 2011. True, the original is famous for its marvelous score and
terrible book—but it's only half terrible. The show's premise was that Mark,
a psychiatrist (John Cullum), treating clairvoyant Daisy (Barbara Harris),
learns that she has been reincarnated, and falls in love with her former self
while Daisy falls in love with Mark. So the rather dreary modern-day scenes
were to be haunted by flashbacks to a fabulously sexy Regency England,
giving the musical a unique tang in the score, the optics, and in Barbara
Harris' dual role, for Daisy was a nice little klutz while her other half was
something of an evil twin. At times, the show visually "collapsed" the two
different time periods together, because the jealous Mark kept interfering
in Harris' affair with a rake (Clifford David). "Quiet!" Harris ordered Cullum, when he threatened to sabotage one of the Regency scenes. Lerner's
script was very funny, too, as when Harris slipped into David's rooms and
found a doxy in his bed:

HARRIS: Are you a friend of Sir Edward?
DOXY: We were at Oxford together.

It was the sort of show that had the audience taking its seats for the second
act eager to see how it turned out.

But Lerner had no second act. He tried to firm it up with a Greek tycoon
interested in reincarnation and a ridiculous plot device linking a shipwreck
in the flashback to a plane crash today, but even at 280 performances *On
a Clear Day* was a disaster, Lerner revised it for the national tour, then
again for the film with Barbra Streisand; neither version worked. Then
the director Michael Mayer "reconceived" it (as his billing put it) with the
Regency flashback moved up to the recent past, thus losing the picturesque
argument between the everyday and the fantastical. And Daisy became
David, though his former self remained a woman. Now Mark would be entertaining trendy bi-curious wonders about what he's attracted to. Is it
David? Or is it the girl David "used" to be? Worse, the score would lose its
zestily mannered Regency numbers for interpolations from the *Clear Day*
film and another Lane-Lerner collaboration, the 1951 Fred Astaire–Jane

Powell movie *Royal Wedding*. In *TimeOut*, David Cote called the result a "Frankenscore," "sewn together" from mismatched parts—and Harry Connick Jr.'s lounge stylings did not justify the music, though Jessie Mueller won praise for her singing of the *Royal Wedding* numbers in the now denuded flashbacks. Gone was the witty visual clashing of eras; the revisal didn't even have sets, playing on furniture pieces in front of vast pointless patterns. Worse, the gender gaming was mystifying, though David Turner, the new "heroine," played his part well. Didn't the show's glamor lie mainly in the bravura of Harris' split personality?

Speaking more broadly, the concentration of revivals—really, the incessant platforming of used music—is an admission that Broadway is running out of sound. Anthology revues like *Ain't Misbehavin'* (1984), a chamber piece made on the "Fats" Waller oeuvre, or the elaborate *Sophisticated Ladies* (1981), on Duke Ellington's catalogue, were unthinkable in earlier years—unnecessary, because so many new musicals were being written, including by Waller and Ellington.

This led to the so-called jukebox musical, another term used variously, though it most often refers to a book show with a new storyline into which pre-existing songs are fitted. This may remind some of that mother of all musicals *The Beggar's Opera*, but, remember, John Gay wrote *new* lyrics to old music; the jukebox score generally uses old lyrics with the old music they originally were written for.

This aesthetic creates a problem when the characters in a show try to address us in songs that established different characters in previous shows. *My One and Only* (1983), billed as "The New Gershwin Musical," really did seem all new, partly because of its spectacular production numbers, its odd look (with constructivist sets), its odd ensemble (black guys, white girls), and its reteaming of the co-director, Tommy Tune, with his colleague from Ken Russell's film of *The Boy Friend*, Twiggy. The score was a fetching mixture of standards ("Strike Up the Band"), semi-standards ("He Loves and She Loves"), and rediscoveries ("Kickin' the Clouds Away") and one number never performed on Broadway, "In the Swim," which was cut from *Funny Face*). So when Twiggy sang the Heroine's Wanting Song sitting in an odd little crescent-moon chair during a press interview, her lyric lines sounding like answers to the journalist's questions, Twiggy's character was truly introducing herself to us. This is because that number, "Boy Wanted," is from Gershwin's little-known London show of 1924, *Primrose*. New Yorkers had never heard it before, and were thus drawn in to share the character's privacy. But if, instead, the character had sung "Someone To Watch Over Me," an old chestnut that for all its charm is dramatically all used up, she would have nothing to share with us, whether in *Crazy For You*

(1992) or *Nice Work If You Can Get It* (2012), two jukebox shows that lamely sought to acquaint us with their heroines using this tired old piece.

On the other hand, some jukebox shows reach beyond classic Broadway for their music, and old pop tunes, however familiar, are not, at least, dramatically exhausted the way old Broadway ones are. *Jersey Boys* (2005), on the lives of Frankie Valli and the Four Seasons, is still playing as I write, and *Jelly's Last Jam* (1992), on Jellyroll Morton, enjoyed the advantage of a fountain of music unknown to the general public. In librettist and director George C. Wolfe's vision, Jelly (Gregory Hines) "preaches" the gospel of jazz piano while haunted by the Chimney Man (Keith David), a Death figure in the form of a *Cabaret*-like emcee. The music, adapted (and expanded) by Luther Henderson and lyricked by Susan Birkenhead, was presented with such artistry that it came off as an entirely new creation.

Jersey Boys was the smash and *Jelly's Last Jam* the arty number. *All Shook Up* (2005) was the camp frolic, a lovable piece with an engaging cast singing numbers associated with Elvis Presley. Joe DiPietro's book and Christopher Ashley's direction recalled the fifties style of show, when charm and spiffy nonsense reigned within the confines of sane storytelling. Interestingly, though *All Shook Up* used many songs that had charted bigtime, that was fifty years before, so even "Love Me Tender" and "Blue Suede Shoes" sounded fresh. Cheyenne Jackson—fitting his pants, as they put it in Texas—played a motorcycling nomad invariably addressed as "the roustabout" (a running gag) who strays into a town ruled by a prudish mayor (Alix Korey). "Attention, citizens!" she cries on her entrance, riding in a car from stage left to right, brandishing a bullhorn. "Freakish dancing, gyrating hips—this is how Rome fell!"

The roustabout brings music and love to the place as a kind of rock-and-roll Music Man, but we knew he would. What sparked this sadly unappreciated show was the way the many Presley numbers were bent into plot action, so that, for example, "Teddy Bear" and "Hound Dog" were mated in a quodlibet as if they were character numbers written for the occasion. A sharp and snazzy production kept everything moving brightly along, as when the roustabout first appeared riding his chopper down a winding road against rolling hills in a trick effect, his ensuing vocal capped spectacularly when someone in the orchestra pit threw a guitar straight up into the air and Jackson caught it one-handed right on the tonic button.

Perhaps the worst aspect of Broadway's attempt to revive bygone art amid a shortage of new work was the staging of movie musicals. Adapting films—as with *Fanny*, *Oh Captain!*, or *Carnival!*—is no different than adapting plays or novels. The problem lies in the lack of adaptation: in the staging of films that already were musicals, as if fulfilling a franchise extension with Stepford shows to function as tourist stops, in the reassurance of the familiar. *Gigi*, lumbered with miscasting, failed, in 1973, but Gower Champion's imaginative reworking of *42nd Street*, in 1980, launched a cycle. *Seven Brides for Seven Brothers*, *Singing in the Rain*, and *Meet Me in St. Louis*—all MGM classics that could not possibly be improved upon—have made it to Broadway, confusing the issue of screen-to-stage transfers of *non*-musical movies simply because they often seem just as hopeless. *Ghost* (2012), an English import, added nothing to the popular film but marching office workers against frantic projections. Charles Isherwood called it "a thrill-free singing theme-park ride," catching exactly the inartistic aspect of "theatre" taking movies literally.

But *Spamalot* (2005), also English, if only in its origin in *Monty Python and the Holy Grail*, used its score to elaborate what was otherwise a carbon of the film, from the bellicose knight who won't stop fighting even after his limbs are hacked off to the man-killing bunny rabbit. Credited to *Python* capocomico Eric Idle and composer John Du Prez, the songs truly enhanced the material, as in a spoof of pop opera's power ballads, "The Song That Goes Like This" (though it was in fact quite compactly sung, without pop opera's screamo approach), or "You Won't Succeed on Broadway," a jest on the concentration of Jewish talent in the theatre, complete with a goof on *Fiddler on the Roof*'s Bottle Dance with the men still in their dark-ages Camelot garb. Interestingly, *Spamalot*'s cast was more comic than musical, from Tim Curry's King Arthur to Hank Azaria's Sir Lancelot (with *Python* co-founder John Cleese's recorded voice as God), leaving only Sara Ramirez's Lady of the Lake to supply vocal tone. Even so, unlike the twice-told *Ghost*, *Spamalot* was not just an excellent show but a very musical one, complete with a catchy cheer-up ditty, "Always Look on the Bright Side of Life." And Ramirez's takeoff on the Vegas lounge singer, nodding with a hammy grin and scatting in her high and low Yma Sumac ranges, was one of the sharpest bits of the season.

Spamalot ran four years, the current standard for a smash hit (and roughly five or six times what a smash hit ran in the 1920s). No doubt the film's zany brio so matched the essential spirit of American musical comedy—albeit in its own English manner—that it was easy to absorb. However, a spate of Disney screen stagings, from *Beauty and the Beast* (1994) and *The Lion King* (1997) to *Tarzan* (2006) and *The Little Mermaid* (2008), has favored the more sober musical play. No doubt some of their appeal (for the first two were vast hits) lies in the public's curiosity to see the cartoons' magic brought to life on stage, as in Julie Taymor's theatricalization of *The Lion King*, no mere movie copy but art all its own. Perhaps the best of the Disney group was *Mary Poppins* (2006), co-produced with

Cameron Macintosh and put on in London first. To fill out the film score, a new team, George Stiles and Anthony Drewe, was brought in to write not only new songs but trio sections and other bits for the existing numbers by Richard M. and Robert B. Sherman. Julian Fellowes, author of the scripts for *Gosford Park* and *Downton Abbey*, wrote *Mary Poppins'* book—proof that Disney and Macintosh saw this project as not just a franchise extender but an opportunity to perfect the material artistically. Then, too, the production, directed by Richard Eyre and Matthew Bourne, went all out in special effects, most notably when Gavin Lee, in Dick Van Dyke's old role, capped a big dance number by tapping up the stage left proscenium, continuing upside down along the top of the stage, and down the stage right side. Sharp eyes could detect the wires supporting him—but how did he maintain the illusion of staying perpendicular to the proscenium surface, against the rules of gravity?

In the title role, Ashley Brown managed to share the aura that Julie Andrews created for Disney's Mary—a lot sweeter than the impenetrably temperamental fay of the original books. That's quite an accomplishment, but then the production was almost recklessly brilliant, rethinking an all but untouchably beloved classic while respecting the reasons why it *is* beloved. To choose one instance among many: in the movie, "Supercalifragilisticexpialidocious" is a duet for Andrews and Van Dyke, processed in live action against a cartoon backup of five buskers. The stage equivalent was a huge production number accommodating a new Stiles-Drew episode in which the ensemble (including the two children) "spelled out" the song's title in body-language rendering of the letters, at first slowly and then mounting to a lightning-strike clip in one of those mad scrambles that had the thespians in the house wondering what the rehearsals must have been like.

Mary Poppins was notable also for the uncluttered simplicity of its singing. The very notion of a "power ballad" makes one wonder if there's something missing from, say, "I Get a Kick Out of You." Is it too . . . dulcet? The song that goes like this is infecting the music just as the staged movie is colonizing the repertory, as the revival is overcoming new work—and the musical might be in danger of losing its salient quality.

Originality.

CHAPTER 17

That Is the State of the Art

Looking at the musical in its early maturity around the turn into the twentieth century, we noted that it had yet to develop almost all the essentials of the Golden Age show: an above all characterful score, an intelligent book, strong principal parts to generate a powerful narrative, imaginative staging, and a nuanced, individual visual style. In other words, *Camelot*'s score, *Fiddler on the Roof*'s book, *The Music Man*'s leads, *West Side Story*'s staging, the look of *Follies*.

Considering the characterful score by itself, we realize how far we've come in the uniqueness of the numbers in musical comedy, always the more conventional mate of the musical play. The Gershwins' *Oh, Kay!*, a very representative item from 1926, runs from standard-make choruses ("The Women's Touch," "Bride and Groom") to charm songs ("Do, Do, Do [what you done, done, done before]") and from ballads ("Maybe") to rhythm numbers ("Clap Yo' Hands," "Fidgety Feet"). They're all wonderful, but in hearing them we realize why numbers dropped from one such show could be resuscitated without a single change for another. It's a genre festival.

However, in a show like *City of Angels* (1989), a crime thriller in a Raymond Chandler tone, the Cy Coleman–David Zippel score precisely mirrors the rufftuff lingo and wise-guy innuendo of Larry Gelbart's book. Respecting the late-forties setting, a radio singing group cuts in with commentary numbers—"Ya Gotta Look Out For Yourself" and "Stay With Me"—and scat vocals, especially useful in the "detective chase music" prologue. Coleman's satiric voice is at its best here, and Zippel's brilliant lyrics make the most of some unusual concepts, such as when detective and guilty lady sing a challenge-flirtation duet of double meanings in "The Tennis Song." (She: "it's not exciting unless the competition is stiff.") An aggressive movie mogul misleadingly named Buddy sings a cross-section on the business "of refuse and nephews" in "The Buddy System," composed in a rare mode, the intimidating waltz. Or consider the gloating merengue of a vicious police detective imagining the execution of the show's detective hero, "All You Have To Do Is Wait," busting the piñata with Tijuana woodwind and castanets.

Some of today's musical comedies strike the traditional poses, as in *Thoroughly Modern Millie* (2002): "How the Other Half Lives," "Only in New York," "What Do I Need With Love?," "Forget About the Boy," "I Turned the Corner (and there you stood)." *Millie's* score was stippled with interpolations from such as Gilbert and Sullivan, Victor Herbert, and its source, the film of the same title. Yet the new numbers were composed by Jeanine Tesori, who is very adept at switching autographs to suit the occasion. She could write her own interpolations.

Another new voice, David Yazbek, writes both words and music and is adept at texturing his scores with touches of pastiche to widen their reach. Each of Yazbek's three Broadway scores was drawn, like *Millie*, from a film, but *Dirty Rotten Scoundrels* (2005) is an exhibition piece on how rich a musical-comedy score can be. Yazbek's first show, *The Full Monty* (2000), was more homogenized; *Dirty Rotten Scoundrels* ranges from country spoof ("Oklahoma?") to manic tango ("The More We Dance"), pausing for sexy-jaunty French wordplay ("Like Zis, Like Zat") and eighties pop-rock ("Love Is My Legs"). This suited the show's plot, centered on the rivalry between two thieves, one super-suave (John Lithgow) and one crass (Norbert Leo Butz), forming a triangle with the heroine (Sherie Rene Scott), apparently naive and sentimental. (Spoiler ahead:) *Apparently*.

Thus, touching all the bases as he provided a batch of plot-situation numbers, Yazbek, in the verse to "All About Ruprecht," gave Lithgow probably the wickedest Noël Coward takeoff ever perpetrated—not just in Lithgow's soigné delivery, but in the very sound of the lyrics, with their cushiony vowels and cut-off consonants. The show itself was intensely funny, with a breezy use of the ensemble and expert playing from the principals, all leading up to a twist ending so startling that, on the cast album, Lithgow himself slipped in at the seventeenth track to warn the unititiated to see the show before listening further. *Apparently*.

The oldest of these new voices was Mel Brooks, songwriter. So ran his billing for *The Producers* (2001), another movie adaptation: "Music and lyrics by Mel Brooks." Here was the most antiqued of millennium titles, almost every number predictable, if tuneful and amusing. There was the flop producer's establishing lament, "The King of (old) Broadway"; the nerd accountant's "wish" number, "I Wanna Be a Producer"; the title song of their joint attempt to outflop even *Carrie*, "Springtime For Hitler." Brooks actually thought to include a genre that had died out in the 1950s, the song that's only there to cover a set change or give an actor a chance to slip into his next costume, "You Never Say Good Luck on Opening Night." With Nathan Lane and Matthew Broderick assuming the parts Zero Mostel and Gene Wilder played on screen, *The Producers* had difficulty replacing them satisfactorily. Somehow, Lane seems to be the last comic who knows how to make joke shtick land; and Broderick's habit of acting within scare quotes, as if demonstrating rather than portraying his character, is frankly inimitable. Still, the show ran almost exactly six years.

Can anyone write a musical—such as those naughty boys from *South Park*, Trey Parker and Matt Stone, who with Robert Lopez, a co-composer of the children's show spoof *Avenue Q* (2003), wrote all of *The Book of Mormon* (2011)? Another "physical adventure" musical, this one followed two missionaries of the Latter Day Saints to Uganda, along the way making allusions to a ton of older musicals. This referential approach could be seen as a defense mechanism, as the dark sort of musical overwhelms the zany shows, and the zany shows got extra-zany—though *The Book of Mormon* includes a brutal murder right on stage.

Perhaps the most intense push back by a funny show against the dark shows was *Urinetown* (2001), itself dark, even brutal, but also deliberately risible and joketastic. Greg Kotis' book looked at a rebellion by the oppressed in a fantasy society in which one pays to pee. Again, we got the references to other musicals—to *Steel Pier*'s slow-mo first-act finale, for instance. But *Urinetown* mainly spoofed the very notion of a musical, with everybody singing and dancing at, really, the most inappropriate times and places. If there could be a gang-war musical or a serial throat-slayer musical, then what *can't* be a musical? *Urinetown*'s score, by Mark Hollman and Kotis, followed the book in ridiculing the story even as it faithfully told it, while John Rando's direction and John Carrafa's choreography brought everything up to fever pitch, as when the rebels' captive, gagged and bound to a chair, helpfully tried to take part in a dance number by kicking her legs in rhythm.

Or consider Officer Lockstock (Jeff McCarthy), costumed very like a member of the Nazi S.S., who nevertheless slipped into campy poses and conversed with a scoffing Little Sally (Spencer Kayden) about the show's curious premise. (In one of their talks, he took her onto his knee for "You see, sometimes, in a musical . . .") The simple set, catwalks overlooking an open space, with a large rectangular piece pulled on and off or rotated to define locations, testified to the work's off-Broadway origin. But if *Little Mary Sunshine* looked back at sweet *Rose-Marie*, *Urinetown*'s point of departure was *West Side Story* and the misery-laden shows that followed.

The referential genre hit its apex in *The Drowsy Chaperone* (2008), about as far as the musical could get from Disney stagings, pop operas, and the Live From Hollywood retreads that have been common of late. A bit reminiscent of *The Boy Friend* in its reanimation of twenties musical comedy, *The Drowsy Chaperone* offered a "Man in Chair" (Bob Martin, co-author of the book, with Don McKellar) narrating, interjecting during, and generally getting a kick out of an old show come to life in his studio apartment. His taste was Jurassic; he summed up the contemporary musical as "Please, Elton John, must we continue this charade?" No, he preferred the company of "a bride giving up the stage for love, her debonair bridegroom, a harried producer, two real gangsters posing as pastry chefs, a flaky chorine, a Latin Lothario, and an aviatrix . . . what we now call a 'lesbian.'" In Casey Nicholaw's clever staging, the evening-long spoof never got tired, and if Lisa Lambert and Greg Morrison's score lacked the tang of *The Boy Friend*'s "twenties" tunes, Nicholaw's cast was sharp and spirited. As the heroine, Sutton Foster dialed down the high energy she ran on in *Thoroughly Modern Millie*, for the ingenue in these takeoffs is the only one who doesn't get the jokes. Thus, Foster's big number, "(I don't want to) Show Off (no more)," found her calmly spinning plates on rods, sharpshooting, playing music on water glasses, charming a snake, getting out of a straitjacket in a chained-up refrigerator, making *surprise!* costume changes, and singing while drinking (via a guide vocal over the sound system, in flawless timing). We laughed; to her, it's just her day job.

Nothing generates excitement on Broadway like a hit musical comedy with a star or two, like *The Producers*. Yet the musical play commanded, as always, superior prestige, in the manner of *West Side Story* and *Follies*. Moreover, following the lead of R & H in those first four mega-hits from *Oklahoma!* to *The King and I*, the musical play was usually an adaptation.

Some musical plays trouble to maintain elements of the silly shows. Rupert Holmes' *The Mystery of Edwin Drood* (1985), a murder case based on Charles Dickens' last (unfinished) novel, was set within a jolly Victorian music-hall frame, and featured an aleatory finale in which the actual audience solved the mystery by a simple vote. A stylish piece with a personality-rich cast, *Drood* was rich also in atmosphere—one advantage that the best musical plays have over musical comedy. The fun shows employ fun music, now music. Musical plays—the reincarnation, after all, of operetta—are always evoking something, taking us to somewhere else.

Similarly, Kander and Ebb's *Kiss of the Spider Woman* (1993), in a Hal Prince production, drawn from Manuel Puig's novel, made much of campy movie spoofs and a few Latin numbers set against the hope/despair of prisoners in an unspecified South American country. The score was foreign, dramatic, impassioned: an exotic show. Chita Rivera, as a movie star adored by the flaming gay prisoner (Brent Carver) to the exasperation of the political prisoner (Anthony Crivello), had to balance a musical-comedy presence with an alternate identity, menacing, seductive: the beauty, so to say, of conformist fascism. In other words, such was the attraction of the musical play that Kander and Ebb, as well as Rivera, so often archons of the merry show—*Flora, the Red Menace, Bye Bye Birdie*—could reveal untapped powers. Tragedy tonight.

New sources of music, in Jason Robert Brown's *Parade* (1998) and Michael John LaChiusa's *Marie Christine* (1999), presented unrelievedly serious musical plays, both original yet based on . . . well, one might say on myth, as Brown's story of the Jewish northerner Leo Frank, lynched in Georgia in 1913 for a murder he did not commit, could be thought of as the American equivalent of what Medea—LaChiusa's model—represented to the Greeks. *Parade*, another Hal Prince production, began with a lowering theme in the brass that continued through the vocal, by a Confederate soldier in 1862 who then morphed into his much older self, in 1913, still in uniform and still singing his folkish number addressed to "my Lila" and celebrating "the old hills of Georgia." The lyrics themselves are harmlessly ceremonial, yet that sullen brass theme sounds as an alarm, and southern xenophobia and its corruption of the human spirit animated the action. By contrast, *Marie Christine* began with a suggestion of Greek ritual theatre, and bleachers at stage right allowed the cast to serve as witnesses to the proceedings, emphasizing the religious nature of Graciela Daniele's staging.

Both *Parade* and *Marie Christine* were Lincoln Center productions; one wondered if the commercial theatre could have made room for two such uncompromising works, very melodic but always dramatically jolting, as when *Parade* builds "The Picture Show" around two teens flirting on a trolley car riding across the stage. The audience at reenactments of myth already know what will happen, but, listening to the two kids going on about nothing to a catchy tune in their picturesque regional accents, no one in the house would have been aware—yet—that she was just about to be brutally murdered and he would lead the lynching party. In *Marie Christine*, LaChiusa, too, includes attractive numbers as if toying with us, humanizing and updating a tale of the most primitive tribalism—but his heroine really is a sorceress, a priestess of womankind attuned to her gender's unique powers. "We were thrown out of Eden," she recalls, "for knowing too much." Both shows gave splendid singing-actress opportunities, to *Parade*'s Carolee Carmello as a housewife rising to greatness trying to save her accused husband, and to Audra McDonald's Marie Christine, the witch herself, living on the tiny line between the hot and cold halves of the moon.

If LaChiusa is the most prolific of the new voices, Richard Rodgers' grandson Adam Guettel has offered only two musicals, the aforementioned *Floyd Collins* and *The Light in the Piazza* (2005)—again, adaptations from, respectively, American reality-myth and fiction. The latter show claims an extremely lyrical yet dramatic score, often tender and troubled in the same number. Even in irresistible waltz rhythm, "Passeggiata" betrays the hero's lack of confidence in a very rainbow of worried harmonic progressions. A sturdy cast, especially Victoria Clark and Kelli O'Hara as an American mother and daughter visiting Florence, gave this odd show the breath of life; like *Marie Christine*, it had virtually no humor, reminding us that the R & H musical play has been supplanted—even by a Rodgers—by a purer musical play, not as dark as parts of *Oklahoma!* yet also not as funny as the rest of *Oklahoma!*, when that Second Couple of Ado Annie and Will Parker gets into dancing and flirting and noodling around. Shows like *The Light in the Piazza* act as though the Second Couple never existed in the first place.

Among the newer voices is one composer who can't get a break, Frank Wildhorn. More than anyone else, he has concentrated on figures of myth; Wildhorn has turned to the Dr. Jekyll/Edward Hyde dual-personality, *The Scarlet Pimpernel*, *Dracula*, and *Alice in Wonderland* for various shows, which tend to get terrible notices and, frankly, often suffer poor work from their wordsmiths. *Jekyll & Hyde* (1997), while running almost four years, was all but incoherent. *Wonderland* (2001), which lasted a single month, seemed noisy more than anything, though Susan Hilferty's costume designs were a hoot.

The problem, perhaps, lies in conceiving shows around how they will sound rather than what they will mean; it certainly sabotaged Wildhorn's best title, *Bonnie & Clyde* (2011). The thirties setting and country-music flavoring provided excellent character material for the two leads (Jeremy Jordan, Laura Osnes), his "This World Will Remember Me" buzzing along with a rustic swank and her "How 'Bout a Dance?" plaintively seductive. Back when Broadway could produce hit tunes the way Renaissance Venice produced paintings, "How 'Bout a Dance?" would have become a standard. Besides, musicals love characters with ambition, and Clyde has plans to fulfill his:

BONNIE: Everybody's got plans.
CLYDE: Everybody's got dreams. *I* got plans.

That could be Curly McLain, Billy Bigelow, Sid Sorokin, Madame Rose, the heroes of *The Golden Apple*, *Man of La Mancha*, *Barnum*, and countless other shows. Unfortunately, Wildhorn's hero was a serial killer, and the attractive music served only to try to make him and his partner attractive, a hopeless task despite Jordan's goofy charm and Osnes' really quite nuanced portrayal.

Of the old voices, Stephen Sondheim remained the undisputed champ, now pursuing collaboration with the librettist and director James Lapine. The Sondheim-Prince era had ended with *Merrily We Roll Along* (1981), a shocking failure in its original production. Narrating its story in reverse chronology (as in its source, the 1934 George S. Kaufman–Moss Hart comedy-drama), *Merrily* was the ultimate "choice" musical, relentlessly chugging back in time to reveal the protagonist's bad life decisions. However, George Furth's book reduced the play's plot-filled chronicle to a few episodes and turned its protagonist into a cipher. Worse, his best buddy, originally a quixotic charmer, became an enraged nebbish. Then, too, the youthful cast—assembled possibly to duplicate Prince's mentor George Abbott's expertise in discovering stars—was, with exceptions, not of Broadway caliber. A George Abbott youth cast is Nancy Walker, June Allyson, William Tabbert, Ellen Hanley, Helen Gallagher, Russell Nype, Red Buttons, Liza Minnelli. Moreover, kids are unable to project the typical Sondheim disillusionment; despair belongs to the aged. To cap it all, the show looked horrible, in a dingy, high-school-sort-of set with sweatshirts (not T-shirts, as often reported) labeled with each character's relationship to the protagonist. At that, the lettering was hard to read past the tenth row.

Sondheim had a mentor, too—a second one. After Oscar Hammerstein died, Leonard Bernstein became, of a sort, an adviser, and when he heard that *Merrily* was to be a popular show, accessible and commercial, Bernstein smiled upon it. After all, in his musicals, Bernstein had combined classical accomplishment with hit tunes—"Ohio," "Tonight," "Maria." And here was Bernstein's former protégé finally deciding to do the same—deciding, choosing, the first virtue in a Sondheim world: we are all guilty of our lives. According to a story that circulated at the time, Sondheim went to Bernstein's apartment in the Dakota to play him the *Merrily* score. Sitting at the piano, Sondheim began by explaining that numbers associated with the protagonist all grew out of an *ur*-theme, and that the rest of the numbers were bonded in the use and re-use of melodic cells, so that one song's A-strain was the B-strain of another song, while the accompaniment to one song would recur as—

And Bernstein slammed his fist on the piano, crying, "We had an agreement! *This* time, *no art!*"

A Sondheim show without art is like one brother Karamazov, and there was plenty of art in *Sunday in the Park With George* (1984), on the creative process, and in *Into the Woods* (1987), on the psychological subtext of fairy tales. *Passion* (1994) at first disappointed some because it lacked the flamboyant theatrical gestures so much a part of the Sondheim oeuvre—for instance the riveting look shared by Len Cariou and Angela Lansbury in the last seconds of *Sweeney Todd*, which might have been Brechtian punctuation or the visual equivalent of "See you in hell!" *Passion*'s score is constricted, like the romance between beauty (Jere Shea) and beast (Donna Murphy), or between his beauty and hers (Marin Mazzie). Only the music for soldiers and a blithely fortune-hunting husband is free and open; all else winds tightly around nameless fears, like a predator lying in wait for itself. In recent years, however, *Passion* is becoming a kind of secondary classic, always difficult and consistently fascinating.

Indeed, the show could be seen as a Compassion Musical, for while it is fiction, it nevertheless sympathizes with an extremely unlikely heroine, for Murphy played a woman isolated, ailing, and unattractive. She didn't simply fall in love with the handsome, sensitive Shea: she obsessed over and stalked him. But then, this was an age of Compassion Musicals. *Side Show* (1997) offered a loving portrait of its Siamese twins (Alice Ripley, Emily Skinner), shyly tackling the problems inherent in trying to maintain normal lives, even love affairs. William Finn's *A New Brain* (1998), about a songwriter (Malcom Gets) diagnosed with a brain tumor (as Finn himself was), gushed—in the best way—with the singular Finn ability to raise music on virtually any topic, as in "Poor, Unsuccessful and Fat" (the lament of a male nurse who, when Gets resents having to take a sponge bath, replies, "Honey, I don't want to be here, either"), "Change" (the shrilling of a homeless woman), and even "Brain Dead."

Scott Frankel and Michael Korie's *Grey Gardens* (2006), amazingly, tenderized the freak-show documentary about two batty dames decaying in an East Hampton ruin—Kennedy relations, at that. The first act, set in the past, began as musical comedy, then turned dire; the second act, today in the ruin, was pure musical play, despite opening with Christine Ebersole's lampoon on fashion, "The Revolutionary Costume For Today." An aficionado's favorite, *Grey Gardens* used its almost old-fashioned melodies and witty, touching lyrics to humanize women who, in the film, seemed irritatingly dotty, especially given that they had once been notables of the leadership class. The show itself made quite a journey, too, from the jaunty, forward-looking First Number, "The Five-Fifteen," to the hopeless, heartbroken "Another Winter in a Summer Town."

Many of the most interesting musicals are now launched institutionally, *Grey Gardens* at Playwrights Horizons and *next to normal* (2009) at Second Stage Theatre. If the former was in large part fanciful, whimsical, the latter was utterly realistic, the first Compassion Musical to treat genuine mental illness—and so sympathetically that by the show's end it seemed as if Diana (Alice Ripley), a "bipolar depressive with delusional episodes," made more sense than her husband (J. Robert Spencer), daughter (Jennifer Damiano), and even doctor (Louis Hobson). Complicating matters was her son (Aaron Tveit), at first a regular member of the family on the three-tiered unit set but eventually revealed as the ghost of a long dead child haunting his parents.

Brian Yorkey's book and lyrics, among the cleverest of the day, were set to Tom Kitt's driving music, at times too rock to deliver character content, though the intricate interlocking of dialogue and song gave the show one of the most integrated scores since *Carousel*. Under Michael Greif's direction, the cast was very strong, Ripley in particular, in her fire-engine red dress and distracted smile, helplessly cogent even as she falls apart. *Next to normal* ended as a hit, almost shockingly so considering its bleak premise, for this lady never does get out of the dark. Still, the racy character development maintained a high energy level, and the topsy-turvy nature of Ripley's family as a whole meant that a line as casual-sounding as "Hi, Dad" was as devastating as *Gypsy*'s "I thought you did it for me, Momma"—because it is the dead son speaking to his father, who has spent the entire time denying him.

The most successful of the modern Compassion Cycle—phenomenally so, with a run lasting twelve years and a busy production history all over the Western world—was Jonathan Larson's *Rent* (1996). A retelling of Puccini's *La Bohème* set in New York's East Village, *Rent* focused on young people of diverse backgrounds, races, and sexuality struggling to survive—literally, as some of them have AIDS. Larson's versions of Colline and Schaunard, now called Tom Collins (Jesse L. Martin) and Angel Schunard (Wilson Jermaine Heredia), are not just buddies but gay and dating, and Larson's Musetta, Maureen Johnson (Idina Menzel), a performance artist instead of a tavern singer, is bisexual. "Tango: Maureen" was in fact given to her latest flames, one male and one female, and *Rent* in general accepted such dissent from state-and-church-approved behavior as the new normal.

As librettist, lyricist, and composer, Larson was able to make *Rent* his personal statement (though he tragically died on the eve of its first performance, a week short of his thirty-sixth birthday). This is another of those expanded scores, bordering on opera, and while the style is occasionally rock or something near to it, Larson found a way to cut character into those insistent rhythms, creating a memorable gallery of individuals. Opera fans must be amused by how near yet far Larson's people are to Puccini's. *La Bohème*'s lead baritone, Marcello, is a painter; Larson's equivalent is Mark (Anthony Rapp), a videographer. The tenor Rodolpho, a poet, becomes

Roger (Adam Pascal), a songwriter, composing on an electric guitar. The bohemians' landlord, Benoit, a stock comic type, is in Larson's hands still a landlord, but Benny (Taye Diggs), with a much larger role, is a suave yuppie with corporate ambitions. Larson's Mimì (Daphne Rubin-Vega) didn't even get a name change, and she meets Roger just as Puccini's Mimì does, in "Light My Candle," which is a good deal more sensual than the same scene in the opera but which ends with Mimi singing (to different music) the very words of Mimì's aria, "Mi Chiamano Mimì": "They call me Mimi."

"Light My Candle" is one of *Rent*'s most potent moments, because—like so much of the *Dreamgirls* score—it is less a "number" than dialogue that happens to be sung. This is a feature of the Fourth Age musical. It was used sparingly in earlier eras—in *Music in the Air* and *Street Scene*, for instance, or in *The Music Man*'s "Piano Lesson." But the present-day musical can turn these musical conversations on and off like spindles. Pop opera of course has adopted the style as well—but it has become an official part of the musical's grammar.

Of the High Maestro stagings, Tommy Tune's *Grand Hotel* (1989) stands out for the breathtaking verve with which it collapsed musical comedy into the musical play. True, Tune's *Nine* did so, too. But *Nine* was less a story than a map of a nervous breakdown, with fanciful costumes and the dramatis personae of a pasha and his harem. *Grand Hotel*, from Vicki Baum's novel and play of five lives intersecting glamorously, ecstatically, and fatally in Weimar Berlin, was a linear narrative with realistic costuming and a full complement of guests and staff, merrymakers and schemers, predators and prey. It was at once the darkest of musical comedies, the lightest of musical plays. Thus, the Baron (David Carroll) and the Accountant (Michael Jeter) could sing the uproarious "We'll Take a Glass Together" just before the Baron is murdered. Or the Baron's scene with his sinister chauffeur could start with the suggestion, from the look of things, that they have just had sex, even as the Baron is about to romance the Ballerina (Liliane Montevecchi). The show's first moments were a shock, as the Doctor (John Wylie) staggered downstage right to shoot up; later, his solo, "I Waltz Alone," treated us to a trippy float through the addict's pacified haze.

More: the Typist (Jane Krakowski) hired by the Businessman (Timothy Jerome) starts penniless and ends larking off to Paris with the Accountant, who has hit it big on the Baron's stock tip. The Accountant had come to Grand Hotel under a sentence of death by poor health. Yet, as he departs with the Typist, he springs with the step of a young man, as if he and the Baron had traded places. Indeed, in the novel, Baum says the Accountant (in Basil Creighton's translation) "may develop fresh resources and remain alive in defiance of every diagnosis."

This is a notion out of Oscar Hammerstein: that fate rules not individuals but clusters of them, some serving as "helpers" in the others' earthly journey. Julie's self-sacrifice for Magnolia in *Show Boat*'s second act (an episode that Hammerstein invented, not to be found in Ferber's novel) is an instance, and *Grand Hotel* is a festival of intertwined fates. It is noteworthy that, when the show's original songwriters, Robert Wright and George Forrest, were slow to give Tune the new numbers he needed during the tryout and Tune called in his *Nine* songwriter, Maury Yeston, for doctoring, Yeston insisted on writing a character number for each of the principals. For *Grand Hotel* is indeed a musical with lead roles but no single lead, no Madame Rose or Tevye. There are others such, of course—*Show Boat* again, *Guys and Dolls*, *Dreamgirls*, *Rent*. But only *Grand Hotel* lavishes character songs on so many principals with such intensity—even one, "Roses at the Station," that expands into several minutes the last few seconds of the Baron's life.

Grand Hotel could be seen also in terms of its staging, in a set made entirely of chairs, chandeliers, and a great revolving door, with the orchestra perched above. As the chairs were shifted about to demarcate various locales within the hotel, the show took on a somewhat cinematic feeling, as if in a movie without sets. Thus, the intermissionless two hours seemed ceaselessly in motion, though there were few dance numbers as such. Rather, the show itself was dancing, in—to quote Baum's novel again— "hunger for life, and knowledge of death."

A multitude of principals filled Stephen Flaherty and Lynn Ahrens' *Ragtime* (1988) as well, in a lively look back at the bygone days of an America not yet absorbing its immigrant subcultures. Flaherty and Ahrens do their best work when a show is set in the faraway, like this one, for like Frederick Loewe, Flaherty responds to the exotic. For Loewe it was the Scots highlands, California of the Gold Rush, or Arthurian Britain; for Flaherty it's the Caribbean of *Once on This Island* (1990), the Dublin of *A Man of No Importance* (2002). With librettist Terrence McNally, Flaherty and Ahrens wrote *Ragtime* on the grand scale, requiring a High Maestro staging, one to bleed together people who, in Concept style, are technically in different parts of the story just as they are in different venues of American life. At one point, an expert in explosives becomes tongue-tied when attempting to join a terrorist gang, and Emma Goldman (who in real life attempted to assassinate J. P. Morgan) magically appears to speak for him, in "He Wanted To Say."

But therein lies a problem, obviously. Drawn from E. L. Doctorow's novel, *Ragtime* treats a fantastical reality populated by both invented characters and historical figures. The explosives expert is invented; Goldman is real. However, as I have said, the music in musicals emphasizes everything it touches. It doesn't merely explain. It glorifies: "Ol' Man River," "Twin Soliloquies," "Send in the Clowns." *Ragtime* the novel is an epic in deadpan, emotionless and abstract in intention. *Ragtime* the musical emotionalizes that epic, not least in singling out one of Doctorow's invented figures, Coalhouse Walker (Brian Stokes Mitchell), as the protagonist. He is the terrorists' leader, and giving a visionary anthem, "Make Them Hear You," to a man who has been blowing up firehouses with the firefighters inside turns an opaque fable into a defense of terrorism.

After which, it's a relief to turn to yet another famous staging, Michael Mayer's of *Spring Awakening* (2006), after Frank Wedekind's play about adolescents in turmoil. To depict a world hemmed in by regulations set down by clueless grownups, Mayer locked the action into a small playing area, with some of the audience (and some of the actors) taking seats on either side. Duncan Sheik and Steven Sater's score, in a guitar-based rock sound, suited the generation war inherent in the story, as rock is, permanently, the voice of the young. But, like *next to normal*, the show offered music as atmosphere and generalized feeling rather than as character revelation.

Of all the shows noted for their staging, none got more attention than *Spider-Man: Turn Off the Dark* (2011), the ill-fated yet so far commercially successful collaboration of the imaginative director-designer Julie Taymor and Bono and The Edge of U2. During nearly seven months of previews, the show's combination of high-flying aerial stunts, an elaborate scene plot, incoherent storytelling, a seventy-five million-dollar tab and numerous performer injuries (including two serious ones) made it a national town topic. Joan Rivers' comedy act included a request for a moment of silence to honor "those Americans risking their lives daily . . . in *Spider-Man*, the musical.*

Exasperated critics, tired of letting the headlines "review" in their place, finally dropped in on the show, mostly to excoriate it—David Cote called it "a theme-park ride that has lost its theme." Even as previews continued, to good houses, the producers determined to remake the show. Ironically, they fired Taymor, whose visual imagination was the only thing that worked—as in the eerily beautiful weaving of a stage-filling red tapestry by seven women to and froing on red cloth swings, the horizontal pieces sliding in to "loom" a curtain behind them. Yet Bono and The Edge were

---

*If nothing else, the accidents reminded the public that performers—usually dancers—imperil themselves while entertaining, something that, before *Spider-Man*, seldom if ever made the news (though *A Chorus Line* focuses on it). While we're footnoting, *Spider-Man*'s subtitle is supposedly based on a sleepytime request from Bono's little boy, who wanted a nightlight on.

retained, though their work was dreary—as when Arachne, a sort of spider goddess, came down to sing against that woven red curtain, her words and music alike unintelligible.

Our tour began almost three hundred years ago with *The Beggar's Opera*, and the historian's etiquette now calls for some statement about how much detail has changed yet how little substance has changed. Nonsense: everything has changed. *The Beggar's Opera* is still playable, true. But it is an artifact nonetheless. Furthermore, the American musical's development was prodigious even *before* a full evening's score, at least mostly by one source, became the rule. The form changed again when the Golden Age added wit and point to the lyrics and trio sections to the numbers to widen their dramatic reach. Then came *Show Boat*: an organically narrative libretto. *Porgy and Bess*: the expansive score. *The Band Wagon, On Your Toes, Oklahoma!*: the integration of dance. *West Side Story*: kinetic set changes for a flowing, unbroken narrative and a thematically unified score, creating a new unity of composition and production.

These are landmarks in the Great Tradition; the musical is still collecting them, even as the unique titles recall earlier works, if only in spirit. Maury Yeston and Peter Stone's *Titanic* (1997) harks back to the spectacle, with its lavish visuals—*The King and I, My Fair Lady, Camelot*. More important, *Titanic* recalls the "big sing" show, expressive as few musicals are: *Carousel, Street Scene, The Most Happy Fella*. One could call *Titanic* a gigantic operetta; even its orchestrations, by Jonathan Tunick, distinguish a career already thought of as one of the most significant.

Yeston's music all but overwhelems the action. Two ur-motifs—a bright Morse code-like jabbing and a brooding alternation of $\frac{4}{2}$ and $\frac{3}{1}$ thirds in the tonic punctuate a score that surges from one set of characters to another—the ship's staff; the passengers, from grandees to proles; the flirtatious young; the bickering middle-aged; the serene oldsters, who refuse the lifeboat to die together. The sentimental, the ambitious, the powerful. In a prologue, the *Titanic*'s architect (Michael Cerveris) explained how art and science together rose to a climax in this stupendous achievement, whose very existence is a cry to God. Then came an elaborate musical scene showing the turning of a page of history in the first boarding of the vessel, technology marrying humanity. Which is the story about—man's search for glory or man himself?

Thus, *Titanic* was one of the few Big Idea musicals, making necessary a truly grand production, designed by Stewart Laing and directed by Richard Jones with, obviously, a startling amount of scenery and a cast of forty-two. And, arguably, one of the greatest scores ever heard, romantic in its anthems, often worried in its ballads, giving way but once to a dance number, "Doing the Latest Rag." The entire ship came alive as though the show were a novel by other means: a stoker (Brian d'Arcy James), a wireless operator (Martin Moran), a steward (Allan Corduner), the captain (John Cunningham), the owner (David Garrison), a star-struck second-class passenger (Victoria Clark) and her weary-of-celebrity-worship husband (Bill Buell), a department-store magnate (Larry Keith) and his wife (Alma Cuervo), and various others, each with a throughline carefully interlocked with the others' throughlines.

For example, stoker and wireless operator shared a strangely touching scene, as the one dictated an offer of marriage to his girl (in "The Proposal"), and the other told how shyness led him to socialize himself, with the rhapsody of a bride, in the thousand voices he picked up on his reception set (in "The Night Was Alive"). The two men then intertwined their love songs as *Titantic* itself intertwined the key themes of technology and humanity. Or: Captain, owner, and architect argued over who was at fault in the disaster, then, as the complex set construction tilted more and more alarmingly through the second act, the architect, alone in the first-class smoke room, desperately redrew his blueprints—yes, *now* she's unsinkable!—as the furniture slid past him, including the grand piano. And at last, survivors and the dead alike gathered in a reprise of their ecstatic hymn, "Godspeed Titanic," and—just as we had seen when the ship first set forth—a little boy came running on with his toy sailboat, thrust it high in the air, and the curtain fell.

In his introduction to the show's published text, Peter Stone commented on how eager the press was to see *Titanic* fail. "They were not only lying in wait," Stone wrote, "they were also drooling over the possibilities of greeting the show with such stored up gems as . . . 'ALL SINGING, ALL DANCING, ALL DROWNING.'" Robbed of their gleeful "sinking" analogies, the critics gave their praise, Stone thought, "grudgingly." Yet the show played two years, and it could surely have lasted another season but for its huge running costs. In a time when unit sets and comb-and-tissue "orchestras" are the norm, *Titanic* remains one of the last of the visual wonders, Big Broadway in every possible meaning.

Along with the grand score, like opera but not like opera, the musical as a form is unique for its pride of character songs, often the most surprising element in a form celebrated above all for surprise. Those cops "raiding" the *Follies* so long ago; *Show Boat* bringing Julie back after she had been apparently swept out of the story; *Carousel* raising its curtain on a pantomime; even the last line of Morales' "Nothing" in *A Chorus Line*. True, there is little surprise in the Heroine's Wanting Song or a comic tripping through his patter. But consider instead the lurid autobiographical confessions of a high-liver as he snorts a line of cocaine in "Breezin' Through Another Day," or the sexual credo of a lady who pays for it—her boy is "guilty where it counts"—in "Black Is a Moocher." Or a lesbian's prayer, in "An Old-Fashioned Love Story," for a Girl Meets Girl, its dark, minor-key verse marked "[Kurt] Weill Slow," or the drunken outcry of a man lost in anger at . . . well, everything, his tune barked out over a walking bass bitten by deadpan chords, the whole thing wrapped up as "Let Me Drown."

These songs are from *The Wild Party*—both of them, for the year 2000 saw two different adaptations of Joseph Moncure March's 1928 poem of the same title,* by Michael John LaChiusa (collaborating with George C. Wolfe on the book) and the other entirely by Andrew Lippa. Both shows are made largely of character numbers, because March's little epic is just what its title implies: a party, and parties have no plot. There is the tiniest narrative movement in that one of the guests makes a play for the hostess, Queenie, and the host, Burrs—her romantic partner—pulls a gun on them only to be shot himself.

A plotless musical? But both LaChiusa and Lippa saw marvelous possibilities in March's parade of party guests. Jackie:

> His hips were jaunty,
> And his gestures too dextrous.
> A versatile lad!
> He was ambisextrous.

Or Eddie, a boxer:

> Aggressive; fast;
> Punishment-proof:
> Each hand held a kick like a mule's hoof.

---

*America's present copyright law, covering works registered from 1978 on, grants protection for life plus fifty years (plus the added twenty years of the so-called "Sonny Bono" amendment). However, the older copyright law, with a protection of a flat seventy-five (plus the amended twenty) years, required a renewal during the term of protection, and March's poem, unrenewed, fell into the public domain. Thus the competing versions. A very few other works have thrown off more than one musical adaptation—*Tom Sawyer*, *Twelfth Night*, *The Importance of Being Earnest*. Booth Tarkington's *Seventeen* sang on Broadway twice, as *Hello, Lola!* (1927) and, under its original title, in 1951, with the future Dame Kenneth Nelson as Willie Baxter.

Or Dolores:

> She was swell to sleep with.
> Her toe-nails were scarlet.
> She looked like—and had been—
> A Mexican harlot.

This is poetry alive with many possibilities—satiric, impish, reckless, cute. And the host is mad and his girl's a beaut. Is he Al Jolson and she Marilyn Miller, the crowd-rouser and the sylph? Offstage, they are less delightful—but it's the rogues' gallery they assemble that gives the piece its content.

LaChiusa and Lippa chose different characters to emphasize, and treated most of them in very different ways. Further, LaChiusa's party was more elaborately staged (by Wolfe) on a turntable presenting a travelogue of the action. Yet both shows hewed closely to the sheer wildness of March's worldview. Blurbing the 1994 edition of March's poem, William Burroughs said, "It's the book that made me want to be a writer"—and Burroughs was the most transgressive of America's novelists, one part pulp, one part sci-fi, and one part sex-snuff. Indeed, it's safe to say that, among the many qualities that mark America's lyric stage as different from that of every other Western nation, no world but that of the American musical could have dreamed up these two shows. The black-comic character songs, the dazzling performances, the jazz-anxious piano filigree of LaChiusa's score and the slashing dance rhythms of Lippa's point up the know-how and guts of our national form.

There is this as well: the balance between star performers and the help has greatly shifted to ensemble casts in which every player is more or less a lead. There really were no ensembles in, for example, the 1920s. A show like *No, No, Nanette*, lacking not only a star but even a designated protagonist, nevertheless played host to Charles Winninger, Blanche Ring, and a few other shtick specialists. It was the musical play that initiated the ensemble in *Oklahoma!* and *Carousel*, though Curly and Billy have over time emerged as star parts. And both *Wild Party*s depended on character painting that *lands*, right through the playbill cast listing, even when LaChiusa's Jackie (Marc Kudisch) was a bubbly sociopath and Lippa's (Lawrence Keigwin) a mute who at one point danced sadly around a roomful of passed-out joy freaks.

Lippa's cast generally featured talent on the rise while LaChiusa's counted more established names, even Eartha Kitt, complete with an eleven o'clock song staged as her personal exhibition spot, "When It Ends." In the 1920s, Burrs and Queenie would have been star roles—that is, if the twenties musical could possibly have allowed anything so provocative as a *Wild*

Party. Lippa had the more accomplished singing Burrs and Queenie in Brian d'Arcy James and Julia Murney, though LaChiusa's Mandy Patinkin and Toni Collette seemed closer to March's characters, he a monster hiding his rage behind the mask of Happy Crazy Show Biz and she a femme fatale in the literal sense: to get close is to court death.

The notion of unmasking corruption in glamorous terrain is another facet of the modern musical, though it has plenty of antecedents—*Gypsy*, *What Makes Sammy Run?*, *Follies*, *Dreamgirls*, *City of Angels* . . . perhaps *A Chorus Line*, in a way . . . and even *Show Boat*, in Julie's throughline. All this runs counter to the American success myth; Florenz Ziegfeld, poet laureate of that myth, could imagine no ending happier than *Sally*'s Orphan Makes Hit on Broadway. But Marvin Hamlisch and Craig Carnelia's unappreciated *Sweet Smell of Success* (2002) unveiled the ugly side of show biz PR by deconstructing the celebrity column once so intrinsic to the entertainment-world infrastructure. Further, modern sensitivities would find the very setting chilling—a vanished New York of men in suits and fedoras having total power and of women viewed as trinkets of various kinds.

Ernest Lehman's novella and his co-written (with Clifford Odets) screenplay, both with the same title as the show, provided *Sweet Smell Of Success* with its material: an ambitious and unscrupulous PR flack (Brian d'Arcy James) courts an all-powerful columnist (John Lithgow), forming the First Couple and leaving the show's sweethearts (Jack Noseworthy, Kelli O'Hara) in the secondary slot. Indeed, in place of the film's ice-cold columnist, played by Burt Lancaster as an enraged Easter Island statue, the musical expanded Lithgow with a warmer attitude. He remained a homicidally dangerous power boss, but the music gave him a vital presence, even—at times—a spirited or tender one. "Welcome To the Night" found him inducting James into the celebrations of Manhattan's dolce vita—the clubs and the clothes, the stars and the style, to put it in columnese. Composer Hamlisch fashioned a wild soundscape for the number, as the frantic choristers, pounding drums, and slithery brass suggested a heathen rite.

Like the movie, the show took place in that nighttime of dangerous glamor, in a unit set dominated by a cyclorama of skyscrapers. John Guare's book found its own equivalent for the spooky vernacular Odets invented for the film, the wit of a warlord and his henchmen, making *Sweet Smell* altogether one of the very darkest of musicals. Yes, *Carousel* is dark, but it has its merry side, as in "June Is Bustin' Out All Over." *Sweeney Todd* is dark, but its woman lead is a Victorian yenta. LaChiusa's *Wild Party* guests known as the "brothers" d'Armano hold forth at the keyboard with "Uptown," on how "black and white" and "gay and straight" are becoming married cultures. It's white hot, lurching along chromatic vocal lines, as reckless as a Bentley full of Column Names scooting up to do the Harlem night-spots: an intellectual's comedy spot, one might say.

But *Sweet Smell of Success* was dark, period. Its one lighthearted number, "Don't Look Now," a softshoe for Lithgow and the chorus, was performed simultaneously with the beating—ordered by Lithgow—of the Second Couple Boy. In this, *Sweet Smell* is like other wholly dark shows—*Marie Christine* and *Parade* come to mind—that tell us how far the evolutionary process has taken us from the Princess shows and *Lady, Be Good!* and their world of youth running hurdles over censorious elders, suspicious but harmless cops, and impedient screwballs.

Even musical comedy now goes dark, or at least serious. David Yazbek's *Women on the Verge of a Nervous Breakdown* (2010) could easily have been a zany show, based as it is on the film by Pedro Almodóvar, one of the zaniest of directors, with a passion for the ridiculous. At that, his *Women* includes plenty of impedient screwballs, and even a couple of suspicious but harmless cops. Jeffrey Lane's book hewed closely to the film script, in its look at a handful of women revolving around a father (Brian Stokes Mitchell) and son (Justin Guarini), the older man a confident womanizer and the younger naive and uncertain. The women include Mitchell's loony ex-wife (Patti LuPone) and the lover he is just now abandoning (Sherie Rene Scott), Scott's dizzy pal (Laura Benanti), an attorney (de'Adre Aziza) who becomes Mitchell's latest flame, and Guarini's disdainful girl friend (Nikka Graff Lanzarone). Add in a merrily garrulous taxi driver (Danny Burstein), a pitcher of gazpacho laced with valium, and those cops, and the musical exactly mirrors Almodóvar's chosen genre: farce about weighty matters.

Indeed, *Women*'s storyline is slightly reminiscent of the zigzaggy plotting beloved in the late First Age and the Second Age that was still in use by the Guy Bolton School of librettists into the 1930s. Couples form and separate capriciously, an outlaw provides menace, law enforcement bumbles about—and in place of Bolton's never-fail stolen jewels is the drugged gazpacho. To show us why Almodóvar's crazy comedy had to be a musical, Yazbek laid out a dazzling suite of songs with a judicious use of pastiche to pump the atmosphere of Madrid into the action. It's comparable to what Frederick Loewe did in *Camelot*: favoring marches and galops out of operetta, with a folkish French *ballade* accompanied by lute, harp, and strings as Lancelot's prelude to "If Ever I Would Leave You" and, for curtain music, a ritualistic anthem of military drums and squealing woodwinds that sounds like Birnam Wood striding up Dunsinane. For *Women*'s Madrid of 1987, Yazbek employed occasional guitar accompaniments, very slight use of flamenco vocal decoration, and the odd Latin beat—in all, a subtle but effective Spanish tinta, compounded by the cast's use of a sibilant "z," as in

LuPone's bravura showpiece, whose recurring title she pronounced as "Invisssible."

Here was another score rich in character numbers. Father suavely gives son a kind of birds-and-bees talk in "The Microphone," while female icons, from geisha to Scheherazade, parade around; when a standing mike shot up from below the stage, Mitchell brandished it as a kind of magic wand, capping the number with a dazzling baritonal high A. Or Benanti, repeatedly trying and failing to reach Scott by telephone in "Model Behavior," dashed through a scatterbrained cyclone of a number, utilizing the production's system of turntables and projections to suggest one of the titular nervous breakdowns.

LuPone's "Invisible" proved a superb solo indeed, a strangely haunting autobiography fit for a diva. In a wonderfully florid performance that combined Mary Boland and Dracula's Daughter, LuPone was the key screwball in a stageful of them. Yet there was darkness in her portrayal as well, as there was darkness in the show—darkness, I say again, in today's musicals generally. True, the book pulled off many a jest, as when Guarini's irritable fiancée, exasperated with Guarini's mother, LuPone, cried, "This is why people marry orphans!," or when LuPone, trying to look into a mirror but accidentally viewing an absurd modernist painting, observed, "God, I look dreadful!" Benanti's character got a lot of mileage out of her sexual vivacity. Learning that she faces legal trouble, Guarini asked if she had a lawyer, and she replied, "I did, but he went back to his wife."

But here is more darkness, for her legal trouble lies in her current live-in lover, an Islamic terrorist. Guy Bolton's lawbreakers were petty crooks; terrorism turns lawbreaking from easy-pickings devilry into genuine evil. But then, Guy Bolton's musical was—again, for this is a key point—musical comedy, a now all but vanished entertainment form made of youth and mischief. It was, above all, *carefree*, which is partly why the intellectual and academic worlds took so very long to start paying attention to it. Just the inclusion of a number like "Invisible" marks the boundary between Guy Bolton's world and ours, for the song cuts past LuPone's energy and wit to look at the world through her character's eyes. We thought her idiotic, irritating, unhinged. And she is; some of the number deals with being institutionalized. But Yazbek makes the moment startlingly honest, even compelling: she may be a loon, but she's his loon—and she does round out the plot nicely by dispatching the terrorist (albeit while aiming for Mitchell). This is the modern musical, artistically capable of tackling even difficult subject matter with nuance and integrity.

Women on the Verge of a Nervous Breakdown suffered dismissive reviews and didn't run long. It did have one flaw, a failure to identify clearly and distinctly—and right at the start—the somewhat cloudy triangle among Mitchell, Scott, and LuPone. The authors and the director, Bartlett Sher, may have been too close to the film to realize how confusing the plot can seem to the uninitiated.

However, another show with unflattering reviews has been running unstoppably: Stephen Schwartz's *Wicked* (2003). Although the setting is L. Frank Baum's Oz back when Dorothy visited by cyclone, the tale is timeless: two young women of very different backgrounds and interests become college pals and eventually play significant roles in the political capital. Belonging to opposing parties, they fall out over a crucial policy issue even while sharing a boy friend who deserts the "pretty" one for the "smart" one. In fact, both are pretty and both are smart, and, in the end, despite their differences, they realize how much they have learned from each other, and remain intensely close friends till the state has the smart one liquidated. (Or so it appears.) The pretty one is left sorrowfully to announce her friend's passing and take the reins of state alone.

It could have been set just as easily in the present time in Washington, D.C. But Oz allows for the transcendent wonder of fantasy—and, in any case, *Wicked* was based on Gregory Maguire's novel, in which his inventions are ingeniously interlocked with particulars of Baum's Oz. Thus, Boq, a Munchkin who shelters Dorothy for a night in the third chapter of the very first Oz book and vanishes thereafter, becomes one of *Wicked*'s college students and a major supporting player. In fact, he then becomes one of the exemplars of the show's fantasy when (contrary to Baum and Maguire) he is transformed into the Tin Woodman.

Maguire's rich storytelling had to be cut way down to suit a three-hour evening, but even so *Wicked*'s narrative is unusually dense for a musical. Perhaps only Sondheim's *Into the Woods* covers more synoptic territory. Then, too, just like *Sweet Smell of Success*, with its alliance of star columnist and stooge, *Wicked* upends the First Couple–Second Couple model, indispensable in all sorts of shows from *Leave It To Jane*, *Rose-Marie*, and *Good News!*, into the R & H era, then past *Follies* and on to *Bonnie & Clyde* and *next to normal*. For *Wicked* centers on the Girl meets Girl of these two friends, Glinda (Kristen Chenoweth) and Elphaba (Idina Menzel), as they learn to share what one thought she never had and the other believed she could live without: vulnerability.

More than *Gypsy* or *The Sound of Music*, *Wicked* is a woman's-story musical. Its other principals, from dashing Fiyero (Norbert Leo Butz), the wheelchair-bound Nessarose (Michelle Federer), and Dr. Dillamond (William Youmans) of the oppressed Talking Animals minority to the manipulative Madame Morrible (Carole Shelley) and the Wizard himself (Joel

Grey), take stage as adjuncts to the Glinda-Elphaba throughline. Are these two roles destined to replace other heroines as the parts young American girls dream of playing? They are oddly sorted, one dark in coloring, gloomy on any occasion, direct, weird, and a belt vocalist, the other fair, effervescent, flirtatious, "normal," and a soprano. Yet the pair are so interdependent that their headline billing was arranged by a trick: Menzel was placed higher but Chenoweth came first.

In truth, it's impossible to say which of the two proved more essential to *Wicked*'s success, for while Menzel had the more intense "track" (as they now put it) to play, Chenoweth had more of an "arc" to fulfill. As the latter outlined in "Popular," when coaching Elphaba in how to command socially, Glinda is the one obsessed with the trivial. Yet she comprehends the spiritual as well—and Elphaba makes that journey along with her. Each is incomplete without the other, half a protagonist, and the two stars were really quite touching in their last farewell, allowing *Wicked* itself to comprehend how enemies can be friends: how the personal matters more than the political.

The most notable breakaway separating the modern musical from much earlier ones lies in the older meaning of "integration": how snugly the score sits inside the story. Ever since the introduction of the trio section and the musical scene with its unbroken wave of underscored dialogue, vocal bits, and outright song, the musical has pursued an alternative opera in which spoken theatre and sung theatre absorb each other's properties. Again, we've noted the landmarks—*Show Boat*'s "Make Believe" scene rather early on and, more recently, *Grand Hotel*, whose script and score Tommy Tune ripped apart to reconstitute as a two-hour musical scene, all talking, all singing, all dancing. This is the musical today, utterly liberated in its ability to pour drama into music even while pouring music back into the drama, water into wine.

Thus, a central number in *Wicked*'s first act, "Dancing Through Life," seems only at first to be a mere charm number with a touch of character song built in: Fiyero revs up the college kids with a salute to living without ambition or ideals, without even a discerning worldview. "Life is fraughtless," he advises, "when you're thoughtless." Two generations ago, the episode would have been a big dance number built around a freshman mixer. But the intricacies of musical-scene integration allow *Wicked* to collapse plot development into the song while expanding the music in subsidiary sections linked by small dialogue scenes. Character conflict: Boq dotes on Glinda, but she manipulates him into romancing the lonely Nessarose. Narrative twist: Glinda fools Elphaba into wearing an ugly pointed black hat—the beginnings of the "wicked witch" outfit we recognize from the

MGM movie. Moving to the mixer itself, dance takes over as Boq wheels Nessarose onto the floor to join the other couples. Now more conflict: Elphaba appears, only to realize that the hat has cursed her with the worst sin an adolescent can commit: being uncool. Sadly defiant, she starts to dance by herself in a weird undulating motion. Another twist: the guilty Glinda—the very arbiter of cool—supports Elphaba in her strange dance. And of course whatever Glinda does instantly becomes the rage, and everyone takes it up, retrieving "Dancing Through Life"'s main strain to cap the number. In something like eleven minutes, what once might have been an empty choreographic exhibition has jumped the libretto through five or six scenes, all the while maintaining the zest of up-tempo melodymaking. It's the heart and soul of what musical comedy does that no other form can rival.

Except *Wicked* offers yet another reminder that musical comedy has not survived in unedited form. As I've said, "A New Musical" is how shows have been billed for over fifty years, as though Broadway welcomed dark shows yet feared to alienate ticket buyers with something more honest, like "A New Sadfest About Abstract Horrors like Racism and Everybody's Suffering and Cute People Die." In fact, "Dancing Through Life" is meant ironically, because Fiyero and the other principals learn that the thoughtless life isn't worth living—in other words, that carefree musical comedy is no longer functional because we expect more from musicals now.

True, like *Women on the Verge of a Nervous Breakdown*, *Wicked* programs many zany moments. In a late confrontation, Elphaba accuses Glinda of complicity in the assassination-by-falling-house of Nessarose. (Elphaba's sister, by the way, just as in the MGM script, though in Baum they are apparently unrelated, and the names are Maguire's invention.) As Glinda sees it, it wasn't homicide, but a "regime change." Anyway, what about Elphaba and that broom of hers? "Riding around," Glinda sniffs, "on that filthy old thing!":

ELPHABA: Well, we can't all come and go by bubble!

To add to the comedy, in the ensuing battle between them, Glinda warms up by twirling her magic wand like a red-state majorette.

Nevertheless, for all its fun *Wicked* is at heart a serious show, and therein may lie its secret power. It's absorbing as entertainment and claims the enduring appeal of a score that is melodious, intelligent, and inventive. But it also gives its audience something to ponder, which the carefree musical seldom did. If *Wicked* lacks anything, it is that isolated memorable event to be talked of long after the show closes—*My Fair Lady*'s spectacular set change from the arrival hall at the Embassy into the ballroom, for which the revolving stage seemed to flip the Mark Hellinger Theatre's auditorium around to change the view. Or Ethel Merman's charging down the aisle on her entrance into *Gypsy*'s backstage "fable." Or simply the way Danny Burstein put his hand on his heart in the 2011 *Follies* during "Waiting for the Girls Upstairs" as he gazed up at Bernadette Peters: the Boy still hopelessly in love with the Girl, though her thoughts be elsewhere.

Ah!: more darkness. It's inescapable, for the musical has grown from the madcap to the sensitive and now, often, to the tragic. The night is alive. Welcome to the night.

FOR FURTHER READING

The musical's bibliography officially begins with Cecil Smith's *Musical Comedy in America* (Theatre Arts, 1950), a formal but not academic history that perforce cut off just when things had been getting interesting, at *South Pacific*. Note Smith's use of "musical comedy" as his portmanteau term for everything from revue to operetta; nowadays, writers prefer the more neutral "musical" to avoid favoring, say, Rodgers and Hart over Stephen Sondheim. Smith makes a readable guide, and he seems to have seen everything that played in his lifetime. However, his opinion of the expansive score—especially anything like Kurt Weill's *The Eternal Road* or the Wright–Forrest–Villa-Lobos *Magdalena*—is often wayward, though Smith was a critic primarily of classical, not popular, music.

After the first history came the first reference work, David Ewen's *Complete Book of the American Musical Theater* (Holt, 1958). Organizing his text around the major writers with an appendix of "Some Other Outstanding Productions," Ewen chose conservatively, including such folk as Ludwig Englander, Louis Hirsch, and Gustav Luders, though by 1958 they were so over they didn't even rate as has-beens. Then, too, Ewen's data were often errant, in misspelled names, incorrect song titles, and miscarried synopses. This may be a problem built into the subject matter, for no other topic has as many sheer details as the musical. Every work comes complete with a host of credits and characters, a tunestack, a storyline, a production history that can take in numerous revisions. Most books on the subject treat so many different shows that even experts can confuse two different people, two different lyrics. In 1970, Ewen put forth a new edition, not a mere updating but a total rewriting, now organized by individual titles from *Adonis* to *Zorbá*, with the writers' bios grouped together at the back. The synopses ran much longer, at times verbosely so, but the dinosaur composers were still on site.

However, Stanley Green had already cut them loose in *The World of Musical Comedy* (Grosset & Dunlap, 1960), only two years after the Ewen first appeared. Englander and company were gone; Green began with Victor Herbert and George M. Cohan. Thus, Green banished *The Belle of New York*, *Robin Hood*, and *King Dodo* from the canon. Like Ewen, Green served as an impartial emcee, never letting on how he personally reacted to the art, but he did at least make very few errors. His output eventually included a little known history of the musical, a study of Rodgers and Hammerstein (and Green ghosted Rodgers' autobiography), a coffee-table book on the thirties musical called *Ring Bells! Sing Songs!* (Arlington House, 1971), and a very useful encyclopedia on the form. However, Green's irreplaceable work is *The Great Clowns of Broadway* (Oxford, 1984), an exhaustively detailed look at Third Age stars from Ed Wynn and Joe Cook to Beatrice Lillie and Bobby Clark. Profusely illustrated, the book is invaluable for its resuscitation of the most ephemeral element in the art, the comics' performing style.

Snatches of scripts bring us back to a time when the audience might laugh not because a joke is funny but because the comic *thinks* it is, as when Green quotes a bit of Willie Howard in *George White's Scandals of 1931*:

WILLIE: I bagged a lion in Africa.
REPORTER: You bagged a lion?
WILLIE: I bagged him and bagged him but he wouldn't go away.

Quite some time ago, my then Oxford editor, Sheldon Meyer, told me he was about to publish a book surveying every Broadway musical from the earliest days on, with a sentence, a paragraph or two, or even a mini-essay on each title. That sounded like science-fiction to me: what writer could encompass so much material? Yet so it was, and Gerald Bordman's *American Musical Theatre: A Chronicle* (first edition, 1978; fourth edition updated by Richard C. Norton, 2010) is arguably the indispensable volume in the canon. Stanley Green told Bordman that he should make a career of it: writing about musicals, Green warned him, wouldn't make you rich, but you'll have a lot of fun. Unlike the dispassionate Green, Bordman had not only fun but opinions. Sheldon told me he had to persuade Bordman to tone down his distaste for Sondheim; not getting the music already told of poor listening skills, but to admit it publicly was to bait ridicule. At that, Bordman's taste was so antique that he timed the musical's decline from right after *Rose-Marie* or so. Of *Carousel* he wrote, in *American Musical Theatre*, "For [some] it was the beginning of an era of pretentious solemnity . . . that attempted to replace the marquee with a steeple." But Bordman took Green's advice, staying with Oxford till his death, in 2011, and going on to smallish works on operetta (1981), musical comedy (1982), and revue (1985). In terms of genre criticism, the operetta book is the most interesting, because while the voyage from comic opera to operetta is relatively direct, that of operetta into the musical play needs detailed explanation. Everyone knows what a musical comedy is: *Anything Goes*. Everyone knows what a revue is: *The Band Wagon*. Everyone knows what an operetta is: *Show Boat*.

Wrong: *Show Boat*'s book is nothing like those of the other very lyrical, romantic twenties shows like *The Student Prince* or *The Vagabond King*. At times, *Show Boat*'s libretto resembles that of a play, as in the Miscegenation Scene. In fact, the writing is that of a melodrama, as Steve cuts Julie's finger and sucks up her blood so he can swear—correctly—that "I have Negro blood in me." At other times, especially in scenes involving Captain Andy and Parthy or Frank and Ellie, *Show Boat* plays like a musical comedy. Today, we think of *Show Boat* as a musical play; Bordman calls that "a meaningless distinction" based on confusion about the genre of the R & H shows. Fair enough. But Bordman thinks of them—the early ones and *The Sound of Music*—as operettas, too. *The Sound of Music* strikes me as a straight play with songs added in as an afterthought—which is exactly what it was, having been conceived as a drama with a folk song or two. Further, in Bordman's view *The King and I*'s "fundamental romanticism" and "exotic canvas" mark it as "consummate operetta." That creates an awfully broad definition. Is *Ragtime* an operetta? *Marie Christine*?

Bordman wrote biographies as well. His *Jerome Kern* (1980) remains the standard work on the man who, with Irving Berlin, concluded George M. Cohan's early work in Americanizing the Broadway score. For his only other bio, Bordman might have chosen a composer comparable to Kern—but nobody was. Instead, Bordman chose the "other" Gershwin, Vincent Youmans, in *Days To Be Happy, Years To Be Sad* (1982), though Youmans was capable of great lyrical expression and intriguing harmonic travelogues. And, like Kern, Youmans was very influential. The varying of accents in the melodic cell of

Gershwin's "Fascinating Rhythm" ("*Fasc*inating *rhy*thm, you've *got* me on the *go* . . .") that gives Gershwin his signature effect of chattering urban anxiety was actually introduced by Youmans in the early 1920s. Sidelined by illness, Youmans wrote for Broadway for little more than a decade. Had he lived on, he might have become as familiar to us as the boldface names of the day.

It happens that one book preceded all of the above, Douglas Gilbert's *American Vaudeville: Its Life and Times* (Whittlesey House, 1940), but it didn't properly enter the canon till republication, in 1963, by Dover. Vaudeville was at once entirely different from and intensely interconnected with the musical—different, obviously, in its lack of narrative and production unity, its proletarian rather than middle-class audience, and its index of forbidden words and subject matter. The musical was protean and ungovernable, run by adventurers. Vaudeville was prudent, relying on the same jokes, the same types of songs and dances, and almost the same acts for its entire fifty-year history (from about 1880 to 1930). So vaudeville and the musical were worlds apart. Yet the musical used those same jokes, borrowed those songs, and raided vaudeville for talent. Gilbert doesn't deal with the connection between Broadway and the national variety show, but his anecdote-stuffed chronicle is very enjoyable, with much use of slangy kennings, as if in Walter Winchell's translation of the *Iliad*. A sad song is a "sobber," an actor "had a large slice of Westphalian" (i.e., was a ham), anything against the rules was "strictly pro" (for "prohibited"). It must have seemed very racy in 1940.

On the minstrel show, Robert C. Toll's *Blacking Up* (Oxford, 1974) is the standard work, filled with detail on how many exceptions teased the rules of the genre. Minstrelsy is remembered for yawk-yawking jokesters and implausibly merry plantation workers, but Toll lists such other personae as "hunters and fishermen thrilling to the joys of the catch; young lovers flirting and courting; black frontiersmen and riverboatsmen . . . and various characters voicing social commentary," including critiques of slavery. We learn that blacks themselves eventually formed their own minstrel troupes, that visual spectacle enlarged the simplicity of the early shows, that many outfits gave up on black subjects altogether even while retaining blackface. Says Toll, the "eye-catching novelty [of the costuming and makeup] became, after the [Civil] War, little more in most cases than a familiar stage convention." This perhaps explains why the last of the leading blackface specialists on Broadway, Frank Tinney, Al Jolson, and Eddie Cantor, employed the look while playing themselves: the smart-alec attitude remained, yet all the rest of the minstrel format had vanished.

Alec Wilder's *American Popular Song: The Great Innovators* 1900–1950 (Oxford, 1972) is a semi-technical analysis of the music of (mostly) Broadway. Except for Irving Berlin, all the subjects were Max Dreyfus' boys at Harms and Chappell, so Oxford was able to make a deal with Warner Bros. Music, Dreyfus' successor in the publishing rights, for countless musical examples. (Berlin withheld permission for his own music; his chapter looks naked without the miniature stavework.) Wilder was to have written a follow-up volume, this time analyzing lyrics, but now Warner Bros. demanded a prohibitive fee. They even told Oxford that the associate who had negotiated for Wilder's first volume had been fired for bargaining too generously.

Two books of the 1970s could be said to have founded genres that have more recently attracted many more titles—the book devoted to a single show and the review of a single artist's (or team's) career. Miles Kreuger's *Show Boat: The Story of a Classic American Musical* (Oxford, 1977) takes us from Edna Ferber's novel through the musical and its 1946 revisal and the three *Show Boat* films, with many photographs to lead the way. Craig Zadan's *Sondheim & Co.* (Macmillan, 1974) has gone through several editions to keep up with the output; here, too, photographs enlarge the record. The book is especially useful because so many of the talents involved in the work chime in—Angela Lansbury on the difficulty in getting Arthur Laurents to see her *Anyone Can Whistle* role her way; Dean Jones on why he left *Company* so soon after the premiere; Ron Field on his dumbfounded exasperation, on *Merrily We Roll Along*, at how unaware Hal Prince was of the amateur night he had erected in place of Big Broadway. "It was like summer stock," says Field, who then utters his famous reply to Michael Bennett during *Merrily*'s previews, when Bennett asks how the show is coming along. "How good could it be?" says Field. "It's *still* backward!" In all, *Sondheim & Co.* offers over 350 pages of bewitching recollections and analyses, making it one of the essential books in the field.

Joined by my own *Broadway Babies: The People Who Made the American Musical* (Oxford, 1983), the foregoing comprises an informal "early library" on the musical. Now I'm going to cite a few works from later years—but the proliferation of studies of all kinds makes it impossible to shape anything like a canon. The following is no more than a modest catalogue of books of interest. A student's shopping list, so to say.

We should start with the father of musical comedy, in *Jacques Offenbach* (Scribner's, 1980), by the British conductor Alexander Faris. A combination of biography and output review, the book contains many musical examples, pointing up Offenbach's relationship to coeval composers, here mocking the grandiose Meyerbeer but there anticipating Bizet and Tchaikofsky. Moving across what the French call "The Sleeve," Audrey Williamson's *Gilbert and Sullivan Opera* (Rockcliff, 1953) is the classic study, updated in 1982—but so lightly that Williamson regrets that the D'Oyly Carte company failed to revive *Princess Ida* after the sets and costumes were lost in a wartime bombing raid. In fact, the company did revive the piece thereafter, in a new staging famous for its outlandish, almost sci-fi designs. (It was seen here on the company's last extended visit, in 1955.) Williamson's writing is generally stuffy, as in "Tights, and especially striped tights, are . . . something that should be used with discretion in the costuming of male singers." Gayden Wren counters with more venturesome discussion in *A Most Ingenious Paradox* (Oxford, 2000), at times surprising in its revisionism. Even if you don't agree with his argument, you'll never see these works the same way again.

Now we cross the Atlantic, for E. J. Kahn's *The Merry Partners: The Age and Stage of Harrigan & Hart* (Random House, 1955), anecdotal and full of atmosphere. The men officiated in the transformation of burlesque into musical comedy (even if their shows were really plays with music), and form a central piece in the historical puzzle. Kahn reminds us that they were as well important enough to function as a major tourist stop. "To many out-of-towners," he writes, "Harrigan and Hart were a New York landmark equal in stature to Broadway."

A century after Harrigan and Hart, Hal Prince comparably officiated in a transformation: of the musical play into the Concept Musical. Foster Hirsch's *Harold Prince and the American Musical Theatre* (Cambridge, 1989), as the title implies, discusses Prince's work in the perspective of the transitions the musical underwent during what the Russians would call "Hal Princeshchina." When Hirsch quotes Stephen Sondheim on how *Allegro*'s "chorus that oversees the action" and "abstract scenic design" haunted him and Prince when they were producing their five masterpieces of the 1970s, we realize that the influence of R & H lay not only in their musical play as a genre but in the spicy theatricality permeating *Allegro*'s staging. The show was R & H's unidentified flying object, a kind of rebellion against their own form and its heightened realism. But then Hirsch quotes Prince observing that "a straight-on realistic musical always seemed to me a contradiction in terms." Among the illustrations is one of *A Doll's Life*, about which Hirsch remarks on "Prince's love of elevation, deep focus, and simultaneous action": the Concept Musical in a single view.

Michael Bennett worked with Prince and Sondheim on *Company* and *Follies*, but then turned away to master his own form, examined in comprehensive detail by my friend Ken Mandelbaum in *A Chorus Line and the Musicals of Michael Bennett* (St. Martin's, 1989). Bennett's early death was a terrible loss to the musical, because like Sondheim—and like Kurt Weill, by the way—Bennett wasn't willing to do the same show twice. A great number of eye-witnesses—actors, writers, those who depended on Bennett and those who mistrusted him, who were often the same people—gave Mandelbaum a piece of their mind, yielding a unique book, part critical history and part mourners' wake. Mandelbaum handles the delineation of Bennett the artist; Bennett's colleagues discuss the person. Nicholas Dante, the co-author of the *Chorus Line* book and the first Paul, the Puerto Rican drag queen, told Mandelbaum that he thought it wrong that Cassie—Donna McKechnie's role—got hired at the show's end. Cassie is too smart and strong for Zach (the "Bennett" role, remember). As Dante puts it, "With Michael, you were out the door if you were a threat." Is that why Cassie and Zach broke up? Yet Bennett and McKechnie married. It's one of *A Chorus Line*'s many paradoxes, as its fact-based storyline creates a fantasy that creates more facts.

Meanwhile, *On the Line* (Morrow, 1990), by Robert Viagas and *Chorus Line* "originals" (as the premiere cast is called) Baayork Lee and Thommie Walsh, is made almost entirely of performers' recollections, which generally reflect the ambivalence toward Bennett that Mandelbaum uncovers. Some figures in the musical's history were hated, and for good reason—Jerome Robbins, Jack Cole, David Merrick. Some were loved—Moss Hart, Oscar Hammerstein. Bennett inspired a rueful affection, perhaps uniquely so. Still, both books assure us that all of the originals found their way into something that, whatever else happened to them, was pivotal in their lives. In a partly indefinable way, the originals embodied their roles, even when playing a character fashioned out of others' confessions.

One feels this especially in the *Chorus Line* movie, which shifted emphasis onto the Zach and Cassie romance even while the director, Richard Attenborough, made a beast out of Michael Douglas' Zach and a pathetic mooning castoff of Alyson Reed's Cassie. Bennett's Zach was efficient rather than angry and his Cassie was valiant. Attenborough has Reed arriving late encumbered by duffel bags as big as China, twittering and hoping and falling down on a rain-drenched pavement, no doubt to heighten her vulnerability. But why demean her? Bennett's Cassie was vulnerable yet winning. (Though Bennett did at first plan to have Zach turn her down for the job at the end, supporting Nicholas Dante's view of it.) Bennett should have made the movie himself, of course—but, says Mandelbaum, the studio wanted "a literal transcription" of the show, and Bennett was too feverishly creative for that. In effect, while on stage his *Chorus Line* nevertheless did everything a movie could. Even the husband of original Carole (later Kelly) Bishop noticed. "The stage version," he says, in *On the Line*, "is more cinematic than the movie."

Like *On the Line*, *Colored Lights* (Faber & Faber, 2003) is an oral history, this one of Kander and Ebb by themselves, "as told to Greg Lawrence." Their lively dialogue, rich in anecdote, is notable above all for their quietly loving tone, a best friendship. How many of those are there? Robert Wright and George Forrest were close their entire adult lives—long ones, too. But more typical is Richard Rodgers' two main collaborations: the increasingly unreliable Hart antagonized him, and he and Hammerstein were really two different breeds of man. Editor Lawrence discreetly keeps out of sight as Kander and Ebb tour us through (as the old cabaret cliché goes) a medley of their hits. This includes a lost line from *Chicago*'s "Class": "Last week my mother got groped in the middle of Mass!" The audience didn't laugh, so they cut it.

Yale and Oxford have each embarked on a series analyzing Broadway's great song-writers. The atmosphere is academic, though Geoffrey Block's *Richard Rodgers* (Yale, 2003) never loses sight of the influence of the staging process on the writing of musicals. Thomas L. Riis' *Frank Loesser* (Yale, 2008) delves into many unknown aspects of this unusual talent, a pop tunesmith who wrote an opera and a mentor and publisher as well. On the question of why *Guys and Dolls'* original librettist, Jo Swerling, was fired, Riis cites the memoirs of Swerling's successor, Abe Burrows (Atlantic, 1980): producers Cy Feuer and Ernest Martin had wanted a romantic musical play in the *South Pacific* manner, then jumped track in favor of sassy musical comedy. However, Loesser had already started writing the score—and it certainly wouldn't have suited a romantic musical play. According to Feuer's memoirs (with Ken Gross, Simon & Schuster, 2003), Swerling's book wasn't workable, and, says Feuer, didn't even include Nathan and Sky's bet that sets the plot (as we now know it) rolling.

Over at Oxford, Jeffrey Magee gives us, in *Irving Berlin's American Musical Theatre* (2012), a solid discussion of *Watch Your Step*, an important show too often scanted by historians. Magee provides also a blueprint of the Roscoe Number in *Ziegfeld Follies of 1919*. It's vintage Ziegfeld: showgirls parade in to famous classical bits enlyricked by Berlin, the sequence bound into "A Pretty Girl Is Like a Melody." Of course we know that one, but here's Berlin's version of Franz Schubert's "Ständchen" ("Serenade"):

> Once to a maid this sweet serenade I sang with feeling and grace.
> I vocalized just how much I prized her form and beautiful face.
> Sad to say the maiden's husband came with a garden spade
> And ruined my serenade.

Philip Lambert's authoritative *To Broadway, To Life!: The Musical Theater of Bock and Harnick* (2011) uses not only lyric quotations but musical examples to analyze both their teamwork and separate careers. (Harnick started as a composer-lyricist; as such he is the sole author of one of the most famous of all revue numbers, *New Faces of 1952*'s "Boston Beguine.") Lambert troubles to correct many common misapprehensions. For instance, it is a truism that Hal Prince wanted Bock and Harnick for *Fiorello!* even after their unexciting debut score, *The Body Beautiful*, because Prince heard something in their style. Lambert reveals that Bock was hired alone, but book-writer Jerome Weidman proved unequal to lyric writing. (At a panel after an Encores! *Fiorello!*, in 2013, Harnick recalled Bock's likening Weidman's lyrics to *Beowulf*.) As Lambert tells it, Prince then asked Stephen Sondheim, who said no. Still Prince hesitated, finally signing Harnick after he and Bock wrote four songs on spec. (That first quartet of numbers can be momentous. It was why Mary Martin turned down *My Fair Lady*, but also how Jerry Herman persuaded David Merrick to let him write *Hello, Dolly!*.) Lambert details the genesis of *The Apple Tree*, as stories by Truman Capote, James Joyce, Henry James, Emile Zola, and Nikolai Gogol among others were considered. At first, the three tales were to be the Twain they ended up with, Bruce Jay Friedman's "Show Biz Connections," and Nathaniel Hawthorne's "Young Goodman Brown."

This is interesting. Though Lambert doesn't go into it, the last two are wild fantasies that would have clashed horribly with the domesticated Twain. Friedman's story is a black comedy in which a nerd is granted the power to dally with doomed women—in an earthquake, a cable-car accident, and so on; but there's a twist ending. And Hawthorne tells of man struck by a vision of all his neighbors—even his wife—engaging in a sort of black Mass.

This trio of tales would have featured a First Couple and a tempter figure, creating a nifty unity. Still, as I say, the tone would be cockeyed—and the Friedman would have been impossible to stage. One can see why Bock and Harnick substituted for it Frank Stockton's "The Lady or the Tiger," for it works in a simple set and has its own twist ending. And perhaps Hawthorne's Colonial setting seemed too "uptight," as the 1960s put it; Jules Feiffer's "Passionella," a fantasy but a mild one, certainly closes off the group suavely. Better, it fixes the evening's chronological arc: first the Bible, then early Anno Domini (at the time of Roman Gaul), then the present day.

Now to bios and memoirs. Neil Gould's *Victor Herbert* (Fordham, 2008), more savvy than previous Herbert volumes, includes notes on every show. John McCabe's *George M. Cohan: The Man Who Owned Broadway* (Doubleday, 1973) gets close to this all-important figure, so misunderstood after portrayals of him as a barnstormer when he was a master of the now all but lost art of underplaying. Harry B. Smith's *First Nights and First Editions* (Little, Brown, 1931) looks back on a career that reached from Reginald De Koven through the first *Follies* on to Sigmund Romberg with almost nothing to say about what Smith actually did. He also has an odd habit of misspelling many names and titles, as if he wasn't paying much attention to the data of his life. The bibliography of my *Ziegfeld: The Man Who Invented Show Business* (St. Martin's, 2008) points out the standard biographies of early Golden Age writers, to which I would add Gary Marmorstein's *A Ship Without a Sail: The Life of Lorenz Hart* (Simon & Schuster, 2012), which has all the Broadway atmosphere that Smith's book lacks. But then George Abbott's *Mister Abbott* (Random House, 1963) is another memoir obsessed with the to and fro of a thoroughly uninteresting life. He does mention "smuggling" a copy of *Quo Vadis* (a forbidden novel, on the Index of a preacher father) to the young Dorothy Thompson, soon to be Abbott's cousin by remarriage and, later, the intrepid journalist and pundit, second in fame, among women, to Mrs. Roosevelt only.

Charles Strouse's *Put on a Happy Face* (Union Square, 2008) is almost all about his shows, with many arresting details: auditioners for *Bye Bye Birdie* sang "Bye Bye Blackbird," as if sensing a connection; Lauren Bacall killed Sidney Michaels' book for *Applause*; Martin Charnin was so determined to direct *Annie* that when Strouse resisted, Charnin broke up the partnership and started working with another composer. Imagine *Annie* with different music for "Tomorrow." And then came *Annie 2*. No one had liked the idea of the original *Annie*, but then, given its flash success, everyone *loved* the idea of *Annie 2*—which closed in tryout. Says Strouse, "The easier it is to acquire backing, the more likely the show will fail." Throughout, Strouse comes off as unnaturally mild-mannered for such a rowdy business. Warren Beatty and Sammy Davis Jr. exasperate him, though only one of Strouse's collaborators causes him finally to blow his top. The curious can find that singular personage named on the last page of the present volume's discography.

It takes performers really to spice things up, however, and Ethel Merman's "as told to" autobiographies, *Who Could Ask For Anything More?* (with Pete Martin, Doubleday, 1955) and *Merman* (with George Eells, Simon & Schuster, 1978) speak in her own tough-broad voice. The earlier book catches Merman more authentically, but Eells, who knew Cole Porter personally and was his biographer as well, fills in the theatre background with aplomb. Mary Martin's *My Heart Belongs* (William Morrow, 1976) is also very personable. But it took *Patti LuPone* (Crown, 2010) to get into all the backstage espionage of show biz. Her pre-Broadway tour of Stephen Schwartz's *The Baker's Wife* (1976), which never came in, is "Hitler's road show," and we see Patti avoiding ensemble work in *Les Misérables* beyond her assigned role of Fantine, the shortest lead in musical history. (In the *Forbidden Broadway* version, Fantine wishes, "I didn't sing one song, then die.") Co-directors Trevor Nunn and John Caird wanted the principals to turn up among the chorus, thus to suggest that all, all are part of the vast horde of helpless, hopeless humankind. Yes. But sly Patti had been slipping out through a secret passage whenever these scenes were rehearsed, till she blundered into the Barbican just as Nunn was setting up the barricade sequence. Patti was dragged into the blocking as a smelter, "not even knowing," she confides, "what a smelter was." Before publication, Patti held a contest for the best title; some wag on a web site suggested *I'd Like To Buy a Vowel*, a reference to Patti's sometimes impenetrable diction.

Among general academic studies, three works offer a kind of synopsis of the full history in discussing a limited number of works: panorama by synecdoche. The biggest is Raymond Knapp's companion volumes, for Princeton, *The American Musical*: the first on *The Formation of National Identity* (2005) and the second on *The Performance of Personal Identity* (2006). There are good insights on, for example, *West Side Story*'s unity of related melodic cells. Bernstein's use of the tritone at the start of "Maria" and "Cool" is well known, but Knapp offers twenty-one musical examples to explore this further. He notes also how the element of magic in *Camelot* fades as humanist idealism reforms a primitive society. The show's *ur*-theme—the three notes that are the first to be heard at the very top of the overture—suggests to Knapp "heroism from a bygone era," a theme "saturated with magic." True enough. Yet one would add that this triadic theme, so boldly diatonic, contrasts with the music associated in the show with sorcery— Nimue's "Follow Me" and the eerily tickling melody of Morgan Le Fey's Enchanted Forest, which is startlingly chromatic. It may be that *Camelot's ur*-theme more truly symbolizes the hero's idealism: it not only opens the show but underlines Arthur's tragedy of noble undertakings as virtually the last thing heard as the curtain falls.

Geoffrey Block's single volume *Enchanted Evenings* (Oxford, second edition, 2009) also uses musical examples, underlining a shift in the historians' format, which now demands the musicological analysis unknown to the Green-Bordman era. Like Knapp, Block blueprints *West Side Story*, even tasting a bit of the aforementioned vocal lines that originally sang to the angular theme at the very start of the prelude. ("How long does it take to reach the moonarooney?") All this exploration suggests that beneath *West Side Story*'s apparently artless continuity, the sheer logic of its wholeness, is a daring and mighty creation. Simply the way the music sounds—modern-jazz-flavored riffs scored in classical technique—warns us how deceptively special it really is. In another part of the forest, both Knapp and Block spend serious time on the movie musical, another aspect that is more and more being seen as integral to the "text" of the musical's history.

The smallest of these three titles is Scott McMillin's *The Musical As Drama* (Princeton, 2006), similarly filled with unique observations on works that have become so familiar we don't recognize the genius that activates them. McMillin suggests replacing "integration" with "coherence," for a great musical is often less interesting in its harmony than in its discords. I see *Porgy and Bess* as an outstanding example, not least in its cheek-by-jowl tournament of the popular ("I Got Plenty O' Nuttin'") and the classical ("Bess, You Is My Woman Now"). But there are many other such shows, deriving energy from the tension of components; *Show Boat* is a classic example, with its hokum comedy and social progressivism, its comic roles and acting roles, its ragtime and "Ol' Man River." One wonders if, eventually, the R & H titles will seem almost ordinary in their aesthetic consistency, while more disorderly works—*On the Town*, *Candide*, *Pacific Overtures*—will continue to feel freakishly vital.

On specific shows, Mark Evan Swartz's *Oz Before the Rainbow* (Johns Hopkins, 2000) is a luxurious tour through the life and times of *The Wizard of Oz*, the many illustrations including even some color, very hard to accommodate when venturing into the early Second Age. More than a narrative about a single title, this is a look at the show biz of its day, as when Swartz points out that *The Wizard* did such good business that "tickets could be purchased four weeks in advance"—virtually unheard of in a time when theatregoers bought on the day of the performance.

No one knows that there is a "making of *Funny Girl*" book, because its author, the show's fired director, Garson Kanin, published *Smash* (Viking, 1980) as a novel. To throw us off, he swapped *Funny Girl*'s set designer, Robert Randolph, for Boris Aronson, whom Kanin knew from *Do Re Mi*. Otherwise, most of the *Funny Girl* people are here (under fictional names), from the book doctor, John Patrick, to the chorus guy who sleeps with the stage manager to understudy a lead. *Smash* is dishy, but Don Dunn's *The Making of No, No, Nanette* (Citadel, 1972) is even dishier. Ted Chapin runs a more discreet outfit in *Everything Was Possible: The Birth of the Musical Follies* (Knopf, 2003). Before his seniority as the head of the Rodgers and Hammerstein organization, Chapin was a go-fer on the *Follies* staff; aficionados favor this title in particular for its inside look at the musical of musicals.

Jeffry Denham's *A Year With The Producers* (Routledge, 2002) is less a "making of" than one actor's relationship with a show, from his audition to going on for Matthew Broderick. So, from *Oz*'s historian to *Funny Girl*'s failed director and *Nanette*'s (if I have the dish correctly) boy friend of the production's PR woman, we come to the narrative of a performer. Thus, we become privy to aspects of Putting On the Show not available in other books. For instance, there is the habit, in R & H-era musicals with a lot of plot and characters, of ensemble multi-tasking, so Denham ends up playing a blind violinist, Scott the choreographer, the "Little Wooden Boy" singer in the auditions for the role of Hitler, and an old lady in the "Along Came Bialy" number, staged with more walkers than at a Paper Mill Playhouse midweek matinee. Or there is the inside joke inserted into the score, when Mel Brooks' musical affiliate, Glen Kelly, at the lyric "I'm the German Ethel Merman, don'tcha know?," adds the four notes of *Gypsy*'s "I had a dream" motif right after, in the brass. Or there are Nathan Lane's improvisations in performance, some of them radical, a last echo of the way comics were expected to behave in shows in the past. Zero Mostel did it, too, in *A Funny Thing Happened On the Way To the Forum* and even *Fiddler on the Roof*, but in cheesy ways that detracted from the performance.

Now to the etcetera. Robert C. Allen's *Horrible Prettiness* (North Carolina, 1991) details the early history of burlesque at the time when it was essentially the forerunner of musical comedy. Allen emphasizes the participation of Lydia Thompson, "dangerously impertinent in [Thompson's mostly-women casts'] mocking male impersonations, streetwise language, and nonsensical humor." Thompson's burlesque "presented a world without limits . . . Meanings refused to stay put. Anything might happen." Does this anticipate the crazy house of *Hellzapoppin*—or, say, *Pal Joey*, with its openly appetitive Society Lady and submissive male sex object?

On vaudeville, another early form (though it flowered just when burlesque went into decline), Douglas Gilbert's already cited pathbreaking survey is joined by *American Vaudeville As Seen By Its Contemporaries* (Knopf, 1984), Andrew Stein's compendium of writing souvenirs from back in the day. These include Edward Milton Royle's general introduction, which notes that the no-no words comprised not only "damn" but "liar," "slob," and "sucker"; the program from Keith & Proctor's 125th Street Theatre (in New York), featuring little Hip, "The Smallest Elephant in the World," and Wm. A Dillon, "The Man of a Thousand Songs," and the next-to-closing, McMahon's Minstrel Maids and Watermelon Girls, and the chaser (the last act, to clear the house for the next show), a set of orchestral renderings; "A Potpourri of Vaudeville Jokes"; and the tale of a man who ran up from the audience to claim a child actor as his long-lost daughter. "Oh, take me away!" she cries—but her "hard-faced" manager refuses to release her.

The house staff must restrain the father as the shocked crowd demands family justice. "Shame! Shame! Give her up!" At last, the man who runs the theatre appears, to bring father and daughter together, to the cheers of the house.

It was all an act; that's show business.

Moving up to the modern era, Ken Mandelbaum's *Not Since Carrie* (St. Martin's, 1991) brings us to another corner of the industry, the flop musical. Drawing on not only extensive research but his own vivid recollections, Mandelbaum covers 1950 to 1990, seeking reasons why the greatest talents can bungle so badly (as with *1600 Pennsylvania Avenue*), or fall in love with unpromising material (*Prettybelle*, the Jule Styne–Bob Merrill–Gower Champion–Angela Lansbury show that closed in Boston, or *A Doll's Life*, the Comden-Green sequel to Ibsen). One reason buffs love this book its comprehensive mastery, from awetastic trivia (as when *Kelly*'s producer, television talk-show host David Susskind, brings psychics onto his program to foretell *Kelly*'s future and all predict success for a work that closed on opening night) and wonderful illustrations (such as all four of *Dear World*'s playbill covers) to lengthy, thoughtful considerations of such enticing items as *The Grass Harp, Juno,* and *Rags*. Those in search of more on the same topic can repair to Peter Filichia's *Broadway Musicals* (Applause, 2010), which covers *the* hit and *the* flop of each season from 1959 to 2009. Filichia offers some surprising titles; it's all in how you read the word *the*. The novelties include a live elephant in the 1974 *Good News!*, seen for two preview performances only. We think back to Little Hip, and wonder.

Picture books are more useful in the musical than in many other fields, because they raise the curtain on vanished productions. Frank Rich and Lisa Aronson's *The Theatre Art of Boris Aronson* (Knopf, 1987), Mary C. Henderson's *Mielziner* (Back Stage, 2001), and Andrew B. Harris' *The Performing Self*, on William and Jean Eckart (North Texas, 2006) blend designs, performance stills, and informative text to reconstruct the physique, so to say, of old shows. It's invaluable in exploring what musicals used to look like and how they behaved. Edmund Burke said, "I must see the Things, I must see the Men." When I got the idea for *Rodgers & Hammerstein* (Abrams, 1992), my first thought was to use the picture-and-text format to create a scene-by-scene "revival" of *Allegro* using the Vandamm stills and snapshots taken during the Boston tryout. Words can go only so far in describing this remarkable work, the cornerstone in the edifice of the Concept Musical. Similarly, Ken Bloom and Frank Vlastnik's *Broadway Musicals: The 101 Greatest Musicals of All Time* (Black Dog & Lebenthal, 2004) is invaluable for its many unusual photographs. One isn't captioned: on page 24 is a shot of *The Wizard of Oz* filling out the *Babes in Toyland* entry. The actual *Babes* shot, on the facing page, is the "Garden Wall" scene mentioned some three hundred pages and a century ago, the "I Can't Do the Sum" number to hold the continuity in place while the stagehands, behind the backdrop, readied the next big set. The two kids in front, incorrectly identified in the caption, are Alan (William Norris) and Jane (Mabel Barrison).

Last, we gaze into *Broadway Song & Story* (Dodd, Mead, 1985), transcriptions of Dramatists Guild panels (by the authors and associates) on both plays and musicals. We get fascinating looks back at *On the Town, West Side Story, Fiddler on the Roof, Cabaret,* and much else. The *Gypsy* panel is especially full of arcane tidbits—other writers tackled the project before Styne, Sondheim, and Laurents; June Havoc vacillated so long on whether to let the production use her name that, in the first performances it was changed from June to Claire and confused actors called her "Baby Clune"; Jerome Robbins hated the overture, generally regarded as the greatest in its line; and Faith Dane, who played the stripper billed as "Mazeppa, Revolution in Dance," was the daughter of Arthur Laurents' high-school history teacher.

To which revelation Sondheim observes, "That's the most startling fact of the afternoon."

DISCOGRAPHY

This is a very selective catalogue, with three purposes: one, to guide the reader to a re-discovery of old music and the styles in which it was originally played and performed; two, to outline the development of the cast album, the single most influential element in the creation of a permanent repertory of works; and, three, to point out recordings both enlightening and entertaining.

If the musical begins with *The Beggar's Opera*, the piece itself starts its modern career with the Frederic Austin arrangements made for the 1920 revival at London's Lyric Theatre, Hammersmith (HMV, World, Past). Delicately vigorous in an antique scoring for strings, woodwinds, and harpsichord (to reflect the production's fashionably obsolete look of three-cornered hats and buckled shoes), the Austin version absorbed its mother work till it was thought—in Britain, at least—to be the authentic voicing of the play. The Lyric cast comes to us in the pale tones of acoustic recording (that is, into a horn), but a Glyndebourne production of 1940 (HMV, Pearl), with opera singers and Michael Redgrave's Macheath, has the advantage of electrical recording (into a microphone, yielding more realistic reproduction, used from 1925 on). The later cast has more espressivo, and Redgrave is surprisingly musical for a supposed non-singer.

Still, to understand how well John Gay united script and song, one should sample modern recordings, which routinely include linking dialogue. The classic performance is EMI's in 1955 under Malcolm Sargent, with John Cameron, Elsie Morison, Monica Sinclair, Owen Brannigan, and other opera singers and, speaking the lines, such wonderful actors as Paul Rogers, Robert Hardy, and Rachel Roberts. The speakers don't sound like the singers, but at least the respective recording levels are equalized—a rare event in these half-talk-half-song disc productions. Hearing the dialogue "place" the songs reveals how aptly Gay lyricked the music, creating a little monster of a solo for Macheath in "O Cruel, Cruel, Cruel Case!," which is actually a medley of four separate songs. (In the Austin version, that is: Gay's original stacked ten melodies atop one another.)

Alternate editions of the music include one made for the West End in 1968 (CBS) by Benjamin Pearce Higgins in a pointedly "now" style that today sounds even more archaic than Austin's Edwardian piping. Nor does this cast control enough vocal tone, though Peter Gilmore's Macheath revels in sexy baritone and Hy Hazell, the delight of many an English musical, from *Lock Up Your Daughters* to *Fiddler on the Roof* (as a replacement Golde), had been playing Mrs. Peachum virtually throughout her career. With only six in the pit, CBS accords with the typical chamber scoring in this work. But Richard Bonynge commissioned an Erich Wolfgang Korngold "Symphony Of a Thousand" orchestration from Douglas Gamley for the all-star lineup of Kiri Te Kanawa, Joan Sutherland (as Lucy), James Morris, Angela Lansbury, and, as Mrs. Trapes, Regina Resnik (Decca). Gamley's arrangements, eclectic in the use of pastiche, upstage the story. Thus, Stafford Dean's "You'll Think, Ere Many Days Ensue" comes off as a drunken music-hall turn, while Sutherland's "Thus When a Good Housewife" fairly twirls with mad-scene coloratura. In all: an unfocused reading, but amusing and very well sung.

For *Beggar's Opera* DVDs, we can pass over one on Arthaus, with Roger Daltrey's anomalous pop twerping and incomprehensible mumbles. Warner Archive rescues Peter Brook's 1953 Technicolor film starring Laurence Olivier in—says Pauline Kael—"one of his most playful, sophisticated, and least-known roles." Brook opened the play up with action scenes and changes in plot, moved numbers around, and used yet another musical setting, this one by the major classical composer Arthur Bliss, for full orchestra but in faithful old style. Bliss even reached over Austin to Gay's original version of "O Cruel, Cruel, Cruel Case!," including nine of the ten melodies used in 1728. The script (by Christopher Fry and Denis Cannan) follows Gay's tone if not all of his words, and generally the movie is superb—dashing, Hogarthian, and so profligate of imagination that a spectacular shot of prison doors opening on a vast crowd hot for a hanging lasts but seconds. Most of the actors were dubbed in the music by opera singers, but not Olivier, who, in the same red coat designed for the 1920 revival, clearly also does his own stunts and horseback riding. This proves invaluable in one of Brook's most arresting inventions: after a robbery, Olivier canters along singing "My Heart Was So Free" till he reaches the summit of a hill and suddenly sees a noosed corpse hanging in full body irons. Most interesting for students of the musical is the reapportioning of dialogue to song: with much less of Gay's full score of sixty numbers, the work suddenly resembles a modern show.

From 1963 comes a BBC telecast (Decca) of the best of all the settings, Benjamin Britten's. Though the spirit is that of Austin (in a twelve-man pit), the reworkings of the vocal lines and the way the orchestra dialogues with them is utterly original. And note how much more playing time Britten gives his band. The Austin version is awfully dry in its stodgy alternating of speech and song; Britten moistens the spaces between till a play with songs becomes—almost—an opera with speeches, and far more integrated than the piece was in 1728 or after. Peter Brook used actors but the BBC offers opera people who can act—Janet Baker, Kenneth McKellar, Heather Harper, and Anna Pollak (who sang Jenny Diver, the Lotte Lenya part, for Malcolm Sargent). Pollak's wily slattern of a Mrs. Peachum is so unlike what the term "opera singer" means that one realizes how infectiously theatrical *The Beggar's Opera* really is. Watch for a Decor Malfunction at 26:45 in the disc's running time, when a closing curtain gets stuck on McKellar's shoulder and Baker deftly flips it free without changing expression.

Gilbert and Sullivan's scores are so much more integrated than Gay's that one can almost follow the action through the lyrics alone. Among the countless recordings, seven series stand out, reissued over the years on various labels. The first is HMV's acoustic albums using recording veterans and some D'Oyly Carte performers; the last unit, a flavorful *Princess Ida* and nearly a D'Oyly Carte cast album with only two non-company singers in minor roles, is the only *Ida* (of four) to include the contralto's "Come, Mighty Must!," apparently because Bertha Lewis was the sole singer to bring this dirge to life. HMV went on to an electric D'Oyly Carte series, featuring one of the best G & S albums of all time, 1927's *Gondoliers*. After the war, Decca made the first LP D'Oyly Cartes, then a stereo group, five with the spoken dialogue; as with the *Beggar's Operas*, this gives the student a chance to see how old the integration of song and story really is. Meanwhile, EMI produced a stero series under Malcolm Sargent with casts very like his *Beggar's Opera* crew. These are less theatrical than the D'Oyly Cartes, in draggy tempos. However, except for George Baker in the Ko-Ko roles—useful in the old 78 sets but by now given to Jurassic-era wheezing—the singers make some very beautiful music. Are these operas (as they were called in their day) or musicals? That is, how much singing is enough singing? High school drama clubs get through them, yet current usage favors plush voices, in both the so-called New D'Oyly Carte series (TER, Sony) and Telarc's spicier runthrough of the favorite titles. TER specializes in reviving cut numbers; the *Patience*, never released in the United States, offers a realization of a lost solo for the Duke. It won't make headlines; but the performance is very well conducted by John Owen Edwards, and the acting and singing, often out of proportion in G & S, is acutely balanced. Some Savoyards find Simon Butteriss' Bunthorne over the top dramatically. But so is the character.

Let us try *The Mikado* on DVD. The 1939 English film (Criterion) with one American, Kenny Baker, is a movie rather than a staging, and a very elaborate one, constantly changing locale and filled with extras. The arrival of the Mikado is filmed as a full-scale parade, with not only officials, guards, and palanquins but a band featuring a horn so long it takes four dwarfs to bear it. Savoyards delight in the preservation of Martyn Green's Ko-Ko and Sidney Granville's Pooh-Bah, and the two do include traditional D'Oyly Carte "business" (presumably handed down from Gilbert's original stage direction). This takes in Green's pixilated dancing in "Here's a How-De-Do" and his turning around at a flute solo in "The Criminal Cried" to see who's playing. We even get one of the "How-De-Do" encores in an alternate staging, a D'Oyly Carte tradition for four generations and a reminder that audiences could demand repetitions in the days before recordings and the "freezing" of productions just before opening night. However, this *Mikado* hacks away at the score quite drastically. The D'Oyly Carte troupe made its own *Mikado* in 1966 (VAI), so stagey that one spies the actors' "bald" makeup. Another stage production, but a much livelier one, is Jonathan Miller's for the English National Opera (A & E), set entirely in the lobby of a resort hotel. The Monty Python's Eric Idle plays Ko-Ko, with updated lyrics for "I've Got a Little List." But the best of the cast—and thoroughly into the spirit of Miller's gentle jiving—is Felicity Palmer as Katisha. Her big solo in the first-act finale is rendered as a recital set piece at the grand piano in full diva kit topped by a fringed silver lamé mobcap with curly tail. The DVD adds touches of trick photography: after "Comes a Train of Little Ladies," the schoolgirls, in hockey outfits, pose around a settee and the view turns as still as a yearbook shot.

Entre Nous: Celebrating Offenbach (Opera Rara) presents two CDs of unusual material—solos, ensembles, and extended scenes—from the man who most definitively put comedy into the musical. The label's typical high-end production offers a dazzling group of soloists under conductor David Parry and a 240-page booklet with texts, translations, and plenty of background on the forty-one selections. This is a great way to take in Offenbach's melodic contours, his piquant orchestrations, and his ability to handle sentiment as well as the grotesque. There is plenty of pastiche, of course, along with music describing how it feels to freeze in a blizzard or roar along like a train. In the second-act finale of *La Diva*, Jennifer Larmore is hosting a party when her boy friend's uncle bursts in to drag him away. The ten-minute sequence is an opera in miniature, as the chorus exhorts the boy to stay by turning his name—Raoul—into a great tearful groan. And when that doesn't work, everyone breaks into a cancan.

On DVD, to see how beautifully Offenbach marries what is sung to what is spoken, try *La Grand-Duchesse de Gérolstein* (Virgin) and *La Belle Hélène* (Kultur), both staged by Laurent Pelly and conducted by Marc Minkowski, with Felicity Lott and Yann Beuron in the leads. These are merrily modern stagings, interpreted rather than gimmicked. Offenbach would have been surprised by all the dancing (that element of the musical hadn't been integrated in his time), and the sets stray from the stage directions—Pelly plays *Hélène*'s first act, laid in a public square in Sparta, in Helen and Menelaus' bedroom. Pelly also encouraged Lott to exaggerate the Grand-Duchess' erotic impulses, all rotating hips and bouncing knees. The work is already a sly cartoon; this makes it a crude one. Still, it does remind us how horrified American audiences were when Offenbach was finally produced in English translation. *That's* what they were about?

To consider how the musical's rich table of contents prompted its creators to experiment with serious themes, try *Les Contes d'Hoffmann*. The Lyons Opera offers a dark and fascinating version (Images, Arthaus), directed by Louis Erlo, that places Hoffmann's tales in a madhouse. Erlo and conductor Kent Nagano used the rediscovered material that transforms a frisky *opéra comique* into something so contemporary in its paradoxically visionary bitterness that Lyons billed the show as *Des Contes d'Hoffmann*— an untranslatable pun meaning both *Some Tales of Hoffmann* and *From the Tales of Hoffmann*. The cast is top, with Natalie Dessay, Barbara Hendricks, and Isabelle Vernet as Hoffmann's loves. Unfortunately, Andy Kaufman plays Hoffmann. Actually, it's tenor Daniel Galvez-Vallejo, but his resemblance to the late comedian is distracting. Veterans Gabriel Bacquier and José Van Dam are also on hand, and Brigitte Balleys plays Nicklausse, the hero's sidekick but, under this disguise, his muse. In the middle of the action, without warning, she rises from the orchestra pit on a platform with the first violinist to sing, to his accompaniment, "Vois sous l'archet frémissant . . ." (See, beneath the trembling bow . . .), on how art consoles the loveless. The scene is at once ghoulish and reassuring, and though it is but a moment in an event-filled staging, it reminds us how densely observant the musical can be when it expands its perspective.

In the variety shows so popular in the nineteenth century, two anthologies instruct us: *Monarchs of Minstrelsy* (Archeophone) and *Legendary Voices of Vaudeville* (Take Two), each furnished with colorfully illustrated notes on the performers and material. The minstrel disc goes back to music taken down in 1902, yet it can be heard easily through the surface buzz. The program opens with a tiny minstrel show, from the local street parade to advertise the bill, one of those ebullient marches so much a part of the old American soundscape—"Minstrels in town!"—through a typical First Part with the Interlocutor and the end men:

INTERLOCUTOR: Why is a dog sittin' on a cake of ice like a young lady?
END MAN: Because it's doggone nice!

and on to the olio acts, with the aid of a close-harmony quartet, a minstrel mainstay. The solos typify the innocence of minstrel content in "Don't Be an Old Maid, Milly" (a suitor's plea), "When You and I Were Young, Maggie," and "My Sweetheart's the Man in the Moon." Note that the last title, a woman's-point-of-view number, is sung by a man. This is partly because minstrel casting was all male, but also because the etiquette allowed for gender-neutral presentation into the start of the band-singer era, in the late 1920s, when discs of men singing even "Can't Help Lovin' Dat Man" and "The Man I Love" could be issued without igniting a marriage-equality firestorm. Note also the spoken intros to a few of the minstrel vocals: some of these cuts come from cylinders, which could not be labeled like the flat discs. Without the announcer, listeners wouldn't know what they were hearing unless they had the packaging handy.

Lew Dockstader, one of minstrelsy's outstanding impresarios, is on this disc, and he also gets mentioned in the first cut of the *Vaudeville* collection, in George M. Cohan's rendition of his own "You Won't Do Any Business If You Haven't Got a Band." This clues us in to an essential difference between minstrelsy and vaudeville, besides the obvious one of co-educational employment: vaudeville's material is racier in general, always eager to try new things, mention the famous, remark upon cultural institutions. Minstrelsy was nostalgic and shy of innovation. Then, too, vaudeville was urban in its outlook, while the minstrel habitually yearned for (southern) country life. True, we hear Marion Harris, in "Sweet Indiana Home," long for "my mammy's arms," and Margaret Young's "Tomorrow" invokes "my mammy's knee." Minstrelsy's influence was pervasive, indeed. Yet Elsie Janis, in "The Darktown Strutters' Ball," reorients the black worldview from Old Folks At Home to the big-city dance hall. "C'mon, honey," she ad libs, resorting to an encoded erotic term. "Ball the jack!"

We should pause to remark these vaudevillians' expansive delivery, reflecting their need to fill auditoriums without miking. Al Jolson isn't here, but others who shared his aggressive style are—Georgie Price, Blossom Seeley, Lou Holtz, Harry Fox (the inventor of the fox trot). Listen to Nora Bayes and her husband, Jack Norworth, duet in "Turn Off Your Light, Mister Moon Man." Each has a solo, but when they get together, Norworth takes the tune while Bayes surrounds him with ad libs, replies, and commentary, almost nagging at the music. Bert Williams; Sophie Tucker; the deep-toned mistress of soap-opera singing Belle Baker; and the racial-stereotype specialists (Gus) Van and (Joe) Schenck are also on hand, as are Vivian and Rosetta Duncan, the Cherry Sisters of the headliner class.* Like everyone else in vaudeville, the Duncans depended on those ad libs to keep the show moving, but theirs were the dumbest in show biz. "Why don't you dance?" asks one, and her sister replies, "I'm waiting for you to get off my foot!"

In *Music From the New York Stage* 1890–1920, a four-box series of three CDs each, Pearl has collected what appears to be every single surviving 78 side featuring an original-cast performance. Some of the discs are so rare that Pearl had to settle for copies with noisy surfaces, but then the program actually reaches back to the Bostonians in *Robin Hood* and *The Serenade*; Marie Cahill in—of course—an interpolation; Lillian Russell; Montgomery and Stone slipping jokes into a number from *The Old Town*; Eva Tanguay as the "I Don't Care" Girl; Eddie Cantor, Bert Williams, and John Steel in *Ziegfeld Follies of 1919*; Edith Day in *Irene*. The song titles themselves revive a long bygone time with sheer guiltless merriment, as in such ethnic concoctions as "Oh, How That German Could Love," "My Little Zulu Babe," "How Can They Tell That Oi'm Irish?," and, addressing a question that had us all waiting for centuries, "Who Played Poker With Pocahontas?" The very fullness of the bill sounds magnificent. However, most of what Victor, Columbia, and the lesser labels were preserving was the specialty number with no relationship to the plot. Thus, the series represents not the musical per se but rather its vaudeville component, the most unstable element in the composition of old shows.

Consider Volume Three, covering 1913 to 1917. We hear two cuts of Eleanor Painter, one of the era's leading sopranos, and a side of Irving Berlin's *Watch Your Step* gives us Charles King and Elizabeth Brice in "I've Gotta Go Back To (dear old) Texas," Brice going into a fluttery descant on the second chorus in a long-forgot style of the time. West End star George Grossmith is amusingly grisly in "Murders," from an English show, *Tonight's the Night*. "Take me away, constable," he urges at the end, oh so calmly. "I am quite ready." Christie MacDonald recalls the central role of her career, in Victor Herbert's *Sweethearts*, in three cuts, her vocalism understated except at the most

---

*The Cherry Sisters were so terrible that they supposedly had to play behind wire mesh for protection from vegetable projectiles. Notorious on the national level, they became a running gag in early talkies.

beseeching climaxes. The more spirited Mizzi Hajos is delightful in *Pom-Pom*; she, too, descants, in yodeling style. Baritone George MacFarlane, an unusually strong singer, offers "My Castle in the Air," possibly the first song ever written by Jerome Kern and P. G. Wodehouse and one of the transitional numbers in the creation of the New Music.

So far, so good. Yet most of the box comprises Al Jolson and his novelties, Chauncey Olcott too-ra-looring, a couple of band cuts, and more silly insert numbers. This isn't the meat of the musical: it's the side orders. Most disappointing of all is a cut of the Duncan Sisters in more Kern, "The Bull Frog Patrol," from *She's a Good Fellow*, in the fourth volume. What we hear is slightly amusing, no more. But on *The Jerome Kern Treasury* (see below), John McGlinn conducts Jeanne Lehmann and Rebecca Luker, a women's chorus, and an orchestra playing the song in its original scoring—and what sounds thin and hokey on the Duncans' 78 suddenly surges with melody. This is the problem with these old discs: they are, more often than not, misleading rather than representational.

Pearl offers another four volume set, this one at least yielding a good sample of each show's core numbers, *Broadway Through the Gramophone*. Here are the (usually) one-sided, twelve-inch 78 medleys that Victor (and, much less often, Columbia and Brunswick) made from 1909 into the 1930s: four minutes of some six or seven numbers sung by a merry little group with the odd solo here and there. Once again, Pearl has been amazingly resourceful in tracking down the rare sides (though the collection ends in 1929, ignoring later two-sided selections from *Jubilee* and *Revenge With Music*, among others). The ancient sound makes it difficult to hear the lyrics on the acoustic sides, but the transfers are so vivid one might almost be in a Victor studio in Camden, New Jersey, as the tiny orchestra bunches up in a corner and the singers crowd around the horn, backing away whenever they hit a high note. Then, too, anyone who wants to hear the difference between acoustic and electric recording has only to apply to Volume Four, wherein the older style gives way to the new on disc one and the voices start to ring out with astonishing realism.

With eight CDs' worth of medleys, we are treated to an immense amount of material. In just four minutes with Victor Herbert's *The Wizard Of the Nile*, we get a ceremonial chorus full of cymbal crashes (difficult to record in those days, for percussion jarred the delicate technology); about twelve seconds of a love song; comic tenor Billy Murray in "That's One Thing a Wizard Can Do":

> I can make politicians resign their positions
> And be just as honest as you . . .

the waltzy hit tune, "Star Light, Star Bright"; Murray again in that ode to a circus freak mentioned in the text, "My Angeline"; and at last the jumpy "A Cheer For Kibosh," with everyone in spread harmony for the penultimate chord, up to high A. It's the entire show in caption form.

THE FIRST AGE

I Wants To Be A Actor Lady (New World) is our only chance to hear even a note of *The Black Crook*, *Evangeline*, *Wang*, and a few other classic historian's titles. A product of the University of Cincinnati's school of music, the disc draws on student forces, including Kim Criswell (in Jerome Kern's first hit, "How'd You Like To Spoon With Me?") and Faith Prince (in the chorus), and everyone's in top form. The title cut (in a total of sixteen), added during a London tour of the black musical *In Dahomey*, outlines the agenda of a stagestruck young woman. It's an endearing piece, filled with references to the theatre of the day, a few of which even the all-knowing Stanley Green, who wrote the extensive liner notes, couldn't place. I'm eager to hear the source of a dramatic line quoted in the lyrics: "Troskeena Wellington, you can't square what you have done!"

What, now, of complete scores? Two very different outfits have produced a slew of titles. The Ohio Light Opera insists on two-disc sets, taped live on stage with the spoken dialogue. This is a drawback, as Ohio's casts are better singers than actors—*and* the discs are overpriced in the first place. Worse, Ohio tends to fiddle with texts. In *Naughty Marietta*, important music has been cut from the opening, the Jeunesse Dorée ball, and the two act finales. Romberg's *Maytime* is unusually well sung for this series, but its New York setting is blithely moved to New Orleans, which makes nonsense of "It's a Windy Day on the Battery." Apparently no one in Ohio knows that the Battery is the southern tip of Manhattan. And one of the show's hits, "Jump Jim Crow," has been bowdlerized into "Do Si Do" to soothe the politically sensitive. This is good censorship but bad history, as "Jump Jim Crow" was created specifically to evoke the earliest days of minstrelsy.

The other outfit is the Comic Opera Guild of Ann Arbor, offering, also live, both narration-and-dialogue but also music-only units of their titles; the group has recorded most of the lesser-known Herbert shows and a lot of early Kern. There is no fiddling: COG plays the text as written, often adding in cut numbers to fill out the evening. Unlike Ohio, with its quite serviceable orchestra, COG performs with two pianos—but the players, Adam Aceto and Patrick Johnson, are vivacious, with a strong response to the authentic Herbert style and its tip-toeing rubatos. At times, the pair pounds away so fervently that you'll hear a few lovable clinkers. The singers, too, may slip out of tune. But they all know how the music should go, while Ohio fields too many bland groups picking their way through scores from a time that liked its vocalists blitzing like opera champs.

That said, Ohio's *Robin Hood* and *El Capitan* are among the best in this field. Nicholas Wuehrmann takes De Wolf Hopper's *El Capitan* bass line up into tenor range—apparently a common practice in this role whenever Hopper wasn't available—while the love-plot tenor, Kyle Knapp, and mezzos Alta Dantzler and Tania Mandzy offer sturdy vocalism in Ohio's liveliest cast, very ably led by conductor Stephen Byess. Wuehrmann's counterpart over at *Robin Hood*, the Sheriff of Nottingham (Frederick Reeder) has to carry the show's comedy while maintaining a near-operatic baritone line. This Reeder does, even matching his singing style to his spoken lines with a Gilbert and Sullivan flourish, right down to his pronunciation of "diamond" in three gleefully fastidious syllables. Robin (Timothy Oliver) and Marian (Dominique McCormack) have far less interesting roles, but they hit all their notes, which take him (like *El Capitan*'s Knapp) up to high C and her to Ds and an E-flat at the finales. J. Lynn Thompson conducts a sound performance, and the cast is good enough if never thrilling. *Robin Hood* is presented in another of Ohio's sneaky "editions," though this time the revision is an improvement, even daring a last-minute joke on the show's hit tune, "Oh, Promise Me." *El Capitan*, a superior piece, appears to be more or less intact.

THE SECOND AGE

One can take the measure of the first half of the era with a comparison of its two outstanding hits, the comic opera *The Merry Widow* and the fairytale extravaganza *The Wizard of Oz*. An excellent reading of the former from 1952 (Columbia, DRG), in the Adrian Ross translation used on Broadway in 1907, offers Dorothy Kirsten and Robert Rounseville under Lehman Engel in an extremely long timing for the LP age, over sixty-two minutes. The other major English-language *Widow* recordings use new translations, not to mention more spirited widows—for instance Patrice Munsel (Victor),

June Bronhill in her most famous role (twice, both for EMI), Beverly Sills (EMI), who sings the lyrics of Broadway's own Sheldon Harnick, and Joan Sutherland (Decca), in an offbeat tunestack that includes the rarely heard "Quite Parisian," written by Lehár and Ross for the comedian of the London premiere, W. H. Berry. Douglas Gamley arranged an overture that is a kind of *Leonore No. 3* of operetta, and Sutherland turns her entrance into *Lucia di Lammermoor*. *Als Gast*, Regina Resnik defies her age to play cocotte in the cancan, with an *"Et moi!"* tasty enough to snack on. But all this lures us away from how the widow sounded to its first American audiences. Today, Ross' English feels stodgy, but Engel's opera singers are very comfortable in his verses, and, indeed, Ross sounds almost suave next to what *Robin Hood's* Harry B. Smith was writing. Engel adds a zither to the so-called "Merry Widow Waltz," an odd but effective touch, and note a bizarre engineering glitch on the CD at the very start of the second verse of "In Marsovia."

The Wizard of Oz claims no modern recording, but the Hungry Tiger Press in San Diego has gathered all the pertinent flotsam into a two-CD set: two-and-a-half hours of flat discs, cylinders (with more of that announcing), piano rolls, and even music boxes of songs from the show, from other Oz shows, and by Oz cast members in other material. Elaborate notes and texts recreate the event, establishing which songs were part of the core score and which joined it during its long touring history. It's a triumph of the absurd, for if *The Merry Widow*, like Gilbert and Sullivan, sings its way right through its plot, the Oz songs refer to anything *but* the plot.

For the English shows so influential in the United States, Hyperion obliges with a bright, enthusiastic performance of *The Geisha*, under Ronald Corp. Is it comic opera? Musical comedy? The score calls it a "Japanese musical play"—but it does demand real singers with a sense of fun, as if comic opera and musical comedy at once. Thus, Christopher Maltman and Sarah Walker get silly while duetting beautifully in "The Toy," about childhood playthings from windups to Punch and Judy. Note that the booklet's excellently detailed synopsis reveals that "The Toy," like many of *The Geisha's* songs, touches the plotline but glancingly. *The Geisha* premiered in 1896, the same year in which the last work by Gilbert and Sullivan; *The Grand Duke*, premiered. But Savoyard integration is already overthrown; one can no longer follow the story through the lyrics. Nevertheless, *Geisha* enthusiasts will brood and scheme till they acquire the long-lost Urania LP of a Radio Berlin broadcast under Otto Dobrindt, featuring Rosl Seegers' melting O Mimosa San (the real geisha) and Ruth Zillgers' rougher voiced Molly (disguised as one), a standard separation of abilities in these old comic operas: the sweetheart and the seriocomic. Hyperion's Molly, Sarah Walker, is full of lovely tone, however, for these old shows are frankly better sung today than they were when new.

The most melodic of all the English imports is the only one still performed today, *The Arcadians*, CD'ed by West End Angel in a compilation of two LPs and with an extremely strong cast headed by June Bronhill and Ann Howard. Original 1909 cast members Florence Smithson, Phyllis Dare, and Alfred Lester turn up in seven bonus tracks. *The Geisha* and *The Arcadians* were American hits, but Edward German's comic opera after Henry Fielding, *Tom Jones*, was not. Naxos' two-CD set, complete with cut numbers, tells why: it's a very musical work, but awfully serious. German completed an unfinished Sullivan score and collaborated with Gilbert, and that's the problem: *Tom Jones* (and German's other famous title, *Merrie England*) is G & S without the sparkle. *The Geisha* and *The Arcadians* typify the generation after G & S, with a leavening of music-hall fun, but German never got out of the Savoy. Those who nevertheless want to hear how Fielding's sexy novel turns into a comic opera might skip Naxos for EMI's old LP of excerpts, much better sung and, on CD, coupled with the Sargent *Beggar's Opera* (see above). And those who prefer the playful side of this territory should enjoy *Lionel Monckton: Songs From the Shows* (Hyperion), twenty-two cuts sung by Catherine Bott and Richard Suart, with chorus and Ronald Corp again conducting. 'The acoustic is spacious, the tympani pounding as if in one of Mahler's doomsday movements, though the songs are pure musical comedy. There's nothing in *Tom Jones* as frivolously pleasant as Monckton's "Two Little Sausages" or "Moonstruck"—yet German and Monckton were almost exact contemporaries, born two months apart in the early 1860s. "I'm such a silly when the moon comes out," sings the "Moonstruck" girl, while *Tom Jones* is all "My Lady's Coach" and "For to-night, for to-night, let me dream out my dream of delight."

For American comic opera, AEI offers a double-bill of core numbers from *The Prince Of Pilsen* and *The Pink Lady*. This was the way many Americans heard the old classics in the 1940s, when stagings were all but unheard of: a half-hour of radio, as actors performed linking dialogue for legit singers (in this case Jessica Dragonette and Charles Kullman, misspelled as "Kuhlman" on the album). It's operetta filet. The LP never made it to CD, yet it's worth mentioning, as these two once imposing titles are otherwise unrecorded. Note, in the spoken cue before *Pilsen*'s finale, one of the very last "Dutch" comics, as Hans Wagner.

In American musical comedy, the go-to figure is George M. Cohan, and Rick Benjamin resuscitates the authentic style in *You're a Grand Old Rag* (New World). Two singers give us Cohan's words and music (mainly in the most famous titles) to balance purely orchestral tracks, such as the overtures to *Little Nellie Kelly* and *The Talk of New York*. Benjamin's male soloist, Colin Pritchard, renders his numbers in a genuine Cohan voice, much less aggressive than we're used to from, for example, Joel Grey in *George M!* (Columbia, Sony). Still, that cast album is a treasury of Cohan songs, with visitations from such obscure shows as *The Little Millionaire*; *Hello, Broadway*; and *The Governor's Son*, which provides the ultra-Cohanesque "Push Me Along in My Pushcart." Unlike Rick Benjamin's CD, the scoring reflects modern usages—and, though the notes are mum about it, lyric revisions make completely new numbers out of *The Merry Malones*' "Tee Teedle Tum Di Dum" (as "Twentieth Century Love") and *Billie*'s "I'm a One Girl Man" (as "My Town"). A future Queen of Broadway, Bernadette Peters, plays Cohan's sister, Josie.

The master of the age, in both comic opera and musical comedy, was Victor Herbert. He is much recorded, but just about everything is flawed—in vocal appeal, performing style, or deceptive revision. Ohio Light Opera offers most of the famous titles, with the usual Ohio problems. In *The Red Mill*, two minor characters get into a nice swing on "You Never Can Tell About A Woman." But the romantic numbers are feeble. One might try Decca's CD reissue of the show, coupled with *Babes in Toyland*, two 78 sets from the 1940s. These are arguably Herbert's most agreeable scores, even cut down to a handful of numbers each. The liner notes do nothing to assist us, getting very busybody about the singers' biographies but, for instance, failing to explain why Kenny Baker, in the third cut of *Babes*, claims to be a gypsy named Floretta. (He's one of the two babes, hiding from their wicked uncle in disguise.) Further, the booklet assures us that the songs have been reordered to conform to the narrative; on the contrary, everything's in the wrong place. Some problems are native to the original discs, as when *Babes*' "Song Of the Poet" omits the *Lucia* spoof so intrinsic to the number's pastiche form, or when, in *The Red Mill*'s "Moonbeams," Eileen Farrell and the chorus smooth out Herbert's meticulous sixteenth notes into eighth notes, robbing the melody of its edgy wistfulness.

Then why recommend the CD? Because this is wonderful music wonderfully sung. And there is an antidote of sorts: orchestral readings of the same two scores (Naxos) in authentic style, sixteenth notes and all. Keith Brion conducts some fifty minutes of *Babes*, including the lengthy prelude of the ocean voyage and shipwreck, which the liner notes incorrectly declare to have been cut. The scene is listed in the New York program.

The Comic Opera Guild recorded most if not all of the Herbert shows Ohio ignored. One might try COG's *Her Regiment*, an unknown but tuneful piece with lyrics by one of the better Broadway writers, William Le Baron, whose day job was running the Paramount studio in Astoria, Queens. (Le Baron wrote also the words of the great score to *Apple Blossoms*, but there is no recording save two 78 sides by John Charles Thomas.) More Herbert: Flapper's *A Victor Herbert Showcase* looks in on the music as it was heard in the years just after Herbert's death. A mixture of vocal and orchestral cuts takes in Herbert's side-career in light-classical pieces, presented here in the lush violations of tempo that mark the true Herbert style. The singers range from Richard Crooks to Jeanette MacDonald (each with a high C), and the players range from violinist Alfredo Campoli to, for that touch of camp, the Yerkes Jazzarimba Orchestra. A *Sweethearts* medley blithely sings the lyrics used in MGM's version (a number here called "Mademoiselle" is actually "There Is Magic in a Smile" in the show), but "Pan Americana," a march with a smashing Latin trio, returns us to pure Herbert. The twenty-one cuts yield seventy-three minutes of music.

THE THIRD AGE

Nothing recalls the 1920s like George and Ira Gershwin, best served by Nonesuch's series of restorations commissioned by Ira's widow, Leonore: first *Girl Crazy*, followed by *Strike Up the Band* (in both versions, though 1927, with 1930 bonus tracks, came out in 1991 and 1930 appeared in full twenty years later), *Lady, Be Good!*, *Pardon My English*, and *Oh, Kay!*. *Tell Me More* and *Tip-Toes* were also taken down, but after Leonore's death the Gershwin heirs apparently lost interest; New World brought the last two out in a double-disc set in 2001. The series oozes class. Casting combines the usual suspects (Rebecca Luker, Brent Barrett, David Carroll, Judy Blazer) with delightful surprises (William Katt, Frank Gorshin, Ivy Austin of the plangent tones, who played the title role in *Raggedy Ann* on Broadway, Adam Arkin). Susan Lucci turns up in *Oh, Kay!* as a very funny Spiteful Fiancée rivaling Dawn Upshaw, who typifies the high level of vocalism that rules the series. (Upshaw made also valuable Nonesuch discs devoted to Rodgers and Hart and Vernon Duke.) Even when the original orchestrations were extant, some restoring was necessary, and it was done ingeniously, mostly by Tommy Krasker. For instance, *Oh, Kay!*'s partly lost first-act finaletto was recomposed by Steve Brown in flawless period style: one new melody (to "Oh, it's perfectly grand") with reprises of refrains already heard ("Don't Ask," "Maybe," "Clap Yo' Hands," "Someone To Watch Over Me") with new lyrics and interspersed with plot glitches in underscored dialogue. Nonesuch's booklets, too, are informative about the shows and the authenticity of the resuscitations. For *Girl Crazy*, Krasker identifies his source material in four pages of very close printing. And when in fact new orchestrations were needed, they were supplied largely by Russell Warner, invariably the first choice for new-old scoring till his recent death.

Nonesuch's Gershwins were not all disc premieres. *Lady, Be Good!* actually got a cast album complete with the Astaires: in London. Since the 1910s, the English casts of American shows had been preserving eight or ten sides per title. Most of the London albums, which start with Irving Berlin's *Watch Your Step*, run through *Oh, Boy!* (with

Beatrice Lillie, billed as *Oh, Joy!*) and *Going Up*, and move on to *Sally, The Blue Kitten, Sunny, No, No, Nanette*, and most of the famous operettas, have been rereleased on various labels and presumably will continue to resurface (though *Going Up* has proved elusive save for a single side by Evelyn Laye). Some of the vocalism is raw. You can tell the musical comedies from the operettas because the musical-comedy men can't sing—and Lillie, who can, nonetheless talks her way through Jerome Kern. Still, these are genuine preservations, made with their pit orchestras a generation before it became the norm on Broadway.

A few DVDs bear preservations as well, more of performing styles than of specific shows. Much of the choreography we see in early talkies is Broadway on a soundstage, and Florenz Ziegfeld's mixture of crazies and fairy princesses haunts us like Sondheim *Follies* ghosts in four films especially. *Sally* (Warner Archive), though greatly changed from what Ziegfeld produced on Broadway, does star Marilyn Miller, and the disc includes Technicolor footage of "Wild Rose"—a real taste of what Miller was like on stage. A Hollywood original, *Be Yourself* (Kino), Fanny Brice's only surviving star vehicle (her first film, the part-talkie *My Man*, is lost), serves as a museum visit to her versatility, with five numbers from comedy to torch. Most Bricean is an opera spoof starting, "Is something the matter with [arts philanthropist] Otto Kahn or is something the matter with me?"—the lament of a would-be diva who then proceeds to flatten the diva's airs with the insight of an outsider with x-ray vision.

A sixth number is missing from the *Be Yourself* print Kino used, and a good two reels' worth of *Rio Rita* (Warner), including at least two numbers, is also missing. But what remains follows the play somewhat closely, even retaining Bert Wheeler and Robert Woolsey from Broadway. While *Rio Rita* is not a great work, it was a great Ziegfeld production, as the damsel and hero blithely operetta around while the two comics zany the place up, the two energies never as much as trading a glance. A third Ziegfeld title, *Whoopee*—still awaiting DVD release—presents another classic Ziegfeldian in Eddie Cantor. Further, the film offers an entire Ziegfeld cast, for the producer sold *Whoopee* to Samuel Goldwyn, who closed the show and brought everyone out to California to play a last performance before the camera. The film dropped about forty minutes of the continuity, featured leads Ruth Etting (for song) and Tamara Geva (for ballet), and most of the score. With camera-provocative choreography by Busby Berkeley, the film *Whoopee* isn't exactly a replica of theatre style, but it comes close. It even includes an authentic Ziegfeldian showgirl number, on an Indian motif, as squaws march (and then ride) onto a stage set wearing less and less with each entrance.

On Golden Age composers, Pearl again assists us, with its *Ultimate* series, each single CD decorated with old sheet-music covers, its contents devoted to original-cast cuts from the 1910s on into the 1940s, but centering on the two middle decades. *The Ultimate George Gershwin* includes London cast albums of the 1920s—*Lady, Be Good!* and *Tip-Toes* on Volume Two and, on Volume One, *Primrose*, an English show in the English manner, Gershwin's New York jazz finally stealing in in "Naughty Baby," later used in *Crazy For You*. Most of the major Broadway songwriters created shows for London, but only Gershwin actually wrote a show in London's style, at times slavishly recreating the sounds of the Monckton years. Leslie Henson's number "When Toby Is Out Of Town" is one of the hippity-hoppity hymns to oneself that Edwardian comics loved to romp through, and Heather Thatcher's "I Make Hay When the Moon Shines" is an homage to the aforementioned "Moonstruck" (on Hyperion's Monckton CD, above). *The Ultimate Irving Berlin*'s first volume takes in *Watch Your Step* and *Stop! Look! Listen!* (given in England as *Follow the Crowd*) from the 1910s, but Volume Two moves into the 1920s with the *Ziegfeld Follies* and *Music Box Revues*, as Roscoe brings on the Weismann girls with "The Girls of My Dreams" and "Lady of the Evening," the Brox Sisters recall the close-harmony sister acts popular into the 1950s, and Grace Moore surpasses everyone in sheer warmth. *The Ultimate Rodgers and Hart* runs to three volumes, *Cole Porter* to four, and rather a lot of movie material creeps in. "Don't Fence Me In" was Porter's biggest hit and Roy Rogers the lad who introduced it in *Hollywood Canteen*: but it takes us far off our mission.

For a taste of twenties musical comedy in modern sound, try *Kitty's Kisses* (PS Classics), from 1926, in which Rebecca Luker, Philip Chaffin, Danny Burstein, and (in a small but very funny role) Victoria Clark revive the old "couple mixups in hotel" routine. The score is by Con Conrad and Gus Kahn—uncelebrated but, here, tuneful and charming. Oddly, this utterly unknown show had a previous recording: on a technicality. In London, *Kitty's Kisses* used the title and two or three songs from another 1926 musical, Rodgers and Hart's *The Girl Friend*. Three generations later, in 1987, a regional English theatre revived this mélange, still fraudulently titled *The Girl Friend* and now offering less of the *Kitty's Kisses* score and more Rodgers and Hart. Though the cast was vocally weak, TER recorded it (on LP only); a comparison of the two discs reveals just how sharp the PS cast is. However, PS interpolated Conrad's New Dance Sensation Oscar winner "The Continental" as a finale; the original finale, "Step On the Blues," can be heard on TER and in the English *Girl Friend* medley in *Broadway Through the Gramophone*, Volume Four.

Among essential twenties musicals, *Good News!* should have had an authentic reading by now. MGM first filmed it in 1930, and the 1947 remake (Warner DVD), faithful to the story though retaining only key numbers, is very personably cast, including the seldom seen Joan McCracken. The studio wanted Van Johnson for the football-hero lead opposite June Allyson, ending instead with the preposterously suave Peter Lawford. But it works. The 1974 Alice Faye revival got a private cast album on two LPs made of audio tapes of various performances. As I said earlier, the show suffered such a pile-on of irrelevant De Sylva, Brown, and Henderson numbers that it was virtually a jukebox musical, yet this was largely the basis for the score used in a lively 1933 Wichita revival (Jay). "Just Imagine" is shunted into the second act, misguising a wishful dream into a torch song, though "The Varsity Drag," invariably used as a late-in-the-second-act raveup after the 1947 film, is back in its original slot in Act One. Further, here's one's chance to collect "On the Campus" and "Today's the Day"—and they even sneaked most of the 1927 opening chorus into the first cue.

Twenties operetta fares better, if only because its more evolved musical narration makes the insertion of extraneous numbers difficult. There are authentic readings of *Rose-Marie* (Victor, Sepia), with Julie Andrews and Giorgio Tozzi, and *The New Moon* (Ghostlight), with Rodney Gilfry and Christiane Noll, from an Encores! concert. Each is ideal: a single disc stuffed with music, a wealth of vocal talent, no dialogue unless dramatically necessary, and no interfering "editions." This *New Moon* is especially rich in vocal glamor, keeping Noll in the original high keys for her numbers; in London, these had to be lowered for Evelyn Laye, as we hear on the 1929 album (World, Pearl).

The most recorded twenties exotic-setting operetta is *The Desert Song*, starting with its only cast album, from the London run at Drury Lane, with Edith Day and Harry Welchman. Their approach is mannered, even fantastical, as operetta folk generally were (especially in England), and the text is authentic. In "Romance," a typo in the vocal score has duped many later Margots into a solecism on "My princes become what I mold them" (to rhyme with "enfold them"). But the Chappell score reads, in a misprint, "would them." Day gets it right, because she learned it direct from parts rather than from the printed score. Then, too, at the climax of "One Flower Grows Alone in Your

Garden," the tenor sails up to high C while the bass dredges out a super-low C—as in Romberg's writing but, to my knowledge, not to be heard on subsequent recordings.

These include Columbia's old mono LP (Flare) with Nelson Eddy and Doretta Morrow, most complete but lacking the comics, Bennie and Susan. Worse, Eddy is at his dullest, outshown by his rival in the love plot, David Atkinson. This LP-era tendency to record operettas with little or no participation by the comedians explains why moderns think of these shows as relentlessly romantic. Typically, Pearl's CD release of the London *Desert Song* tacks on London's *New Moon* while omitting the comics' two sides, though the disc is filled out with *The Blue Train*, an adaptation of Robert Stolz's *Mädi* and an out-and-out musical comedy with lots of drollery. Note, however, that both the *Rose-Marie* and *New Moon* cited just above made sure to keep the funny characters in place.

English studio *Desert Songs* include Bennie, whose main contributions are a "Help! She's vamping me!" duet, "One Good Boy Gone Wrong," and a salute to Elinor Glyn's old term for sexual charisma, "It." On a World LP, John Hewer sings both—and note tenor Peter Hudson's unique rendering of "One Flower," in an intense near-screech suggesting calls to prayer from the minaret, much as at the end of "Sands Of Time" in *Kismet*. Another English LP, on Saga, with Mary Millar and Robert Colman, offers not only Bennie but Susan as well. Millar sings the incorrect "would" in "Romance," but she does sample the rare "clockwork" encore to "The Sabre Song," enlivened by anachronistic xylophone runs. The best known of the English *Desert Songs* (EMI) stars June Bronhill and Edmund Hockridge; Bronhill sings "would," too. The performance is woefully untheatrical, though Bronhill is as exquisite as ever.

My favorite *Desert Song* is Decca's 1945 set with Kitty Carlisle and Wilbur Evans. Ten sides exclude the comics, but the reading sounds like a cast album, complete with cue-in dialogue (mostly not from the show). "One Flower," sung by Felix Knight, is sweet rather than abrasive, and Carlisle makes "The Sabre Song" confidential rather than a big showpiece: operetta with nuances. Offstage, Carlisle habitually referred to one of her children as "My daughter, the doctor," as though there were something unique about the profession. It was Carlisle who was unique: the suavest of operetta singers and one of Broadway's best-liked people. There's something simply endearing about her singing; one hears it, say, in the twee chic of her "ra-ta-ta-ta"s in the "French Military Marching Song." Note her descant on "One Alone" in the last cut; by 1945, the practice was about to disappear. The CD release includes a little-known Decca *New Moon* album.

To follow the rise of the New Music, start with Joan Morris' *Vaudeville* (Nonesuch), with her husband, William Bolcom, at the piano, to get a fix on popular song at the turn of the century—and note the long verses and short choruses. The revolution starts shyly, in *Jerome Kern: Lost Treasures* (Centaur), Anne Sciolla's review of Kern's first six years or so. It's a somewhat dainty recital, as Sciolla is subtle and her accompanist, Brian Kovach, plays straight from the published sheets, without fireworks. The lyricists are all from Kern's pre-Wodehouse days; they lack brilliance. The music has charm, though, as when, in "Whistle When You're Lonely," tootling is written into the melody.

The other leader of the revolution was Irving Berlin, and the key work is *Watch Your Step*, on CD in the aforementioned London production but also in its own 2001 off-Broadway cast album (OC). An ingratiating kid ensemble and excellent keyboard work from Mark Hartman bring the show back to life. When Julian Brightman, in Vernon Castle's old role, sings "I'm a Dancing Teacher Now," he demonstrates waltz and tango as others watch and comment; one almost sees him in motion. It's fun to hear Berlin trying out a genre he would make his own, in the "I love to hate you" sweethearts' nag (called, in fact, "I Hate You") and the quodlibet counterpoint duet, in "(Won't you play

a) Simple Melody." Stepping out of the show itself, the company borrows Berlin's two other famous quodlibets, *Annie Get Your Gun*'s "Old Fashioned Wedding" and *Call Me Madam*'s "You're Just in Love," for a wonderful stunt. "Now," cries an announcer, "we will attempt, perhaps for a first time, to sing his most famous three [quodlibets]." Not one after the other: all at once, six different strains in harmonious war. Further, we can track Berlin's next four years in *Keep On Smiling* (Oakton), Benjamin Sears' recital, to Bradford Conner's piano. Anne Sciolla's Kern is so innocent that "Ballooning" pleads, "And up above/We'd just make love,/If you'd only go ballooning with me." But Sears' Berlin is ethnic stereotypes and wartime strains, and he and Conner work on the grand scale. It's a bit of Jolson, perhaps, to Sciolla's Christie MacDonald.

We jump back to Kern in the 1959 off-Broadway *Leave It To Jane* (Strand, DRG, AEI), very much in style, even including the plotty ensembles so much a part of Second Age scores. Louis Hirsch, a Kern acolyte, gets a superb showcase in *Midnight Frolic* (New World), like New World's Cohan CD using period orchestrations and a handful of vocals. Hirsch's most famous tune, oddly, is the theme of *The George Burns and Gracie Allen Show*, which started out as "The Love Nest," from *Mary*. You'll hear it sung, along with Hirsch's second famous number, "Hello, Frisco!" (complete with the interjections mentioned in the text) from *Ziegfeld Follies of 1915*, whose eleven-minute overture is included. Note the Roscoe Number, "A Girl For Each Month of the Year."

This brings us to just about 1920, when Kern, Berlin, Cole Porter, and Hirsch are joined by Vincent Youmans, the Gershwins, Rodgers and Hart, and De Sylva, Brown, and Henderson, as the Golden Age takes wing. A bit of backtracking, now, with another elusive item, *Early Kern* (Shadowland). First issued on cassette and only later on CD (with extra tracks), this invaluable retrospective takes Kern from his start ("Never Marry a Girl With Cold Feet") through his all-important *Girl From Utah* and Princess eras, then on to such long-lined ballads as "The Land Where the Good Songs Go" and "Weeping Willow Tree." Save for one cut sung by an out-of-place has-been, the performances are all of the first division, led by Judy Kaye, David Carroll, George Dvorsky, Rebecca Luker, and other stalwarts in the revival of Broadway Melody. The closing cut, Paige O'Hara's "Alice In Wonderland," is illustrated in this book's picture section.

To complete Kern's journey to *Show Boat*, try the Comic Opera Guild's reading of *The Stepping Stones* and New World's *Sitting Pretty*, a John McGlinn project with Judy Blazer and Paige O'Hara in roles intended for the Duncan Sisters. In the difference between the cute little ditties on Anne Sciolla's Kern disc and these broadly limned vocal sequences lies the saga of how the musical reinvented itself finally, in *Show Boat*. The first-choice recording is McGlinn's labor of love and passion, EMI's three-CD box in crossover style, with numbers dropped during composition, rehearsals, or tryouts, and forget-me-nots added in various restylings: a *Show Boat* symposium. I detailed a *Show Boat* discography in an earlier book, a biography of Florenz Ziegfeld, so for now let us consider *Show Boat* questions in a single disc, EMI's 1959 English studio cast, most recently on Classics For Pleasure with, as a bonus, core numbers from Kern's *Roberta* and *Music in the Air*.

Every production of *Show Boat*—even every studio recording—must deal with a host of issues, mainly dramaturgical but also political and of course musical. As early as the second staging (in London, in 1928), the spot just before the finale's reprise of "Ol' Man River" got a completely new number, and virtually every major revival finds something different to do in that slot. Political considerations start with the show's very first line, "Niggers all work on the Mississippi." Our EMI recording changes the danger word to "darkies," which is still pretty dangerous. (In more correct times, the 1994 New York staging settled on "Colored folks work . . .") More pertinent is the casting of Julie, unmasked as a mulatto after having "passed" (i.e., for "white") all her adult life. Obviously, she must look Caucasian. But, for the last generation, the role has become unofficial black property, which creates politically correct story nonsense. If Julie looks black, how did she pass? This shouldn't come into play in recordings, of course, but in 1959 Shirley Bassey's singles were charting for EMI, and this *Show Boat* was to be her first LP. True, she had only two numbers, but she was featured alone on the cover in a color photo, costumed on a mockup of a slice of boat deck. As Bassey was half-Nigerian, this stretched credibility—as did MGM's casting of Lena Horne as Julie in the tab *Show Boat* we see in *Till the Clouds Roll By* or the occasional appearances of Dorothy Dandridge in the role in regional productions. At that, Bassey makes no attempt create a "stage" Julie, tying "Can't Help Lovin' Dat Man" to an "after hours at the blues club" trumpet riff for a nightclub feeling or singing "Bill" with a smile.

But then, the entire album is a somewhat pop *Show Boat*, with arrangements so big they suggest volcano explosions. The two romantic leads, Don McKay and Marlys Watters, were just then playing Tony and Maria in the London *West Side Story*, and they are wonderful singers—EMI gave the pair a *West Side Story* EP single all their own. They clearly could have gone right into a *Show Boat* revival, if *Show Boat* revivals weren't routinely casting seasoned veterans in these parts. Magnolia is seventeen when *Show Boat* begins, but stage Magnolias are often crowding forty. Meanwhile, for the sidekick comic, Ellie, normally a dancer, EMI brought in the daffy Dora Bryan, billed on the cover as "guest artiste," as if her day job busied her with Shakespeare and the classics.

In all, this *Show Boat* lacks theatre bite, as a string of unrelated songs. At least EMI added in Joe and Queenie's "I Still Suits Me," from the 1936 film. Without this duet, the characters are disembodied singers, their "Ol' Man River" and "Can't Help Lovin' Dat Man" robbed of their thematic and narrative significance.* At that, enlarging the *Show Boat* tunestack is traditional. In 1958, with but a single LP side to work with the (*No, No, Nanette* took the obverse), the Fontana label slipped in another of the 1936 film numbers, "I Have the Room Above." No other major American show except *Follies* counts so many add-ons.

The 1930s was the last great decade of the revue, and no recording is more apropos than Decca Broadway's *Ziegfeld Follies of 1936*, one of the greatest studio recreations in its wealth of melody and authentic orchestrations. Ironically, it is too well sung, for the Vernon Duke–Ira Gershwin songs were not performed this capably in 1936, when functional (as opposed to attractive) voices were common and lyrics were often chanted rather than sung. Decca includes no sketches. It's all music, and from the very first notes of the third number, "My Red-Letter Day," Karen Ziemba and the Walton brothers, Jim and Bob, raise up a contagious con brio in their close harmony with woodpecking accompaniment. Later, Ruthie Henshall counters with jaded-lady verse in "That Moment Of Moments." She asks, "What was there to do?," noting that "The opera was getting dull." So she moves to the lobby and meets her heart match, Howard McGillin. In romance comic books, you get what is called a "kiss panel"; in musicals, they love duet.

Revues loved songs that spoofed the famous. Thus, in "I Can't Get Started (with you), Peter Scolari and Christine Ebersole turn a good-night smooch into a review of the leadership class—FDR and MGM, Garbo and the Prince of Wales, *The New Yorker*

---

*EMI's Joe, Inia Te Wiata, sings "Ol' Man River" in C Major, the score key, though Joes now prefer B-flat, simply because Paul Robeson sang it thus. Still, it sounds brighter in the higher key, and William Warfield, in the 1966 Lincoln Center revival (Victor), sang it a half-step higher than that. He sounds marvelous.

and *Time*. He's the wonder boy of the age, yet she feels nothing. (Is *she* in for a surprise!) Meanwhile, in Fanny Brice's numbers, Mary Testa goes to town in "Modernistic Moe," a goof on Modern Dance from Brice's familiar viewpoint of the nice Jewish girl bewildered by but game for the latest twist in WASP sophistication. Note the number's emphasis on pastiche and cultural reference, with quotations of Gertrude Stein, the old Karl Hoschna musical *Madame Sherry*, and the pop tune "Dancing With Tears in My Eyes." And the dance break is mock-Shostakovich.

We can sample the small-scaled revue in the union show *Pins and Needles* (Columbia), one of Barbra Streisand's best albums. True, this is a show recording accompanied by a jazz-flavored quartet and with the composer-lyricist, Harold Rome, in four numbers. But Streisand dominates the survey in six cuts. "She doesn't know a thing about the period," said Rome at the time, "and yet she gets into the songs as if she'd been born to them." The project came about in 1962, when Streisand was crashing into fame. According to her biographer Randall Riese, Columbia honcho Goddard Lieberson didn't want Streisand even after taping her with the rest of the original cast in another Rome work with a thirties labor background, *I Can Get It For You Wholesale*. Streisand dominated that recording, too, from a genuine showstopper, the comic lament "Miss Marmelstein," to "What Are They Doing To Us Now?," a powerful humanist outcry in the style of "Brother, Can You Spare a Dime?" and "Remember My Forgotten Man." Lieberson's resistance is bizarre, especially when *Pins and Needles* offers Streisand the "Miss Marmelstein"-like "Nobody Makes a Pass at Me," which utterly overcomes even the original-cast 78 of Millie Weitz (local 22, Dressmakers) when *Pins and Needles* was new, in 1937.

In the thirties book show, *Face The Music* (DRG) catches the buffoonish worldliness of the post–Victor Herbert era, as in the prostitute's "Torch Song" referred to in the text, put over with amusingly naive yet knowing commitment by Felicia Finley. She is, so to say, contradicted by an interpolated revivalist hymn, "If You Believe," led by Judy Kaye at her most superb. The entire cast is marvelous, with great orchestra playing under Rob Fisher.

Another of PS Classics' excellent restorations, Kay Swift's *Fine and Dandy* (1930), gives us the star-comic show. That comic, Joe Cook, was in only one number, the title song, which Mario Cantone and Carolee Carmello put over with giddy aplomb. Carmello really takes stage with her two solos, "Can This Be Love?" and the second-act torcher, "Nobody Breaks My Heart": her vocal timbre is loaded with personality, at once plaintive and determined, and she knows how these old ballads go. Note the odd role of a certain Miss Hunter—Eleanor Powell, in the original—who is on hand simply to lead production numbers.

On Your Toes brings us to the dance show, a fixture of the 1930s from *The Band Wagon* to Rodgers and Hart's *Too Many Girls*, in 1939. Columbia's mono *On Your Toes* suffers from sleepy tempos and Portia Nelson's inappropriately operatic delivery of the ingenue role. It's a pleasant jolt to switch to the 1954 revival (Decca, MCA), where Elaine Stritch, in a different part, reinstates musical-comedy style. Producer-director George Abbott gifted her with a Rodgers and Hart interpolation (from *Present Arms*), "You Took Advantage of Me"; don't be fooled by Stritch's placid opening, as her second chorus thoroughly jazzes up the joint. Further, Columbia completely omits one of *On Your Toes'* most delightful touches, when the protagonist and his precocious jazz-classical composer student plan the orchestration of the title song even as the ingenue is about to sing it and the ensemble interpret it in a hoofing-versus-ballet challenge dance. "Let's start the melody on the piano," it begins. "Then I'd sneak in a trumpet solo . . ." And so it continues, with each addition sounding in the pit as the actors announce it: the wire swish, the strings in an inner-voiced counter-melody, the woodwinds. "Then the whole band!" as the tutti explodes with joy. "And then I'd sing the song!" cries 1954's Kay Coulter. The sequence comes through even better in the 1983 revival (Jay), in slightly different words, now with Christine Andreas. A game cast, excellent conducting by John Mauceri, and a rare Broadway attempt to bring back an old show in nearly its original form (even in its brilliant orchestrations, by Hans Spialek) make this *On Your Toes* one of the very best of revival albums. "Slaughter on Tenth Avenue," at more than seventeen minutes, is, to my knowledge, recorded complete for the first time.

The essential thirties musical is *Anything Goes*, and while we have 78s from Ethel Merman and from the original London leads (both on *Ultimate Cole Porter* Volume Two), there was no cast album per se till the 1962 off-Broadway revival (Epic). The very engaging cast rallies behind Eileen Rodgers' almost implausibly resounding instrument, a sharp little band offers nifty brass playing, and there are choral arrangements not heard elsewhere. Alas, when this version made it to London seven years later, a crew of nobodies ham-and-egged its way through the score (Decca, TER) with a lack of charm so extreme it could be called fascinating, led by probably the only Reno Sweeney in history to sing in a Vegas lounge-act croon. Yet the disc has one other distinction: till its LP rerelease, it was the all-time rarest cast album of an American show, edging out Victor's television *Lady in the Dark* and the 1964 London *She Loves Me* (EMI). As legend tells, Decca's *Anything Goes* was pressed and packaged, then abruptly cancelled—but one box was shipped to South Africa. When it sold out, fewer people owned it than saw Eve Arden in *Moose Murders*.

The superb 1987 Lincoln Center revision has generated numerous cast albums. Patti LuPone in New York (Victor) and Elaine Paige in London (First Night), both with Howard McGillin, return us to the land of belting Renos, but I'm going to play eccentric and confess a fondness for the Australian cast (EMI), with Geraldine Turner, Simon Burke, and Peter Whitford. This is the snazziest of *Anything Goese*s, very bright in sound with stereo effects so marked they're less separation than geography. Is it that conductor Dale Ringland's tempi are a hair faster than others'? Did the cast all fall in love that morning? But John McGlinn, as always, recalls to us the original (EMI) in an archive package, with a year's worth of liner notes by Miles Kreuger (including annotations on Porter's lyrics), the 1934 orchestrations (with a flourish at the overture's start that anticipates Richard Rodgers' *Victory At Sea*), a photo-offset of the 1934 playbill cover and credits, and "Where Are the Men?," led by Judy Kaye in occult billing. (It's her married name.) Frederica Von Stade and Cris Groenendaal take the love plot, Jack Gilford matches his usual humblebumble with that of his 1934 predecessor Victor Moore, and Kim Criswell's Reno sings "I Get a Kick Out of You" exactly as Porter wrote it, in a seesaw between quarter notes and half-note triplets that suggests a serene flight of the heart over mundane trifles. We should note as well a live 1954 television *Anything Goes* (Entertainment One), with Merman, Frank Sinatra, and Bert Lahr. The production itself is nugatory, but as a preservation of what Merman was like on stage it is more valuable than any of her movies. You'll even see her acting a bit, as if training for *Gypsy*.

The 1930s is the decade in which the American recording industry began to issue show albums. These were not cast albums in the modern sense; Victor's twenty minutes of *The Band Wagon* (Sepia, with *Inside U.S.A.*) on an experimental long-playing disc used Fred and Adele Astaire, but in non-theatre arrangements. Similarly, Jack Kapp, then at Brunswick, made full-scale albums of *Show Boat* and *Blackbirds of 1928* (in 1932 and 1933, respectively), using mixtures of cast members and ringers, again with studio charts. *Show Boat* suffers from this disembodied rendition, as it's an extraordinarily narrative show for its era. But *Blackbirds*, as a revue, features songs that create their own theatre vibe—and the performances, by Ethel Waters, Bill Robinson, Adelaide Hall, Cab Calloway, the Mills Brothers, and Duke Ellington's band, are extremely juicy. Waters pulls off an in-crowd homage on "I Can't Give You Anything But Love," closing on an ascending scale exactly as Louis Armstrong had done on his single of the number.

Now comes an insert into history: someone privately recorded, live in New Haven on the post-Broadway tour, *Ziegfeld Follies of 1934* (AEI). The sound varies from distant to tornado, but one can pick up a great deal of what musicals sounded like in the theatre. Note Eve Arden (unbilled) *Sprechstimme*-ing her way through "That's Where We Come In." And is that indeed Ethel Merman we hear on two important numbers in an undocumented substitute gig? The author of the liner notes, David Cunard, thinks it *migh*t be. On the night this *Follies* was taken down, Merman was still in the cast of *Anything Goes* in New York and was not to leave for another four months or so. Still, listening through the sonic camouflage, Cunard says, "The similarity is so vivid." On certain phrases, it unquestionably is.

The best of all these early show albums is Victor's *Porgy and Bess* of 1935, another half-and-half: half original people (the conductor and chorus) and half guests (Lawrence Tibbett and Helen Jepson of the Met). Gershwin himself supervised, getting Victor to include "The Buzzard Song," cut in the theatre to protect Todd Duncan's eight-performances-a-week energy level. Tibbett is stupendous and Jepson pale, but these eight twelve-inch sides started a debate that continues today: is *Porgy and Bess* better served by opera singers or theatre singers?

In 1938, the preceding year's *The Cradle Will Rock* was recorded exactly as it played on stage (Musicraft, American Legacy), making it the first American cast album, albeit-piano-accompanied when the work had in fact been orchestrated.* Succeeding albums, however, continued to filet shows, like Decca's *Boys From Syracuse*, with cover art splashed with tasty stage shots but using Hollywoodians Rudy Vallee and Frances Langford, in six cuts, dully sung. Decca's *Panama Hattie*, similarly theatrical in its appearance, offered only four numbers—but sung by the star, Ethel Merman, in topmost form. Then in the early 1940s, Decca made two *Porgy and Bess* albums, the first with the original leads, Todd Duncan and Anne Brown, singing everyone's roles just like Victor's Tibbett and Jepson. The second album brought in more singers; combined on a single LP, the two sets constituted the first (sort of) cast album with orchestra, as every soloist (and the conductor) had performed the opera on stage, all but one in the original company, in 1935.†

The first genuine Original Cast Album—that is, a souvenir of what was heard in the theatre, and, unlike *The Cradle Will Rock*, with its orchestration intact—happened by accident. Failing to conclude a royalty agreement with the recording industry in 1942, the musicians' union declared a strike; no new recordings could be made, even with a

---

*Worse, this piece eventually collected three more cast recordings (MGM, Jay, Lockett-Palmer) with piano only, which seems to me an affectation. Is this work doomed to play its damn-the-torpedoes first night over and over, as if on *The Twilight Zone*? Enough already.

†As Todd Duncan had recorded Sporting Life's "It Ain't Necessarily So" in the original sessions, MCA's CD *Porgy* release thought to append a bonus track of a real Sporting Life, Avon Long of the 1942 cast, in the same number. Unfortunately, the engineer pulled the wrong master, and the CD offers Avon Long in "I Got Plenty O' Nuttin'"—Sporting Life singing *Porgy's* number.

Cradle Will Rock piano. Victor and Columbia, with stockpiles of unreleased classical performances, held firm. Decca, however, exclusively pop in content, had to keep abreast of a volatile market; a prolonged strike would bankrupt it. The union's chief, toil-and-troubling James Caesar Petrillo, tolerated no exception to his ban, but there was a loophole. Anything related to the war effort was exempt, and Jack Kapp, now at Decca, seized Irving Berlin's all-soldier revue, *This Is the Army*, and had a hit. Further, its batch of five discs meant that every sale was a gross sale—and the Big Broadway cast album was born.

Then *Oklahoma!* opened. The restless Kapp negotiated a separate settlement with Petrillo in late 1943 and raced Rodgers and Hammerstein's western into the studio. Realizing what an industry-changer the cast album would prove, Kapp didn't wait to see how *Oklahoma!* would sell: he knew how it would sell. Even before *Oklahoma*'s release, he captured Broadway's next hit, *One Touch of Venus*; the choruses from a straight play, the Air Force's complement to *This Is the Army*, Moss Hart's *Winged Victory*; *The Merry Widow* (in a studio rendering with Kitty Carlisle and Wilbur Evans); and the revival of *A Connecticut Yankee*. This was all before New Year's Day, 1944, with *Carmen Jones* recorded just after. Decca was to take down over a dozen new shows during the 1940s, also following up on *The Merry Widow* with a brace of studio cast operettas (including *The Desert Song* and *Babes in Toyland*, already cited).

The rest of the recording industry settled the strike in November of 1944, though Victor had already competed with Decca, issuing a 1942 studio cast of *This Is the Army* with a house tenor and baritone, adding in Fats Waller for a single cut. The eight sides contained two numbers not on the original-cast discs, the interpolated "Mandy" and "That Russian Winter" (on Hitler's disastrous Eastern campaign), which amusingly fits the title's two last two words to the first four notes of "The Volga Boatman's Song." With a good-sized band very much featuring harp and piano as well as a men's chorus, Victor's *This Is the Army* is almost indistinguishable from Decca's, perhaps explaining why the earlier recording survived well into the LP era (and, later, made it onto CD), while Victor's was quickly withdrawn, becoming one of the most unknown of show albums.

After the strike was settled, Victor challenged Decca to dueling *On the Towns*. Decca (on CD as a bonus with *Wonderful Town*) offered cast members with Mary Martin ringed in for the ballads, while Victor (Pearl, Naxos, MCA) had Leonard Bernstein conducting his ballets, the vocals left to unnamed soloists and a chorus. More swordplay: Decca's *Up in Central Park* was virtually a cast album (with ringers Eileen Farrell and Celeste Holm), but Victor (Encore) had Jeanette MacDonald.

Victor also founded its own operetta line to counter Decca's, starting in the mid-1940s, all under Al Goodman conducting extremely untheatrical arrangements for radio singers in smoothed-out forties style. Earl Wrightson, Donald Dame, Frances Greer, and Mary Martha Briney were the usual soloists, but Elaine Malbin, a soprano with blitz, also took part. She tears the pants off *The Firefly* with Allan Jones, in the original 1912 numbers but inevitably including the film's interpolation of "The Donkey Serenade" in its MGM arrangement. After a few years, Goodman took on the latest shows as well as classics. This led to a curiosity: Goodman's was the sole recording of one of the last really antiqued operettas, *Polonaise*, by a bizarre writing team, Chopin and John Latouche. Goodman recorded even the latest revivals. When a 1951 *Music in the Air* flopped, Victor gave up on making the cast album and shunted the title over to Goodman's outfit (Sepia). Retaining Jane Pickens of the revival as the only voice against a chorus, Goodman varied his approach, emphasizing vocals where he had previously hogged the ear with instrumentals. Then, too, Pickens is more individual than the Goodman regulars, with a warm high mezzo used sensitively, if without the extravagance of the old-time operetta star. Her "The Song Is You" is elegant—oddly so, considering that, two years before, she played the overtly destructive title role in *Regina*, Marc Blitzstein's Broadway opera based on *The Little Foxes*. *Music in the Air* is Goodman's best album—and, to this date, the only recording, however skimpy, of this important score.

Columbia joined the movement when Victor did, running up a *Song Of Norway* with its star, Irra Petina, in another of those untheatrical packages, although the album is very listenable as sheer Grieg. Decca made the *Song Of Norway* cast album, replacing Petina with Kitty Carlisle. Like *Carmen Jones*, *Song Of Norway* occupied six twelve-inch 78s, unusually long for the day; the LP release left out bits here and there. At that, Decca's *Bloomer Girl* ran to eight ten-inch discs. On CD (MCA), it bears a unique sound, not only in orchestration but its wide range of singing styles, from Mabel Tagliaferro's gilded-cage flutterings through the somewhat acidic tones of Celeste Holm and Joan McCracken to the black glee of the jailhouse trio in "I Got a Song." This was the decade when operetta turned into the "musical play" and when Broadway began seriously to implement racial integration, and everything's in transition. *Bloomer Girl* also boasts E. Y. Harburg's best set of lyrics, lovely in "Right As the Rain," whimsical in "The Eagle and Me" (with a line that tickles Stephen Sondheim: "Ever since that day when the world was an onion"), and scathingly satiric in "Sunday in Cicero Falls," the typical second-act opening broken into warring halves, as Holm rags on sanctimonious churchgoers. First you get the Chamber of Commerce, then Kathy Griffin.

Another long 78 set was Columbia's *Street Scene*, a full-scale original-cast preservation of a title that, Goddard Lieberson had to know, was not commercially imposing. Lieberson had it in mind to make his label the master of the show album just when these discs were emerging as an instrument of cultural priority: Victor had Toscanini, but Columbia would have The Musical. Further, Columbia seized industry leadership from Victor in 1948, when it offered the LP for national consumption. (Victor fought back with the 45, a kind of dainty little 78 with the same short side timings and with technical defects in the thin vinyl—and the boxes notoriously fell apart even under normal use. Columbia added injury to insult with sturdier packaging for its 45 sets.) Unfortunately, Lieberson's plans—and the introduction of the LP—fell in the middle of a second Petrillo strike, which lasted right through 1948 till the third week of December.

This time, the industry was ready. With January 1, 1948, looming as the strike's departure point, Decca and Victor rushed three shows into the studio before they had opened, the former *Look, Ma, I'm Dancin'* and the latter *Inside U.S.A.* and *Bonanza Bound*. *Dancin'* had to drop two numbers recorded but cut during tryouts (they're on Decca's CD release), and Victor's *Inside U.S.A.* (Sepia), taken down four months before the premiere, is another of those forties cast albums with a character disorder: using the stars, Beatrice Lillie and Jack Haley, in non-show arrangements with supporting people they may not have met, much less played with. More picturesquely, *Bonanza Bound*, a Comden-Green (and Saul Chaplin) show, closed in Philadelphia and has never been officially released. Sepia's *Inside U.S.A.*, rich in bonuses as always with this label, includes not only the Astaires' *Band Wagon* cuts but a *Band Wagon* from a little known 1950s Victor series of sixteen 45 EPs (also paired on ten-inch discs) devoted to classic titles from *Shuffle Along* to *Kiss Me, Kate*. There were two Victor Herberts, two Rodgers and Harts, and so on; each show got four cuts by the best voices around— John Raitt, Doretta Morrow, Lisa Kirk, Jack Cassidy. The discs must have been thrown together with little rehearsal; on *The Band Wagon*'s "New Sun In the Sky," Harold Lang twice sings, incorrectly and ungrammatically, "Yesterday my heart sung a blue song." It's *sang*.

With the strike finally ended, Columbia moved as quickly as Decca had in 1943, speeding the just opened *Kiss Me, Kate* into the studio and following up with *South Pacific* in the spring of 1949. As bestsellers, the two titles convinced consumers still running a Victrola* to switch over to the LP, creating a sales avalanche and affirming Lieberson's position as a business wizard as well as a supporter of art. There was a third best seller in this saga, part of a Columbia series that ran into the 1960s to a tally of some twenty units: Lieberson's *Pal Joey*, a studio rendering sounding very much like a cast album, with the original Vera, Vivienne Segal and—this was odd—a dancer who could sing, the just mentioned Harold Lang, instead of a singer, period. What difference did it make on a record whether the Joey could dance or not? But what Lieberson's *Pal Joey* revealed, above all, was that *Oklahoma!*, *Annie Get Your Gun*, and *Brigadoon* were not the first shows with wonderful scores from beginning to end—as Lieberson's ensuing releases, of Rodgers and Hart and the Gershwins, demonstrated. Thus, the *Pal Joey* can be seen as one of the most influential of show albums, inspiring preservation, dissemination, revival.

Mary Martin dominated early units in this series; she was the only soloist in *Anything Goes* and *The Band Wagon* (together on DRG), and her participation on *Girl Crazy* and *Babes In Arms* is as "out of show" as her two ballads in Decca's old *On the Town*. However, some of Lieberson's releases were more theatrical, despite his distaste for dialogue cues or spoken repartee between choruses. His 1951 *Porgy and Bess* (Naxos, Sony), though heavily cut, remains even now the most dramatic of all, by a company so stage-routined that some were alumni of the 1935 original. Oddly, at virtually the same time, Victor recorded a *Porgy* with Risë Stevens and Robert Merrill in that same old approach of two (white) singers taking all the leads. There are only eight cuts, including odd bits, as when members of the Robert Shaw Chorale sing the solo lines in "Gone, Gone, Gone," including those of Porgy and Bess. Merrill's voice comes up like dawn in Mandalay, but mezzo Stevens has to take "My Man's Gone Now" down two whole steps, to c minor, robbing the piece of its keening ecstasy. Later *Porgy*s would avoid using white singers, though one of the very best of the single-disc versions (Victor) once again let the leads, Leontyne Price and William Warfield, monopolize the solos and duets.

As Lieberson's review of the great scores got more dramatic, it lost the feeling of An Evening With Mary Martin that pervaded the first releases. It helped that Lieberson's music director throughout the series was Lehman Engel, the most exciting of all conductors then working on Broadway.[†] Even foreign works were put into rotation—the aforementioned Dorothy Kirsten *Merry Widow* and two Noël Coward titles, *Conversation Piece* (Must Close Saturday, Phantom), with its dialogue, on two LPs, starring Coward and Lily Pons and featuring Richard Burton in a non-singing part; and a *Bitter Sweet* with Portia Nelson and Robert Rounseville. Coward so disliked the performance of the latter that Columbia cancelled its release, though it's hard to hear what Coward objected to. Was it the American pronunciation of "Zigeuner" and "Heigh-ho" as *Zagoynerrr* and *Hi-ho*? The performance is actually quite good, with a lot of the between-the-big-numbers musical scenes that were omitted on the two English studio casts and a real Viennese cimbalom for Nelson's "Zigeuner."

---

*This word was the name of the reproducing equipment manufactured by Victor, but it came to denote any firm's record player, in 78 days. As with Kleenex (for "tissue") and Frigidaire (for "ice box"), the brand name became the substantive.

[†]One title was denied Engel. He rehearsed Lieberson's *On the Town*, a gala reunion of most of the original principals, but—Engel himself told me this—just before the taping, Lieberson announced that Bernstein himself wanted to lead the band and they both hoped that Engel would, as one of the show's songs puts it, "understand."

One of the best of Columbia's "reassessment" line was *Brigadoon* (DRG) with Shirley Jones and Jack Cassidy (and the original Broadway replacement Meg Brockie, Susan Johnson). Has anyone else got as much out of a mere B above middle C as Johnson does on her first note, a Scots sales spiel bit in "Down on MacConnachy Square" ("Now-www . . .")? The mono sonics, constricted even for 1957, obscure the counterpoint of "MacConnachy" in both chorus and orchestra, but Engel's brisk baton work and the soloists (Frank Poretta sings Charlie Dalrymple) are excellent. They do not outshine the original cast (Victor), but Columbia has three songs Victor omitted, including "The Chase," following perhaps the most dramatic first-act curtain of all time with the most intense second-act opening. Because choreography had become so intrinsic to the structure of the forties musical—and to its prestige—Victor did include some of the dance music to "I'll Go Home With Bonnie Jean" and "Come To Me, Bend To Me." Columbia skipped all the dance music, but John McGlinn's recording (EMI), eighty minutes to Columbia's forty-five, has so much *Brigadoon* in it that even the non-singing characters get a look in, supporting the very vocal Brent Barrett, Rebecca Luker, Judy Kaye, and John Mark Ainsley. As so often with McGlinn, the smallest parts are cast for plush, with Gregory Jbara, Donald Maxwell, Rosemary Ashe, Susannah Fellows, and irrepressible Shirley Minty. Hearing all the dance music—especially good in this show—and interstitial bits really gives one the feel of the work, as when the trip back from haunted Scotland to jaded Manhattan is rendered by the orchestra's slapping "Bonnie Jean" with a boogie-woogie piano beat.

Before we leave the 1940s, let's consider *Sweet Bye and Bye* (PS Classics), a glimpse into the future that closed in tryout in 1946. Another product of the Secaucus Dig— the rediscovery of Golden Age writing and performing materials in the Warner Bros. music warehouse in Secaucus, New Jersey, in 1982—*Sweet Bye and Bye* is a genuine curiosity, a superb one. The Vernon Duke–Ogden Nash score is brilliant (sample rhyme: "wish to abscond" and "a bank and a blonde"), and Jason Carr's ingenious new eleven-piece orchestration sounds like a full pit, with none of the canned yelping of the synthesizer. With so many revivals depending on smaller scoring, Carr is the man of the future. A vital reading and informative liner notes substantiate this ghost for us: a must-hear for aficionado and debutant alike.

The acculturation of the LP enhanced the musical's commercial strength to a fabulous degree, for the sleek new discs were so much easier to play than 78s that they became essential middle-class leisure tools. Decca's *The King and I* is probably the least highly regarded cast album of a major show in the postwar decade, lacking the energy of *Oklahoma!*, the hammy grandeur of *Kiss Me, Kate*, the variety of *South Pacific*, with its burlesque-show "Bloody Mary" dance and *basso cantante*'s "This Nearly Was Mine." Decca formatted its *King and I* LP to be compatible with ten-inch-78 sides, so the label cut the score down to only core numbers, some very much truncated at that. Later albums busily filled in the gaps, each with a different selection till the 1996 revival (Varèse) had to collect piquant leftovers (such as "Royal Dance Before the King") just to stay at the party. Decca had as well the problem that singing was not Gertrude Lawrence's forte, and she sounds even less absolute as Anna in that her successors include Barbara Cook (Columbia), Julie Andrews (Philips), and, best of all, June Bronhill (Music For Pleasure, EMI). Yet that first *King and I* brings us back to a time when these classic titles were innocent of the incrustations of historical importance, production annals, and analysis they would acquire. Today they are canonical, but they were innovative when new; heard in their earliest incarnation, they communicate more directly to us, as something that, once, was a surprise rather than a landmark.

Of course, the 1950s is filled with original-cast releases of historical power, as in *My Fair Lady*, *The Most Happy Fella*, and *Candide*, all on Columbia in 1956. The first of the trio marked a high point in the musical's importance in national commerce, for Goddard Lieberson, sensing that *My Fair Lady* would be a smash of smashes, convinced CBS to capitalize the show, giving the label access to one of the biggest-selling records in history. To hear it is to return to a time when show music was the lingua franca of pop. Yet the London cast, also produced by Lieberson on Columbia, is better. Stereo burnishes the sound (the Broadway cast was in mono), even if the orchestra is now strangely distanced. With the four original leads and the same musical program recorded in New York, the London disc is not *that* different (though there are completely new lyrics for the second A of the second chorus of "Show Me"). Yet the whole thing sounds more theatrical. For example, "I Could Have Danced All Night," in its theatre reading rather than the studio modifications Lieberson favored in New York, carries far more of Eliza's exultant sense of achievement than before.

As for the other two titles, Lieberson reaffirmed his gift in combining the documentation of an art with sheer business flash. Jack Kapp's relationship with the cast album was Boy Meets Girl; Lieberson's was Boy Gets Girl. For *The Most Happy Fella*, Lieberson made complete and highlights versions, emphasizing—as he had done with his *Porgy and Bess*—that great scores are great all the way through. And *Candide* presented a novelty in that the show failed but the music was a hit; the disc proved one of Columbia's biggest albums.

Indeed, the 1950s invented Broadway's equivalent of Roswell's Area 51, the cult musical: the show closes Saturday night and the music runs forever. *The Golden Apple* (Victor), *Flahooley* (Capitol, EMI), and *Ankles Aweigh* (Decca) are favorites, though the first is a truly excellent piece, the second a silly one with a lovely score, and the last a derivative goulash of guilty pleasures. Note, however, *Ankles'* gala choral singing, relentlessly pushing everyone to the upper limits of his range, a standard feature of the fifties show. This is but one element of the vocal style developed by arranger Hugh Martin, heard at his best in two Jule Styne scores, *Gentlemen Prefer Blondes* (Columbia, Sony) and *Hazel Flagg* (Victor, Sepia). A perfect sample of the Martin style is *Blondes'* "Sunshine," Eric Brotherson and Yvonne Adair's number . . . at first. Then Martin's choristers sweep in, riffing on two of the song's phrases, "C'est la vie" and "Oo la la," in a burst of harmonic and rhythmic devilry. Jule Styne and Leo Robin wrote the *Blondes* score, but, for two minutes or so, the author is Hugh Martin. There's even more Martin to be heard on the Encores! *Blondes* (MasterworksBroadway), one of the best revival discs of all time. Martin's own music and lyrics can be heard in *Make A Wish* (Victor, Sepia)—a Sondheim favorite, by the way—with typical musical-comedy First and Second couples in Nanette Fabray (the heroine, versatile as a rule: she played everything from an Amazon to the First Lady, and could whistle through her teeth), Stephen Douglass (the baritone, and if he seems stolid, he did create London's Billy Bigelow, so he must have had something), Helen Gallagher (the dancer sidekick with goofy charm and a *pow!* belt), and our old friend Harold Lang.

We should note some more or less direct-from-Broadway fifties movie preservations. Johnny Mercer's *Top Banana* (1951) gives us the star-comic vehicle, and, unlike most of his predecessors, Phil Silvers could sort of sing. The show was filmed (Warner) in Los Angeles in a theatre semblance with the original sets and costumes by the entire New York cast. (The film's romantic juvenile, Danny Scholl, replaced Lindy Doherty during the New York run.) United Artists supposedly took down the entire show, but the surviving print is incomplete, missing, for instance, "A Dog Is a Man's Best Friend," in which the animals howl through the vocal. ("Just wag your tail!" Silvers orders.) Yet the dogs are in the movie's curtain calls. Paramount's *Li'l Abner* is the next best thing: a stagey adaptation retaining Michael Kidd's choreography, even for a minor number like "Rag Offen the Bush," a museum piece in the best sense. For *Shinbone Alley* (1957), a sound-system audiotape of the complete show (Legend) preserves fifties style, albeit in the example of an unconventional work. It was an expansion of a smaller piece drawn from Don Marquis' episodic poetry collection *archy and mehitabel*, on the adventures of, respectively, a cockroach and a cat, and though *Shinbone Alley* failed, it makes for lively listening. There is even an actual show-stopper, in "Flotsam and Jetsam," for stars Eddie Bracken and Eartha Kitt. They clearly have a ball with Joe Darion's insouciant lyrics and George Kleinsinger's merry melody. At the first applause spot, the two give an encore; at the second, Kitt tries to pick up the next spoken line, but the public won't stop clapping, and the two have to fill in with ad libs. Says Bracken, as archy the cockroach, "Two of my feet are tired."

This is as good a place as any to consider *Lost In Boston*, an indispensably brilliant set of four CDs (Varèse Sarabande) on the cut number, mainly from the 1950s and 1960s. Broadway's best singers make this a delight as well as an education, because hearing what authors rejected leads us to comprehend how they relate to their narratives. A few numbers are simply wrong—*The King and I*'s bizarre trio "Waiting," when Anna confronts the King and Kralahome about their business arrangement; or "When Messiah Comes," for *Fiddler On the Roof*'s Rabbi and later reassigned to Zero Mostel, which treats eliminationist anti-Semitism humorously. Most of the selections, however, are as listenable as anything in the finished scores—"Thirty Weeks of Heaven," from *By the Beautiful Sea*, set to the breakneck tempo of a no-frills vaudeville tour; or the original opening of *The Mystery of Edwin Drood*, "An English Music Hall," used in the recent revival. Kaye Ballard will stop the show in your home with the typical alcoholic's lament, "Say When," from *On the Town*. (Ready for a wee drinkie, she sweetly tells a passing waiter, "You can use my water glass.") Lynette Perry takes control of the greatest number never heard: "Flaemmchen," from *Grand Hotel*. Ron Raines dives into "Inside My Head," one of the many numbers Harvey Schmidt and Tom Jones wrote while trying to figure out exactly who the sheriff in *110 In the Shade* really is. There's a nifty surprise in "You Don't Have To Kiss Me Goodnight," from *The Music Man*; who would have guessed that Zaneeta Shinn (the mayor's daughter) and Tommy Djilas had a song of their own? By the time *The Music Man* reached Broadway—copping the Majestic Theatre because *Happy Hunting*'s ticket sales had slumped—Zaneeta and Tommy were little more than part of the Merry Villager body count. Presumably, they would have been a Second Couple if Meredith Willson hadn't given Winthrop the show's subplot. Steven Orich scores "Goodnight" (on *Lost in Boston III*) for a combination of forties swing band and ragtime, and it's another showstopper. Orich has a sense of humor, too. In "Travellin' Light," cut from *Guys and Dolls* because Sam Levene couldn't grasp the number's slithery pulse, Malcolm Gets imagines domestic life complete with "the sound of Junior practicing violin"—and Orich fiddles us Jack Benny's old television sign-in theme.

The 1960s brings us to the first truly dark musicals—not musical comedies with dark patches, like *Show Boat*, nor dark shows with, all the same, a lot of comedy, like *Carousel*. The truly dark musical, which would culminate in *Marie Christine*, *Parade*, *Kiss of the Spider Woman*, *Spring Awakening*, and others such, first turns up in the 1960s in such titles as *Zorbá*, *A Time For Singing*, *The Yearling*, and, slipping over into the 1970s, *Cry For Us All*. The genre may be sampled handsomely in *Golden Boy* (Capitol, Bay Cities, Angel, Razor & Tie, DRG). In his memoirs, Charles Strouse observes that, at the end of an extended tryout, Sammy Davis Jr. was "near total exhaustion," his voice "hoarse and strained"—and so he sounded on the cast album. At some point early on, four of his tracks were rerecorded, and he sounds much better, though some feel that his espressivo was muzzled. Unfortunately, all four CD issues use the retakes, so it's nearly impossible for the curious to audition the differences. The *Golden Boy* album is nevertheless amazing. Taking in these very dramatic songs, it's hard to believe that Strouse and Adams are primarily known for "Put on a Happy Face" and "Once Upon a Time." There's one odd note, sounded in a neighborhood jamboree called "Don't Forget 127th Street," but this bleak story needed a first-act pick-me-up, and Davis' ability to don comic voices ties the number to the rest of the score. Hearing Davis' broad dramatic range, rich palette of vocal colors, and valiant phrasing, I wonder why the entire world thinks Frank Sinatra was the outstanding pop singer of postwar America. Note as well Billy Daniels' velvet iniquity on "This Is the Life" and "While the City Sleeps," the latter a paean to the dolce vita unknown to "Scarsdale squares."

Hello, Dolly! and *Cabaret* represent two sixties opposites, unrevised musical comedy and the dark show that nevertheless retains certain musical-comedy attitudes (albeit only in *Cabaret*'s original version). In the former title, Victor's original cast is a glory of the catalogue, not only because of Carol Channing's star turn but because her supporting players are so characterful that, after all this time, no one has rivaled them. This is especially true in London with Mary Martin (Victor). Martin outsings Channing—in fact, Martin reminds us what a fine singer she was (signed, we should note, by Decca strictly for her vocal charm in the early 1940s, before she had revealed her gamine personality). But her London support is lame, and Martin's replacement at Drury Lane, Dora Bryan (EMI, with her Horace, Bernard Spear), similarly left an inconclusive souvenir of what was hailed as a great performance. EMI recorded also Beryl Reid in one of the great Why? recordings, because Reid, so treasurable as Connie Sachs in the two BBC Le Carré *Smiley* series, was, in 1965—the year of the *Dolly!* recording—a nonsinger known only for her stage run in *The Killing Of Sister George*. (The movie came out three years later.) Notable, though, is Reid's support, which includes Patricia Routledge, a sumptuous Irene. Too sumptuous, even operatic. Later, she slimmed her tone for *Darling Of the Day* (Victor), in one of the great assumptions of a decade rich in them—Inga Swenson, Barbra Streisand, Barbara Harris, Gwen Verdon, Lotte Lenya. The black-cast *Hello, Dolly!* (Victor) is astonishingly different from all other *Dolly!* discs, and not for the better. Cab Calloway's Horace pranks like Sporting Life—completely wrong for this joyless shopkeeper, specifically meant as a foil for the life-loving Dolly. And Bailey is Lazy Mae, back-phrasing and hashing up the meaning of her lyrics.

Cabaret's original cast offers interesting bonuses on Sony's CD release: Fred Ebb (singing) and John Kander (playing and adding in bits) in cut numbers from their audition LP. The London cast (Columbia) is overpowered—wonderfully—by Judi Dench in what may be the most underpraised of the great star turns in the musical. There are just so many the public can absorb before it goes all giddy from exposure to genius, as if the arts cops, to protect us, had drawn their guns to say, "Step away from Patti LuPone." Yet it is one of the musical's qualities that it is rich in topmost talent. Returning to *Cabaret*, we learn great respect for Don Walker's orchestrations in hearing the 1986 London revival with Wayne Sleep (First Night), a regional staging brought in with its merely functional cast and *Teeny Todd* scoring (which does at least drop an amusing bit of "Deutschland Über Alles" into the finale). On Jay, a two-CD *Cabaret* gives us bonus tracks of the "extra" songs, for, as with *Show Boat* and *Follies*, this work's score has expanded over time. But Jay's cast is a Grand Hotel of styles, from Maria Friedman's feverish Sally to Gregg Edelman's Broadway suave. He gets to sing an added number he introduced, "Don't Go" (from the 1987 New York revival), heard also on the Dutch cast

(Disky) as "Blijf Hier." Jay's Schneider and Schultz are Judi Dench and Fred Ebb. Yes, that Fred Ebb. As performers, the two are so far apart, even in their duets, that they suggest an *I Do! I Do!* starring Lady Bracknell and King Farouk.

In the 1970s, DVDs of the original stagings of *Pippin* and *Sweeney Todd*, both caught on tour with cast changes, preserve the work of two very different super-directors, Bob Fosse and Hal Prince, the former overruling a composition with his staging and the latter staging the composition. On CD, *A Little Night Music* and *Chicago* serve us as models for the musical play and musical comedy, though other than in completeness of program all *Chicago*s are alike. *Night Music* offers a rare instance of a later production outranking the original one (Columbia), for a 1990 English studio cast (TER) using some principals and the twelve-man scoring (adding a percussionist) from a Chichester Festival revival is very, very beautifully sung by a mixture of opera singers (Bonaventura Bottone and Jason Howard, a Wotan as Carl-Magnus), actors with real voices, and a Desirée (Siân Philips) without one. Elisabeth Welch, who dates so far back in show biz that she introduced the charleston (in *Runnin' Wild*, 1923), makes an elegant Madame Armfeldt, and everything flows wonderfully under John Owen Edwards. Philips was graduated to the older role in the National Theatre production of 1995 (Tring), to Judi Dench's Desirée (and the Swiss chocolate heir Laurence Guittard, Carl-Magnus on Broadway in the first *Night Music* cast, now moved up to Frederick). This disc is better acted than sung, though it is abundantly musical, with eighteen players (to the original's twenty-five) and lashings of extra melody in the movie version of "The Glamorous Life" and the cut "My Husband, the Pig." Dench outclasses even Glynis Johns, setting a tone of cunning sophistication to lead a truly theatrical rendering. It peaks in a breathless "Weekend In the Country," so avid in knotting up the show's plot strands that one virtually sees the curtain falling on Act One. TER gives us the most musical *Night Music*, Tring the most characterful.

Yet doesn't it begin to seem that, after the mid-1970s, all casts in new shows seem more or less the same stylistically? Is it because character writing in the better musicals is now so precise—so definitive—that it leaves little room for performer initiatives?

For instance, going back to the 1940s, I find a lot of play in how a work can be recorded. Take *Pal Joey*. The touchstone is Goddard Lieberson's aforementioned studio disc with Vivienne Segal and Harold Lang, in print without a break for more than sixty years as I write. The ensuing 1952 revival starred Segal and Lang, so its "original cast" LP (Capitol, EMI) had to replace them, with Jane Froman and Dick Beavers, both substantial singers. It's a sexy coupling, too; for once, "Den Of Iniquity" sounds not sportive but sinful. A 1980 London "fringe" staging (TER) was moved into the Albery Theatre with its tiny band, though it was able to generate a very fulfilled quotation of *The Rite of Spring* at "Zip"'s mention of Stravinsky. The small cast took in only girls in the chorus, all directed to sing with the raucous vivacity of the bottom feeder; for once, we realize how lowdown Joey's career really is. Siân Philips, though classy as ever, delivers Vera as a kind of triumphant disaster, for, unlike Desirée, Vera is a singing role. Philips forges through it with nine parts authority and one part voice. As Joey, Denis Lawson uses an aggressive American accent that seems designed to emphasize the character's mooching self-love; this puts Lawson closest of all Joeys to John O'Hara's stories. Peter Gallagher, in Encores!'s 1995 concert (DRG), is suave but flavorless, tilting the story toward Patti LuPone's formidable Vera. So there is a lot of room for the interpretation of these characters, and for varying attitudes in how a staging looks at Joey's world.

In the musical play, let's try *Carousel*. Billy is its most dramatic (and thus interpretable) role, because Julie has nothing comparable to the "Soliloquy." John Raitt dominates this part, having created (Decca) and then restamped it (Victor), in a Lincoln Center revival twenty years later. Interestingly, Raitt doesn't vary his delivery much from song to song yet still seems unchallengeable in the role, with a sweet yet virile sound that tries to mask Billy's irritated vulnerability while revealing it. Victor's LP yields more of the score than Decca's five twelve-inch 78s, though Decca was actually quite clever in rearranging numbers to squeeze in as much as possible. Thus, "Mister Snow" ends not as on stage but with the girls' interjections from its reprise, and "You'll Never Walk Alone" starts as on stage but then switches to the finale setting with full chorus. Further, the "Soliloquy" was spread over two sides for a complete reading, including the transition to the ballad-like final section ("When I have a daughter . . ."), which was recorded also by Frank Sinatra (Columbia), then cut from the text and never heard again.

In 1955, the first crossover recording of all time gave *Carousel* opera singers and Florence Henderson, with an extended reading of the Bench Scene, cut down to "If I Loved You" by itself on the Decca 78s. This and Victor's *Show Boat* in 1956 appear to be Victor's imitation of Goddard Lieberson's Columbia series of classic scores, with generous LP sides, little or no cue-in dialogue, and Lehman Engel conducting. But *Carousel* needs a more driving Billy than the impersonal Robert Merrill. The other singers mirror the original portrayals, as does another opera crew in 1962 (Command). This one is the show-off *Carousel*, with interferingly noticeable new orchestrations and vocals so grand they sound pushy. Even Alfred Drake, the Billy, gets into it, sounding like Robert Merrill trying to act. New York City Opera stalwarts Claramae Turner and Norman Treigle are vivid as Nettie and Jigger, but this is the least theatrical of *Carousels*.

Still, opera singers haunt this work. MCA's 1987 disc, with the score reorchestrated by five names unknown to me, is the glamor *Carousel*, with Samuel Ramey's absurdly cultivated Billy and David Rendall's Mr. Snow offering too heroic a tenor for this pompous goon. The label filled its LP sides at over an hour in nonetheless spacious sonics, but, again, this is a singing and not a dramatic *Carousel*. A telling error: MCA gave Arminy's sarcastic solo in "What's the Use of Wond'rin'" to the Julie, Barbara Cook, pulling her completely out of character.

Billy underwent extreme tempering in Nicholas Hytner's 1993 staging for Great Britain's National Theatre, a revisionist interpretation of the entire work in its ecumenical Christian exhortation. Michael Hayden, Billy in both London (First Night) and New York (EMI) casts, is a singing actor rather than an opera singer or, like Raitt, a *singing* actor, but he arrestingly emphasized Billy's hair-trigger defensiveness and fumbling wish to better his lot. Volatile as he leaped from tenderness to anger, Hayden caught Hammerstein's (actually Ferenc Molnár's, in *Carousel's* source, *Liliom*) paradox of the slap that bears frustrated love in every scene of his portrayal. He lacked vocal wallop, but that only underlined his vulnerability—especially as the London disc includes anchoring dialogue, most effectively where "The Highest Judge of All" had been before Hytner cut it. The New York disc, which makes many different choices about what music to program, is better sung overall, especially by Sally Murphy as Julie, Audra (Ann) McDonald as Carrie, and opera glamor diva Shirley Verrett as Nettie. However, both Jiggers have ugly rasps in lines conceived for a baritone. Does Jigger have to sound unmusical to be believable as a crook?

Still, there is clearly a lot of variation potential in the playing of classic musicals. But when we reach the Big Sing pieces that rose up in the 1970s—pop operas and shows under their influence—there appears to be only one way to perform them correctly. Thus, vital and imaginative dramatic leads like Davis Gaines and Howard McGillin find a way to cut themselves down to disappear into the constipated grandeur of the title role in *The Phantom Of the Opera*. To state it another way: there are many recordings of this work, but they vary only in language or whether they are one or two discs. In sheer performance, they are all exactly alike.

THE FOURTH AGE

Pop opera is essentially European; the American counterpart is something like *Dream-girls*, best heard in the all-star 2001 concert (Nonesuch), for the original cast (Geffen, Decca) takes in very little of the work's unique sung dialogues. In the 1980s, *La Cage aux Folles* (Victor) and *My One and Only* (Atlantic) typify musical comedy old-fashioned and newfangled—the latter, ironically, with old songs. In the musical play, *Sunday In the Park With George* was made for DVD (Image), because so much of it is visual, less a musical play than a musical painting. *Grand Hotel* (Victor) is at once sunny and dark, for each of its principals bears personal information that could erupt in a number either intense or merry at almost any moment. Try comparing the aforementioned "Flaemmchen" (in *Lost In Boston II*) with its replacement, "I Want To Go To Hollywood," with which Maury Yeston textured Wright and Forrest as Brecht might texture Shirley Temple's Storybook—though both portions of this co-written score are equally brilliant.

We now move into the present generation, when, as so often in the musical's history, serious works face off against silly ones. The two *Wild Partys* (Decca; Victor) offer extremely intense performances from all concerned in profusions of the character songs that—I say again and again—distinguish American light opera from all other forms. A piece like *Spamalot* (Decca), for all its amusements, makes no history because its score treats not its characters but its own spoofy gusto.

We should close with an essential title; I wonder if the Fourth Age has one as good as the Third Age classics. Perhaps, then, *Gypsy* will serve, as it is arguably our most timeless show, independent of revision (unlike *Show Boat* and *Follies*), and trim and tight compared with the grandly scaled titles of the Rodgers and Hammerstein approach. Interestingly, *Gypsy* discs center an already very centered show, for Herbie and Louise, Rose's foils, have relatively little to sing. On records, *Gypsy* is *Rose*: the part is our Isolde or Norma, out of the reach of many nonetheless gifted stars and the platform from which the diva ascends to immortality. Luckily, each of the five Broadway Roses has left us a cast album, of course starting with Ethel Merman, all but unmatchable in a part that was written around her.

No one thinks of Merman as a revolutionary, but it was she—and the producers who hired her and composers who made their music on her—who led the revolution into genuinely singing casts in musical comedy in the 1930s. As I've said, surviving recordings by musical-comedy stars such as George M. Cohan, Montgomery and Stone, Elsie Janis, and countless others, reveal how dodgy the vocalizing was. The true voices gravitated toward comic opera, then operetta, then the musical play—whichever format was in season at the time. Musical comedy accepted "Broadway" voices, meaning anything from *Sprechstimme* to people like Fred and Adele Astaire or Bert Lahr, who could put over the right material in the right way without fielding luminous vocal tone.

So *Gypsy* was a triumph for Merman in not only her acting but her singing, as a kind of historical affirmation of how Merman's revolution in musical comedy had forced its way into the musical play. This first *Gypsy* album has been on the short list since its release, even if Goddard Lieberson—as always with the hit shows—fiddled with the arrangements, creating false intros and even changing details of orchestration. This is a great score, but it's also a great Merman score, showing off while not testing her limited versatility: the establishing number, "Some People," in the blazing belt of the Queen Of Broadway, singing as she always did on the melody rather than on the words but with a wonderfully nasty explosion on "rot." Then the sentimental piece, "Small World," blunt and loud but offering a tiny chuckle on the second "Lucky," acknowledging how boldly she's seducing by syllogism. Now the comedy spot, which goes by various titles (it's

"Mr. Goldstone" in the published score), with an extra helping of the Merman mordents and her patented "oo," a vowel unknown to all other speakers of English. Then the Jule Styne Swing Number, "You'll Never Get Away From Me," which Merman delivers instrumentally, each phrase reflecting every other phrase, though she lightens the tone at "Come dance with me."

And so on. Sony's latest CD issue even gives Merman "Little Lamb" on a bonus track, though she cannot connect with the woebegone Louise, created by the excellent Sandra Church. A photograph of Church on the rear of the jewel case, in full stripper kit, impishly pulling at both ends of her long white glove, presents the femme fatale: picture at an exhibition. Yet her face is that of a kid, too young to be confident and too sweet for the tease burlesque requires. No: she's the little lamb, truly lost, and I've never seen any other Louise pull that off. They always seem to know how the show will end, like the characters in *Merrily We Roll Along* knowledgable before their time. But then, everyone in theatre knows *Gypsy* now. Church, of the first cast, got to the material virgo intacta, and you hear it in her cuts.

Angela Lansbury's Rose (Victor) has been overpraised, though she is unquestionably one of our foremost singing actresses. Hers was a great Rose, no question—but an odd one, because Rose is a dumb but shrewd willImakeit? and Lansbury could not hide her innate intelligence and chic, the qualities that gave her top stardom (after some twenty years in show biz) in *Mame*. True, she turned into a proletarian wretch in *Sweeney Todd*. But Mrs. Lovett is a clown set into a Greek tragedy—a cartoon, really. Think of her blithely loony "By the Sea" compared with, for instance, all of Todd's music. Rose isn't a cartoon.

Lansbury's *Gypsy* opened in London. Crossing the Atlantic to become the Very Next Rose after Merman, Lansbury enlarged the character, bringing more variety—especially more fun—to her line readings. In "Mr. Goldstone," when Rose catalogues the stone phyla, from "curbstones" to "gallstones," Merman simply presented the list. Lansbury acts the moment, scoring each example as if fielding flies. But Lansbury's singing failed the part. Styne composed Rose for a four-wheel-drive sound that so dominates the auditorium that everyone else is the undercard. Lansbury so to say "manages" her way through Rose's vocals. It's not Absolute Rose.

Tyne Daly (Electra) was an unexpected Rose, lacking a substantial music-theatre background. It's worth noting that Lansbury's replacement in London was Dolores Gray, one of the outstanding singers in Broadway history, and so imposing a presence that when *Carnival In Flanders* (1953) closed after 6 performances in early September, Gray's nine numbers and stand-and-deliver acting style won her the Best Actress Tony way at the end of the season, an astonishing achievement. Rose is Singer's Property. Monumental Dolores, stacked and shellacked, with her "don't touch me don't even look" eye flashes, would have been less a force of nature—like Merman—than a power plant giving off rays of voice-entitlement electricity.

Gray never recorded the role, and Daly was in uncharacteristically poor voice for her disc. Still, her authority and—this is important—charm come through, and though we cannot "watch" a CD, the booklet's photos remind us how great Daly looked in the period clothes. Further, it's really only her first cut, "Some People," that finds her in difficulty. The song lies low, where the notes don't sound; after, Daly rebounds. She gets a lot out of "You'll Never Get Away From Me"—also low-lying, but smoother on the vocal cords. Note her little laugh at the end, when Jonathan Hadary's Herbie warns her that she is too controlling: Rose blithely bats away anything that thwarts her will. Note, too, that Hadary was let into the score more than his predecessors, taking some of Rose's lines. Later Herbies will do as much, or more. Crista Moore's Louise doesn't seize the role, but Robert Lambert's "All I Need Is the Girl" is a highlight.

Daly's replacement, Linda Lavin—a very interesting but uncharismatic Rose, all charmless ambition—did not record the part, and the next Broadway Rose, Bernadette Peters (Angel), is the one least well served on disc, for hers is not a natural Rose voice; much of her fascination lay in her line readings, the most rangy of all the Roses. Peters' rich characterization added sexiness and, at moments, the shadow of a vast inner despair to the standard Rose applications.

Rose is more than domineering: crafty and reckless, a villain. It's not a Peters part. Still, every artist brings something different to the role, and Peters created a very physicalized Rose, with more body language than anyone else. This Rose had a rack, hips, moves; she uses men. "No arguments," she tells Herbie, "shut up and dance"—and Peters drawls out "dance" in a rough intimacy that reminds us that these two are all but married at this point.

Gypsy is not an especially pictorial show, but Peters' director, Sam Mendes, built around her an eye-filling concept production using a miniature proscenium to frame the onstage numbers and drawing the ensemble into shifting scenery. It brought home the notion that everyone in America is in show biz, even if most of them are working the small time: real life. Mendes also featured June more than most directors do, as when, in the important scene between her and Louise after the farm sequence, "dainty" June most undaintily lit a cigarette with an air of sheer disgust on Kate Reinders' pretty face. As Sartre tells us, hell is other people, especially your mother. My favorite bit of the Mendes production—another instance of how visually he saw the piece—occurred when Rose and her troupe passed through the stage door of their Wichita booking. Way upstage, we glimpsed the silhouettes of two baggy-pants comics—an etch-a-sketch of burlesque and the objective-correlative of Rose's doom. She has hit (as the caption sign placed near the wings states it) "The Bottom."

Thus, without Mendes' staging and Peters' book scenes, her CD is less alluring than the others. Still, as the first *Gypsy* recorded for a CD's extensive playing time, it is more complete than its predecessors. Daly's, one of the last show albums to appear on LP, clocks in at fifty-four minutes. Peters' disc has ten more minutes, allowing for such niche items as the Entr'acte (which then skips the second act's opening "traveling music" to present the Toreadorables' act), Rose's deflated reprise of "Small World" when Herbie leaves her, a lengthy version of "The Strip," and even a bit of the last dialogue scene that preserves Peters' view of Rose as a born star who could do everything in show biz except make it. Then, too, Peters' is the most lovingly sung of Roses, especially in "Small World," in an unusually upbeat tempo. It's radiant. When Herbie (John Dossett) joins in at the end, you can hear their chemistry mixing.

There's something fascinating in the 2008 Patti LuPone Encores! revival (Time/Life). No, I mean besides LuPone. It's an appendix of seven songs dropped from *Gypsy* either before or during rehearsals and, in one case, on the eve of the first tryout performance, in Philadelphia. Sony's CD issue of the Merman cast includes two of these sung by "demo" specialists. Time/Life has recorded them anew with the LuPone cast (and, when needed, fresh orchestrations by Jonathan Tunick), so we collect these numbers as they would sound in the theatre. Truth to tell, most of them are of minor interest, though Herbie's "Nice She Ain't" (one of the Sony bonuses, by the way) reminds us that this role might well have been cast with a singer—George Wallace, say. At least "Smile, Girls," a tango for Rose while directing the Toreadorables (thus the song's Latin rhythm), is rather amusing, and a great Merman number with its blend of sarcasm and pep.

Of greatest curiosity is the often mentioned quodlibet: Rose woos Herbie with "Small World," her daughters make remark in their own little duet, then the two songs are sung simultaneously. Styne must have thought a lot of the latter number, for it was included in the first selection of titles to be offered as sheet music before the New York premiere, as "Mama's Talking Soft." (Yes, with the show's insistent "Momma" respelled thus.) Legend tells us that the staging placed the girls on a platform, one had a fear of heights, and, in the usual mad rush to get a production on its feet in full true for the first time, the song was dropped, leaving "Small World" on its own.

I wonder, though, if that's all there is to it. Hearing the quodlibet sung for the first time—this is its first recording—one realizes that the two melodies simply don't complement each other. In fact, they clash. In a two-part quodlibet, one tune should be silent or sustaining long notes while the other tune is busy. Think of the quodlibet in *Call Me Madam*, "You're Just In Love"—the one that *Watch Your Step* turned into an Irving Berlin quodlibet festival near the start of this discography. The two melodies disarm each other, one so smooth ("I hear singing and there's no one there . . .") and the other so bouncy ("You don't need analyzing . . ."), each operating at strength only when its partner is at rest. *Gypsy*'s quodlibet is a shambles; you hear everything at the same time. I'm guessing that more than a fear of heights led to its being dropped.

As for the LuPone *Gypsy* proper, it may be the best since the original. Certainly, LuPone is vocally the most qualified of Merman's successors—and her instinct for the telling detail is fiercely at work. As I've said, Rose is not only a Great Role but one that attracts great performers, each discovering something unique. I think LuPone discovered Rose's vulnerability. Her last dialogue scene, when she virtually admits that she gave her life away for nothing, was truly shattering. (It actually got recorded, for Barnes & Noble offered a special two-disc *Gypsy* with odds and ends on the second record, including that final scene.) All along, LuPone gave hints that Rose is not the invincible powerhouse she seems, as in "You'll Never Get Away From Me," wonderfully brought off with a very able Boyd Gaines. If you heard them out of context, you'd take them for a Boy Meets Girl love couple with no fault line in their relationship and no quake to come.

The entire cast is fine, with an effervescent "If Momma Was Married"—better on disc, without the "every line enacted in charade" staging that director (and, of course, book writer) Arthur Laurents imposed on it. Conversely, Tony Yazbeck's wonderful "All I Need Is the Girl" is starved for its staging. It's a no-fail number anyway, but somehow Yazbeck's dancing and commentary ("Now I'm more debonair") personalized it. The whole disc is alive, even so. Bill Raymond, uttering Pop's words in "Some People" ("You ain't getting eighty-eight *cents* from me, Rose!") is a jolt of narrative intensity; this is one of the few men who see right through her. Stephen Sondheim originated this line on the Merman LP, because the actor playing Rose's father had not been called for the recording session. Immortally, Sondheim fumbles the line's meaning. He says, "You ain't getting eighty-eight cents from *me*, Rose," as though withdrawing from a pool of contributors.

We are closing with *Gypsy* because, of all the Great American Musicals, it is the one unencumbered by the baggage of extra considerations. *Show Boat* is too big. *Follies* is hard to perfect. Other titles, from *Oklahoma!* and *Brigadoon* to *Fiddler on the Roof* and *Hello, Dolly!*, require the resuscitation of the original choreography or some genius substitution. *Gypsy*, on the other hand, is a simple show, trim and uncluttered. It sums up much of what happened to the musical during the Golden Age—the development of the overture as a kind of prefatory tone poem (at first in *Show Boat*, more commonly in the 1930s), the growing importance of realistic character development (in the 1940s), the rise of the director-choreographer (in the 1940s and 1950s), the revolution in fast-moving set changes (in the 1950s especially).

Above all, *Gypsy* demonstrates the power of smart, funny, naturalistic book continuity. More and more, *Gypsy* looks like the ideal show, if not the greatest nevertheless the one without flaws. Yet Arthur Laurents did find fault with one of *Gypsy*'s aspects, and was always scheming to improve it by erasing the huge box at the bottom of the show's credits: "ENTIRE PRODUCTION DIRECTED AND CHOREOGRAPHED BY JEROME ROBBINS." Laurents staged three of *Gypsy*'s four revivals, relentlessly throwing crazy dust on the very memory of a "Jerome Robbins *Gypsy*," presumably because Robbins thus maintained eternal authority—even in death—over Laurents' only two unqualified successes in the musical, *West Side Story* and then *Gypsy*. Laurents went after both of them, at last unleashing "his" *West Side Story* (in 2009) with some of it translated into Spanish.

But why stop there? Why not *The Desert Song* in French and Rifian Berber, *The Boys From Syracuse* in Ephesian Greek, *Camelot* in Old English with Beowulf signing at stage left? We've covered so much people territory in this book, with fizzy entertainers from Weber and Fields and Marilyn Miller right up to Patti LuPone, with writers as diverse as De Sylva, Brown, and Henderson and Jonathan Larson, from *The Wizard of Oz* to *The Wild Partys*. It's tiresome to end with a personality as mean-spirited as Laurents, forever nosing around to place your insecure spots so he could mug them at whim. But an intimate anecdote will give us a crisp little departure, and show biz does love a good story. The diva advises the young actress on the rise, "When you exit, take everything with you, including the grand piano." We'll be humble and take almost nothing as we slip out: I once asked Anne Kaufman, a neighbor of Laurents' at Quogue who knew him well, how anyone so unpleasant could attract and hold a lover as handsome, built, and blond as Tom Hatcher, and Anne replied, "The blond was even worse."

INDEX

Aarons, Alex A., 113, 115, 133, 158,
    160–61
Abbott, George
    and *Fiorello!* 190
    and *Merrily We Roll Along*, 264
    and *New Girl in Town*, 166, 167
    and *The Pajama Game*, 202
    and *On the Town*, 178
    and *A Tree Grows in Brooklyn*, 168
Academy of Music, 15–16
Adams, Edith, 175
Adams, Lee, 208, 213, 214, 232
adaptations
    of films, 255–56
    television musicals as, 174
Adler, Richard, 75n, 189, 202
Adonis, 29–30, 55
African Americans
    and *Cabin in the Sky*, 150–51
    and *In Dahomey*, 128
    and *Finian's Rainbow*, 177
    and *Follies*, 99, 101
    headliners, 190–91
    and integrated shows, 177
    and opera pool of Broadway, 155
Ah, Wilderness! (O'Neill), 60
Ahrens, Lynn, 268
Ain't Misbehavin', 254
Akers, Karen, 242
Aladdin, 174–75
Alberghetti, Anna Maria, 175, 191
Alda, Alan, 207
Alda, Robert, 192
Aldredge, Thomas, 190
Alessandrini, Gerard, 231
Alice in Wonderland, 76, 263
Allegro
    characters of, 158–59, 162

choices of characters in, 224
and Concept Musicals, 220–21, 224,
    240
dancing in, 212, 240
influence of, 224
as integrated show, xi
and R&H's management style, 164
score of, 238
set design in, 109
setmakers of, 159
theme of, xi
Allen, Fred, 137
Allen, Robert C., 20
All Shook Up, 255
Almodóvar, Pedro, 275
Ameche, Don, 174
The American Idea, 63–64
Anderson, Maxwell, 147
Andrews, Julie, 164, 194, 196, 199, 200,
    257
Andrews Sisters, 235
animal fable song genre, 64–65
Ankles Aweigh, 244
Anna Christie (O'Neill), 166–67
Annie, 232–33
Annie 2, 132
Annie Get Your Gun, 135, 172, 180, 192
Anyone Can Whistle, 207
Anything Goes, 140–42
    as classic of the 1930s, 180
    and *Follies*, 227
    and Merman, 90, 134
    revival of, 192, 249–50
    script of, 140n
Applause, 232
Apple Blossoms, 55–56, 79
The Apple Tree, 207
The Archers, 12

Aristides, John, 167
Arlen, Harold, 83, 164–65, 191
Aronson, Boris, 150, 159, 225, 228
Around the World, 109
Artists and Models, 105
Ashford, Rob, 252
Ashley, Christopher, 255
Astaire, Adele
    and *The Band Wagon*, 137, 138
    in England, 115–16
    influence of, 56
    and *Lady, Be Good!* 114
    and *Stop Flirting*, 115–16
Astaire, Fred
    and *The Band Wagon*, 137, 138, 139
    in England, 115–16
    and *Gay Divorce*, 135, 136
    Hepburn's comment on, 79
    influence of, 56
    and *Lady, Be Good!* 114
    and Rodgers and Hammerstein, 161
    and *Stop Flirting*, 115–16
As Thousands Cheer, 132, 138
At Home Abroad, 138
Atteridge, Harold, 65
Avenue Q, 260
Ayers, Lemuel, 157–58
Azaria, Hank, 256
Aziza, de'Adre, 275

Babes in Arms, 90, 133, 139, 180
Babes in Toyland, 45–47
    adventure theme in, 218
    as extravaganza, 41, 77
    and *Little Nemo*, 78
    pastiche in, 46, 64
    sets in, 79, 110
Bacall, Lauren, 232
Bailey, Pearl, 191
Balanchine, George, 139, 150, 212
Baldwin, Kate, 251–52
Ball, Lucille, 63, 169
ballad operas, **3**, 4, 5
Ballard, Kaye, 175, 187
ballets, 139–40. *See also* Dream Ballets
Ballroom, 240
The Band Wagon, 137–39, 270
Barker, John, 138
Barnabee, Henry Clay, 35
Barnum, 241

Barras, Charles M., 14, 16, 17–18
Barrison, Mabel, 45
Barry, Gene, 233
Barstow, Richard, 185
Battles, John, 178
Baum, L. Frank, 41
Baum, Vicki, 267
Bay, Howard, 217
Beaton, Cecil, 194, 195
Beauty and the Beast, 256
The Beauty Spot, 66
Beggar's Holiday, 177, 186
The Beggar's Opera, 3–4, 5, 7, 141, 157,
    254, 270
The Begum, 28, 36
Belasco, David, 39
The Belle Of Bond Street, 65
The Belle Of New York, 34
Bells Are Ringing, 172, 179, 182
Benanti, Laura, 275, 276
Ben Franklin in Paris, 206, 209
Bennett, James Gordon, 15
Bennett, Michael, 238, 239
Bennett, Robert Russell, 136, 157, 162,
    226, 240
Bergman, Ingmar, 227
Berkeley, Busby, 248
Berlin, Irving
    and *Annie Get Your Gun*, 172
    and *Call Me Madam*, 185
    and co-composed shows, 55
    and Cohan, 60
    and *Face the Music*, 130
    first narrative show of, 130
    and Herbert, 75
    interpolations from, 103
    success of, 194
    and *As Thousands Cheer*, 132, 138
    and *Watch Your Step*, 85
Bernstein, Leonard, 76, 178, 187, 197,
    198, 232
Besoyan, Rick, 215
Best Foot Forward, 215, 215n
Bicknell, George, 17
Big Boy, 68
Big Deal, 243–44
Bigley, Isabel, 192
Big River, 236–37
biographical musicals, 190
Birkenhead, Susan, 255

Bishop, Carole, 239
Bissell, Richard, 202
Bitter Sweet, 227
Björnson, Maria, 231
Blackbirds of 1928, 101
The Black Crook, 13–17
   adventure theme in, 218
   and *The Girl in Pink Tights*, 186
   performance run of, 15, 22
   revivals of, 29, 247
blackface, 68
Blaine, Vivian, 192
Blake, Eubie, 101
Blane, Ralph, 215, 215n
Bledsoe, Jules, 126, 128
Blitzstein, Marc, 76, 148–49, 216, 229
Block, Geoffrey, 126
Bloomer Girl, 164–65
Blossom, Henry M., Jr., 52, 72, 77, 86
Blossom Time, 120, 121, 123n, 125
Blyden, Larry, 207
Bock, Jerry, 190, 207, 216, 219,
   232, 235
The Body Beautiful, 235
Boland, Mary, 131, 276
Bolton, Guy, 69, 87, 88, 91, 114, 140,
   141, 276
Bonnie & Clyde, 263–64
Bono, 269–70, 269n
The Book of Mormon, 218, 260
books and bookwriters. *See* librettos and
   librettists
Booth, Shirley, 168
Bordman, Gerald, 23, 55n
Borodin, Alyeksandr, 186
Boston Ideal Opera Company, 31
Boucicault, Dion, 27
Bourne, Matthew, 257
The Boy Friend, 111, 261
The Boys From Syracuse, 180, 215n
Braham, Dave, 27
Bramble, Mark, 241
Brand, Phoebe, 146
Brennan, Eileen, 218–19
Brian, Donald, 56, 57, 84
Brice, Fanny
   in *Funny Girl*, 209
   name of, 99n
   in *Ziegfeld Follies*, 59, 99, 101, 103,
     104, 145

Brigadoon, 166, 194, 197, 253
Bring Back Birdie, 132
Broadway
   and blacks in musical theater,
     155
   cultural centrality of, 175
   erotic material of, 135
   and the *Follies*, 106
   and Great Depression, 133
   new authors on, 235
   as pinnacle of American theatre,
     106
   and Third Age, 82
Broderick, Helen, 137
Broderick, Matthew, 252, 260
The Brook, 23, 29
Brooks, Mel, 259–60
Brown, Anne, 155
Brown, Ashley, 257
Brown, Jason Robert, 262
Brown, Joe E., 70, 83
Brown, John Mason, 138
Brown, Lew, 105, 118, 133, 249
Bryan, Vincent, 42
Brynner, Yul, 162
Buck, Gene, 103
Buckley, Betty, 244
Buell, Bill, 271
A Bunch of Keys, 24
Burch, Shelly, 242
The Burgomaster, 35
burlesque, 19–32
   defined, **19**
   development of the form, 51
   end of, 30
   fun associated with, 31
   and musical comedy, 51, 98
   return of, 39
   revival of, 29–30
Burnett, Carol, 182, 190
Burns, David, 218
Burns, Ralph, 210, 211
Burrows, Abe, 192, 193, 233
Burstein, Danny, 275, 280
Burton, Richard, 199, 200
Buster Brown (comic strip), 78
Buttons, Red, 264
Butz, Norbert Leo, 259, 277
Buzzell, Eddie, 121
Bye Bye Birdie, 212–14, 262

Cabaret, 220–22
  blended forms in, 51
  as integrated show, xi
  pastiche in, 10
  revivals and revisions of, 252–53
Cabin in the Sky, 116, 150–51
Caesar, Irving, 110
Caesar, Sid, 206–7
Cahill, Marie, 66–67, 68, 209
Caldwell, Anne, 95, 95n
Calin, Mickey, 197
Callahan, Bill, 184
Callas, Maria, 216
Call Me Madam, 185
Camelot, 51, 94n, 198–200, 258, 270,
  275
Can-Can, 167, 174, 212
Candide, 187, 188, 197, 231, 248
Cantor, Eddie
  and Chicago, 238
  and The Desert Song, 121
  and traditional casting, 68
  in Ziegfeld Follies, 99, 101, 102, 104
Capote, Truman, 191
Capp, Al, 234
Cappy, Ted, 185
Carey, Macdonald, 153
Cariou, Len, 229, 265
Carnelia, Craig, 274
Carnival! 191, 217, 255
Carousel
  characters of, 158, 161–62, 173
  character songs of, 271
  couples of, 174
  darkness as theme in, 274
  and evolution of musicals, 227
  influence of, 170, 270
  opening sequence of, 160
  producers of, 163
  success of, 88, 106
  surreal component of, 165
Carrafa, John, 260
Carrie, 244, 260
Carrington, Katherine, 131, 136–37
Carroll, David, 267
Carroll, Diahann, 186
Carroll, Earl, 105
Carte, Richard D'Oyly, 28
Carver, Brent, 262
Caryll, Ivan, 52, 53, 58, 94–95

Casey, Warren, 235
Cassidy, Jack, 214
cast albums, 175, 182, 199
Castle, Irene, 85
The Cat and the Fiddle, 136–37
Cats, 230, 231
Cavendish, Millie, 14, 16
Cawthorn, Joseph, 84, 85
Celebration, 216
The Century Girl, 76
Cerveris, Michael, 270
Champion, Gower
  and Bye Bye Birdie, 213, 214
  and 42nd Street, 256
  and Hello, Dolly! 217, 220
  and I Do! I Do! 206
  and Irene, 248
  and Rodgers and Hammerstein, 161
  and Sweet Charity, 211
Chanfrau, F. S., 13
Channing, Carol, 149, 218, 220
Channing, Stockard, 251
Chapin, Ted, xi, 139n
Chaplin, Sydney, 209
Chappell publishing imprint, 83, 283
character songs, 271
Charnin, Martin, 232
Chasen, Dave, 116
Chee-Chee, 112, 114
Chenoweth, Kristen, 277–78
Chevalier, Maurice, 63
Chicago, 8, 164, 235, 237–38, 250
Chilpéric, 9
The Chocolate Dandies, 42
choreographers
  from classical dance world, 139
  director-choreographers, 41, 186, 210,
    212, 217, 237, 240, 243–44
  staging by, 150
  star choreographers, 185
  See also specific choreographers,
    including Fosse, Bob
A Chorus Line, 238–40, 269n, 272, 274
Church, George, 170
Cimarron, 126
Cinderella, 164, 174, 175
Cinderella At School, 33
City of Angels, 258–59, 274
Clark, Bobby, 117, 132, 171, 247
Clark, Victoria, 263, 271

Clayton, Jan, 158
Cleese, John, 256
Close, Glenn, 241
Cochrane, June, 112
Coco, 169, 183
Coco, James, 249
The Cocoanuts, 130
co-composed shows, 55
Cohan, George M., 59–64
   and *George M!* (biographical
      production), 241
   and *I'd Rather Be Right*, 143–45
   and Irish character of early Broadway,
      13, 91
   and *Mary*, 92
   and minstrel shows, 10
   and Rodgers and Hart, 144
   use of pastiche, 8
Cole, Jack, 191
Cole, Lester, 111
Coleman, Cy, 207, 210, 211, 232, 241,
   258
Collette, Toni, 274
Collins, Dorothy, 226
Collins, Russell, 146
Comden, Betty
   and *The Baroness Bazooka*, 118
   and *Do Re Mi*, 189
   and *New Faces of 1952*, 185
   and *Say, Darling*, 202
   and *On the Town*, 178, 179–80
   and *On the Twentieth Century*, 232
   and women writers, 95n
comic opera, **29**
   development of the form, 5–6, 51, 56
   European comic opera, 33
   and musical comedy, 51–52
   and musical plays, 51
   and operetta, 46–47, 51, 55
   popularity of, 30–31
   prestige associated with, 31
comics, 116–17, 133–34
Company, xi, 223, 224, 225, 225n, 227,
   240
Compassion Musicals, 145, 265–67
*Complete Book of the American Musical
   Theater* (Ewen), 55n
Comstock, F. Ray, 87
Concept Musicals, 63, 176, 220–22,
   223–24, 228, 230, 237, 240

A Connecticut Yankee, 112, 247
Connick, Harry, Jr., 254
The Conquering Hero, 213
Convy, Bert, 222
Cook, Barbara, 188, 216, 244
Cook, Joe, 116–17
coon-song genre, 66, 127
Cooper, Martin, 5–6
copyright law, 272n
Cordelia's Aspirations, 27
Corduner, Allan, 271
Corey, Irwin, 11
Cornell, Katharine, 151
Corthell, Herbert, 124
Cote, David, 254, 269
Cotsirilos, Stephanie, 242
Courtney, Inez, 118
Coward, Noël, 195, 227, 259
Crabbe, Buster, 153
The Cradle Will Rock, 148
Crater, Allene, 45
Craven, Frank, 91
Crazy for You, 254
Crivello, Anthony, 262
Crouse, Russel, 140–41
Crouse, Timothy, 250
Cuervo, Alma, 271
Cullum, John, 253
cultural prestige of musicals, 169
Cumming, Alan, 252
Cunningham, John, 271
Curry, Tim, 256
curse of the sequel, 132
Curtains, 235
Cypher, Jon, 164
Cyranose de Bric-a-Brac, 39

Dale, Alan, 44–45, 121
Dale, Jim, 241
Daly, William, 115
Dames at Sea, 215
Damiano, Jennifer, 266
Damn Yankees, 167, 186, 212
dance-song genre, 65–66
Dancin,' 243
dancing
   in *Cabin in the Sky*, 150
   in the Golden Age, 270
   and musical plays, 197
   styles of, 186

dancing (*continued*)
  in the Third Age, 150
  in *On the Town*, 178
  in *Watch Your Step*, 85
  in *West Side Story*, 198
  See also Dream Ballets; New Dance
    Sensation genre
Dancing Around, 68
Daniele, Graciela, 250, 262
Daniels, Billy, 208
Daniels, Frank, 37–38
Darion, Joe, 216
darkness theme, 274–76, 279, 280
Darling, Jean, 158
da Silva, Howard, 170
Das Land des Lächelns, 57
Davenport, Harry, 34
David, Clifford, 253
David, Keith, 255
Davis, Bette, 182, 183–84
Davis, Jessie Bartlett, 31
Davis, Sammy, Jr., 191, 208
Dawn, Hazel, 53, 80
Day, Edith, 91, 92
A Day and a Night in New York, 24
The Day Before Spring, 165
Dearest Enemy, 111
Dear Sir, 94
death theme, 166, 168
De Koven, Reginald, 31, 32, 35,
  36, 66
Delicious (1931), 64
De Luce, Virginia, 184
De Mille, Agnes
  ability and range of, 212
  and *Allegro*, 159
  and *Bloomer Girl*, 165
  and *Brigadoon*, 166
  choreography of, 139
  and *Goldilocks*, 186
  and *Oklahoma!* xii, 164
  and *One Touch of Venus*, 164
  and *Paint Your Wagon*, 188
  and Rodgers and Hammerstein, xi
Denier, Tony, 23
De Paul, Gene, 234
Der Rosenkavalier, 96
The Desert Song, x, 80, 121–23, 123n,
  125, 140
Destry Rides Again, 189

De Sylva, B. G., 69, 83, 103, 105, 118,
  133, 154, 249
Die Dollarprinzessin, 57
Die Lustige Witwe, 56, 56n
Diener, Joan, 216
Die Rheinnixen, 9
Dietrich, Marlene, 54
Dietz, Howard, 94, 137–38, 195, 206
Diggs, Taye, 267
Dillingham, Charles, 55, 72, 75, 85, 94,
  95, 96–97
DiPietro, Joe, 255
director-choreographers, 41, 210, 217,
  237, 240, 243–44
Dirty Rotten Scoundrels, 259
Dishy, Bob, 209
Disney screen stagings, 256–57
Divina Commedia (Dante), 6n
Dixey, Henry E., 21, 29–30, 33, 35
Doctorow, E. L., 268
Do I Hear a Waltz? 162
The Dollar Princess, 57
A Doll's Life, 179
Do Re Mi, 189
Douglass, Stephen, 187, 216
Dowling, Eddie, 102
Dowson, Ernest, 173
Dracula, 263
Drake, Alfred, 170, 173, 174–75, 206,
  216
Dream Ballets
  in *The Band Wagon*, 139
  in *The Day Before Spring*, 165
  in *Flower Drum Song*, 197
  in *Goldilocks*, 212
  in *I'd Rather Be Right*, 144
  in *New Girl In Town*, 167
  in *Oklahoma!* 164
  in Porter productions, 140
  and Rodgers and Hammerstein, 157,
    163
  in *On the Town*, 178, 179, 180
  in *A Tree Grows in Brooklyn*, 167
  in *West Side Story*, 197
  in *What's Up?* 165
The Dream Girl, 111
Dreamgirls, 240, 267, 268, 274
Drewe, Anthony, 257
Dreyfus, Max, 83–84, 96
The Drowsy Chaperone, 261

Dr. Syntax, 33
Du Barry Was a Lady, 7, 149, 172
Dubin, Al, 215
Du Bois, Raoul Pène, 248
Dude, 230
Duff-Gordon, Lady (Lucile), 100, 101
Duke, Vernon, 150, 182, 183–84
Dumont, Margaret, 130
Duncan, Todd, 150, 155
Dunham, Katherine, 150
Dunlap, William, 12
Du Prez, John, 256
Durante, Jimmy, 117, 189
Dussault, Nancy, 189

Earl Carroll's Vanities, 105
Ebb, Fred
    and *Cabaret*, 221
    and *Chicago*, 237–38
    and *Curtains*, 235
    and *Flora, the Red Menace*, 209, 210,
        262
    and *Kiss of the Spider Woman*, 261
    and *The Scottsboro Boys*, 10
Ebersole, Christine, 265
Eckart, Jean, 216
Eckart, William, 216
The Edge, 269–70
The Ed Sullivan Show, 175
Edward B. Marks Company, 84
Edwards, Sherman, 216–18
8½ (film), 241–43
El Capitan, x, 36, 157
Elg, Taina, 242
Ellington, Duke, 177, 254
Elliott, William, 87
Emmet, J. K., 29
Emmett, Dan, 10
Encores! 250, 251
Engel, Lehman, 191
English musicals, 57–59
ensemble casts, 273–74
Equity Strike of 1919, 97
Erlanger, Abraham, 40
Errol, Leon, 69, 99
establishing numbers, 18n
The Eternal Road, 146
ethnicity, 101, 106, 145, 234
Evangeline; or, The Belle of Acadia, 21–22,
    29, 31

Evans, Charles Evan, 24
Evans, Harvey, 226
Evans, Wilbur, 171
Ewen, David, 55n
expressionism, 111–12
extravaganzas, **41**
    of Herbert, 77–79, 94
    and musical comedy, 98
    as a performer's medium, 47
Eyre, Richard, 257

Fabray, Nanette, 176
Face the Music, 130–31, 132–33, 143
Fade Out Fade In, 182
Fairbanks, Douglas, 103
Faison, George, 236
Fall, Leo, 57
Falsettoland, 234
Falsettos, 234
Fancy Free, 178
Fanny, 166, 167, 168–69, 255
The Fantasticks, 216, 235
farce, **23–24**, 26, 31
Faust, 6n, 9
Faye, Alice, 249
Fearnley, John, xi, 162, 191–92
Federer, Michelle, 277
Feiffer, Jules, 190
Fellini, Federico, 70–71, 210, 241, 243
Fellowes, Julian, 257
feminist movement, 234
Ferber, Edna, 126
Feuer, Cy, 163
Fiddle-Dee-Dee, 39
Fiddler on the Roof, 219–20
    book of, 258
    director-choreographer of, 217
    final curtain for, 220
    music of, 219
    performance run of, 220
    revival of, 249
    stereotypes of, 22
Field, Ron, 220, 248
Fields, Dorothy
    and *Blackbirds of 1928*, 101
    and *Mexican Hayride*, 171
    success of, as lyricist, 114
    and *Sweet Charity*, 210, 211
    and *A Tree Grows in Brooklyn*, 166, 168
    and women writers, 95n

Fields, Herbert
  blue material of, 111, 135
  and *Dearest Enemy*, 111
  and *Face the Music*, 131
  humor of, 133
  influence of, 131
  and *Mexican Hayride*, 171
  and *The New Yorkers*, 135
  and Rodgers and Hart, 114–15
  success of, as librettist, 114
Fields, Lew, 67
Fields, W. C., 99
Fierstein, Harvey, 233
Fifty Miles From Boston, 64
Finian's Rainbow, 7, 177–78, 180,
  251–52
Finn, William, 234, 265
Fiorello! 189, 190
The Firefly, 53, 54
first American musical, 13–17
Fitzgerald, Christopher, 252
Flaherty, Stephen, 268
Flora, the Red Menace, 162, 209–10, 262
Florodora, 58, 59
The Florodora Girl (1930), 59
Flower Drum Song, xi, 162–63, 197
Floyd Collins, 236, 263
Flying Colors, 137, 138
Flying High, 90, 133–34
Follies, 226–27
  blended forms in, 51, 52
  corruption theme in, 274
  and masterpieces of Sondheim, 223
  memorable events in, 280
  and old song genres, 238
  pastiche in, 10
  and Roscoe Number, 103
  style of, 258
  See also *Ziegfeld Follies*
Follow the Girls, 88, 177
Forbidden Broadway, 231
Ford, Helen, 111–12
For Goodness Sake, 115
For Me and My Gal, 239
Forrest, George, 186, 206, 268
Fortescue, George K., 21
The Fortune Teller, 38
42nd Street, 256
Forty-Five Minutes From Broadway,
  60–61

Fosse, Bob
  and *Big Deal*, 243–44
  and *Chicago*, 237–38
  and *The Conquering Hero*, 213
  and *Damn Yankees*, 186
  and *Dancin,'* 243
  and director-choreographer model,
    243–44
  influence of, 212
  and *Little Me*, 206
  and *New Girl in Town*, 166
  and *The Pajama Game*, 185–86
  and *Pippin*, 158
  and *Redhead*, 186
  and Russell Nype's audition, 164
  and *Sweet Charity*, 210–11, 237n
  and Verdon, 167, 186, 212
Foster, Hernandez, 14, 17, 23
Foster, Sutton, 261
Fox, George L., 23, 69
Foxy, 102
Foy, Eddie, Jr., 185
Frankel, Scott, 265
Frederick, Pauline, 67
Freedley, Vinton, 113, 115, 133, 158,
  160–61
Frey, Nathaniel, 168
Friml, Rudolf, 47, 53, 55, 65, 83, 103,
  120, 123
Fritz, Our Cousin German, 29
Frohman, Charles, 57, 84
Frost, Thomas, 36
Fuller, Hernandez, 14
The Full Monty, 259
Funny Face, 113, 116
Funny Girl, 209–10
*A Funny Thing Happened on the Way To the
  Forum*, 208
Furth, George, 225, 264

Gallagher, Helen, 211, 248, 264
Garber, Victor, 229, 249
Garbo, Greta, 174
Garcia, Adam, 180
Gardella, Tess, 126, 127
Gardenia, Vincent, 240
Garland, Judy, 239
The Garrick Gaieties, 84, 112
Garrison, David, 271
Gatti-Casazza, Giulio, 153

Gaunt, Percy, 25
Gautier, Dick, 214
Gaxton, William, 61, 132, 149
Gay, John, 3–4, 5, 6, 254
gay characters, 233–34
Gay Divorce, 135–36, 248
The Geisha, 58
Gelbart, Larry, 208, 258
Gennaro, Peter, 185
genres, 64–68, 162–63
Gentlemen Prefer Blondes, 182, 203
George M! 60, 241
George White's Scandals, 105, 154
Gershwin, George
    and Aarons and Freedley, 113
    and co-composed shows, 55
    and Cohan, 60
    in England, 116
    and *For Goodness Sake*, 115
    and Herbert, 75
    and *Let 'Em Eat Cake*, 132
    memorable music of, 113–14
    musical style of, 113
    and off-Broadway musicals, 214
    and *Oh, Kay!* 258
    and *Pardon My English*, 133
    partnership of, 194
    and political satires, 131, 132
    and *Porgy and Bess*, 153, 154
    and *Strike Up the Band*, 131
    style of, 113
    success of, 194
    and T. B. Harms, 83
    and *Of Thee I Sing*, 132
    and *Ziegfeld Follies* format, 105
Gershwin, Ira
    and Aarons and Freedley, 113
    in England, 116
    and *For Goodness Sake*, 115
    and Herbert, 75
    and *Lady in the Dark*, 151
    and *Let 'Em Eat Cake*, 132
    and moon theme, 64
    and off-Broadway musicals, 214
    and *Oh, Kay!* 258
    and *Pardon My English*, 133
    partnership of, 194
    and political satires, 131, 132
    and *Strike Up the Band*, 131
    style of, 113

    success of, 194
    and T. B. Harms, 83
    and *Of Thee I Sing*, 132
Gervais, Ricky, 183
Gest, Morris, 87
Gets, Malcom, 265
Geva, Tamara, 249
Ghost, 256
Ghostley, Alice, 175, 184
Gibson, William, 208
Gielgud, John, 248
Gigi, 256
Gilbert, W. S., 4–5, 7, 10, 18n, 27–28
Gilbert & Sullivan
    and burlesque, 12
    devolution of format, 58
    and establishing numbers, 18n
    and *HMS Pinafore*, 27–28, 29, 247
    and Hopper, 36
    imitators of, 33
    influence of, 10, 27
    integrated shows of, 157
    interpolations from, 247, 259
    partnership of, 5
    and *Patience*, 28
    and *The Pirates of Penzance*, 29, 249
    popularity of, 249
    style of, 7
    success of, 28
Gilford, Jack, 222
Gillette, Priscilla, 187
The Gingham Girl, 218
Gingold, Hermione, 228
Ginzler, Robert, 202
Girl Crazy, 113, 134
The Girl Friend, 112
The Girl From Utah, 84–85
The Girl in Pink Tights, 186
A Glance at New York in 1848, 13
Glaser, Lulu, 77
Going Up, 91, 93, 134
Golden Age
    and *Apple Blossoms*, 56
    attacks on traditions of, 238
    beginning of, 84, 109, 112
    essentials of productions from, 109,
        258, 270
    and Herbert, 82
    and likeness/unlikeness to life, 7
    and the New Music, 93

Golden Age (*continued*)
  and New York style, 216
  set design in, 159
The Golden Apple, 186–87
Golden Boy, 208, 209, 213, 250
Goldilocks, xi, 186, 212
Goldman, James, 226
Goodman, Dody, 216
Good Morning, Dearie, 93–94, 113
Good News! 117–19, 124, 174, 216, 249
Goodwin, J. Cheever, 21, 29
Gore, Michael, 244
Gormé, Eydie, 212
Goulet, Robert, 199, 200
The Governor's Son, 62
Grand Hotel, 267–68, 278
The Grand Tour, 233
Gray, Dolores, 182–83, 184, 207
Grease, 220, 235, 237
The Great Clowns of Broadway (Green),
  116
Green, Adolph
  and *The Baroness Bazooka*, 118
  and *Do Re Mi*, 189
  eccentricities of, 181
  and *New Faces of 1952*, 185
  and *Say, Darling*, 202
  and *On the Town*, 178, 179–80, 179n
  and *On the Twentieth Century*, 232
Green, Paul, 146, 147
Green, Stanley, 55n, 116, 147, 195, 203
Greenberg, Richard, 250–51
Green Grow the Lilacs, 159
Greenwich Village Follies, 105
Greif, Michael, 266
Grétry, André, 6
Grey, Joel, 60, 221, 241, 277–78
Grey Gardens, 265
Griffith, D. W., 75, 127
Grimes, Tammy, 209
Groody, Louise, 94
Grossman, Barbara, 99n
Group Theatre, 131
Guare, John, 274
Guettel, Adam, 236, 263
Guys and Dolls, 7, 80, 192–94, 268
Gypsy, 203–6
  burlesque in, 19
  corruption theme in, 274
  director of, 240

memorable events in, 280
performers in, 209
revival of, 249

Hair, 229–30
Hall, Bettina, 136, 141
Hallelujah, Baby! 182
Hamlisch, Marvin, 240, 274
Hammerstein, Jamie, xi
Hammerstein, Oscar, II
  characters of, 140
  and *The Desert Song*, 121–23, 140
  on fate, 268
  heroines of, 80
  influence of, 115
  and *Music in the Air*, 136, 137, 140
  and *Oklahoma!* xii
  and revues, 182
  and *Rose-Marie*, 120
  on second acts, 166
  and *Show Boat*, 90, 126, 127, 128
  and Sondheim, xi, 224
  and themes of songs, 122–23
Handel, George Frideric, 3
Haney, Carol, 185, 212
Hanley, Ellen, 184, 264
The Happy Time, 217
Harbach, Otto, 53, 65, 110, 120, 121,
  136
Harburg, E. Y., 83, 165, 177, 191, 195
Harms. *See* T. B. Harms publishing
  imprint
Harnick, Sheldon, 190, 207, 216, 219,
  232, 235
Harrigan, Edward, 13, 26–27, 29, 91
Harrigan and Hart
  culture of, 27
  and founding of American musicals,
    26–27
  influence of, 40, 91
  and Irish character of early Broadway,
    13, 26, 43, 91
  music of, 27
  sequels of, 132
Harris, Barbara, 207, 253
Harris, Charles K., 24
Harris, Julie, 169
Harris, Sam H., 62–63, 83, 105, 131
Harrison, Rex, 194, 196
Hart, Lorenz, 162

Hart, Moss
  and *Camelot*, 199, 200
  and *Face the Music*, 130
  on feeling like an amateur, 196, 207
  and *I'd Rather Be Right*, 143
  and Kaufman, 264
  and *Lady in the Dark*, 151–52, 153
  and *My Fair Lady*, 196
  and *As Thousands Cheer*, 132
Hart, Tony
  and Cohan, 60, 144
  and Dreyfus, 84
  and founding of American musicals, 26–27
  and Herbert, 75
  and Irish character of early Broadway, 13, 26, 91
  and *My Fair Lady*, 195
  and T. B. Harms, 83
Harvey, Georgette, 155
The Harvey Girls, 234
Hauptman, William, 236
Have A Heart, 87
Haverly's Mastodon Minstrels, 12
Havoc, June, 171, 204
Haworth, Jill, 221–22
Hayes, Richard, 190
Hazel Flagg, 145–46
Heads Up! 112
Hearn, George, 233
Hearst, William Randolph, 101
Held, Anna, 24, 104
Hellman, Lillian, 187
Hello, Dolly! 217–19
  director-choreographer of, 217
  driveline for, 123
  final curtain for, 220
  and likeness/unlikeness to life, 7
  and Merman, 135
  and off-Broadway revues, 216
  performance run of, 220
  revival of, 249
  romantic leads of, 80
  success of, 106
Hellzapoppin, 145
Henderson, Florence, 168
Henderson, Luther, Jr., 162–63, 255
Henderson, Ray, 83, 105, 118, 133, 249
Henner, Marilu, 235
Hepburn, Katharine, 79, 169, 183, 248

Herbert, Victor, 75–82
  and *Babes in Toyland*, 46
  and Blossom, 72
  and Cahill, 66–67
  and co-composed shows, 55
  and dances, 96n
  and *The Dream Girl*, 111
  early productions of, 37
  extravaganzas of, 77–79, 94
  interpolations from, 103, 259
  musical style of, 113
  and *The Only Girl*, 85–86
  and Smith, 37, 38, 78
  and Trentini, 53
  use of pastiche, 8
  and Ziegfeld, 76
Herman, Jerry, 135, 216, 218, 223, 233
Hervé (Florimond Ronger), 8–9
Heyward, Du Bose, 153, 154–55
Hickey, John Benjamin, 252
High Button Shoes, 182
Hight, Sue, 184
Hilferty, Susan, 263
Hines, Gregory, 255
Hirsch, Louis, 91, 92–93, 96, 103
Hirschfeld, Al, 194
Hirson, Roger O., 158
His-Mud-Scow Pinafore, 28
Hitchcock, Raymond, 52, 68, 105
Hitchy Koo, 105
Hitler, Adolf, 133
hits and flops, standards for, 225
Hit the Deck! 110
HMS Pinafore, 5, 27–28, 29, 31, 55n, 58
Holiday, Bob, 214
Holliday, Judy, 182
Hollman, Mark, 260
Holloway, Stanley, 13, 194
Holloway, Sterling, 112
Holman, Libby, 137
Holmes, Rupert, 261
The Honeymoon Express, 68
Hood, Basil, 56n
Hooker, Brian, 123
Hopper, De Wolf, 33, 36–37
Horne, Lena, 191, 203
Horton, Robert, 216
Hoschna, Karl, 65
House of Flowers, 191
Howard, Ken, 232

How To Succeed in Business Without Really
    Trying, 207, 252
Hoyt, Charles H., 24, 25
Humpty Dumpty, 22–23, 29
Huston, Walter, 147

I Am a Camera (Van Druten), 220
Idle, Eric, 256
I Do! I Do! 206, 216, 217
The Idol's Eye, 37–38, 66
I'd Rather Be Right, 143–45
immigrants in America
    casting of, 68, 91–92
    portrayals of, 26–27
    stereotypes of, 13, 22, 26
    as subject of musicals, 91–92
    and Ziegfeld's acts, 101, 234
The Importance of Being Earnest, 272n
improvisation, 102
In Dahomey, 128
Ingram, Rex, 150
integrated shows, x–xi, 66, 157, 278
interpolations, 66–68, 96
"intimacy" in musicals, 137–38
Intolerance (1916), 127
Into the Woods, 264
Iolanthe, 36
I Remember Mama, 232
Irene, 91–92, 248
Irish immigrants, 13, 26, 43, 91
Isherwood, Christopher, 220, 256
It Happened in Nordland, 66, 67, 110n
It's a Bird It's a Plane It's Superman,
    214–15
Ixion!; or, The Man At the Wheel, 19–20

Jack O'Lantern, 94
Jackson, Cheyenne, 251–52, 255
Jacobi, Victor, 55
Jacobs, Jim, 235
Jacobson, Irving, 216
Jamaica, 191, 203
James, Brian d'Arcy, 271, 274
James, Lester, 216
Jarrett, Henry C., 14, 15–18
jazz, 82, 113, 198
Jelly's Last Jam, 255
Jennie, 206
Jersey Boys, 255
Jesus Christ Superstar, 230

Jeter, Michael, 267
Johann, Cameron, 242
Johnny Johnson, 146–47
Johns, Glynis, 228
Johnson, Albert, 138, 159
Johnson, Bill, 165
Johnson, Susan, xi, 188
Johnston, Johnny, 168, 170
Jolson, Al, 68–69, 154–55, 209
Jones, Dean, 225
Jones, Richard, 270
Jones, Sidney, 58, 84
Jones, Tom, 206, 216, 235
Judy Forgot, 67
jukebox musicals, 254–55
Julia, Raul, 242, 243
Juno, 216

Kahn, E. J., 26
Kander, John
    and Cabaret, 221
    and Chicago, 238
    and Curtains, 235
    and Flora, the Red Menace, 209, 210,
        262
    and Kiss of the Spider Woman, 261
    and minstrel shows, 10
    use of pastiche, 8
Karin, Fia, 216
Karnilova, Maria, 219
Kaufman, Anne, 193–94
Kaufman, George S., 130, 131, 143,
        193–94, 264
Kayden, Spencer, 260
Kaye, Danny, 153, 232
Kaye, Judy, 231
Kean, 206
Keeler, Ruby, 248
Keigwin, Lawrence, 273
Keith, Larry, 271
Kelley, Peter, 184
Kelly, 244
Kelly, Gene, 149, 239
Kelly, Jude, 180
Kelly, Patsy, 248
Kerker, Gustave, 34, 43
Kern, Jerome
    and co-composed shows, 55
    and Cohan, 60
    and dancing, 65

and De Sylva, 103
and *The Girl from Utah*, 84–85
and the Golden Age, 112
and Hammerstein, 126, 127, 128
and Herbert, 75
influence of, 87, 92–97
and integrated scores, 136
and interpolations, 57, 96, 103
and lyricism in musical comedy, 124
and *Music in the Air*, 137
and Hammerstein, 127–28, 137, 158, 194
and *Sally In Our Alley*, 69, 70
and *Show Boat*, 94, 97, 126, 127, 128
and T. B. Harms, 83, 96
and Wodehouse, 88–90
Kidd, Michael, 177–78, 186, 240
Kiley, Richard, 186, 216
Kimball, Chad, 42
King, Dennis, 124
King, John Michael, 195–96
The King and I
    as adaptation, 261
    book of, 123
    character development in, 161–62
    choices of characters in, 224
    composition of, xi
    couples of, 173
    influence of, 270
    love story of, 193
    performance spots in, 128
    revival of, 249
    tragedy in, 166
    and *Uncle Tom's Cabin*, 165
King Cotton; or, The Exiled Prince, 20–21
King Dodo, 35
Kirk, Lisa, 173
Kismet, 179n, 186
Kiss Me, Kate, 65, 140, 172–73, 174, 180
Kiss of the Spider Woman, 261–62
Kitt, Eartha, 184, 273
Kitt, Tom, 266
Kleban, Ed, 240
Klein, Charles, 36
Knickerbocker Holiday, 147
Kopit, Arthur, 241
Korey, Alix, 255
Korie, Michael, 265
Kotis, Greg, 260
Krakowski, Jane, 267

Kreisler, Fritz, 55
Kreuger, Miles, 141
Kudisch, Marc, 273

La Cage aux Folles, 233–34
LaChiusa, Michael John, 272, 273, 274
Lady, Be Good! 113–14, 116, 124, 158, 161, 275
Lady in the Dark, 106, 116, 151–53, 224, 234
The Lady Of the Slipper, 94
Lahr, Bert, 102, 117, 133–34, 149, 161, 182–83
Laing, Stewart, 270
Lane, Burton, 177, 234, 253
Lane, Jeffrey, 275
Lane, Nathan, 260
Lang, Harold, 173
Lansbury, Angela, 207, 229, 265
Lapine, James, 264
Larroquette, John, 252
Larson, Jonathan, 266
Latouche, John, 150, 186
Laurents, Arthur, 134–35, 197, 204
Lavin, Linda, 214
Lawrence, Carol, 184, 197
Lawrence, Gertrude, 106, 114, 152, 161, 162
Laye, Evelyn, 124
Layton, Joe, 186, 241
Lazar, Aaron, 180
Leave It To Jane, 87, 89–90, 96, 248
Leave It To Me! 149, 216, 218
Lebowsky, Stanley, 237
Lee, Gavin, 257
Lee, Gypsy Rose, 203–4
Lehár, Franz, 56, 57
Leigh, Mitch, 216
Lenya, Lotte, 146–47, 222
Lerner, Alan Jay
    and *Camelot*, 198, 199
    and *On a Clear Day You Can See Forever*, 253
    and *The Day Before Spring*, 165–66
    death of, 231
    and *Li'l Abner*, 234
    and *Love Life*, 176
    marriages of, 240
    and minstrel shows, 10
    and *My Fair Lady*, 12n, 195–96

Lerner, Alan Jay (*continued*)
  and *Paint Your Wagon*, 188
  and *Phantom of the Opera*, 231
  and *1600 Pennsylvania Avenue*, 232
  and *What's Up?* 165
Les Contes d'Hoffmann, 9–10
Les Misérables, 230, 231
Let 'Em Eat Cake, 132
Levene, Sam, 192
The Light in the Piazza, 263
"likeness and unlikeness to life" concept
  of Trussler, 4, 7, 141
Li'l Abner, 31, 186, 234–35, 240
Liliom, 159
Lillie, Beatrice, 138
Limón, José, 139
Lindsay, Howard, 140–41
The Lion King, 256
Lippa, Andrew, 272–73
Lithgow, John, 259, 274
Little Johnny Jones, 61–62
Little Mary Sunshine, 215, 260
Little Me, 206–7, 249
The Little Mermaid, 256
Little Nemo, 77–79, 81
A Little Night Music, 8, 223, 224, 227,
  228, 242
The Little Show, 137
Loesser, Frank, ix, 75n, 187–88, 189,
  192, 193, 207
Loewe, Frederick
  and *Brigadoon*, 166, 194
  and *Camelot*, 198, 199, 275
  and *The Day Before Spring*, 165–66
  love songs of, 166
  and *My Fair Lady*, 195–96
  and *Paint Your Wagon*, 188
  success of, 194
  and T. B. Harms, 83
  and *What's Up?* 165
  See also Lerner and Loewe
Logan, Ella, 177
Long, Shorty, 188
Long, William Ivey, 242
Lopez, Priscilla, 239
Lopez, Robert, 260
Lorraine, Lillian, 99
Losch, Tilly, 138, 139
Lost in the Stars, 197
Loudon, Dorothy, 233, 240

The Love Letter, 115
Love Life, xi, 10, 175, 176–77, 220–21,
  240
Love Never Dies, 132
Luders, Gustav, 34–35, 64
Lund, Art, 188
LuPone, Patti, 230, 250, 276
LuPone, Robert, 239
Lynde, Paul, 184, 213, 214

MacDermot, Galt, 229
MacDonald, Christie, 80, 135
MacDonald, Jeanette, 53
MacDonough, Glen, 46, 66, 110
Macintosh, Cameron, 224, 257
Mack and Mabel, 233
Madame Sherry, 65
The Madcap Duchess, 81
Maguire, Gregory, 277, 279
Maid Marian, 35
Makarova, Natalia, 249
Make a Wish, 123
Make Mine Manhattan, 206
Mame, 207, 249
Mamoulian, Rouben, xii, 155
Mandel, Frank, 110, 121
Mandelbaum, Ken, 231, 244
Man of La Mancha, 216–17, 249
A Man of No Importance, 268
Mantello, Joe, 250
Marbury, Elisabeth, 87
March of the Falsettos, 234
Marie Christine, 262, 275
Marlowe, 230
Martin, Barney, 238
Martin, Bob, 261
Martin, Ernest H., 163
Martin, Hugh, 215
Martin, Mary, 149, 163, 182, 206, 207,
  215n
Marx Brothers, 209
Mary, 92, 93
Mary Poppins, 256–57
Masteroff, Joe, 221
The Matchmaker (Wilder), 220
Mates, Julian, 10, 12
Mature, Victor, 153
May, Edna, 43
Mayer, Michael, 253, 269
Maytime, 54–55, 55n, 56, 79

Mazzie, Marin, 265
McCarthy, Jeff, 260
McDonald, Audra, 262
McDowall, Roddy, 200
McGlinn, John, 141
McHugh, Jimmy, 101
McKechnie, Donna, 239
McMartin, John, 226
McNally, Terrence, 268
Me and Juliet, 128, 162, 163
Medford, Kay, 213
Meehan, Thomas, 233
Meet Me In St. Louis, 34, 215n, 256
Meilhac, Henri, 56n
Mendes, Sam, 252
Menotti, Gian Carlo, 184–85
Menzel, Idina, 277–78
Mercer, Johnny, 234
Merman, Ethel
    and *Annie Get Your Gun*, 135, 192
    and *Anything Goes*, 90, 134, 141, 142
    and *Call Me Madam*, 185
    and *Gypsy*, 204, 280
    and *Hello, Dolly!* 135
    and Laurents, 134–35
    and Porter, 134, 149, 172
    professionalism of, 135
    and *Something For the Boys*, 172
    and *Take a Chance*, 167
Merrick, David, 203–4, 206
Merrill, Bob, 166, 206, 209, 217
Merrily We Roll Along, 264
The Merry Widow, 29, 56, 56n
Messel, Oliver, 191
*Met-A-Mora; or, The Last of the
    Pollywogs*, 20
Mexican Hayride, 170–71
Michaels, Sidney, 206
Michener, James, 160
Middleton, Ray, 172, 176
Mielziner, Jo, 159, 250
The Mikado, 28, 57
Milk and Honey, 162
Miller, Buzz, 185
Miller, Marilyn, 42, 69, 102, 135, 207, 238
Miller, Roger, 236
Mills, Stephanie, 236
Minnelli, Liza, 209–10, 215, 264
minstrel shows, **10–12**, 68
Miss Dolly Dollars, 76, 77

Miss Innocence, 104
Miss Saigon, 231
Mitchell, Brian Stokes, 269, 275
Mitchell, David, 232
Mitchell, Julian, 41–44, 45, 53
Mlle. Modiste, 76
Monckton, Lionel, 58
Montevecchi, Liliane, 242, 267
Montgomery, Dave
    and extravaganzas, 47, 94
    The Red Mill, 72, 74–75, 80
    and traditional casting, 68
    The Wizard of Oz, 43, 44, 45
Monty Python and the Holy Grail, 256
Moon Song genre, 64
Moore, Grace, 123n
Moore, Victor, 61, 63, 114, 132, 149
Morgan, Helen, 126, 238
Morison, Patricia, 173
Moross, Jerome, 147, 186
Morris, Anita, 242
Morrison, Greg, 261
Morse, Robert, 207
Morse, Woolson, 29, 33
Morton, Hugh, 34
Morton, Jellyroll, 255
Mostel, Zero, 208, 219
The Most Happy Fella, ix–x, xi, 187–88,
    193, 270
movie musicals, 255–57
Mr. Wonderful, 191
Mueller, Jessie, 254
Muller, Harrison, 212
The Mulligan Guards shows, 27, 132
Mura, Corinna, 171
Murney, Julia, 274
Murphy, Donna, 265
musical comedies, **33**, 109–19
    and burlesque, 51, 98
    as classics of the 1930s, 180
    and comic opera, 51–52
    development of the form, 51–53, 210
    and extravaganzas, 98
    in French music theatre, 6
    and sex and eroticism, 181
    and *Show Boat*, 129
musical plays
    as classics of the 1940s, 180
    and comic operas, 51
    and dancing, 197

Music Box Revues, 105

Music in the Air, 128, 136–37, 140, 248, 267

The Music Man, 169–70, 206, 258, 267

My Fair Lady, 194–95
   cast album of, 175
   influence of, 270
   librettos of, 12n
   memorable events in, 279
   musical style of, 235
   pastiche in, 8, 235
   performance run of, 220
   revival of, 249
   score of, 194
   success of, 106

My Maryland, 120–21

My One and Only, 254

The Mystery of Edwin Drood, 261

The Naiad Queen; or, The Mysteries of the Lurlie Berg! 13, 14

naturalism, 86, 143, 150, 197

Naughty Marietta, 31, 53, 79–80

Nelson, Gene, 226

Nelson, Kenneth, 272n

The Nervous Set, 189, 190, 198

Neuwirth, Bebe, 250

A New Brain, 265

New Dance Sensation genre, 65–66
   in *Face the Music*, 130
   in the *Follies*, 104
   in *George White's Scandals*, 105
   in *Goldilocks*, 212
   in *Good News!* 119
   in *Mary*, 92
   in *Runnin' Wild*, 101

New Faces of 1952, 184–85

New Girl In Town, 51, 166–67, 168–69, 212

The New Moon, 56, 80, 120, 122, 123n, 125

New York As It Is, 13

The New Yorkers, 135

next to normal, 265–66

Nice Work If You Can Get It, 255

Nicholaw, Casey, 261

Niesen, Gertrude, 177

Nine, 241–43, 267, 268

No, No, Nanette, 110–11, 248, 249, 273

No For an Answer, 148–49

Norton, Richard C., 55n, 56n

Noseworthy, Jack, 274

No Strings, 162, 186

Nype, Russell, 164, 185, 264

O'Casey, Sean, 229

O'Connor, Caroline, 180

Odets, Clifford, 208, 274–75

Odyssey, 187

off-Broadway musicals, 215

Offenbach, Jacques
   and development of musical comedy, 51
   early productions of, 27
   influence of, 10
   integrated shows of, 157
   and *Les Brigands*, 5
   rivals of, 8–9
   on role of music in theatre, 141
   style of, 7–8
   and translations, 29
   use of establishing numbers, 18n

Of Thee I Sing, 7, 113, 132, 180, 190n

Oh, Boy! 87–88, 89, 90

Oh, Captain! 169

Oh, Kay! 88, 113, 114, 248

Oh, Lady! Lady!! 87, 90, 92, 128

Oh, My Dear! 91, 93

O'Hara, John, 149, 150, 250

O'Hara, Kelli, 263, 274

O'Haughey, M., 238

Oh Captain! 255

Oh! Oh! Delphine, 52–53

Oklahoma!
   as adaptation, 261
   ballet of, 224
   blended forms in, 51
   characters of, 158
   costuming of, 158n
   couples of, 173
   dancing in, 178, 270
   elements of, 197
   ensemble cast of, 273
   as family show, 163–64
   first production of, 157–58
   influence of, 116, 170, 209
   as integrated show, xi
   opening sequence of, 160
   and Pulitzer award, 190n
   reactions to, xii

revival of, 249, 252
romantic leads, 80
success of, 88, 194–95
tragedy in, 166
Olcott, Chauncey, 13
Oliver, Edna May, 125
Oliver, Thelma, 211
On a Clear Day You Can See Forever, 253–54
Once on This Island, 268
Once Upon a Mattress, 123, 189–90
110 in the Shade, 216
O'Neill, Eugene, 60, 166–67, 212
One Touch of Venus, 164, 218
The Only Girl, 85–87
On the Town, 7, 25, 162, 178–81, 248
On the Twentieth Century, 232
On Your Toes, 139, 249, 270
opéra bouffe, 5
opera buffa, 5
opéra comique, 5–6, 6n
operas, 5, 6n, 175
opera seria, 3–4
operetta, 120–29
　and classics of the 1920s, 180
　comedy in, 121
　and comic opera, 46–47, 51, 55
　development of the form, 47, 51,
　　54–55
　early productions, 54–56
　and erotic themes, 136
　heyday of, 57
　love plots of, 122–23
　scripts in, 119
　themes of, 122
　See also Herbert, Victor
Orbach, Jerry, 135, 238
Osato, Sono, 178
O'Sullivan, Michael, 214
Our Miss Gibbs, 59
Our Town, 91
Out of This World, 174
Over Here!, 235

Pacific Overtures, 223, 224, 228–29
Paint Your Wagon, 31, 166, 188–89, 194
The Pajama Game, 8, 75n, 185, 189, 202
Pal Joey, 149–50
　characters of, 162, 224
　influence of, 116
　revivals of, 192, 250–51

Panama Hattie, 149, 204
pantomime, 22–23, 33, 98
Parade, 22, 147–48, 216, 262, 275
Pardon My English, 133
Parker, Trey, 260
A Parlor Match, 24, 30, 104
Pascal, Adam, 267
The Passing Show, 98, 105
Passion, 223, 265
pastiche composition, 7, 8, 10, 64
Patinkin, Mandy, 230, 274
Peggy-Ann, 111–12, 218
Pennington, Ann, 99
Pepusch, Johann Christian, 3–4
Peter Pan, 182
Peters, Bernadette, 223, 248, 280
Peterson, Kurt, 226
Petina, Irra, 188
The Phantom of the Opera, 110, 132, 230
The Pink Lady, 52, 53
Pins and Needles, 145–46
Pinza, Ezio, 168
Pipe Dream, 128, 162, 163, 191–92
Pippin, 10, 158
The Pirates of Penzance, 29, 249
Pitchford, Dean, 244
Pixley, Frank, 34–35, 64
Plimpton, Martha, 251
pop opera, 230–31, 267
Porgy and Bess, 153–56
　as Big Broadway production, 106
　operatic aspect of, 186
　revival of, 247, 249
　score of, 270
Porter, Cole, 140–42
　and *Anything Goes*, 134, 140–42
　characters of, 140
　and Cohan, 60
　erotic material of, 135
　and *Gay Divorce*, 135–36
　and *Kiss Me, Kate*, 174
　and Merman, 134, 149, 172
　and *Mexican Hayride*, 170–72
　and *My Fair Lady*, 195
　and *The New Yorkers*, 135
　and off-Broadway musicals, 215
　production power of, 149
　revue of music, 250
　and stars, 149
　success of, 174–75, 194

Porter, Cole (*continued*)
    and T. B. Harms, 83
    use of pastiche, 8
    wit of, 112, 142
Powell, Jane, 248
Present Arms, 111, 112
Presley, Elvis, 255
Presnell, Harve, 209
Preston, Robert, 169, 206
Prince, Hal
    and *Cabaret*, 220
    and *Candide*, 248
    and *Company*, 225, 225n
    and *Evita*, 230
    and *It's a Bird It's a Plane It's Superman*,
        214
    and *Kiss of the Spider Woman*, 261
    and *Parade*, 262
    and *The Phantom of the Opera*, 231
    and *Show Boat*, 252
    and Sondheim, 76, 223, 264
The Prince of Grand Street, 206
The Prince Of Pilsen, x, 35
The Princess "Pat," 76–77
Princess Theatre, 86–94, 96
The Producers, 51, 259–60, 261
Prud'homme, Cameron, 167, 168
Puck, Eva, 125

Queen High, 113

racism, 161, 177, 213
Radcliffe, Daniel, 252
Rado, James, 229
rag genre, 65, 77, 104
Ragtime, 268–69
The Rainbow Girl, 93
The Rainmaker of Syria, 28
Rain or Shine, 116
Raitt, John, 158, 189
Ramin, Sid, 202–3
Ramirez, Sara, 256
Randall, Carl, 90
Randall, Tony, 169
Rando, John, 260
Rapp, Anthony, 266
Rasch, Albertina, 130, 139
Raye, Martha, 248
Reardon, John, 189
Redhead, 186, 211, 212

The Red Mill, 72–75
    as integrated show, x, 157
    revivals of, 247
    romance in, 80
    success of, 81
Reilly, Charles Nelson, 216, 218
Reinking, Ann, 235
Rent, 266–67, 268
revivals and revisals, 215, 247–57
revues, 98, 138, 182–83, 215–16, 254.
    See also *Follies*
Rex, 232
Reynolds, Debbie, 92, 248
Rhodes, Erik, 136
rhythmic dialogue, 112
Rice, Edward E., 21, 30
Rice, Tim, 230, 231
Rich, Frank, 236
Richardson, Natasha, 252
Rigby, Harry, 248, 249
Riggs, Lynn, 158–59
Ring, Blanche, 67
Ripley, Alice, 265, 266
Rip Van Winkle, 31
Risch, Matthew, 251
Ritchard, Cyril, 175
Ritter, Thelma, 168
Rivera, Chita, 212, 238, 250, 262
The Robber Bridegroom, 236
Robbins, Jerome
    and *Call Me Madam*, 185
    and *Fiddler on the Roof*, 219
    and *Gypsy*, 204n, 240
    and Rodgers and Hammerstein, 161
    and *On the Town*, 178
    and *Two's Company*, 184, 185
    and *West Side Story*, 197, 198
Roberta, 133
Roberts, Joan, 170
Robin Hood, x, 31–32, 36, 157
Rob Roy, 35
Robyn, Alfred G., 52
Rockaby Hamlet, 230
rock music and rock musicals, 229–30,
    235
Rodgers, Mary, 189
Rodgers, Richard
    and *Babes in Arms*, 139n
    and *Carousel*, 191
    and Cohan, 60, 144

and Dreyfus, 83, 84
and Herbert, 75
and *I Remember Mama*, 232
on microphones in musicals, 191
and *No Strings*, 186
and *Oklahoma!* xii, 225
performance spots in productions of, 128
and *Rex*, 232
on sets and orchestrations, 228
and T. B. Harms, 83
and *Two By Two*, 232
Rodgers and Hammerstein, 157–81
    and *Annie Get Your Gun*, 172
    artistic emphasis of, 181
    auditions with, 164
    books and scripts of, 213
    characters of, 158, 161–62, 173–74, 206, 213
    and de Mille, xi
    deviations from family-show emphasis, 211
    genres of, 162–63
    influence of, 170
    integration of musicals, 157
    love songs of, 112
    management style of, 164
    and *My Fair Lady*, 195
    partnership of, 194
    rules for show business, 158–66
    and stars, 160–61
    success of, 157, 194
    and T. B. Harms, 83
Rodgers and Hart
    and audience's tastes, 95
    and *Babes in Arms*, 90, 139, 139n
    and Bolton, 88
    and *The Boys From Syracuse*, 215n
    and *Chee-Chee*, 112
    and Cohan, 60
    and *A Connecticut Yankee*, 112
    and *Dearest Enemy*, 111
    and Dreyfus, 84
    and Fields, 114–15
    and *The Garrick Gaieties*, 84, 112
    and *The Girl Friend*, 112
    and *Heads Up!*, 112
    and *I'd Rather Be Right*, 143–44
    and *Pal Joey*, 149–50, 251
    and *Present Arms*, 112

and set design, 111
and *Simple Simon*, 98
songs of, 149
success of, 194
and T. B. Harms, 83
Rogers, Ginger, 79, 134
Rogers, Gus and Max, 40–41
Rogers, Will, 99, 101–2
Rolph, Marti, 226
Romberg, Sigmund, 47, 53–54, 55, 69, 83, 120, 186
Rome, Harold, 166, 168, 189
Ronger, Florimond (Hervé), 8–9
Ronstadt, Linda, 249
Roosevelt, Franklin D., 143–45, 147, 148
Rose-Marie, 56, 120, 123n, 125, 260
Rosenfeld, Sydney, 52
Rosenthal, Laurence, 170
Ross, Adrian, 56n, 57, 189
Ross, Herbert, 167
Ross, Jerry, 75n, 202
The Rothschilds, 232
Routledge, Patricia, 232
Rubin-Vega, Daphne, 267
Runnin' Wild, 101
Russell, Lillian, 39, 40
Russell, Rosalind, 169
Ryskind, Morrie, 131–32, 133

Saidy, Fred, 177
Sally In Our Alley, 67, 69–70, 88, 207, 274
Salsbury, Nate, 23, 24
Sanderson, Julia, 84
Sandifur, Virginia, 226
Sater, Steven, 269
satire, 51, 76–77, 234
Savo, Jimmy, 165
Savoy, Bert, 103
Savoy operas, **4–5**
Savoy style, 28–29
Say, Darling, 202–3
The Scarlet Pimpernel, 263
Scheff, Fritzi, 80
Schmidt, Harvey, 206, 216, 235
Schönberg, Claude-Michel, 230
Schubert, Franz, 120
Schwab, Laurence, 118
Schwartz, Arthur, 137–38, 166, 168, 195, 206
Schwartz, Charles, 154–55

Schwartz, Stephen, 158, 277
Scott, Sherie Rene, 259, 275
Scotto, Renata, 228, 229
The Scottsboro Boys, 10
The Second Little Show, 137
See-Saw, 93
Segal, Vivienne, 90, 122, 149
Sell, Janie, 235
sequels, 132
The Serenade, 38
Sergava, Katherine, 170
set design, 78–79, 109–10, 216–18, 270
The Seven Sisters, 12
Seventeen, 272n
1776, 217
sex and eroticism
    and musical comedy, 181
    and Rodgers and Hammerstein, 211
    in the Third Age, 111, 135–36,
        137–38, 167
Sextet, 234
Shea, Jere, 265
Shean, Al, 77
Sheik, Duncan, 269
Shelley, Carole, 277
She Loves Me, 216
Sher, Bartlett, 277
Sherman, Richard M., 235, 257
Sherman, Robert B., 235, 257
Shevelove, Burt, 208, 248
Shimono, Sab, 228
Short, Hassard, 130–31, 152
Show Boat, 125–29
    Act Two of, 128
    as all-American musical comedy, 129
    blended forms in, 51
    characters of, 125–26, 158, 224
    character songs of, 271
    composition of, xi
    corruption theme in, 274
    epic story of, 201
    and fate, 268
    integrated score of, 278
    and Kern, 94, 97, 126, 127, 128
    music of, 42, 70, 90
    narrative libretto of, 270
    opening of, 31
    revivals and revisions of, 192, 247–48,
        252
    romantic storyline in, 162

specialties and interpolations in, x
use of pastiche, 10
use of story ballad, 24
Shubert, Lee and J. J., 53–54, 105
Shuffle Along, 101, 234
Side Show, 265
Silk Stockings, 174
Sillman, Leonard, 184
Silvers, Phil, 189
The Silver Slipper, 59
Simon, Neil, 206, 210, 237n
Simple Simon, 98
Sinbad, 68
Singing in the Rain, 256
Sissle, Noble, 101
Sitting Pretty, 94
1600 Pennsylvania Avenue, 232
Skinner, Emily, 265
Skyscraper, 169
Slezak, Walter, 136, 168
Sloane, A. Baldwin, 42, 52
Small, Neva, 206
Smalls, Charlie, 236
Smiles, 116
Smiles of a Summer Night, 227
Smith, Alexis, 226
Smith, Harry B.
    bilingual lyrics of, 77
    and De Koven, 35
    disdain for, 38–39
    and Herbert, 37, 38, 78
    and humor, 121
    influence of, as librettist-lyricist,
        38–39, 72, 115
    and *Robin Hood*, 31
    and *Watch Your Step*, 85
    on Ziegfeld's unreliability, 100
Smith, Oliver, 159, 194, 217
Smith, Rex, 249
Something For the Boys, 172
Sondheim, Stephen, 223–44
    and *Anyone Can Whistle*, 207
    artistic emphasis of, 264–65
    and Bernstein, 264
    Concept Productions of, 223–24
    endings of, 224
    and *A Funny Thing Happened on the
        Way To the Forum*, 208
    and *Gypsy*, 204
    and Hammerstein, xi, 224

and hits/flops, 225
masterpieces of, 223
and Prince, 76, 223, 264
reactions to, 224–25
rules for show business, 223–24
success of, 264
variety in music of, 227
and *West Side Story*, 197, 198
song genres, 64–68
Sophisticated Ladies, 254
The Sound of Broadway Music
    (Suskin), 202
The Sound of Music, 128, 163, 224
Sousa, John Philip, 36
South Pacific
    and choreography, 161
    couples of, 173
    elements of, 197
    heroine of, 207
    music of, 199
    opening sequence of, 160–61
    performance spots in, 128
    and Pulitzer Prize, 190n
    set design in, 109
Spamalot, 256
Spencer, J. Robert, 266
Spider-Man: Turn Off the Dark, 269–70,
    269n
Spring Awakening, 269
Stamper, Dave, 102–3
stars and star shows, 208–9, 273–74
Steel, John, 99, 101, 102, 105
Steel Pier, 260
Stein, Joseph, 219
Steinbeck, John, 163
The Stepping Stones, 95–96, 96n, 218
stereotypes, 22, 26–27
Stewart, Michael, 212, 218, 241
Stiles, George, 257
Stone, Dorothy, 95, 97
Stone, Fred
    and extravaganzas, 47, 94
    The Red Mill, 72, 73, 74–75, 80
    and traditional casting, 68
    The Wizard of Oz, 43–44, 45
Stone, Matt, 260
Stone, Peter, 270, 271
Stop! Look! Listen! 130
Stothart, Herbert, 120
Strauss, Richard, 8, 29, 92

Street Scene, 175–76, 186, 229, 267, 270
Streisand, Barbra, 209–10, 253
Strike Up the Band, 31, 113, 131–32
Stritch, Elaine, 225n, 229
Strouse, Charles, 208, 213, 214, 232
Stuart, Leslie, 58, 59
The Student Prince, x, 36, 56, 80, 120,
    125, 166, 227
Styne, Jule, 145, 182, 189, 202,
    203, 204
Sullivan, Arthur, 4–5, 7, 10, 18n, 27–28,
    76. *See also* Gilbert & Sullivan
Sumac, Yma, 256
Summerville, Amelia, 30
Sunday in the Park With George, 264
Sunny, 42
Suskin, Steven, 202
Suzuki, Pat, 197
Swartz, Mark Evan, 44
*Sweeney Todd, the Demon Barber of Fleet
    Street*, 223, 229, 265, 274
Sweet Adeline, 96, 128
Sweet Bye and Bye, 184
Sweet Charity, 210–11, 237n
Sweethearts, 79, 81–82, 247
Sweet Smell of Success, 274–75, 277
Swenson, Inga, 216

Tabasco, 28
Tabbert, William, 168, 264
Take a Chance, 167
The Tales of Hoffmann, 18n
The Talk Of New York, 61
Tangerine, 113
Tarkington, Booth, 272n
Tarzan, 256
The Tattooed Man, 38
Tatum, Marianne, 241
Tauber, Richard, 57, 124
Taymor, Julie, 256, 269
T. B. Harms publishing imprint, 83–84,
    96
television
    impact on Broadway, 182
    television musicals, 174–75
Tenderloin, 162
Terris, Norma, 125, 127
Tesori, Jeanine, 236, 259
Theatre Syndicate, 40
Third Little Show, The, 137

Thompson, Fred, 114
Thompson, Lydia, 19–20, 68, 69, 167, 181, 234
Thoroughly Modern Millie, 24, 259
The Threepenny Opera, 215
Three's a Crowd, 137
Tibbett, Lawrence, 123n
Tierney, Harry, 92
Tietjens, Paul, 41, 52
Tiller Girls, 96
TimeOut, 254
Tip Top, 94
Titanic, 270
Todd, Mike, 163–64, 171
Toll, Robert C., 11
Tom Sawyer, 272n
Tone, Richard, 216
Too Many Girls, 133
Traubel, Helen, 163, 191–92
Travolta, John, 235
A Tree Grows in Brooklyn, 162, 167–68, 169, 170, 175
Trentini, Emma, 53, 54
Tricks, 230
A Trip To Chinatown, 24, 25–26, 55
Trussler, Simon, 4, 7, 141
Tucker, Sophie, 149, 238
Tudor, Anthony, 165
Tune, Tommy, 241–42, 254, 267–68, 278
Tunick, Jonathan, 8, 228, 270
Turner, David, 254
Tveit, Aaron, 266
Twelfth Night, 272n
Twiggy, 254
Twirly Whirly, 39, 40
Two By Two, 232
Two For the Show, 64
Two on the Aisle, 182–83, 185
Two's Company, 182, 183

Ullmann, Liv, 232
Umeki, Myoshi, 197
The Unsinkable Molly Brown, 209
Urban, Joseph, 100, 127
Urinetown, 260

The Vagabond King, 80, 123–25
Van, Gus, 99, 102
Van Druten, John, 220
Van Dyke, Dick, 213

Van Dyke, Marcia, 168
Verdon, Gwen
    and *Chicago*, 237, 238
    and *Damn Yankees*, 212
    emphasis on music, 213
    and Fosse, 167, 186, 212
    and *New Girl in Town*, 166, 212
    and *Redhead*, 186, 212
    and *Sweet Charity*, 210, 211–12
    talent of, 211–12
Vereen, Ben, 230
Very Good Eddie, 87
Very Warm For May, 128
Via Galactica, 230
Violet, 236
Virginia Minstrels, 10–11

Waldman, Robert, 236
Walker, Don, 203
Walker, Nancy, 179, 189, 264
Wallace, George, 167, 168, 225n
Waller, "Fats," 254
Wang, 28–29
Wanting Songs
    in *Brigadoon*, 166
    in *Good News!* 118
    in *Gypsy*, 204
    in *Lady in the Dark*, 151
    in *The Most Happy Fella*, ix, x
    in *Primrose*, 254
Warfield, David, 34, 39
Warren, Harry, 215
Watch Your Step, 85, 130, 218
Waters, Ethel, 132, 138, 150, 234
Wayne, David, 177
Wayne, Paula, 208
Webber, Andrew Lloyd, 230, 231
Weber, Joe, 22, 39–40, 44, 67, 86
Weede, Robert, 188
Weidman, Charles, 139, 144
Weidman, John, 228, 250
Weill, Kurt, 175–77
    background of, 146
    and *Johnny Johnson*, 146–47
    and *Lady in the Dark*, 151
    and *Love Life*, 175, 176–77
    and minstrel shows, 10
    and *One Touch of Venus*, 164
    and *Porgy and Bess*, 153
    and revues, 182

scoring of shows, 75
and *Street Scene*, 175–76, 229
and T. B. Harms, 83
West Side Story, 197–98
  influence of, 260
  music of, 137
  revival of, 249
  romantic leads of, 80
  set design in, 270
  staging of, 258
  and tragedy in musicals, 162
What Makes Sammy Run? 274
What's Up? 165
Wheatley, William, 14, 15
Wheeler, Hugh, 228
Where's Charley? ix, 193, 243
Whirl-i-Gig, 40
The Whirl of New York, 34
The Whirl Of Society, 68
White, George, 105
White, Miles, 157
White, Onna, 170
White, Sammy, 125, 127, 200
White, T. H., 199
The White Fawn, 18, 19
Whiting, Jack, 146, 187
Whitton, Joseph, 14, 15
Wicked, 277–80
Wildcat, 63, 169
Wilder, Thornton, 190n, 220
Wildflower, 110
Wildhorn, Frank, 263
The Wild Party, 272–73, 274–75
Williams, Bert, 99, 101, 102, 234, 238
Williams, Treat, 235
Williamson, Nicol, 232
Willson, Meredith, 169, 170, 209
Wilson, Dooley, 150
Wilson, Francis, 21
Wilson, Mary Louise, 252
Wilson, Sandy, 111
Winchell, Walter, 164n
Winninger, Charles, 125
Wittop, Freddy, 218
The Wiz, 236, 237
The Wizard of Oz, 41–45
  adventure theme in, 218
  influence of, 56
  and "Little Nemo and His Bear," 77
  songs and song genres in, 46, 64, 66

The Wizard of the Nile, 37
Wodehouse, P. G., 69, 87–91, 95, 114,
  140, 141
Wolfe, George C., 255, 272, 273
*Women On the Verge Of a Nervous
  Breakdown*, 275–77, 279
women writers, 95n
Wonderful Town, ix, 31, 169, 179,
  188–89, 198
Wood, Peggy, 54
Woodland, 35, 66
Wright, Robert, 186, 206, 268
Wylie, John, 267
Wynn, Ed, 63, 98, 116–17
Wynn, Rhoda, 147

The Yankee Consul, 52, 72
Yankee Doodle Dandy, 60, 61, 63
Yazbek, David, 259, 275
Yeston, Maury, 241, 268, 270
Yorkey, Brian, 266
Youmans, Vincent, 55, 60, 83, 95n, 110
Youmans, William, 277
Young, Rida Johnson, 54

Ziegfeld, Florenz
  background of, 100
  and ethnic subcultures, 101, 106
  first Broadway production of, 24
  happy endings of, 274
  and Herbert, 76
  influence of, 106
  origins of producing career, 30
  publicity machine of, 101
  rules for show business, 100
  and *Sally In Our Alley*, 69–70
  and *Show Boat*, 126, 128, 129
  showmanship of, 100
  and *Smiles*, 116
Ziegfeld Follies
  character songs of, 271
  comics of, 98–99, 101
  dancing in, 65
  duration of, 98
  and ethnic subcultures, 99, 101, 106,
    145, 234
  and *Florodora* Sextette, 59
  imitators of, 105 (see also *Follies*)
  impact on Broadway, 106
  influence of, 104–5, 106

Ziegfeld Follies (*continued*)
    and management style of Ziegfeld,
      100
    and Miller, 69
    and Mitchell, 42
    music of, 42, 102–4
    name of, 99, 104n
    parodied by Moross and Latouche, 187
    publicity machine of, 101
    and revue format, 215
    sexual component of, 167
    showgirls of, 98, 100
    showmanship in, 100
    spontaneity of, 102
    success of, 104
Zip! Goes a Million, 87
Zippel, David, 258
Zorina, Vera, 249